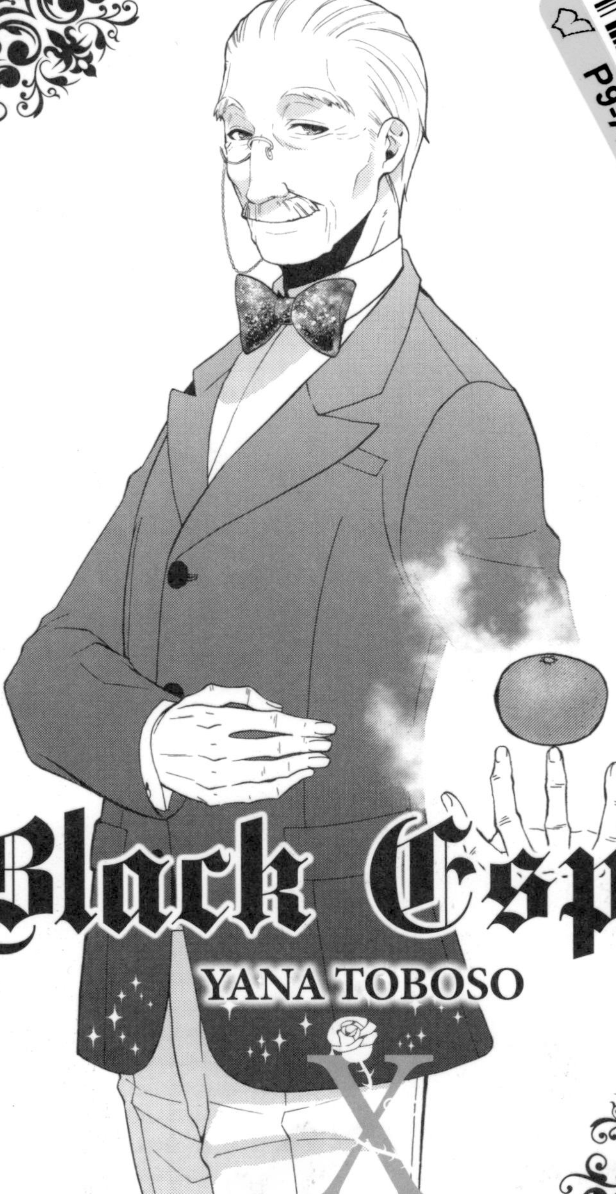

Black Esper

YANA TOBOSO

X

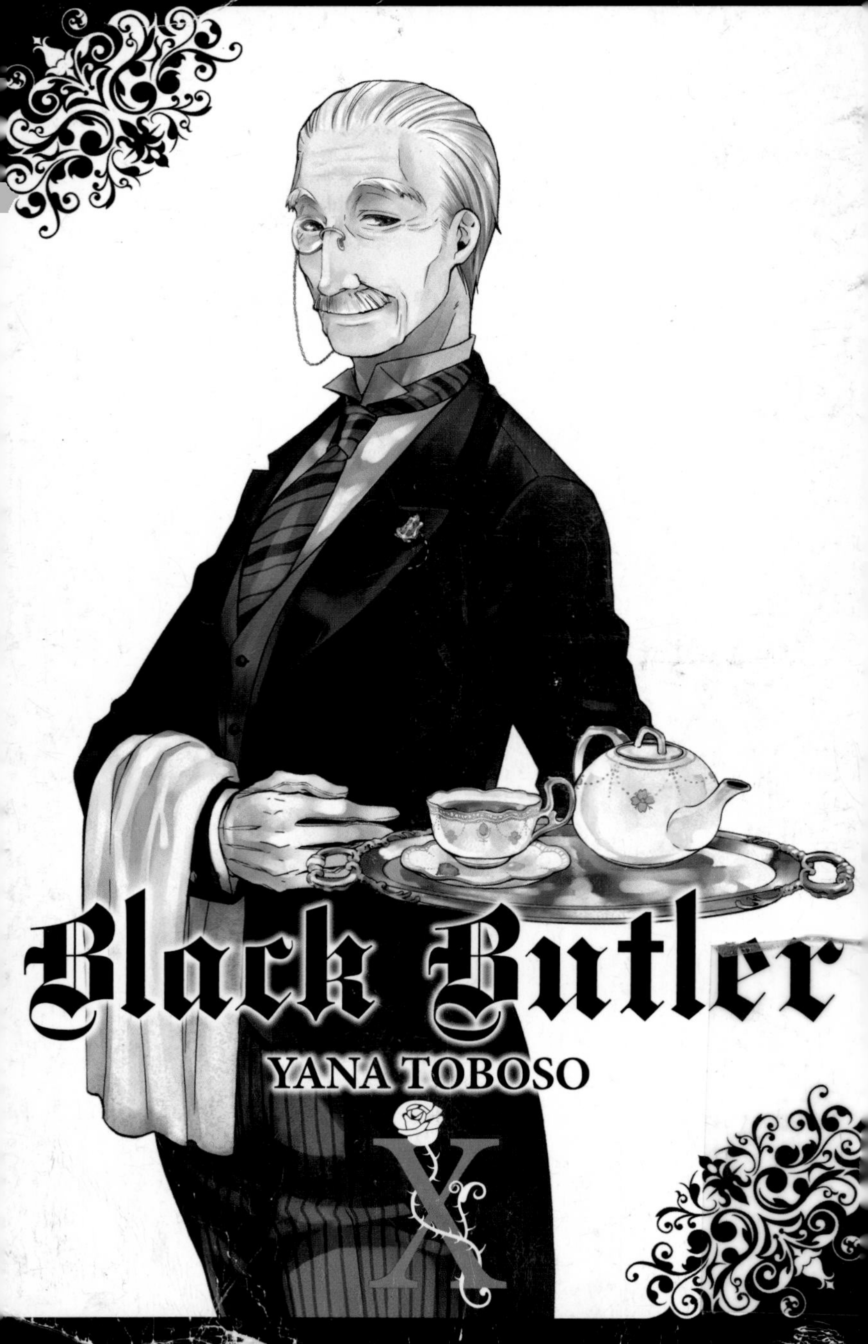
Black Butler
YANA TOBOSO
X

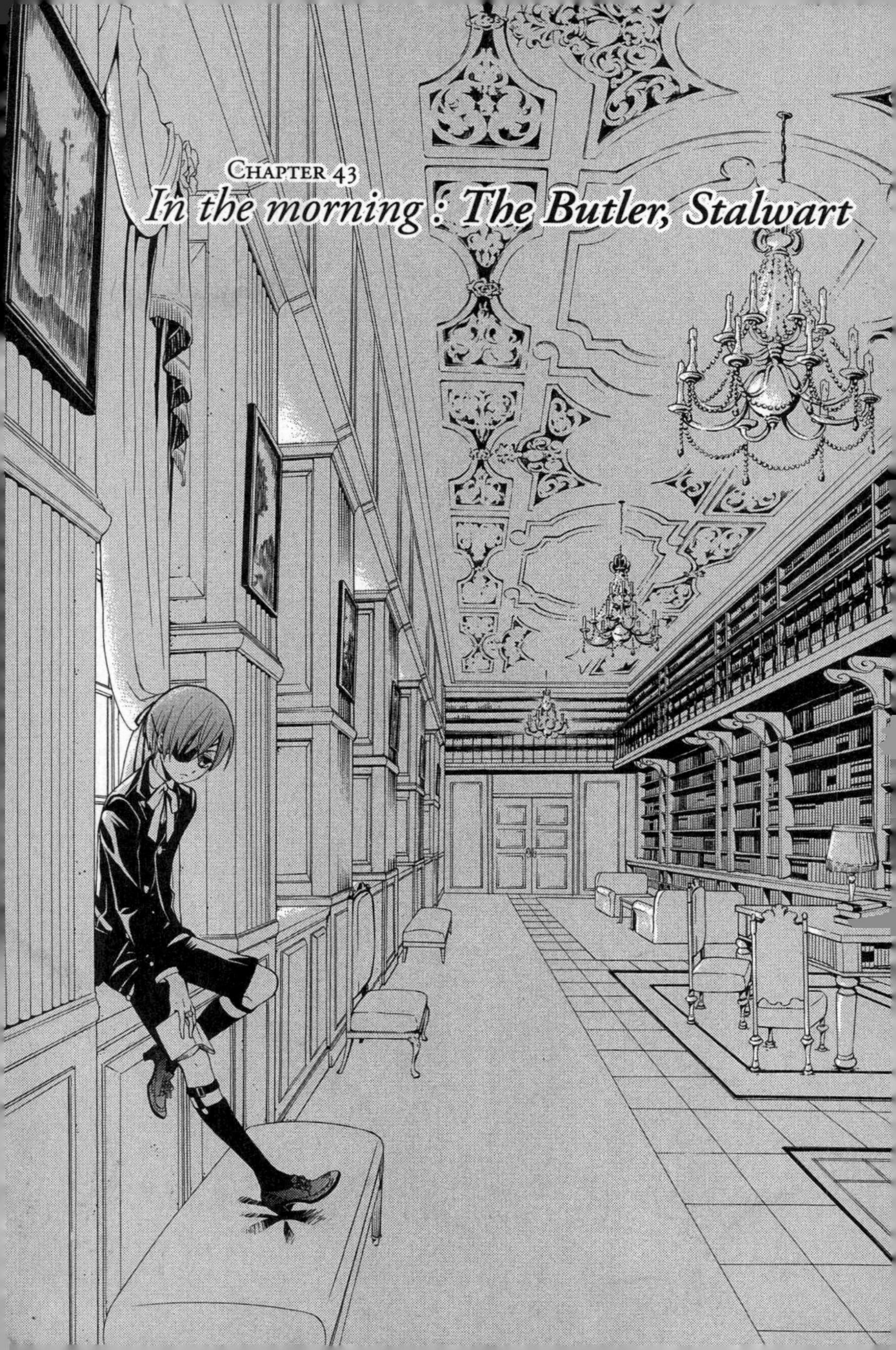
CHAPTER 43
In the morning : The Butler, Stalwart

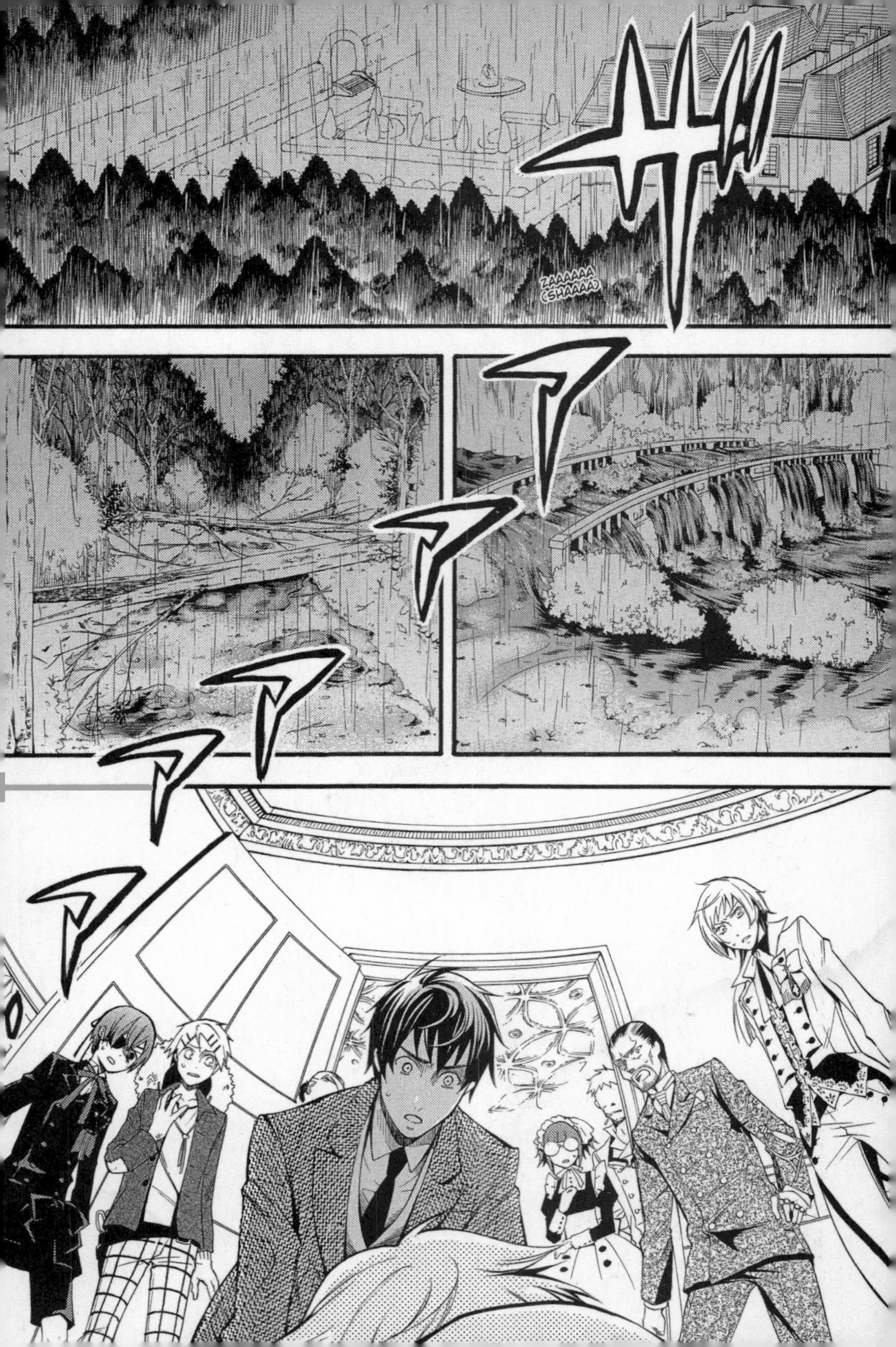
ZAAAAAA
(SHAAAA)

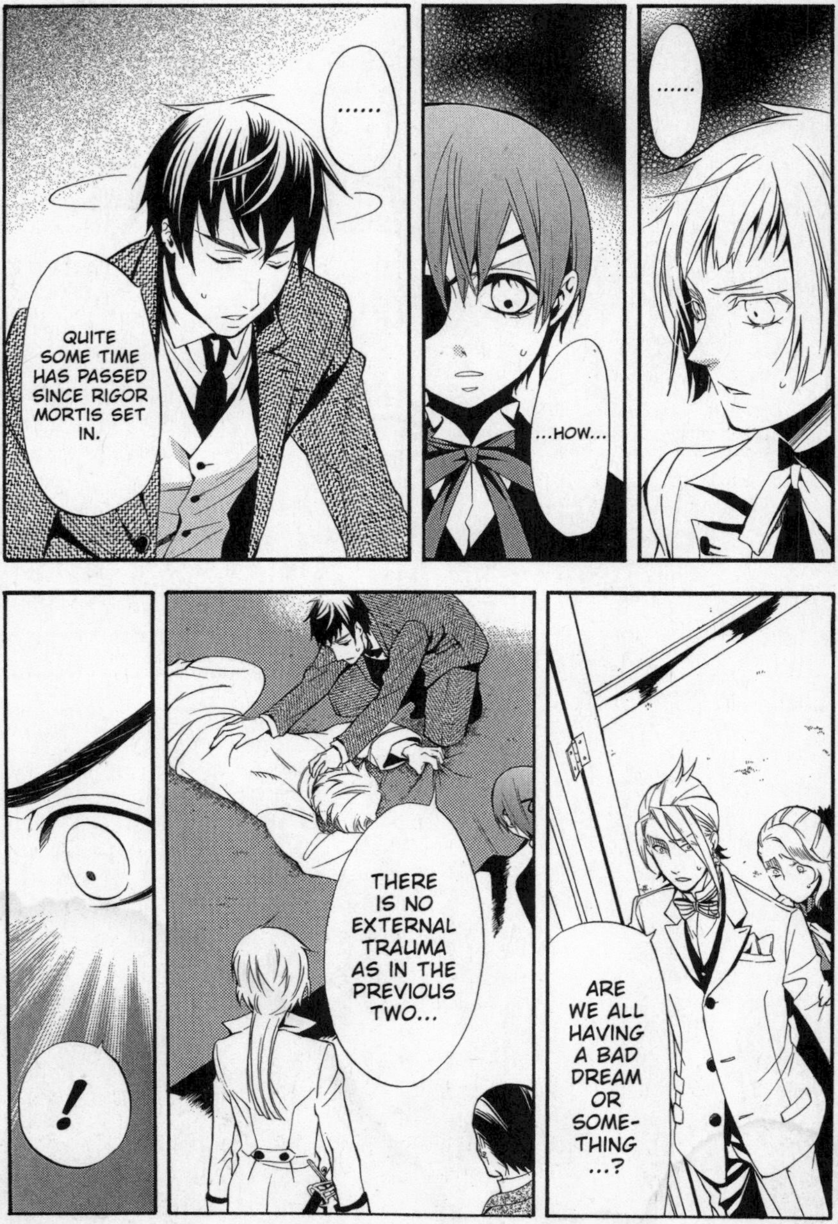
......
...HOW...
......
QUITE SOME TIME HAS PASSED SINCE RIGOR MORTIS SET IN.
ARE WE ALL HAVING A BAD DREAM OR SOME-THING ...?
THERE IS NO EXTERNAL TRAUMA AS IN THE PREVIOUS TWO...
!

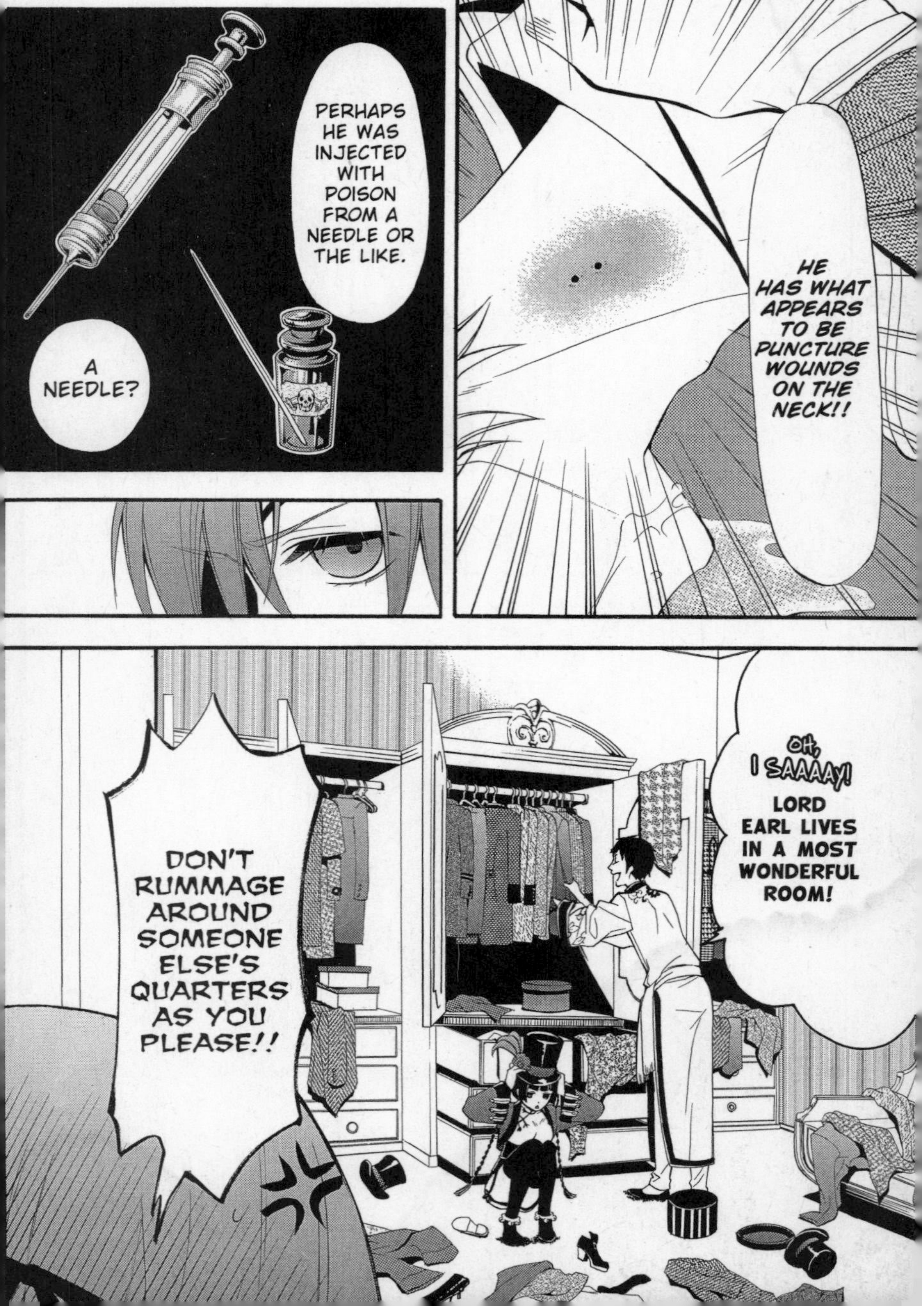
HE HAS WHAT APPEARS TO BE PUNCTURE WOUNDS ON THE NECK!!
PERHAPS HE WAS INJECTED WITH POISON FROM A NEEDLE OR THE LIKE.
A NEEDLE?
OH, I SAAAAY!
LORD EARL LIVES IN A MOST WONDERFUL ROOM!
DON'T RUMMAGE AROUND SOMEONE ELSE'S QUARTERS AS YOU PLEASE!!

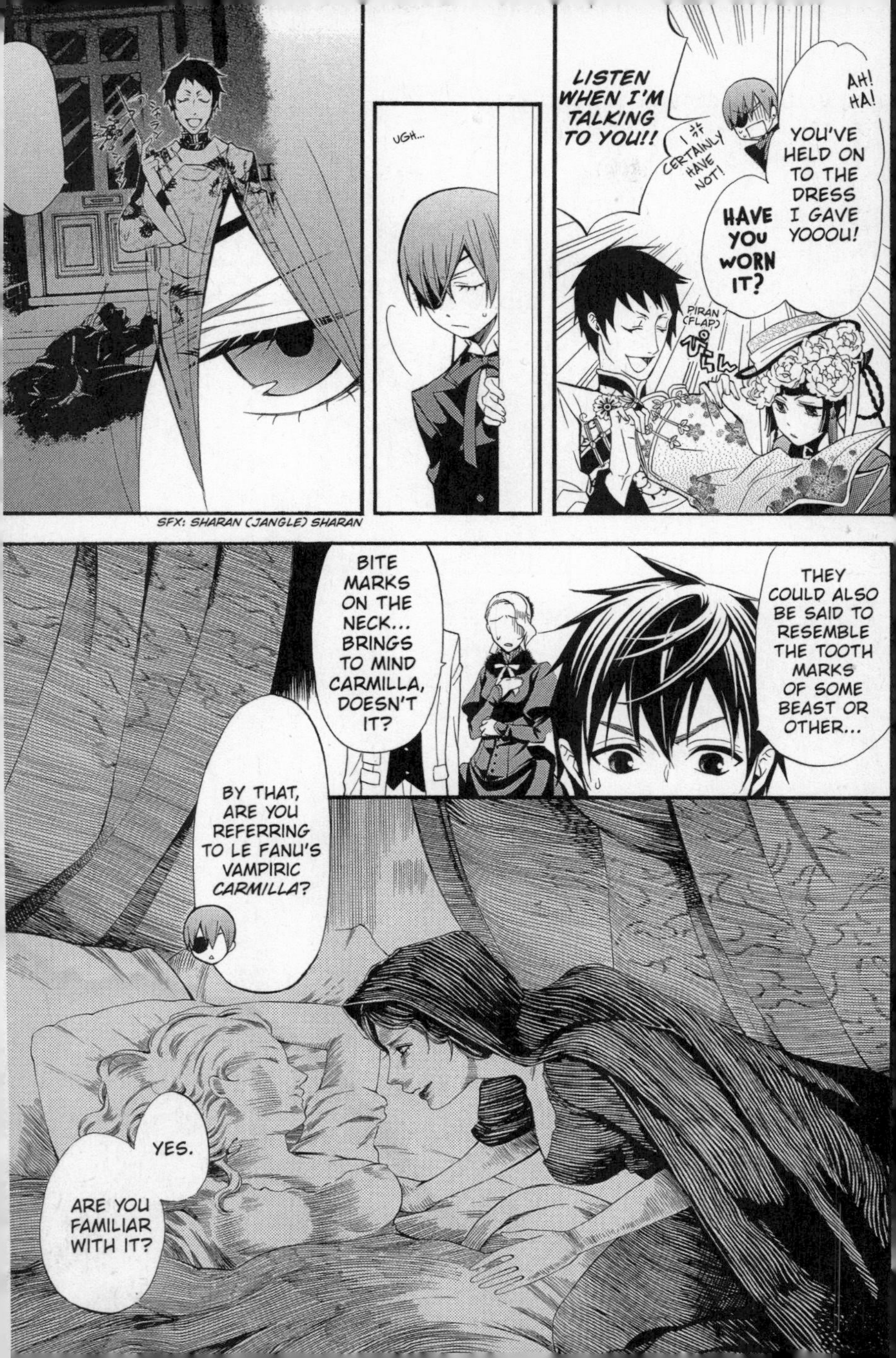
AH! HA!
YOU'VE HELD ON TO THE DRESS I GAVE YOOOU!
HAVE YOU WORN IT?
PIRAN (FLAP)
I CERTAINLY HAVE NOT!
LISTEN WHEN I'M TALKING TO YOU!!
UGH...
SFX: SHARAN (JANGLE) SHARAN
THEY COULD ALSO BE SAID TO RESEMBLE THE TOOTH MARKS OF SOME BEAST OR OTHER...
BITE MARKS ON THE NECK... BRINGS TO MIND CARMILLA, DOESN'T IT?
BY THAT, ARE YOU REFERRING TO LE FANU'S VAMPIRIC *CARMILLA*?
YES.
ARE YOU FAMILIAR WITH IT?

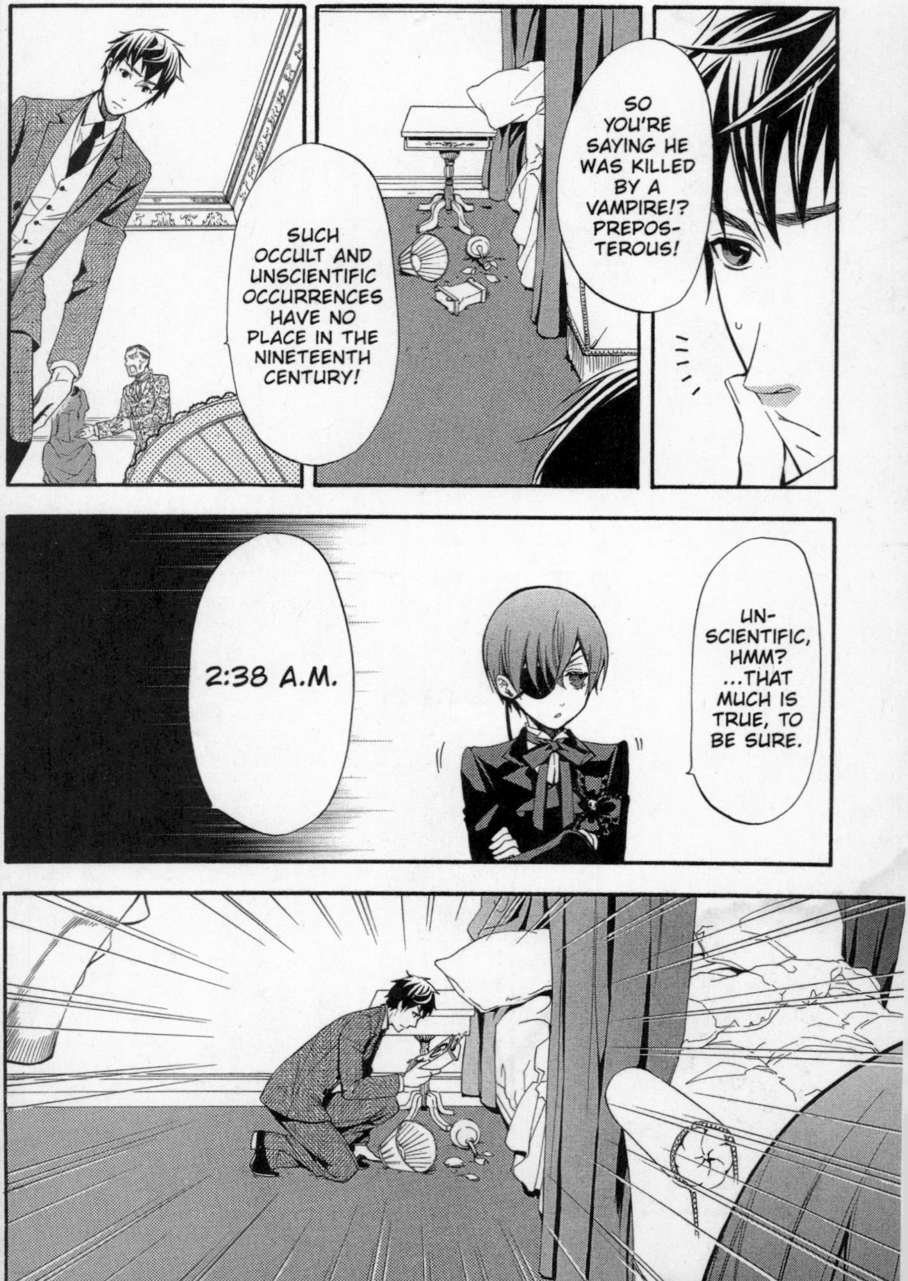
SO YOU'RE SAYING HE WAS KILLED BY A VAMPIRE!? PREPOSTEROUS!
SUCH OCCULT AND UNSCIENTIFIC OCCURRENCES HAVE NO PLACE IN THE NINETEENTH CENTURY!
UN-SCIENTIFIC, HMM? ...THAT MUCH IS TRUE, TO BE SURE.
2:38 A.M.

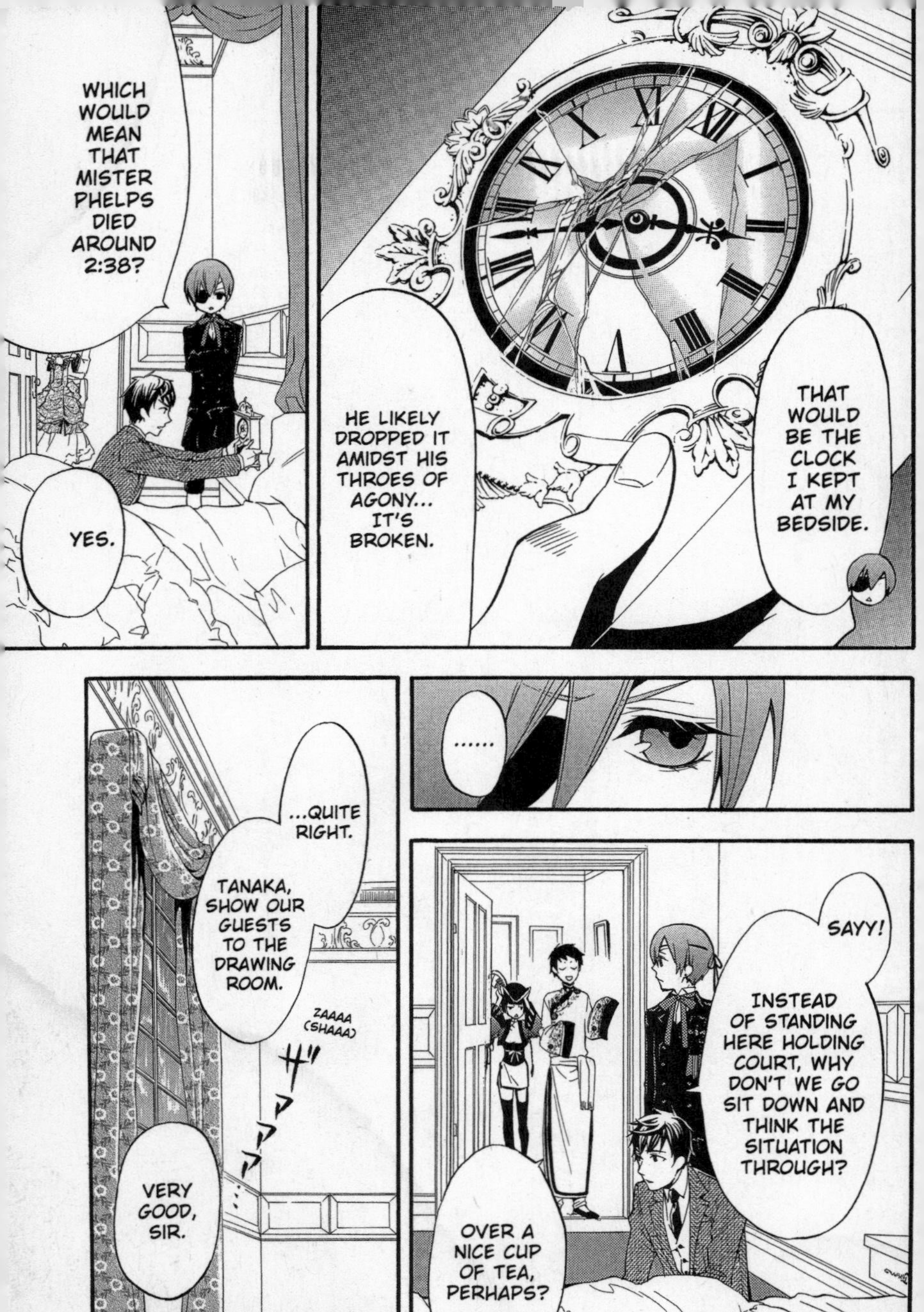
THAT WOULD BE THE CLOCK I KEPT AT MY BEDSIDE.
HE LIKELY DROPPED IT AMIDST HIS THROES OF AGONY... IT'S BROKEN.
WHICH WOULD MEAN THAT MISTER PHELPS DIED AROUND 2:38?
YES.
......
SAYY!
INSTEAD OF STANDING HERE HOLDING COURT, WHY DON'T WE GO SIT DOWN AND THINK THE SITUATION THROUGH?
OVER A NICE CUP OF TEA, PERHAPS?
...QUITE RIGHT.
TANAKA, SHOW OUR GUESTS TO THE DRAWING ROOM.
ZAAAA (SHAAA)
ザァァァ
VERY GOOD, SIR.

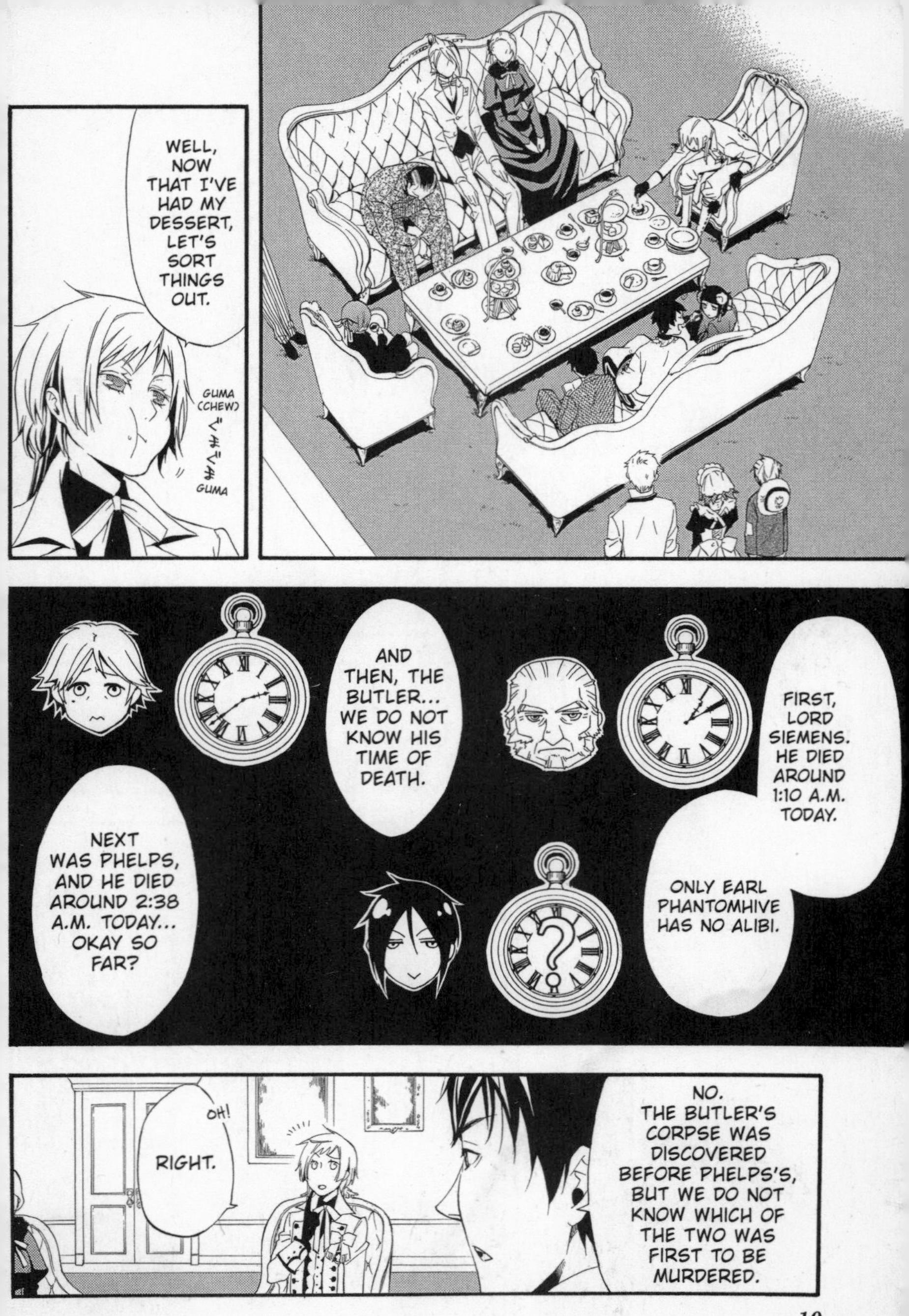
WELL, NOW THAT I'VE HAD MY DESSERT, LET'S SORT THINGS OUT.
GUMA (CHEW)
GUMA
FIRST, LORD SIEMENS. HE DIED AROUND 1:10 A.M. TODAY.
AND THEN, THE BUTLER... WE DO NOT KNOW HIS TIME OF DEATH.
ONLY EARL PHANTOMHIVE HAS NO ALIBI.
NEXT WAS PHELPS, AND HE DIED AROUND 2:38 A.M. TODAY... OKAY SO FAR?
NO. THE BUTLER'S CORPSE WAS DISCOVERED BEFORE PHELPS'S, BUT WE DO NOT KNOW WHICH OF THE TWO WAS FIRST TO BE MURDERED.
OH!
RIGHT.

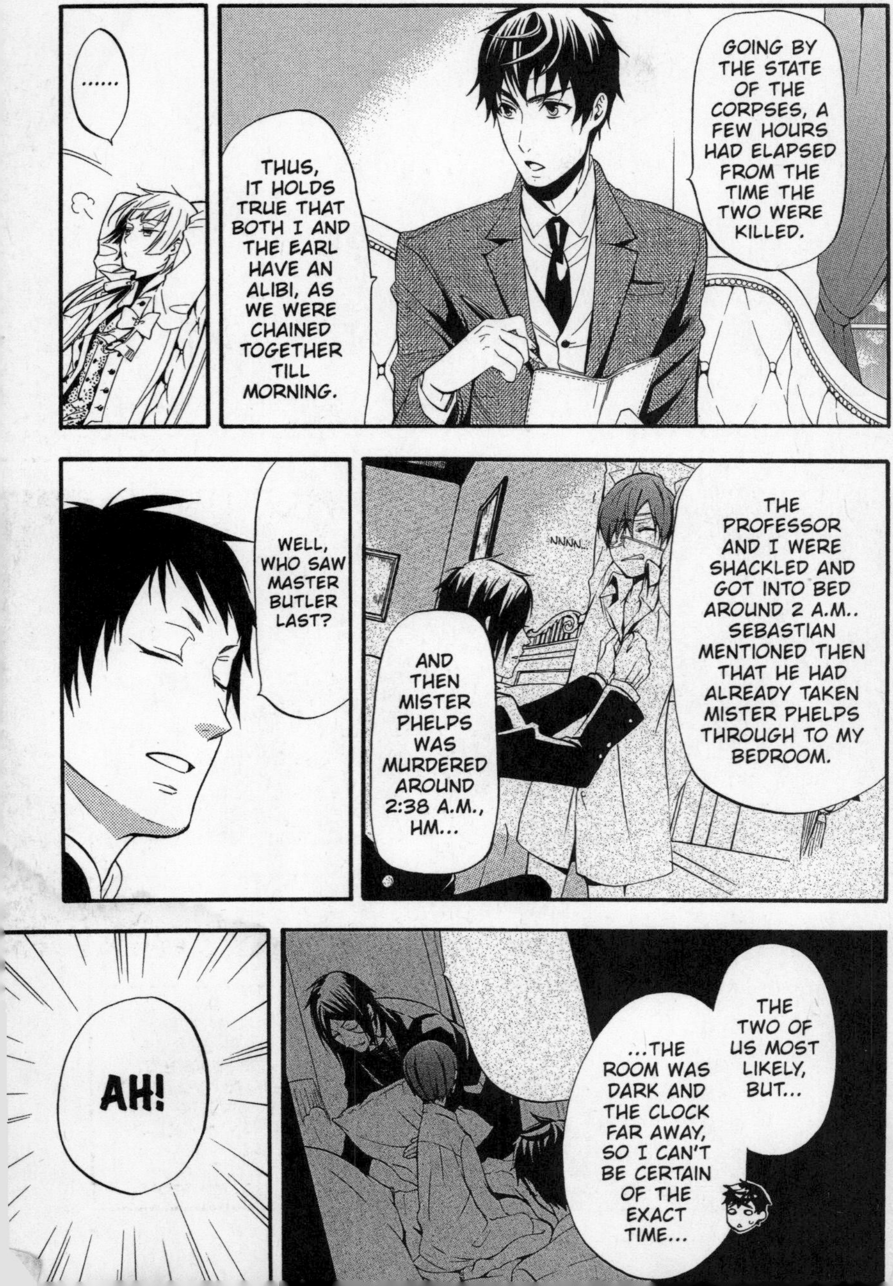
GOING BY THE STATE OF THE CORPSES, A FEW HOURS HAD ELAPSED FROM THE TIME THE TWO WERE KILLED.
THUS, IT HOLDS TRUE THAT BOTH I AND THE EARL HAVE AN ALIBI, AS WE WERE CHAINED TOGETHER TILL MORNING.
......
THE PROFESSOR AND I WERE SHACKLED AND GOT INTO BED AROUND 2 A.M.. SEBASTIAN MENTIONED THEN THAT HE HAD ALREADY TAKEN MISTER PHELPS THROUGH TO MY BEDROOM.
NNNN...
AND THEN MISTER PHELPS WAS MURDERED AROUND 2:38 A.M., HM...
WELL, WHO SAW MASTER BUTLER LAST?
THE TWO OF US MOST LIKELY, BUT...
...THE ROOM WAS DARK AND THE CLOCK FAR AWAY, SO I CAN'T BE CERTAIN OF THE EXACT TIME...
AH!

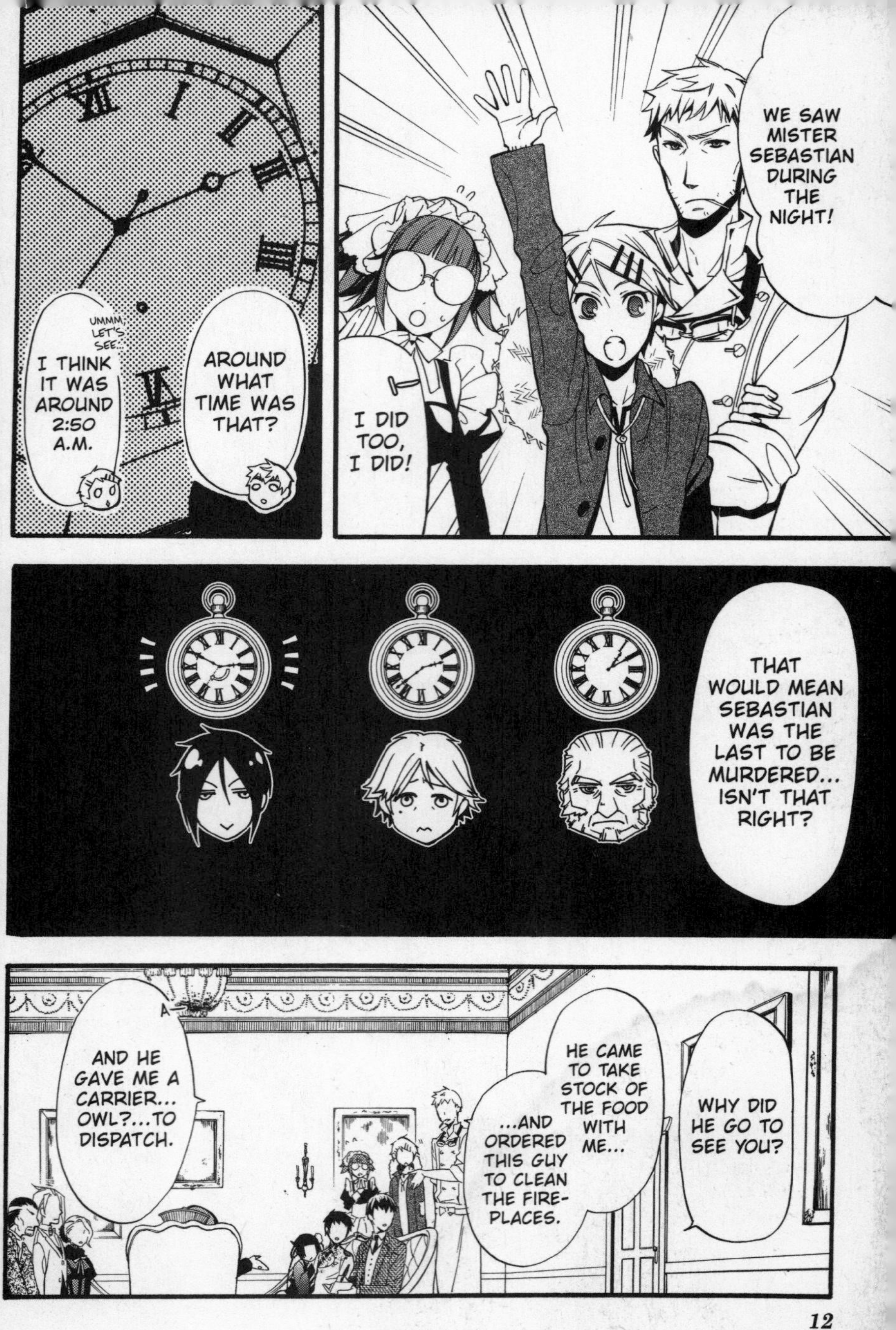
WE SAW MISTER SEBASTIAN DURING THE NIGHT!
I DID TOO, I DID!
AROUND WHAT TIME WAS THAT?
UMMM, LET'S SEE...
I THINK IT WAS AROUND 2:50 A.M.
THAT WOULD MEAN SEBASTIAN WAS THE LAST TO BE MURDERED... ISN'T THAT RIGHT?
WHY DID HE GO TO SEE YOU?
HE CAME TO TAKE STOCK OF THE FOOD WITH ME...
...AND ORDERED THIS GUY TO CLEAN THE FIRE-PLACES.
A—
AND HE GAVE ME A CARRIER... OWL?...TO DISPATCH.

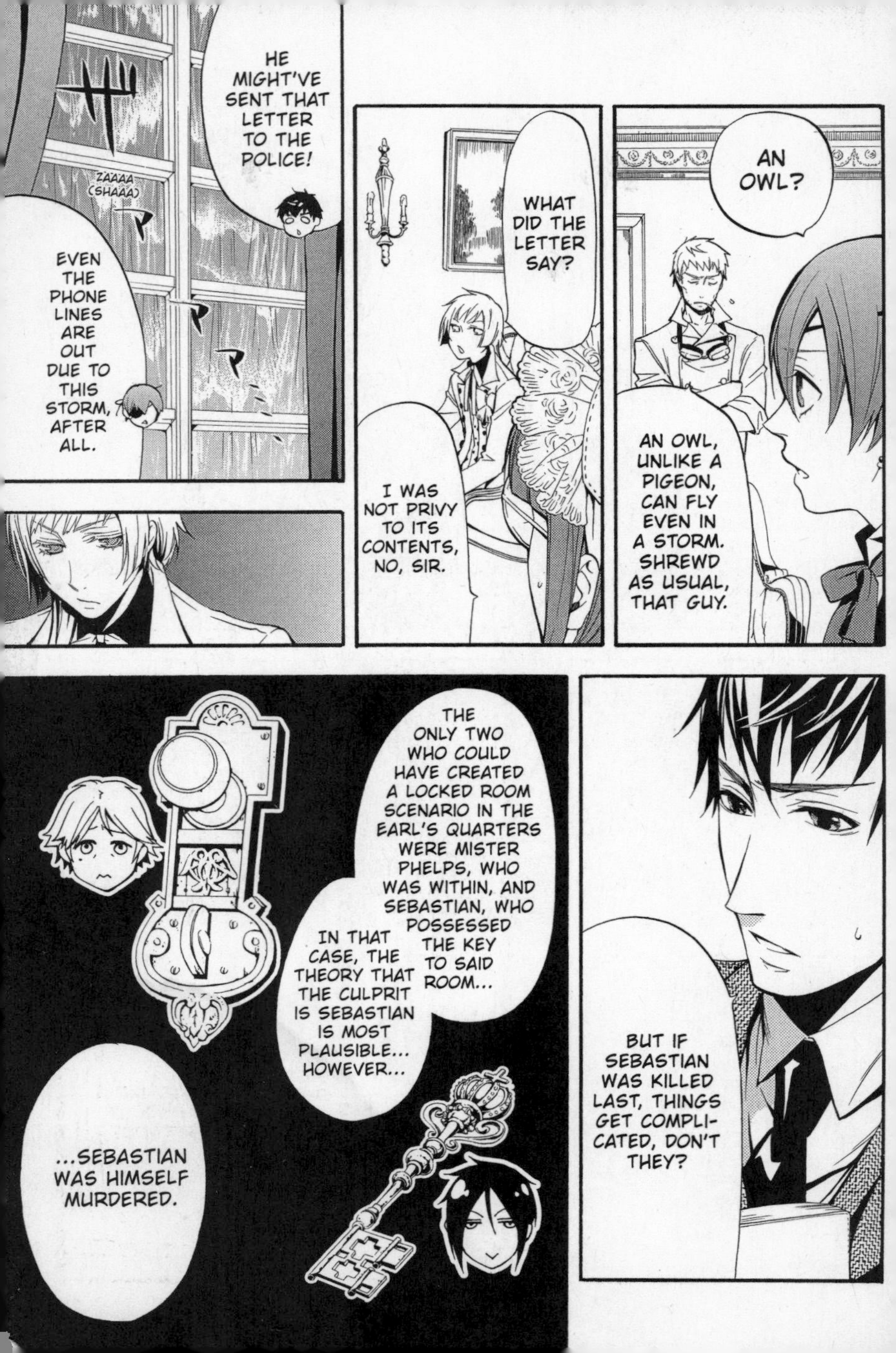

AN OWL?
AN OWL, UNLIKE A PIGEON, CAN FLY EVEN IN A STORM. SHREWD AS USUAL, THAT GUY.
WHAT DID THE LETTER SAY?
I WAS NOT PRIVY TO ITS CONTENTS, NO, SIR.
HE MIGHT'VE SENT THAT LETTER TO THE POLICE!
ZAAAA (SHAAA)
EVEN THE PHONE LINES ARE OUT DUE TO THIS STORM, AFTER ALL.
BUT IF SEBASTIAN WAS KILLED LAST, THINGS GET COMPLICATED, DON'T THEY?
THE ONLY TWO WHO COULD HAVE CREATED A LOCKED ROOM SCENARIO IN THE EARL'S QUARTERS WERE MISTER PHELPS, WHO WAS WITHIN, AND SEBASTIAN, WHO POSSESSED THE KEY TO SAID ROOM...
IN THAT CASE, THE THEORY THAT THE CULPRIT IS SEBASTIAN IS MOST PLAUSIBLE... HOWEVER...
...SEBASTIAN WAS HIMSELF MURDERED.

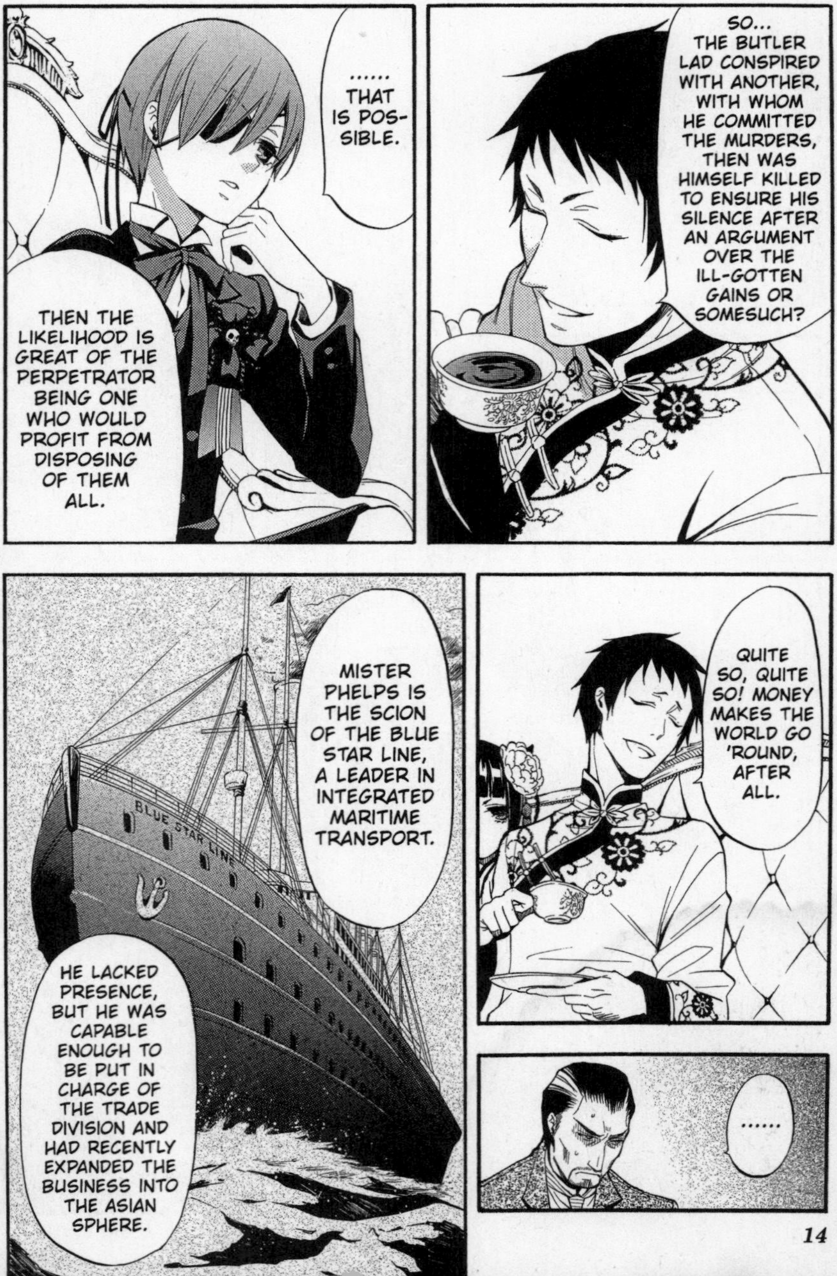
SO... THE BUTLER LAD CONSPIRED WITH ANOTHER, WITH WHOM HE COMMITTED THE MURDERS, THEN WAS HIMSELF KILLED TO ENSURE HIS SILENCE AFTER AN ARGUMENT OVER THE ILL-GOTTEN GAINS OR SOMESUCH?
...... THAT IS POS-SIBLE.
THEN THE LIKELIHOOD IS GREAT OF THE PERPETRATOR BEING ONE WHO WOULD PROFIT FROM DISPOSING OF THEM ALL.
QUITE SO, QUITE SO! MONEY MAKES THE WORLD GO 'ROUND, AFTER ALL.
......
MISTER PHELPS IS THE SCION OF THE BLUE STAR LINE, A LEADER IN INTEGRATED MARITIME TRANSPORT.
BLUE STAR LINE
HE LACKED PRESENCE, BUT HE WAS CAPABLE ENOUGH TO BE PUT IN CHARGE OF THE TRADE DIVISION AND HAD RECENTLY EXPANDED THE BUSINESS INTO THE ASIAN SPHERE.

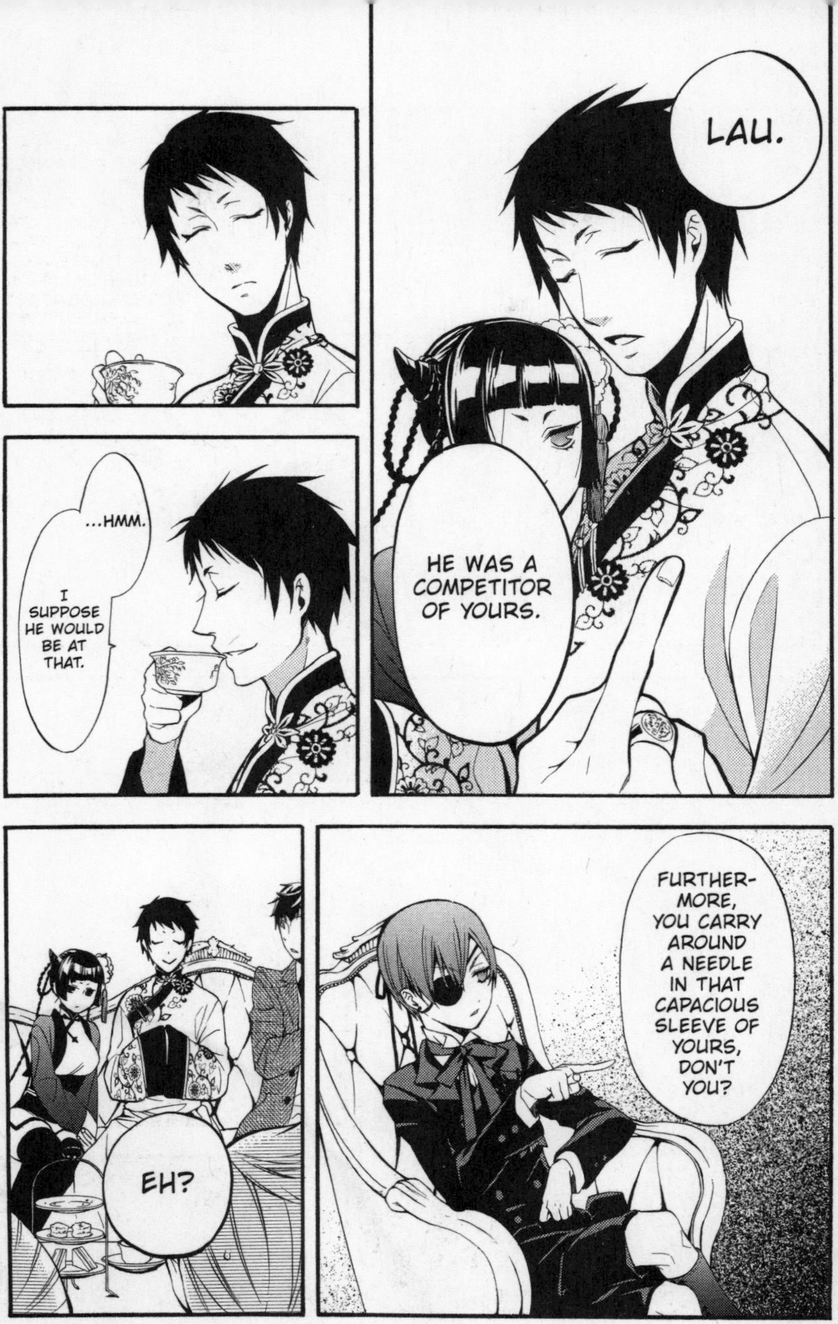
LAU.
HE WAS A COMPETITOR OF YOURS.
...HMM.
I SUPPOSE HE WOULD BE AT THAT.
FURTHERMORE, YOU CARRY AROUND A NEEDLE IN THAT CAPACIOUS SLEEVE OF YOURS, DON'T YOU?
EH?

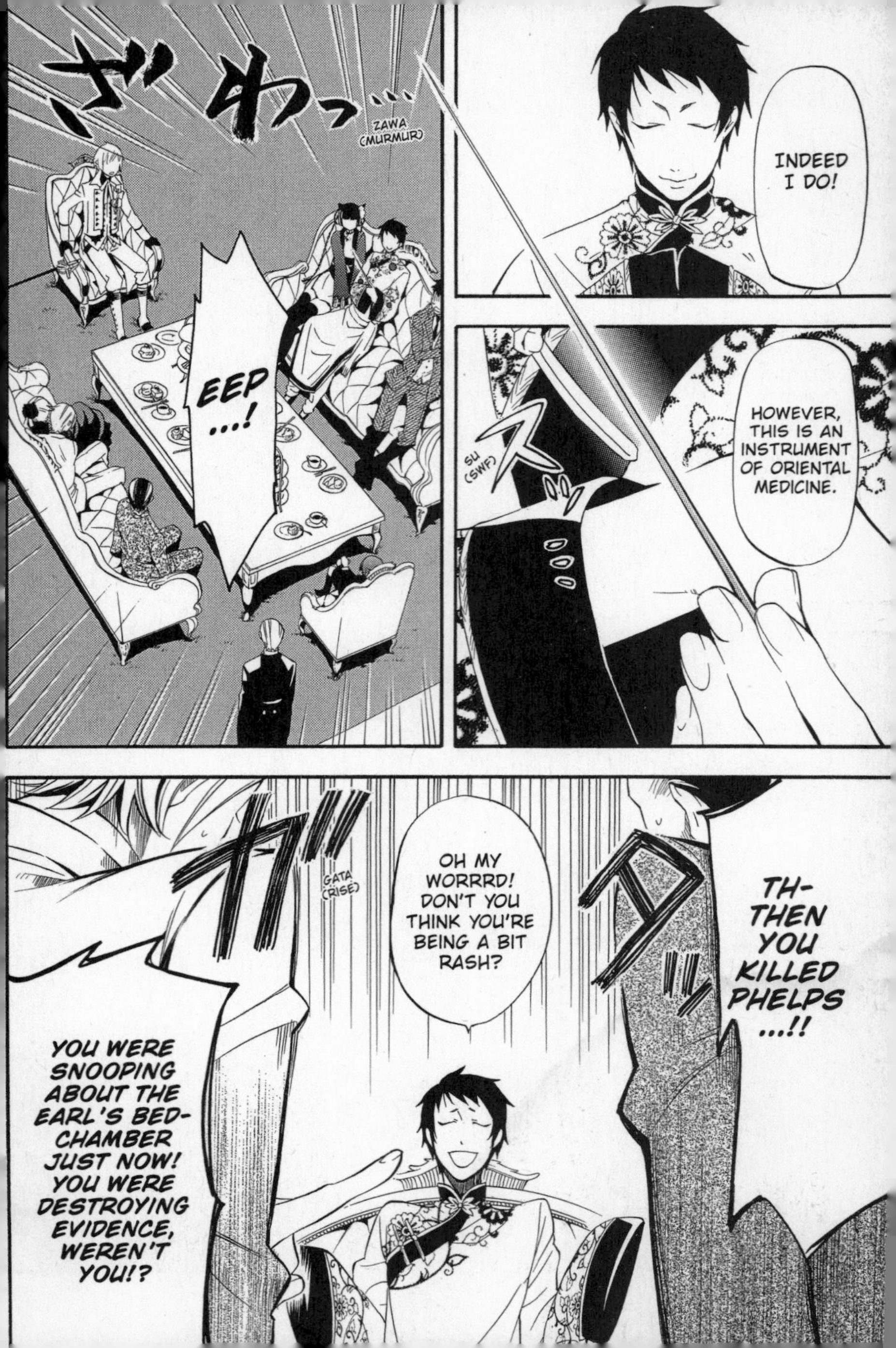
INDEED I DO!
HOWEVER, THIS IS AN INSTRUMENT OF ORIENTAL MEDICINE.
SU (SWF)
ざわっ…
ZAWA (MURMUR)
EEP ...!
TH- THEN YOU KILLED PHELPS ...!!
OH MY WORRRD! DON'T YOU THINK YOU'RE BEING A BIT RASH?
GATA (RISE)
YOU WERE SNOOPING ABOUT THE EARL'S BED-CHAMBER JUST NOW! YOU WERE DESTROYING EVIDENCE, WEREN'T YOU!?

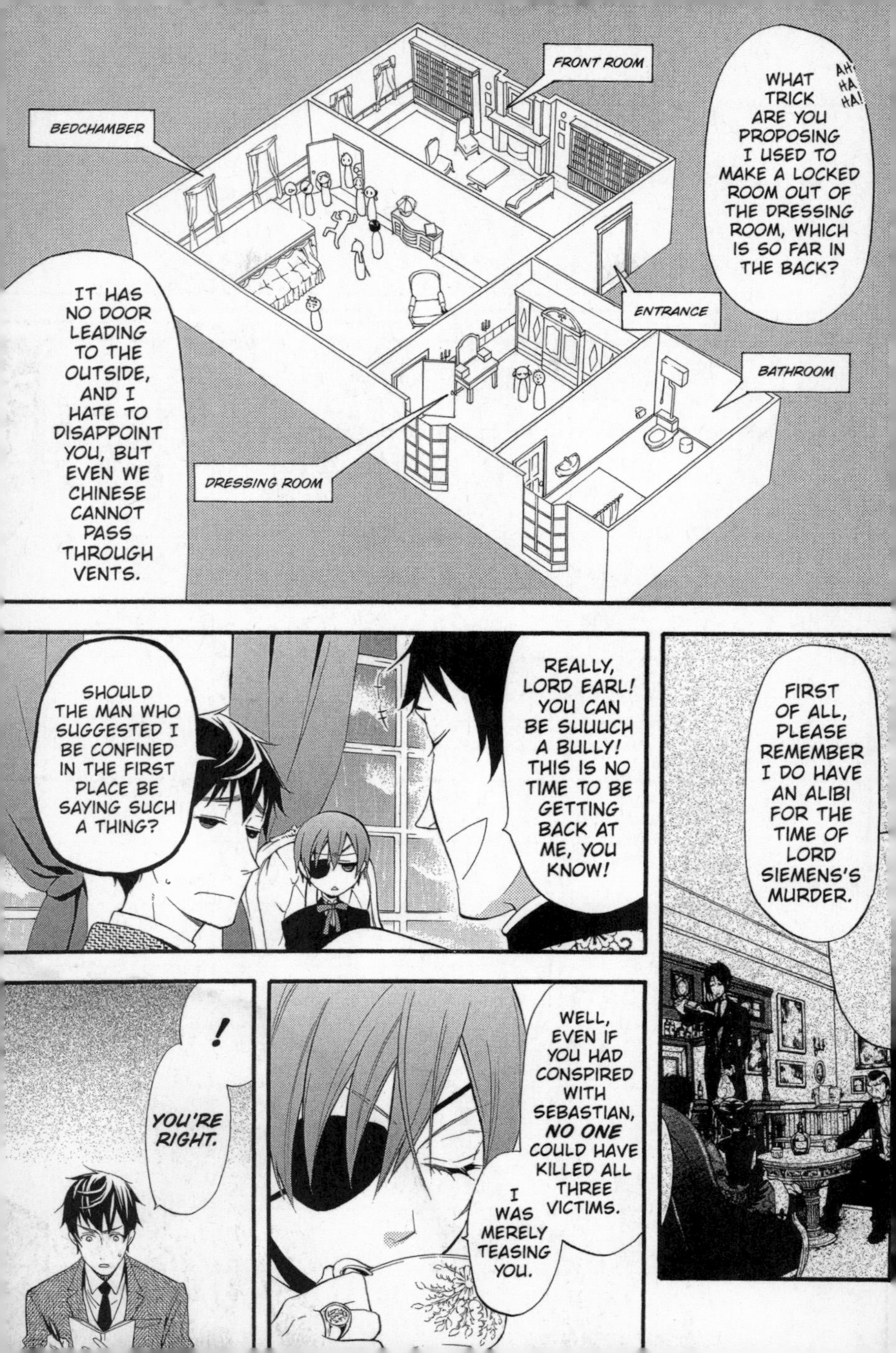

AH HA HA!
WHAT TRICK ARE YOU PROPOSING I USED TO MAKE A LOCKED ROOM OUT OF THE DRESSING ROOM, WHICH IS SO FAR IN THE BACK?
FRONT ROOM
BEDCHAMBER
ENTRANCE
BATHROOM
DRESSING ROOM
IT HAS NO DOOR LEADING TO THE OUTSIDE, AND I HATE TO DISAPPOINT YOU, BUT EVEN WE CHINESE CANNOT PASS THROUGH VENTS.
FIRST OF ALL, PLEASE REMEMBER I DO HAVE AN ALIBI FOR THE TIME OF LORD SIEMENS'S MURDER.
REALLY, LORD EARL! YOU CAN BE SUUUCH A BULLY! THIS IS NO TIME TO BE GETTING BACK AT ME, YOU KNOW!
SHOULD THE MAN WHO SUGGESTED I BE CONFINED IN THE FIRST PLACE BE SAYING SUCH A THING?
WELL, EVEN IF YOU HAD CONSPIRED WITH SEBASTIAN, ***NO ONE*** COULD HAVE KILLED ALL THREE VICTIMS.
I WAS MERELY TEASING YOU.
!
YOU'RE RIGHT.

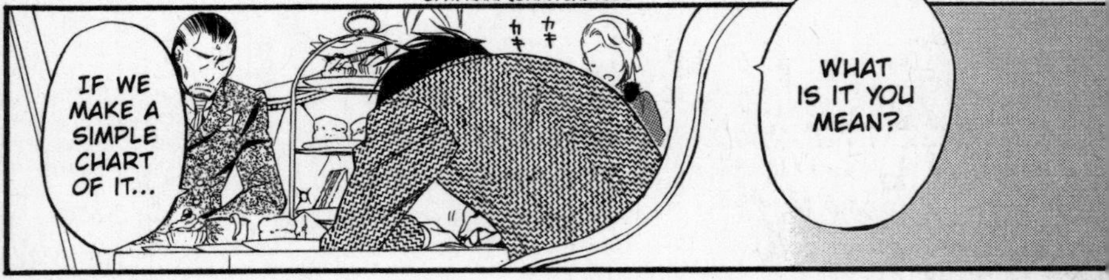
SFX: KAKI (SKRITCH) KAKI
カキ カキ
WHAT IS IT YOU MEAN?
IF WE MAKE A SIMPLE CHART OF IT...

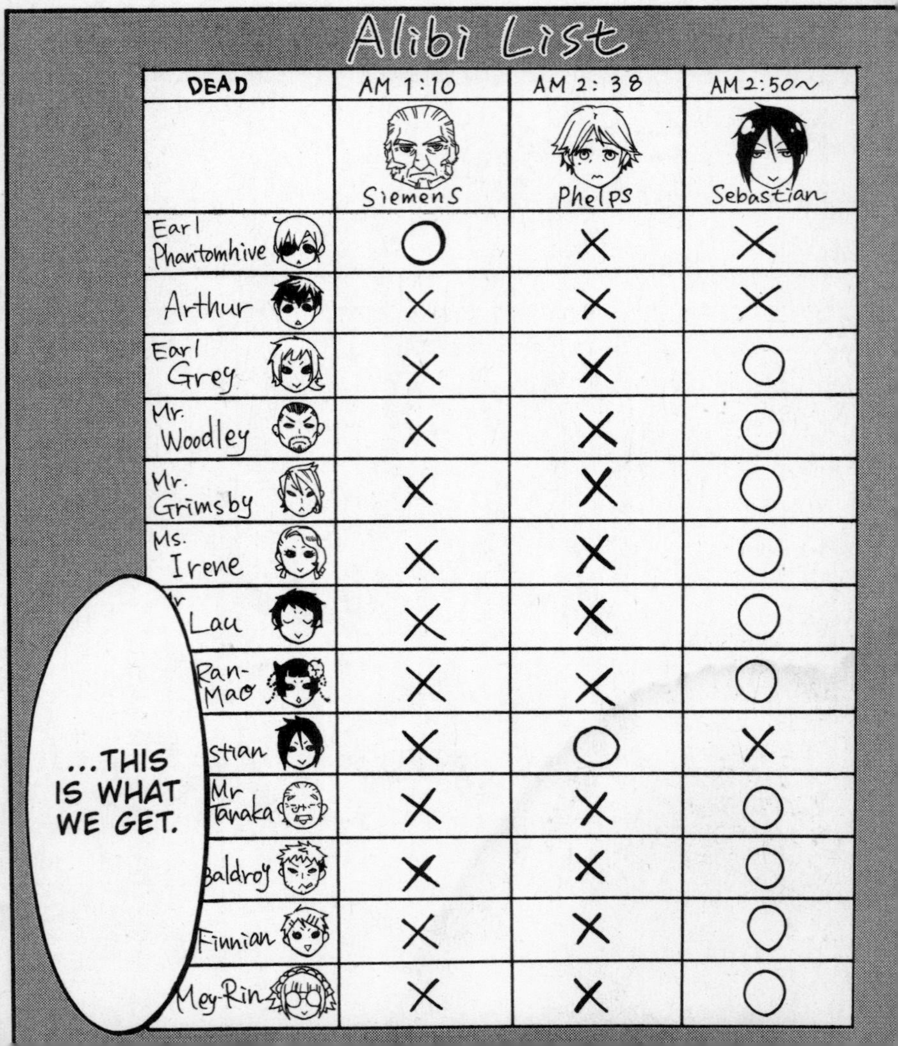
...THIS IS WHAT WE GET.

Alibi List

DEAD	AM 1:10 Siemens	AM 2:38 Phelps	AM 2:50～ Sebastian
Earl Phantomhive	○	×	×
Arthur	×	×	×
Earl Grey	×	×	○
Mr. Woodley	×	×	○
Mr. Grimsby	×	×	○
Ms. Irene	×	×	○
Lau	×	×	○
Ran-Mao	×	×	○
stian	×	○	×
Mr Tanaka	×	×	○
Baldroy	×	×	○
Finnian	×	×	○
Mey-Rin	×	×	○

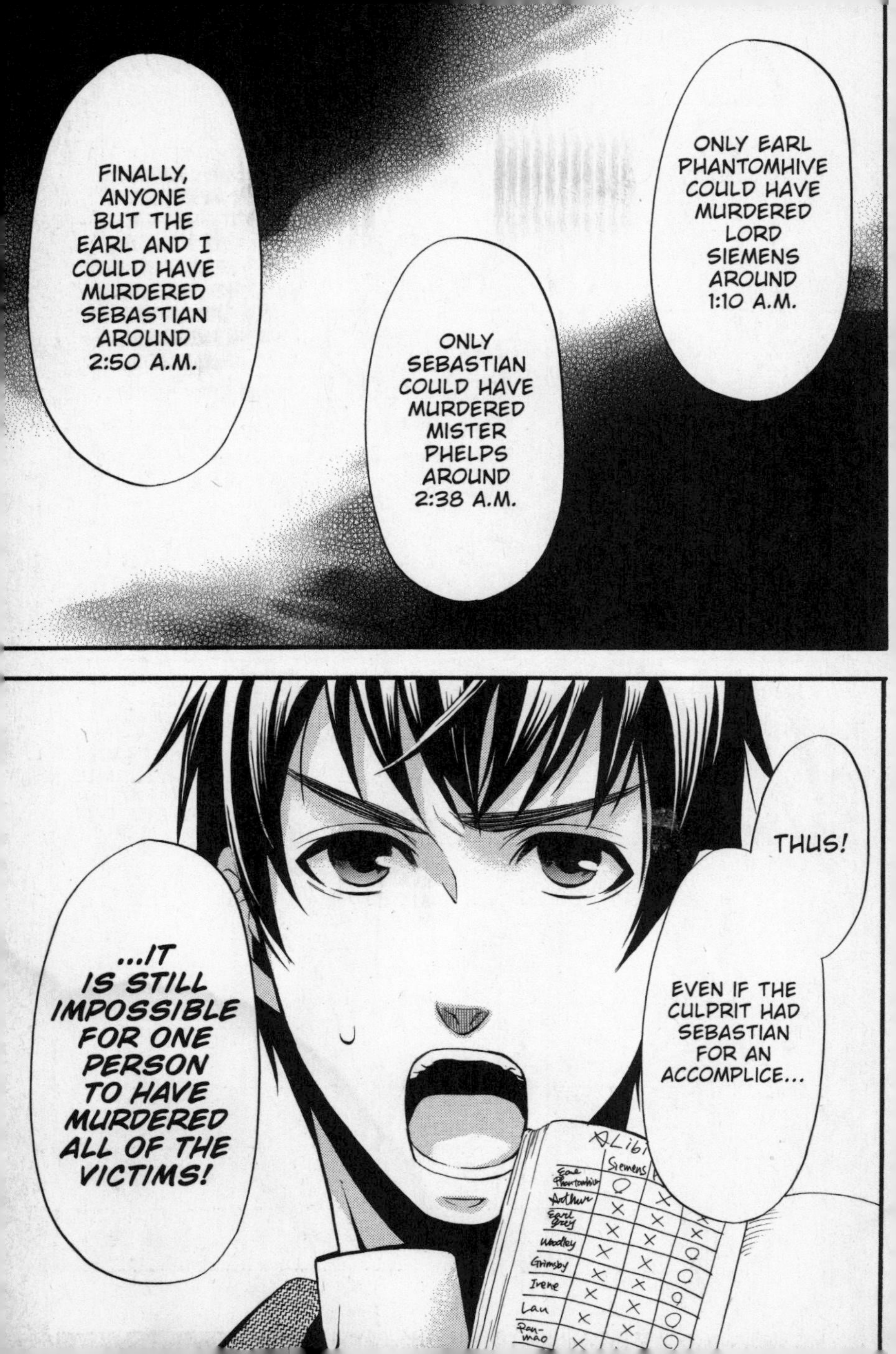
ONLY EARL PHANTOMHIVE COULD HAVE MURDERED LORD SIEMENS AROUND 1:10 A.M.
ONLY SEBASTIAN COULD HAVE MURDERED MISTER PHELPS AROUND 2:38 A.M.
FINALLY, ANYONE BUT THE EARL AND I COULD HAVE MURDERED SEBASTIAN AROUND 2:50 A.M.
THUS!
EVEN IF THE CULPRIT HAD SEBASTIAN FOR AN ACCOMPLICE...
...IT IS STILL IMPOSSIBLE FOR ONE PERSON TO HAVE MURDERED ALL OF THE VICTIMS!
Siemens
Arthur
Earl Grey
Woodley
Grimsby
Irene
Lau
Pan-mao

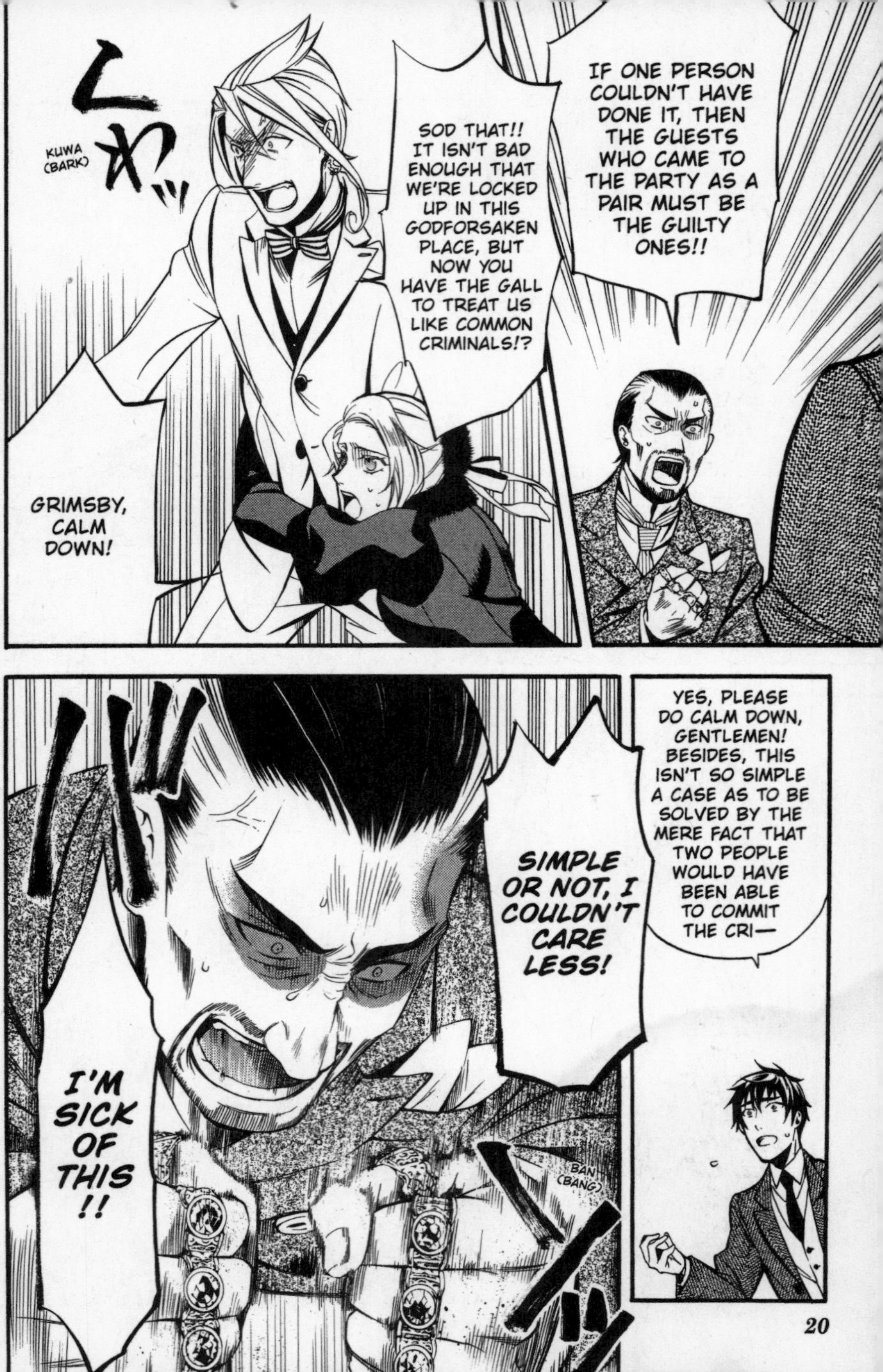
IF ONE PERSON COULDN'T HAVE DONE IT, THEN THE GUESTS WHO CAME TO THE PARTY AS A PAIR MUST BE THE GUILTY ONES!!
SOD THAT!! IT ISN'T BAD ENOUGH THAT WE'RE LOCKED UP IN THIS GODFORSAKEN PLACE, BUT NOW YOU HAVE THE GALL TO TREAT US LIKE COMMON CRIMINALS!?
KUWA (BARK)
GRIMSBY, CALM DOWN!
YES, PLEASE DO CALM DOWN, GENTLEMEN! BESIDES, THIS ISN'T SO SIMPLE A CASE AS TO BE SOLVED BY THE MERE FACT THAT TWO PEOPLE WOULD HAVE BEEN ABLE TO COMMIT THE CRI—
SIMPLE OR NOT, I COULDN'T CARE LESS!
BAN (BANG)
I'M SICK OF THIS!!

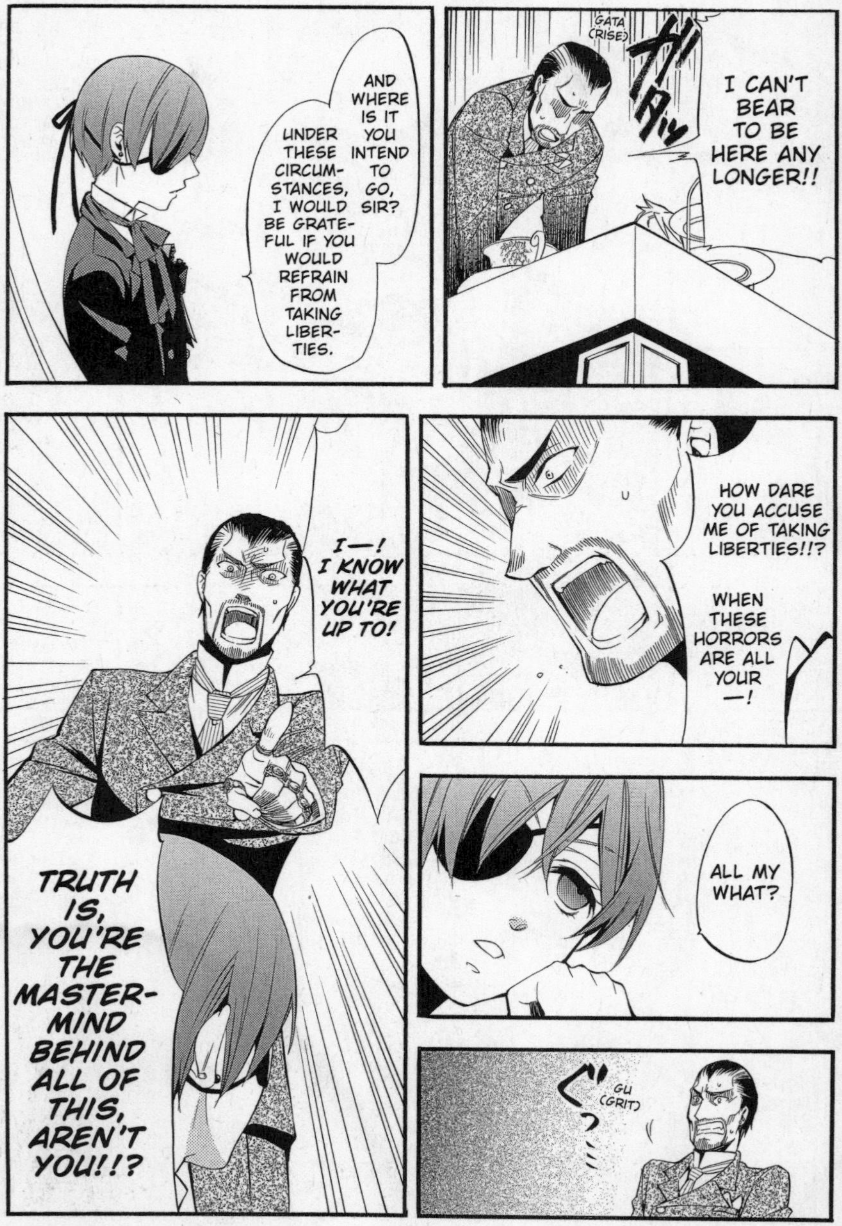

ガタッ
GATA (RISE)
I CAN'T BEAR TO BE HERE ANY LONGER!!
AND WHERE IS IT YOU INTEND TO GO, SIR?
UNDER THESE CIRCUM-STANCES, I WOULD BE GRATE-FUL IF YOU WOULD REFRAIN FROM TAKING LIBER-TIES.
HOW DARE YOU ACCUSE ME OF TAKING LIBERTIES!!?
WHEN THESE HORRORS ARE ALL YOUR —!
ALL MY WHAT?
ぐっ
GU (GRIT)
I—! I KNOW WHAT YOU'RE UP TO!
TRUTH IS, YOU'RE THE MASTER-MIND BEHIND ALL OF THIS, AREN'T YOU!!?

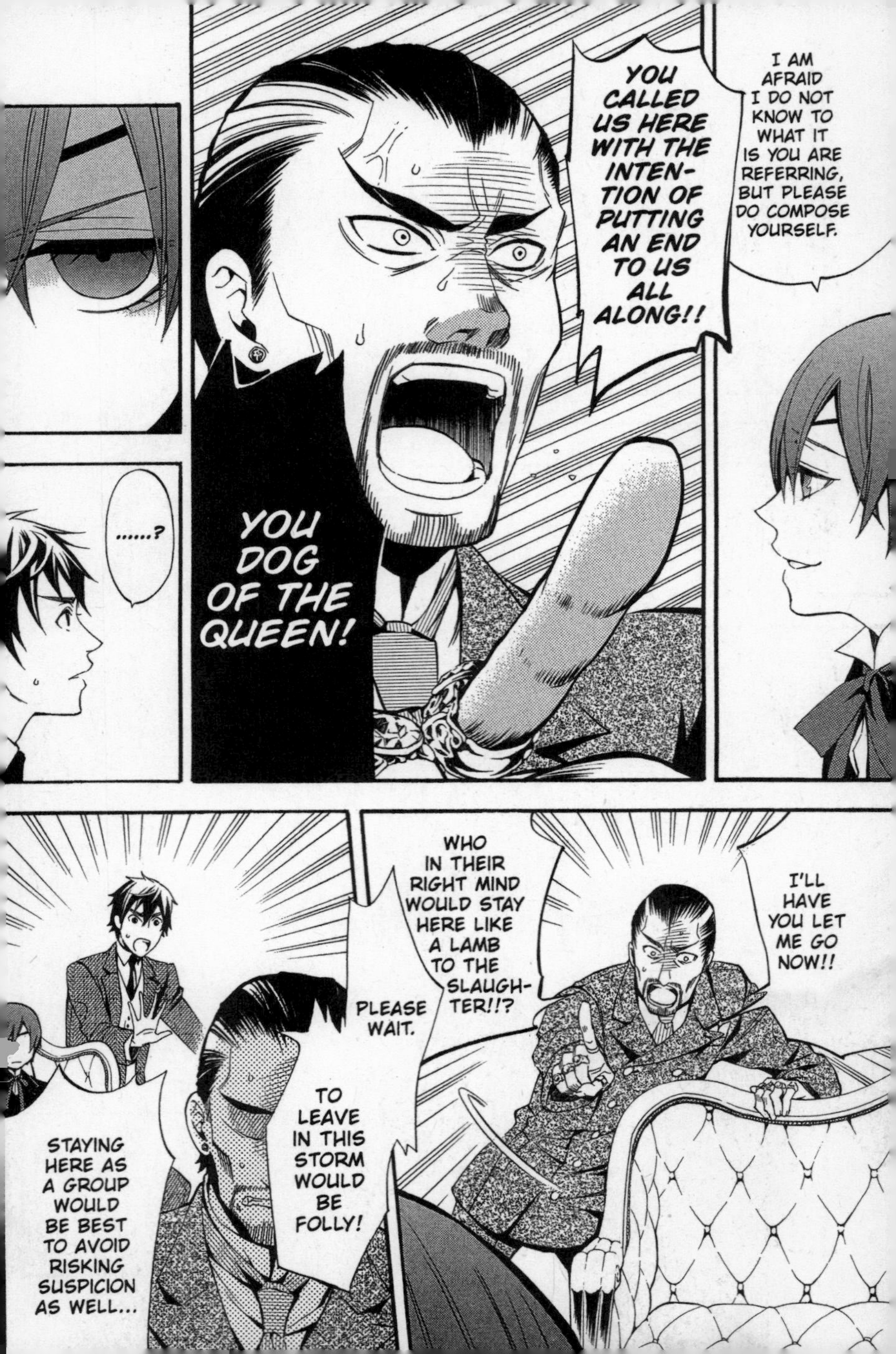
I AM AFRAID I DO NOT KNOW TO WHAT IT IS YOU ARE REFERRING, BUT PLEASE DO COMPOSE YOURSELF.
YOU CALLED US HERE WITH THE INTEN-TION OF PUTTING AN END TO US ALL ALONG!!
YOU DOG OF THE QUEEN!
......?
I'LL HAVE YOU LET ME GO NOW!!
WHO IN THEIR RIGHT MIND WOULD STAY HERE LIKE A LAMB TO THE SLAUGH-TER!!?
PLEASE WAIT.
TO LEAVE IN THIS STORM WOULD BE FOLLY!
STAYING HERE AS A GROUP WOULD BE BEST TO AVOID RISKING SUSPICION AS WELL...

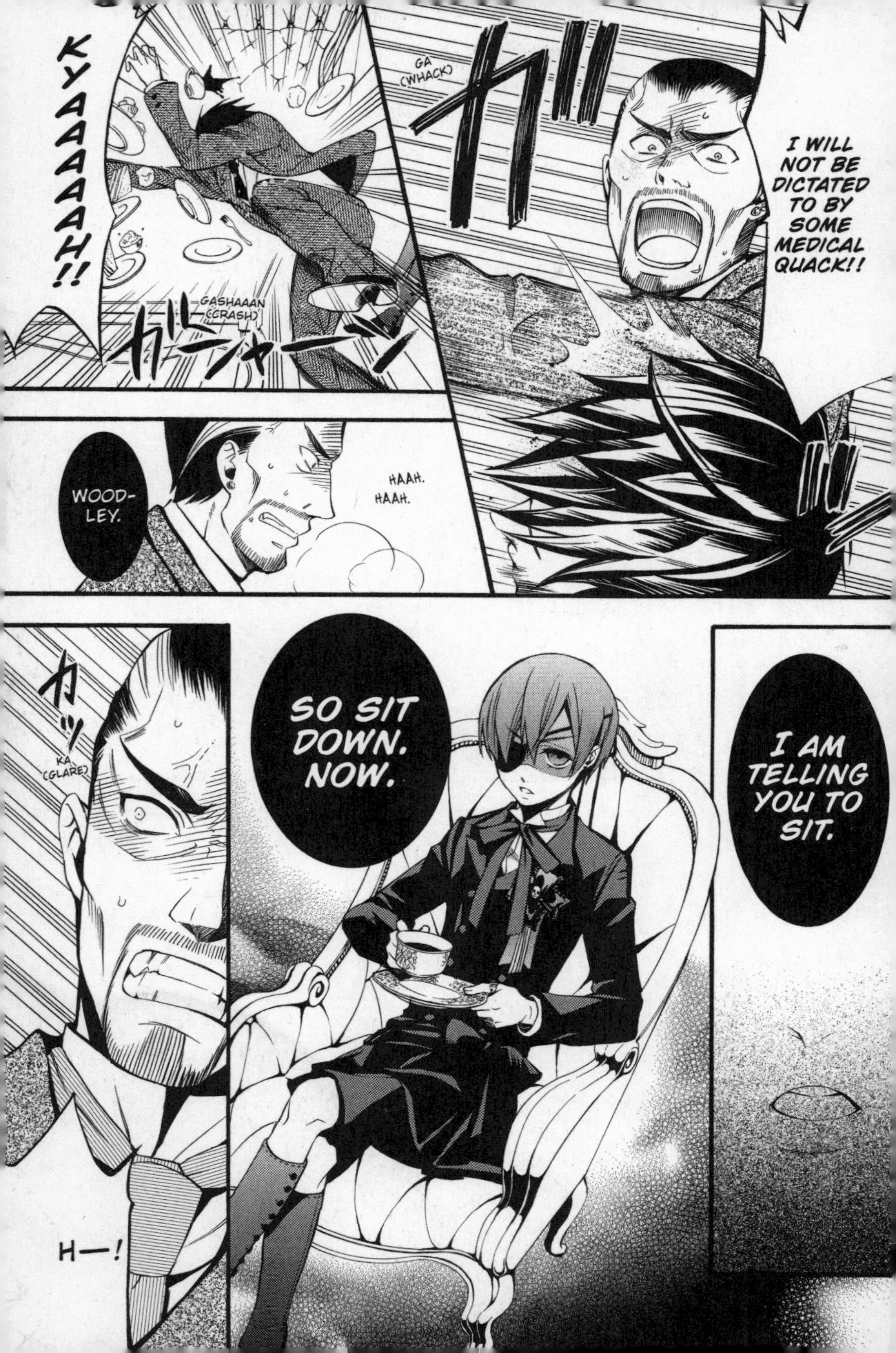
GA (WHACK)
I WILL NOT BE DICTATED TO BY SOME MEDICAL QUACK!!
KYAAAAAAH!!
GASHAAAN (CRASH)
HAAH. HAAH.
WOOD-LEY.
I AM TELLING YOU TO SIT.
SO SIT DOWN. NOW.
KA (GLARE)
H—!

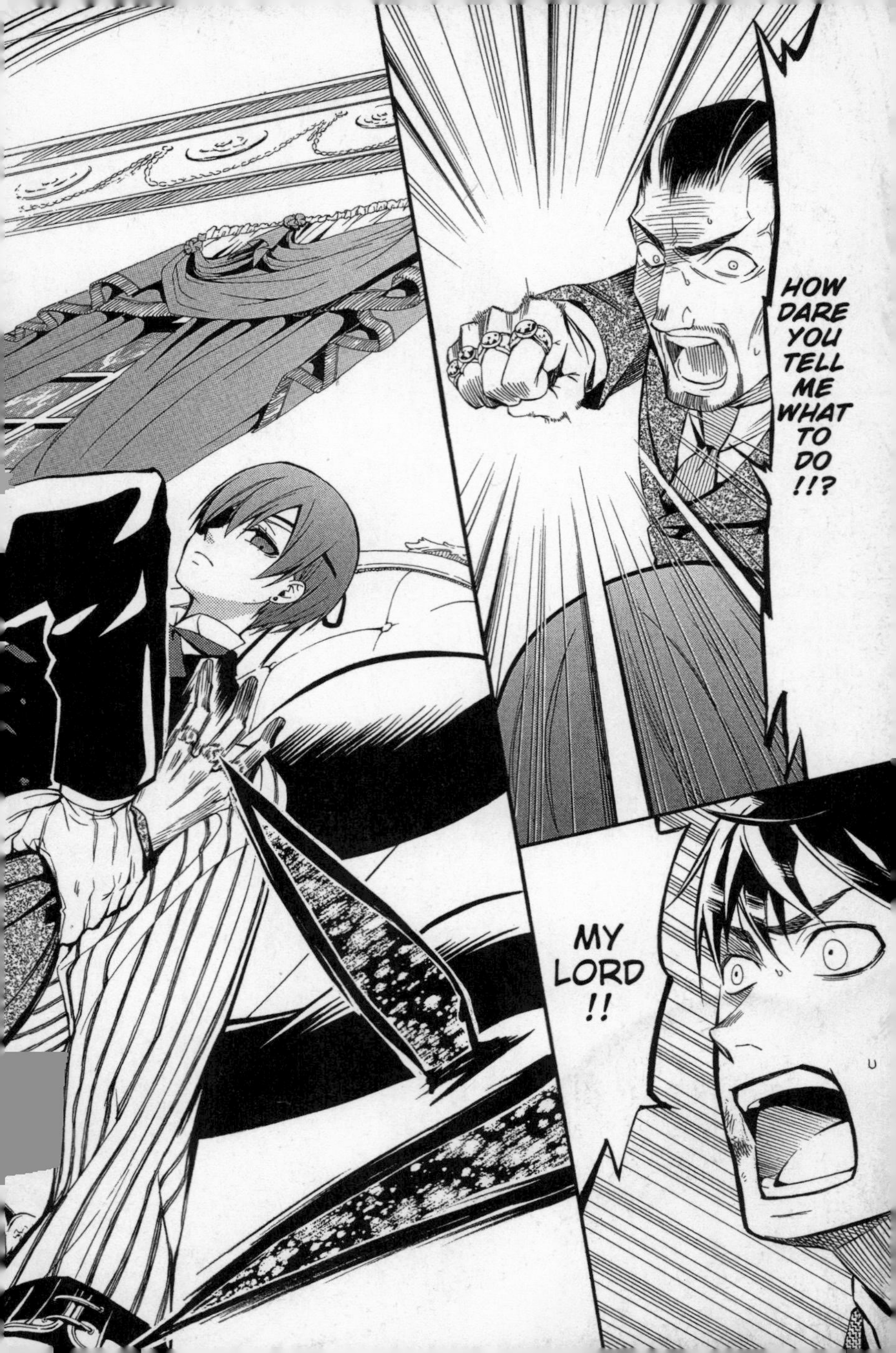
HOW DARE YOU TELL ME WHAT TO DO!!?
MY LORD!!

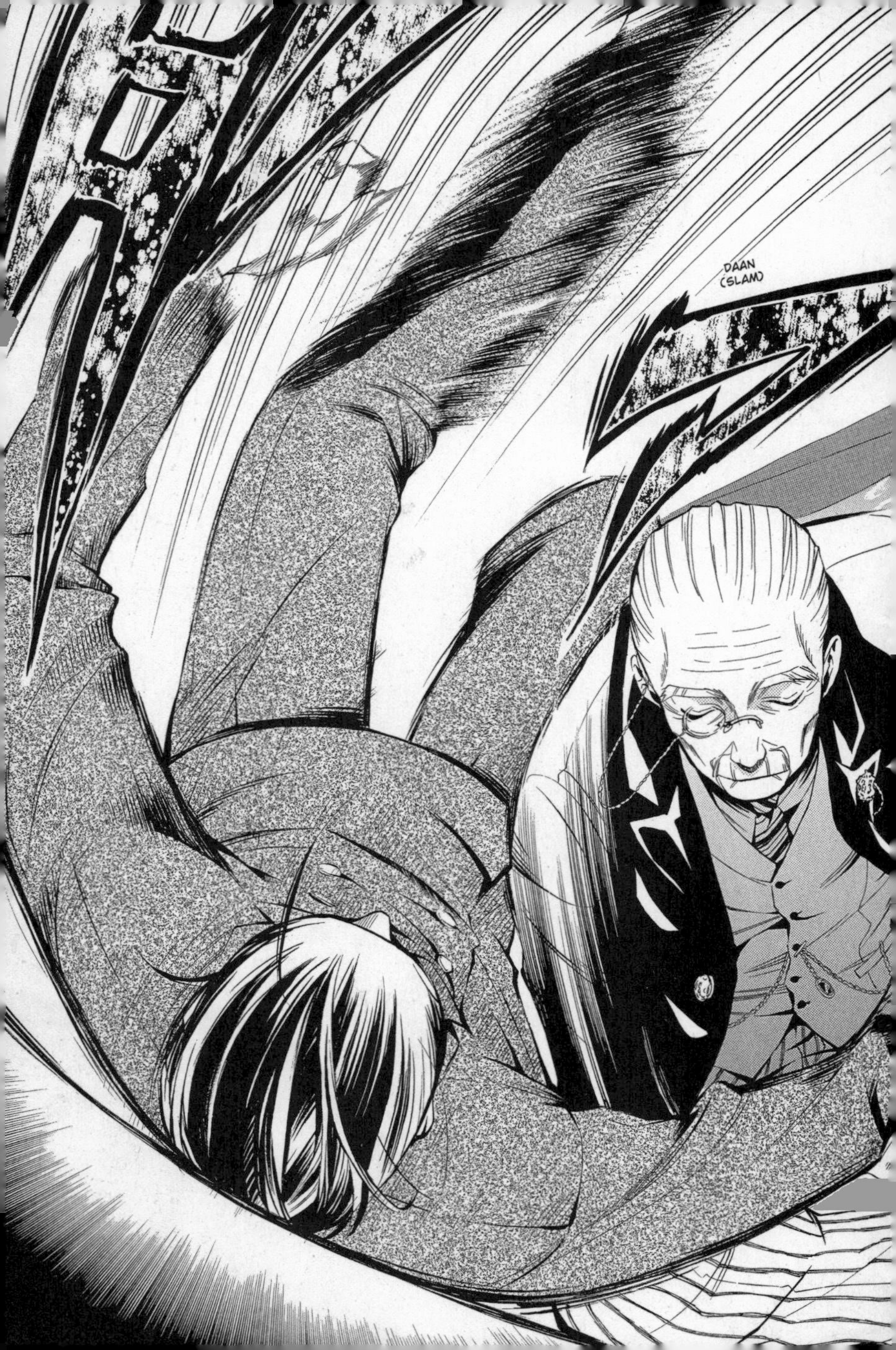
DAAN
(SLAM)

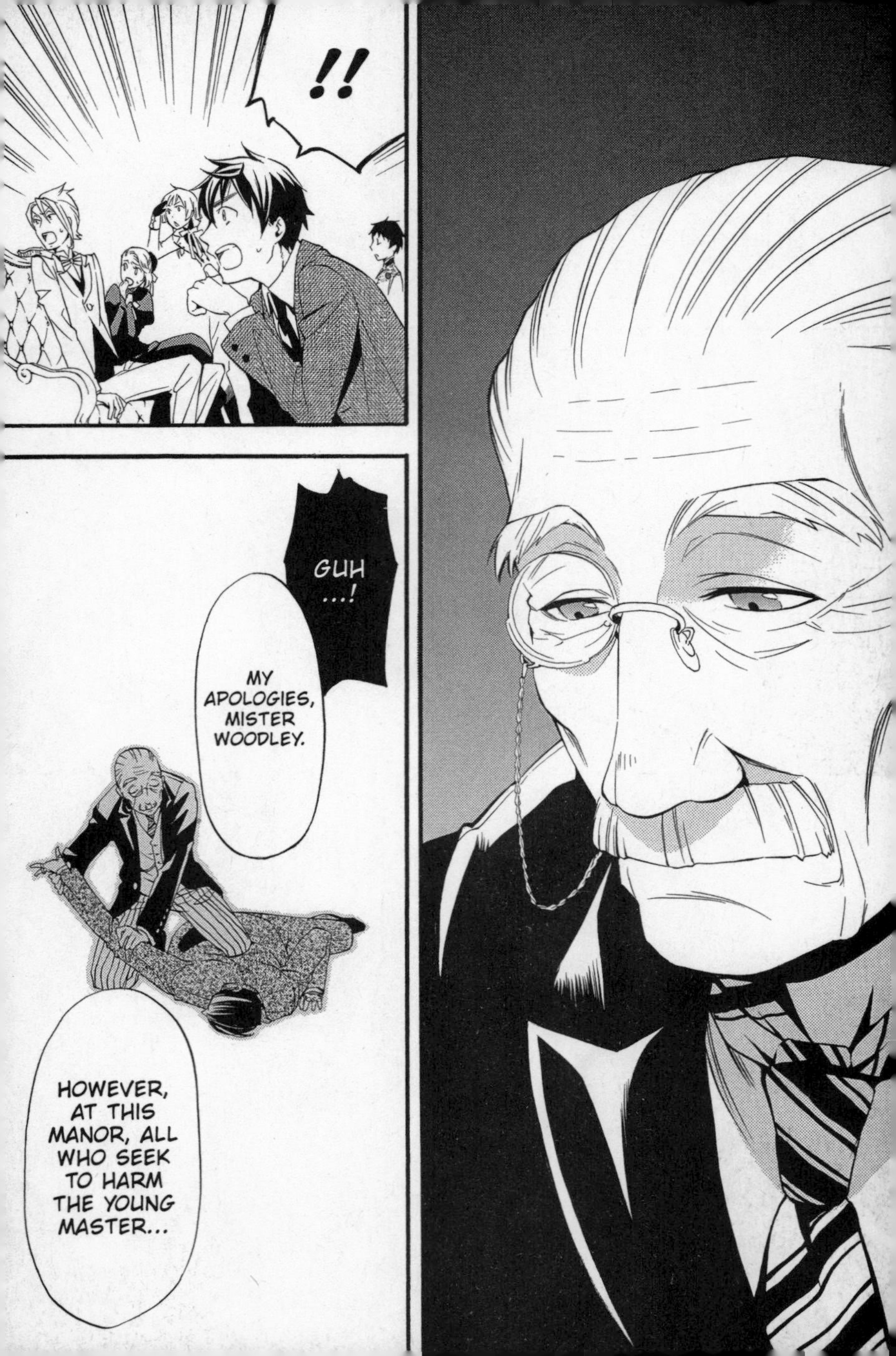
!!
GUH ...!
MY APOLOGIES, MISTER WOODLEY.
HOWEVER, AT THIS MANOR, ALL WHO SEEK TO HARM THE YOUNG MASTER...

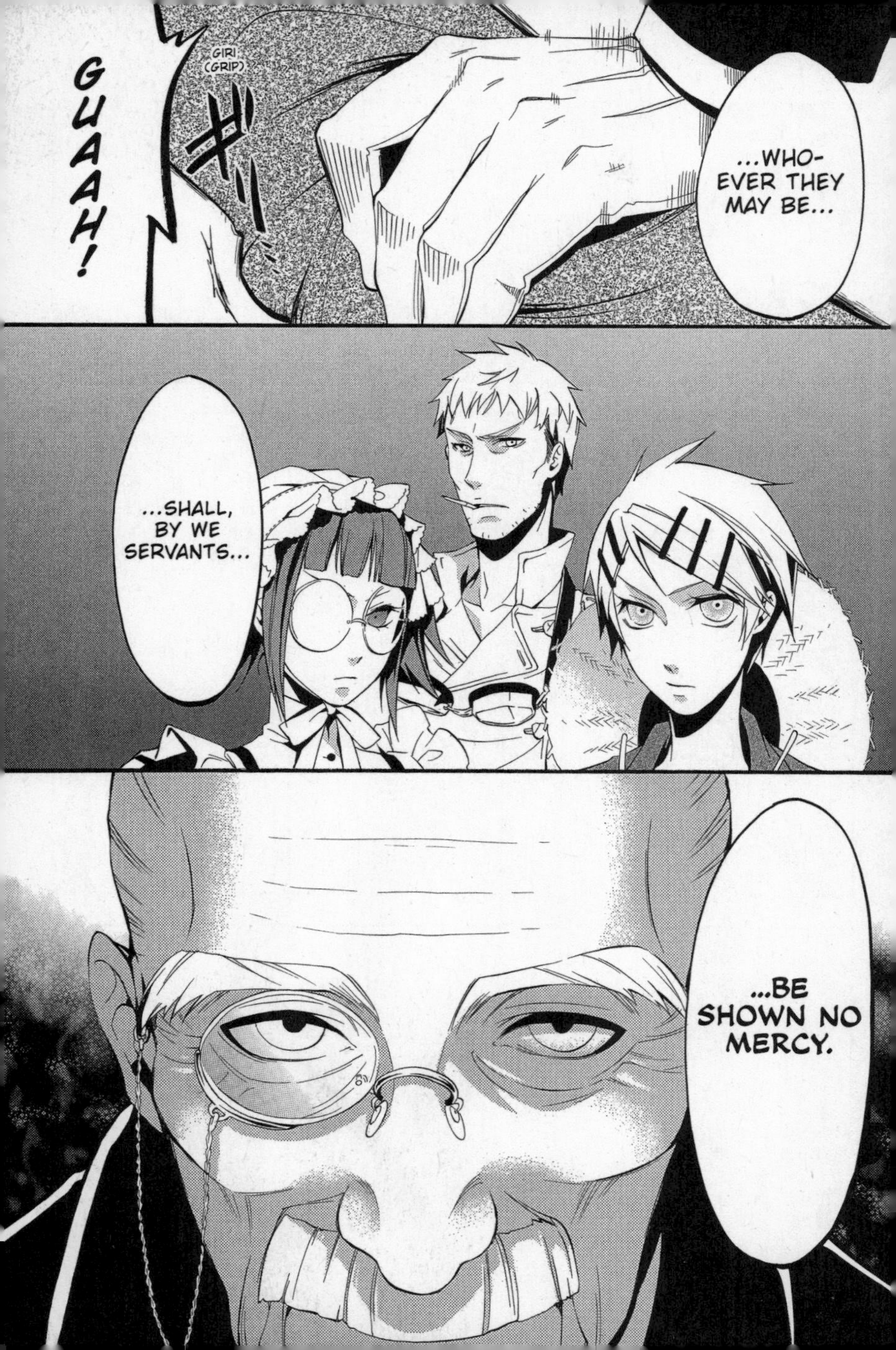
...WHO-EVER THEY MAY BE...
GIRI (GRIP)
GUAAAH!
...SHALL, BY WE SERVANTS...
...BE SHOWN NO MERCY.

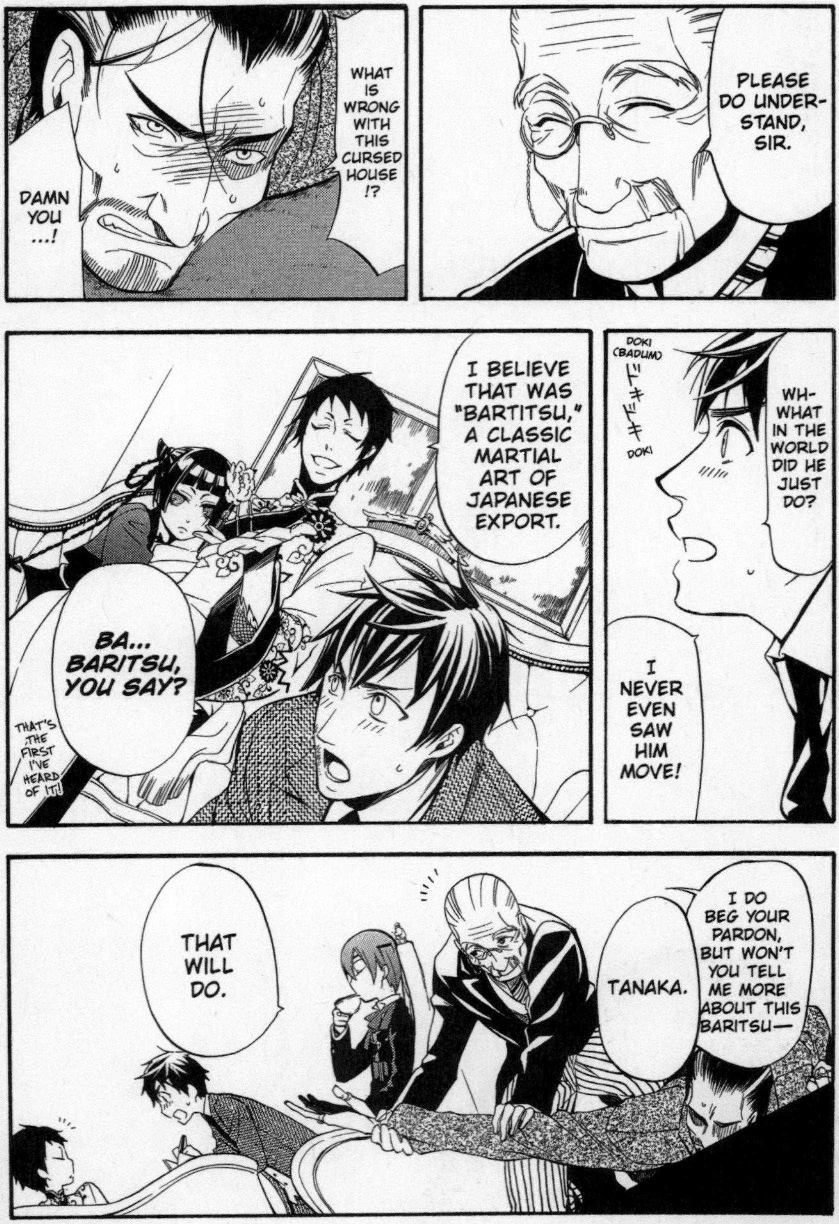
PLEASE DO UNDER-STAND, SIR.
WHAT IS WRONG WITH THIS CURSED HOUSE!?
DAMN YOU ...!
DOKI (BADUM) ドキドキ DOKI
WH-WHAT IN THE WORLD DID HE JUST DO?
I NEVER EVEN SAW HIM MOVE!
I BELIEVE THAT WAS "BARTITSU," A CLASSIC MARTIAL ART OF JAPANESE EXPORT.
BA... BARITSU, YOU SAY?
THAT'S THE FIRST I'VE HEARD OF IT!
I DO BEG YOUR PARDON, BUT WON'T YOU TELL ME MORE ABOUT THIS BARITSU—
TANAKA.
THAT WILL DO.

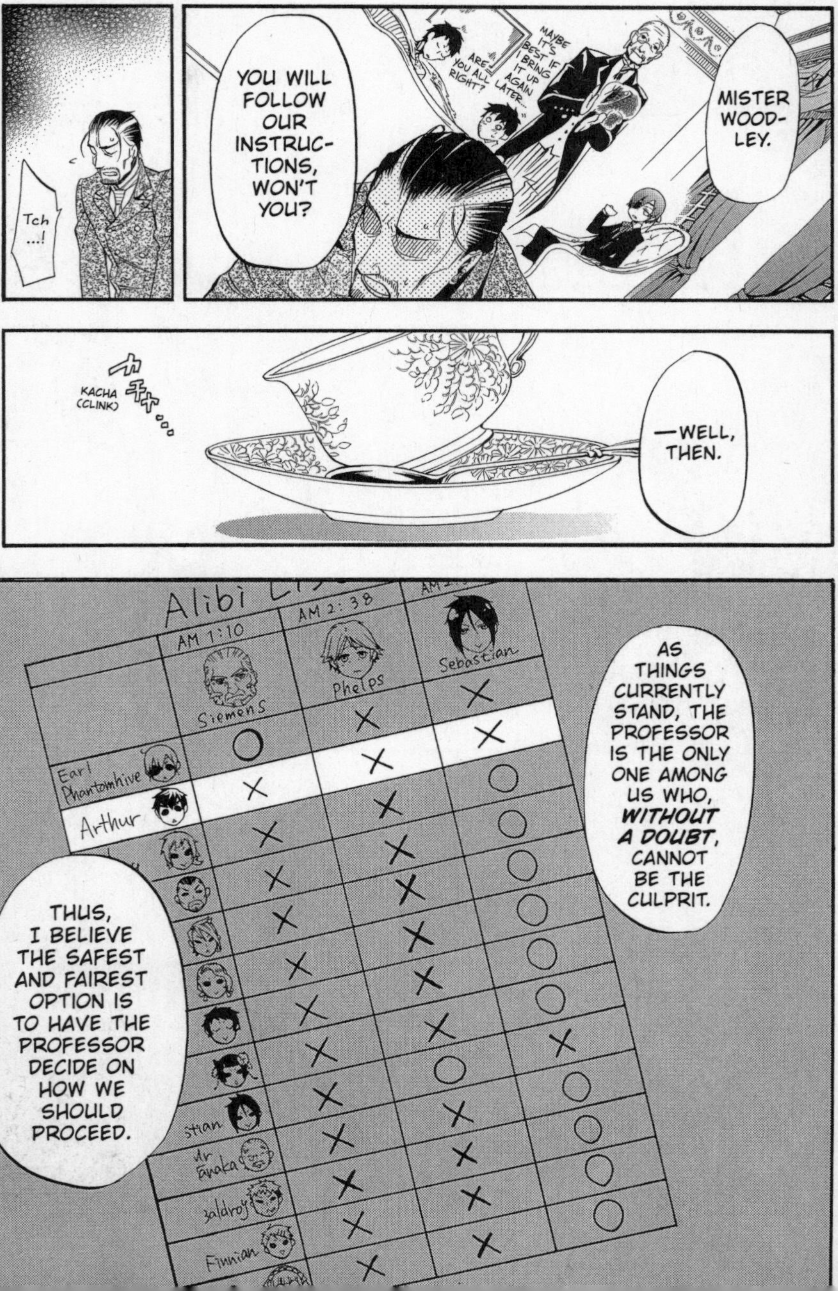
MISTER WOODLEY.
YOU WILL FOLLOW OUR INSTRUCTIONS, WON'T YOU?
MAYBE IT'S BEST IF I BRING IT UP AGAIN LATER...
ARE YOU ALL RIGHT?
Tch ...!
—WELL, THEN.
KACHA (CLINK)
AM 1:10
AM 2:38
Siemens
Phelps
Sebastian
Earl Phantomhive
Arthur
Finnian
AS THINGS CURRENTLY STAND, THE PROFESSOR IS THE ONLY ONE AMONG US WHO, ***WITHOUT A DOUBT***, CANNOT BE THE CULPRIT.
THUS, I BELIEVE THE SAFEST AND FAIREST OPTION IS TO HAVE THE PROFESSOR DECIDE ON HOW WE SHOULD PROCEED.

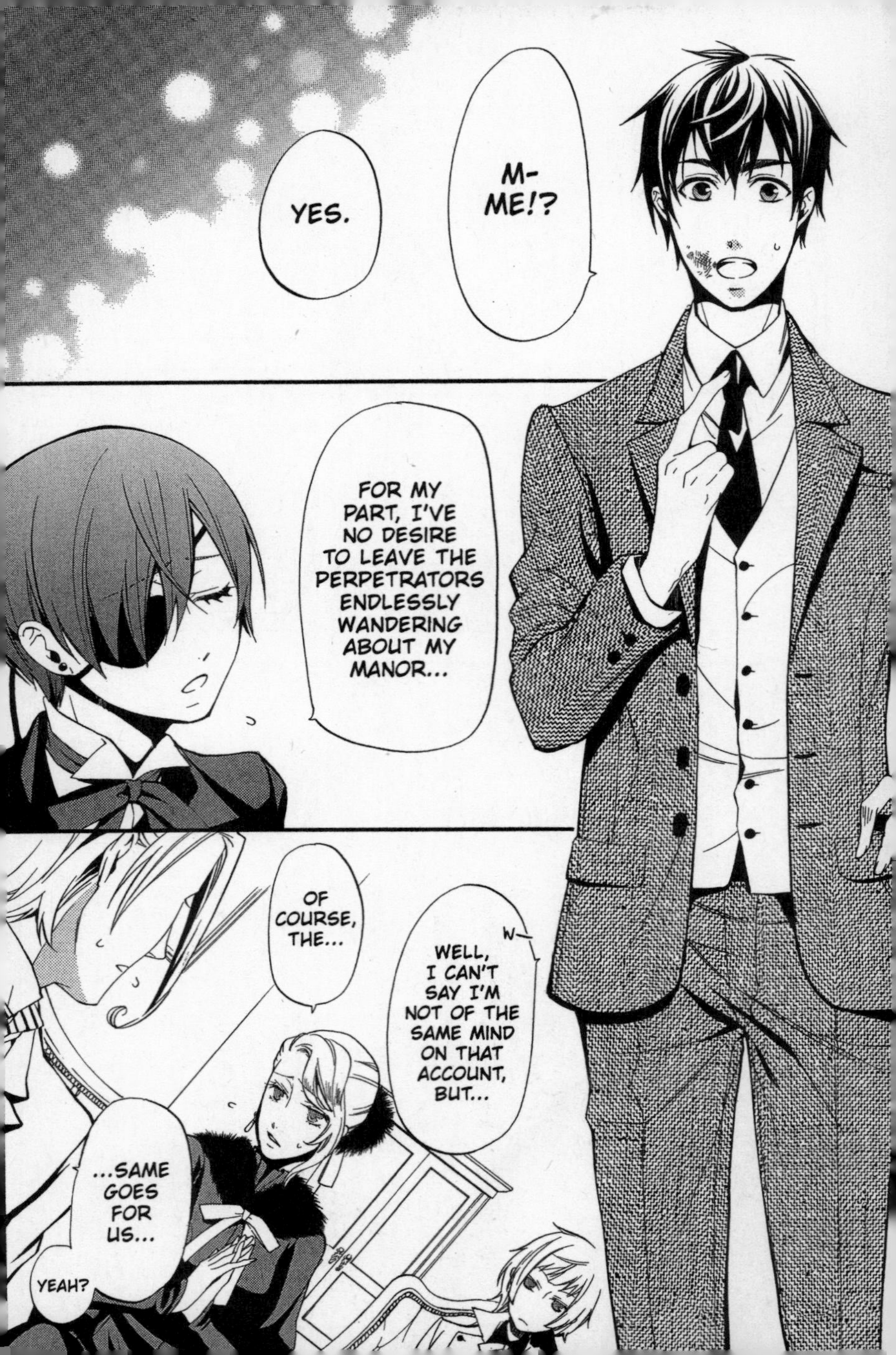
M-
ME!?
YES.
FOR MY PART, I'VE NO DESIRE TO LEAVE THE PERPETRATORS ENDLESSLY WANDERING ABOUT MY MANOR...
W—
WELL, I CAN'T SAY I'M NOT OF THE SAME MIND ON THAT ACCOUNT, BUT...
OF COURSE, THE...
...SAME GOES FOR US...
YEAH?

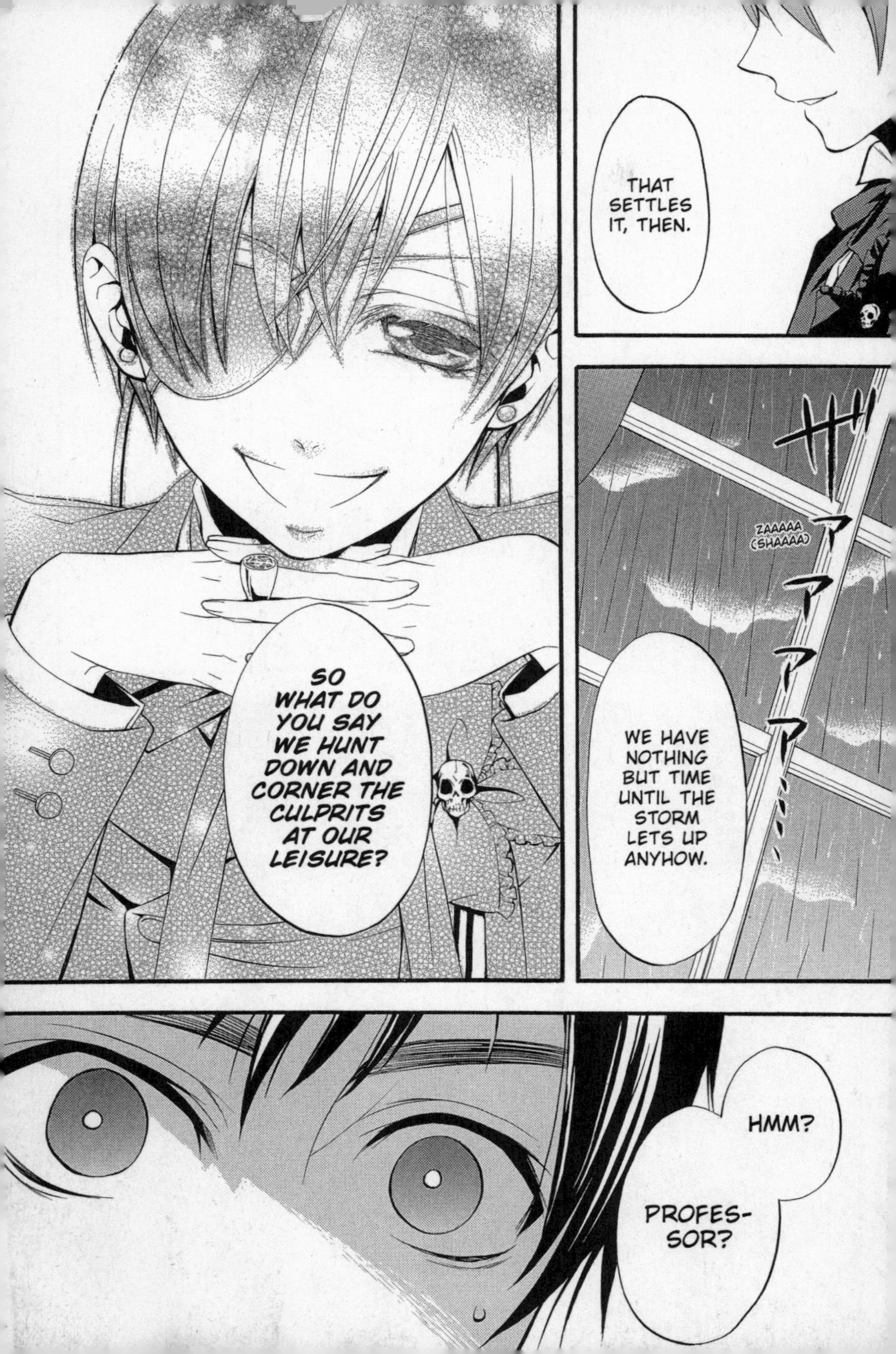
THAT SETTLES IT, THEN.
ZAAAAA (SHAAAA)
WE HAVE NOTHING BUT TIME UNTIL THE STORM LETS UP ANYHOW.
SO WHAT DO YOU SAY WE HUNT DOWN AND CORNER THE CULPRITS AT OUR LEISURE?
HMM?
PROFES-SOR?

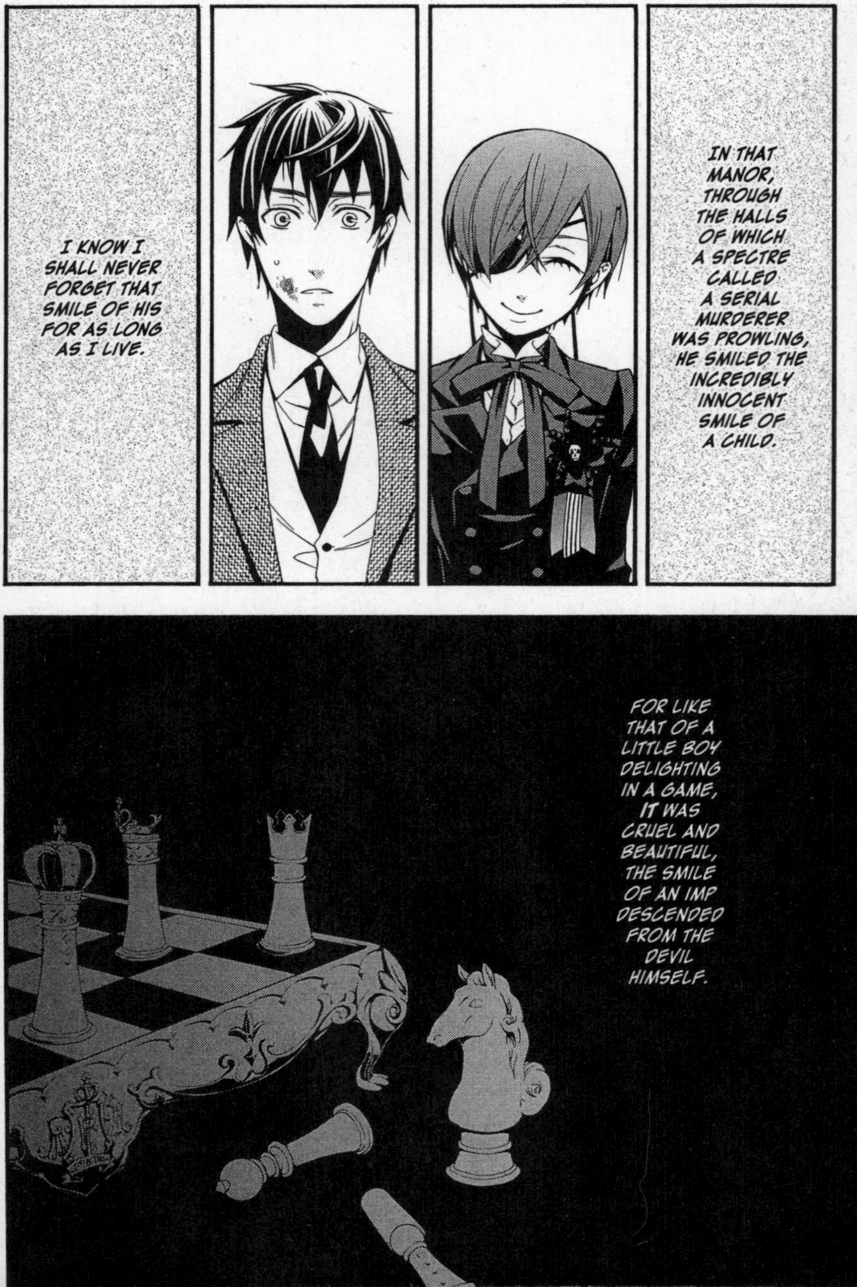
IN THAT MANOR, THROUGH THE HALLS OF WHICH A SPECTRE CALLED A SERIAL MURDERER WAS PROWLING, HE SMILED THE INCREDIBLY INNOCENT SMILE OF A CHILD.
I KNOW I SHALL NEVER FORGET THAT SMILE OF HIS FOR AS LONG AS I LIVE.
FOR LIKE THAT OF A LITTLE BOY DELIGHTING IN A GAME, IT WAS CRUEL AND BEAUTIFUL, THE SMILE OF AN IMP DESCENDED FROM THE DEVIL HIMSELF.

Black Butler

Chapter 44
At noon : The Butler, Wailing

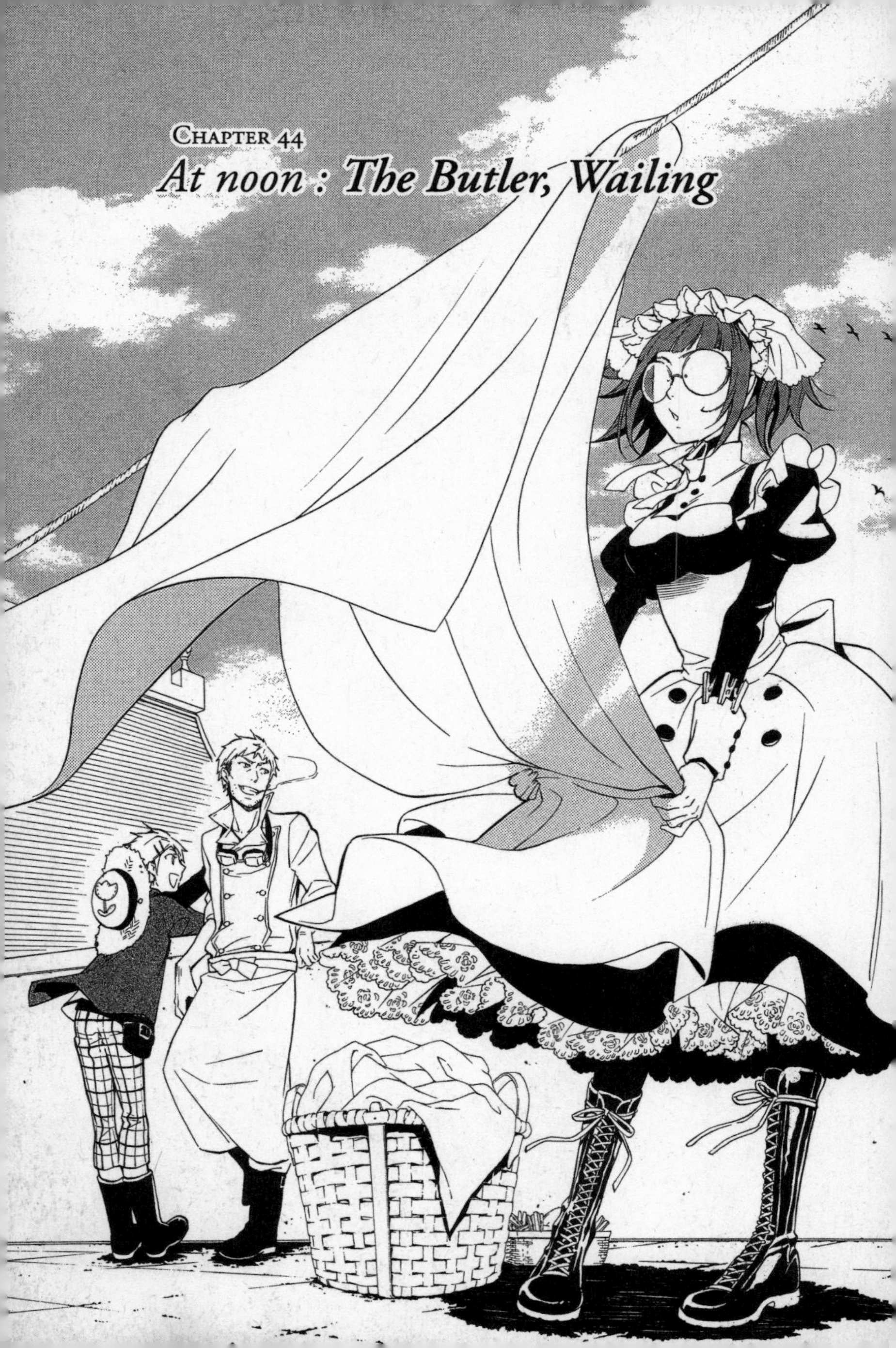

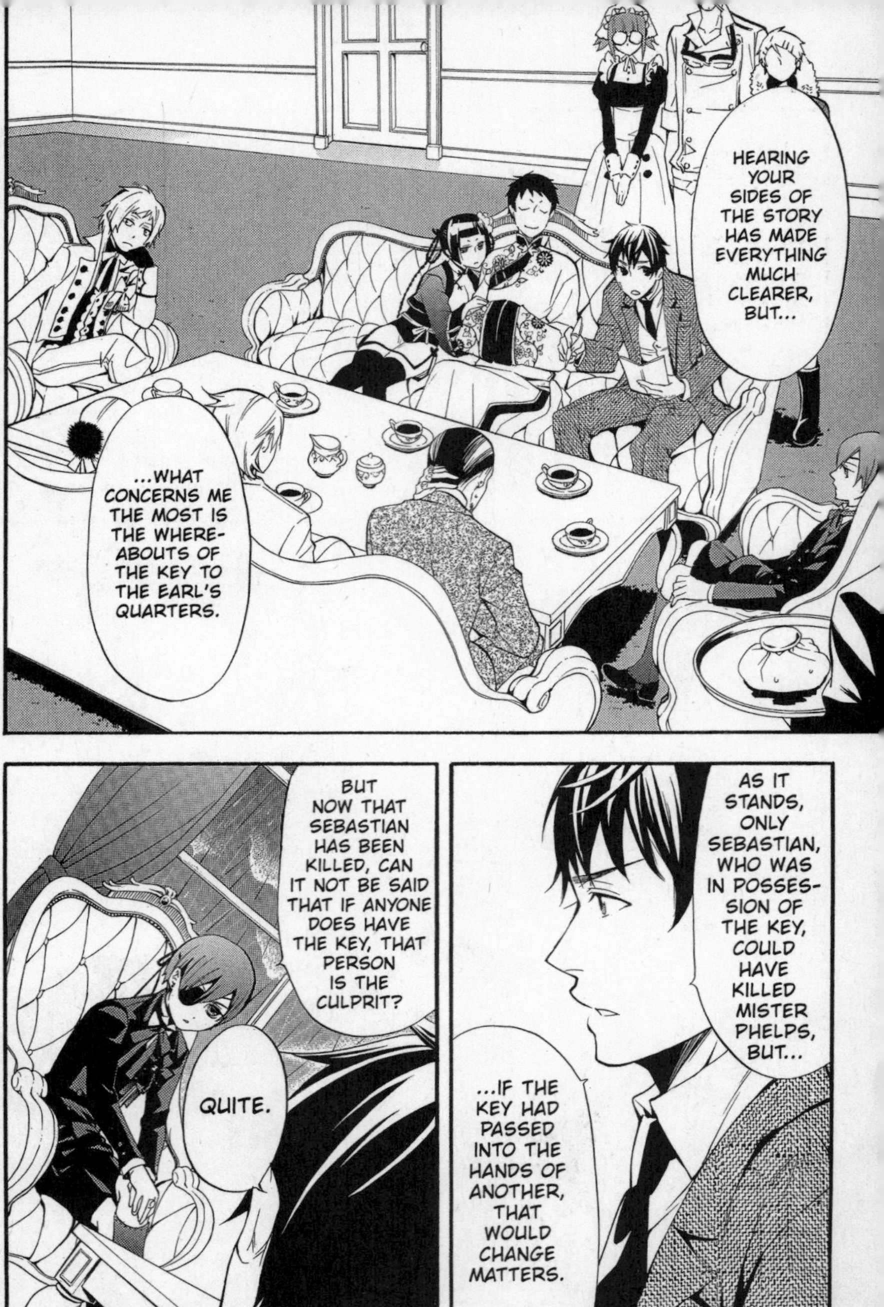
HEARING YOUR SIDES OF THE STORY HAS MADE EVERYTHING MUCH CLEARER, BUT...
...WHAT CONCERNS ME THE MOST IS THE WHERE-ABOUTS OF THE KEY TO THE EARL'S QUARTERS.
AS IT STANDS, ONLY SEBASTIAN, WHO WAS IN POSSES-SION OF THE KEY, COULD HAVE KILLED MISTER PHELPS, BUT...
...IF THE KEY HAD PASSED INTO THE HANDS OF ANOTHER, THAT WOULD CHANGE MATTERS.
BUT NOW THAT SEBASTIAN HAS BEEN KILLED, CAN IT NOT BE SAID THAT IF ANYONE DOES HAVE THE KEY, THAT PERSON IS THE CULPRIT?
QUITE.

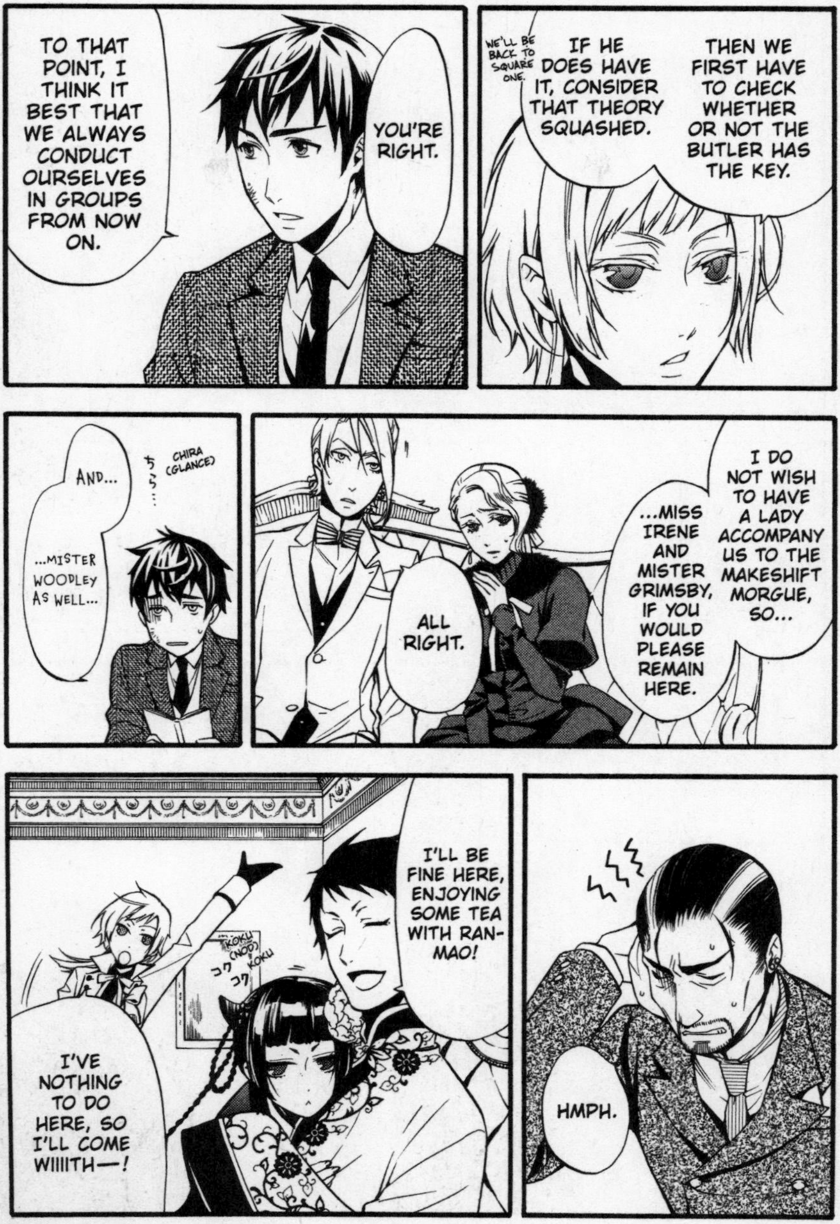
THEN WE FIRST HAVE TO CHECK WHETHER OR NOT THE BUTLER HAS THE KEY.
IF HE DOES HAVE IT, CONSIDER THAT THEORY SQUASHED.
WE'LL BE BACK TO SQUARE ONE.
YOU'RE RIGHT.
TO THAT POINT, I THINK IT BEST THAT WE ALWAYS CONDUCT OURSELVES IN GROUPS FROM NOW ON.
I DO NOT WISH TO HAVE A LADY ACCOMPANY US TO THE MAKESHIFT MORGUE, SO...
...MISS IRENE AND MISTER GRIMSBY, IF YOU WOULD PLEASE REMAIN HERE.
ALL RIGHT.
ちら…
CHIRA (GLANCE)
AND...
...MISTER WOODLEY AS WELL...
HMPH.
I'LL BE FINE HERE, ENJOYING SOME TEA WITH RAN-MAO!
コク コク
KOKU (NOD) KOKU
I'VE NOTHING TO DO HERE, SO I'LL COME WIIIITH—!

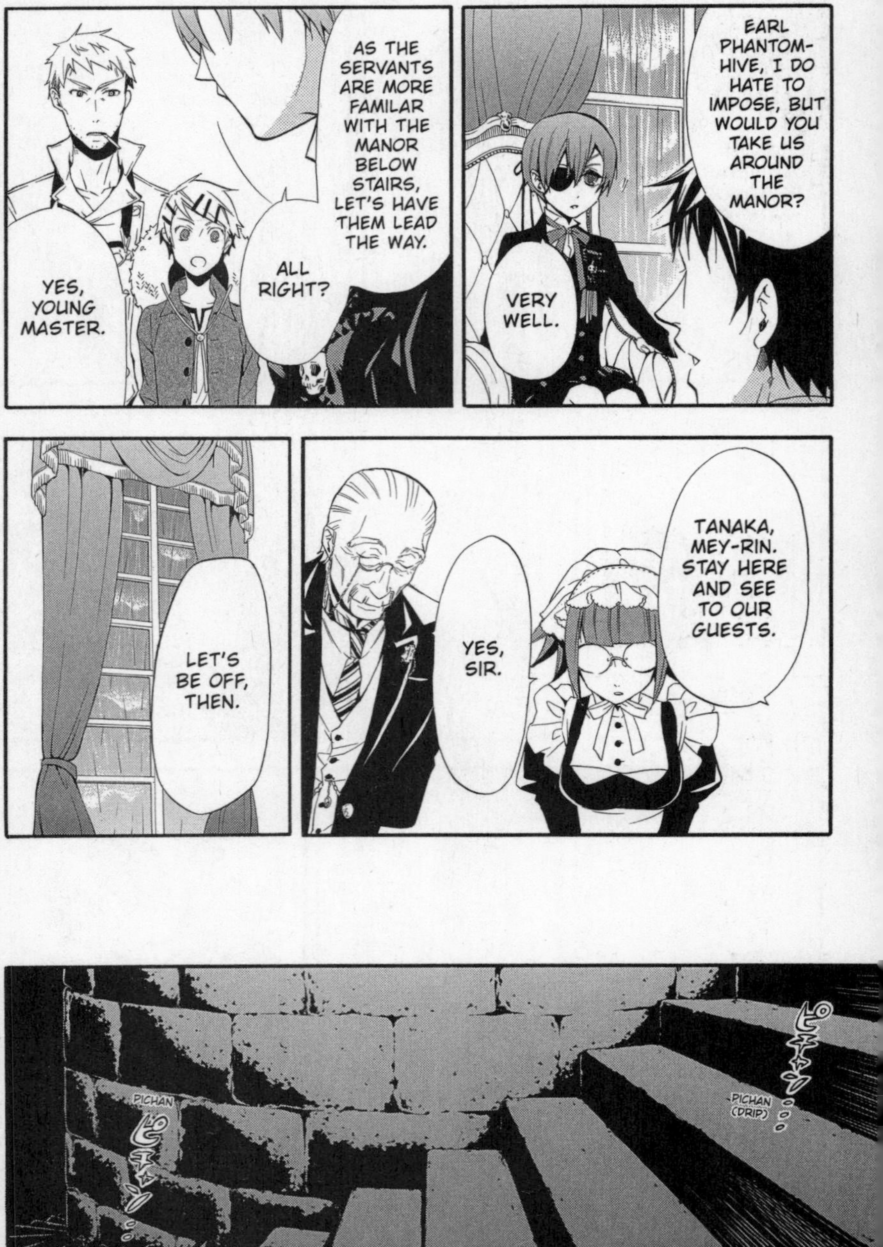
EARL PHANTOM-HIVE, I DO HATE TO IMPOSE, BUT WOULD YOU TAKE US AROUND THE MANOR?
VERY WELL.
AS THE SERVANTS ARE MORE FAMILAR WITH THE MANOR BELOW STAIRS, LET'S HAVE THEM LEAD THE WAY.
ALL RIGHT?
YES, YOUNG MASTER.
TANAKA, MEY-RIN. STAY HERE AND SEE TO OUR GUESTS.
YES, SIR.
LET'S BE OFF, THEN.
PICHAN (DRIP)
PICHAN

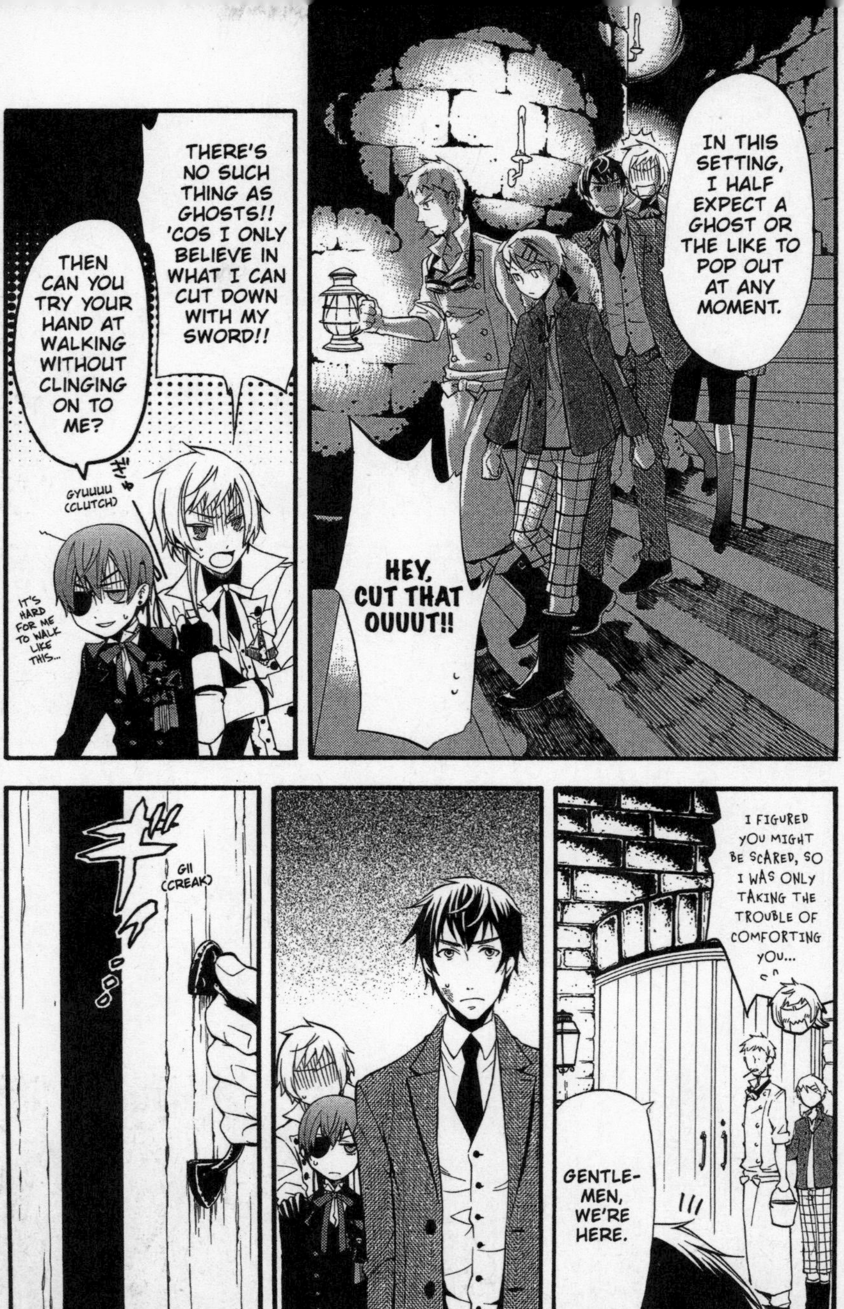
IN THIS SETTING, I HALF EXPECT A GHOST OR THE LIKE TO POP OUT AT ANY MOMENT.
HEY, CUT THAT OUUUT!!
THERE'S NO SUCH THING AS GHOSTS!! 'COS I ONLY BELIEVE IN WHAT I CAN CUT DOWN WITH MY SWORD!!
THEN CAN YOU TRY YOUR HAND AT WALKING WITHOUT CLINGING ON TO ME?
GYUUUU (CLUTCH)
IT'S HARD FOR ME TO WALK LIKE THIS...
I FIGURED YOU MIGHT BE SCARED, SO I WAS ONLY TAKING THE TROUBLE OF COMFORTING YOU...
GENTLE-MEN, WE'RE HERE.
GII (CREAK)

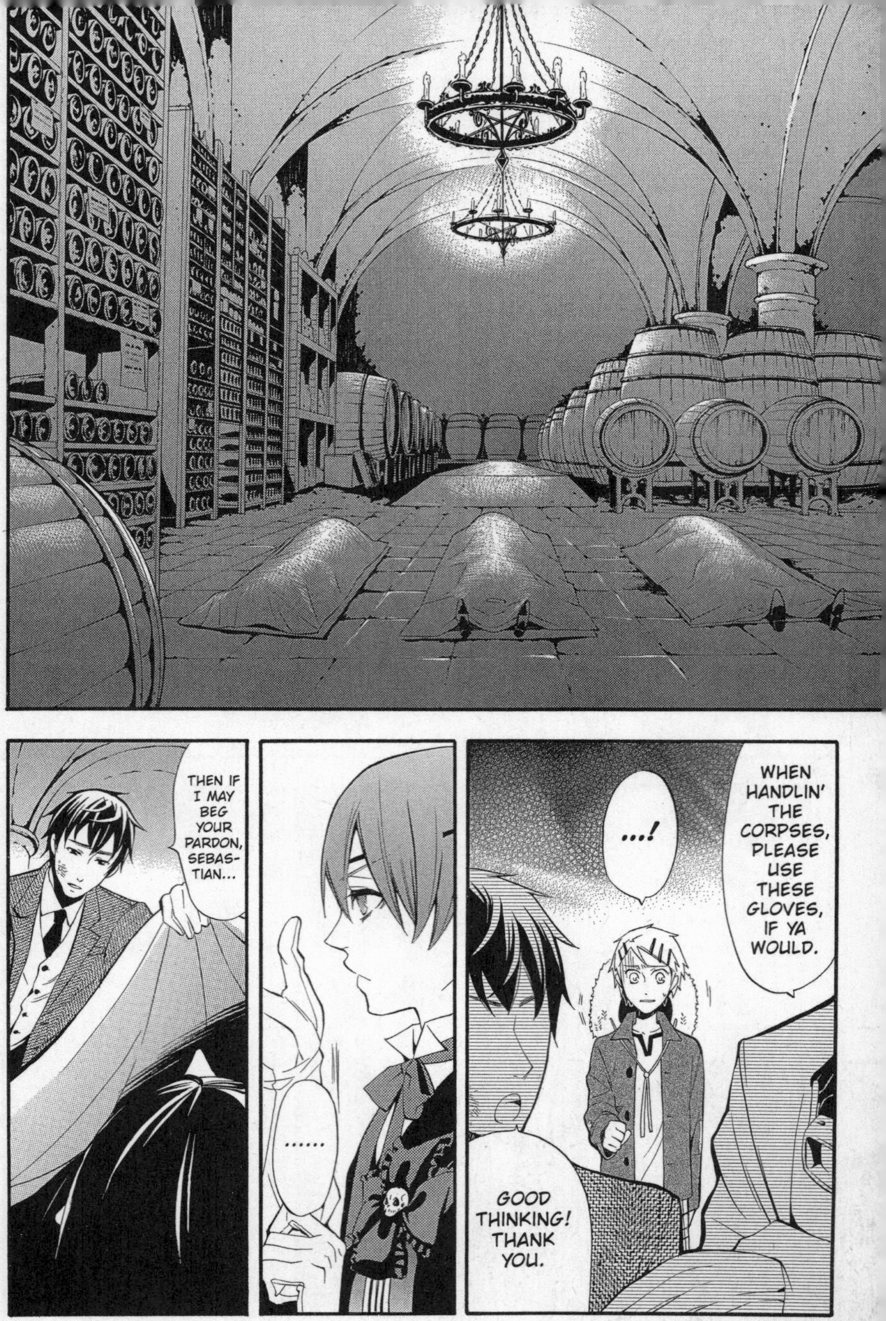
WHEN HANDLIN' THE CORPSES, PLEASE USE THESE GLOVES, IF YA WOULD.
...!
GOOD THINKING! THANK YOU.
......
THEN IF I MAY BEG YOUR PARDON, SEBAS-TIAN...

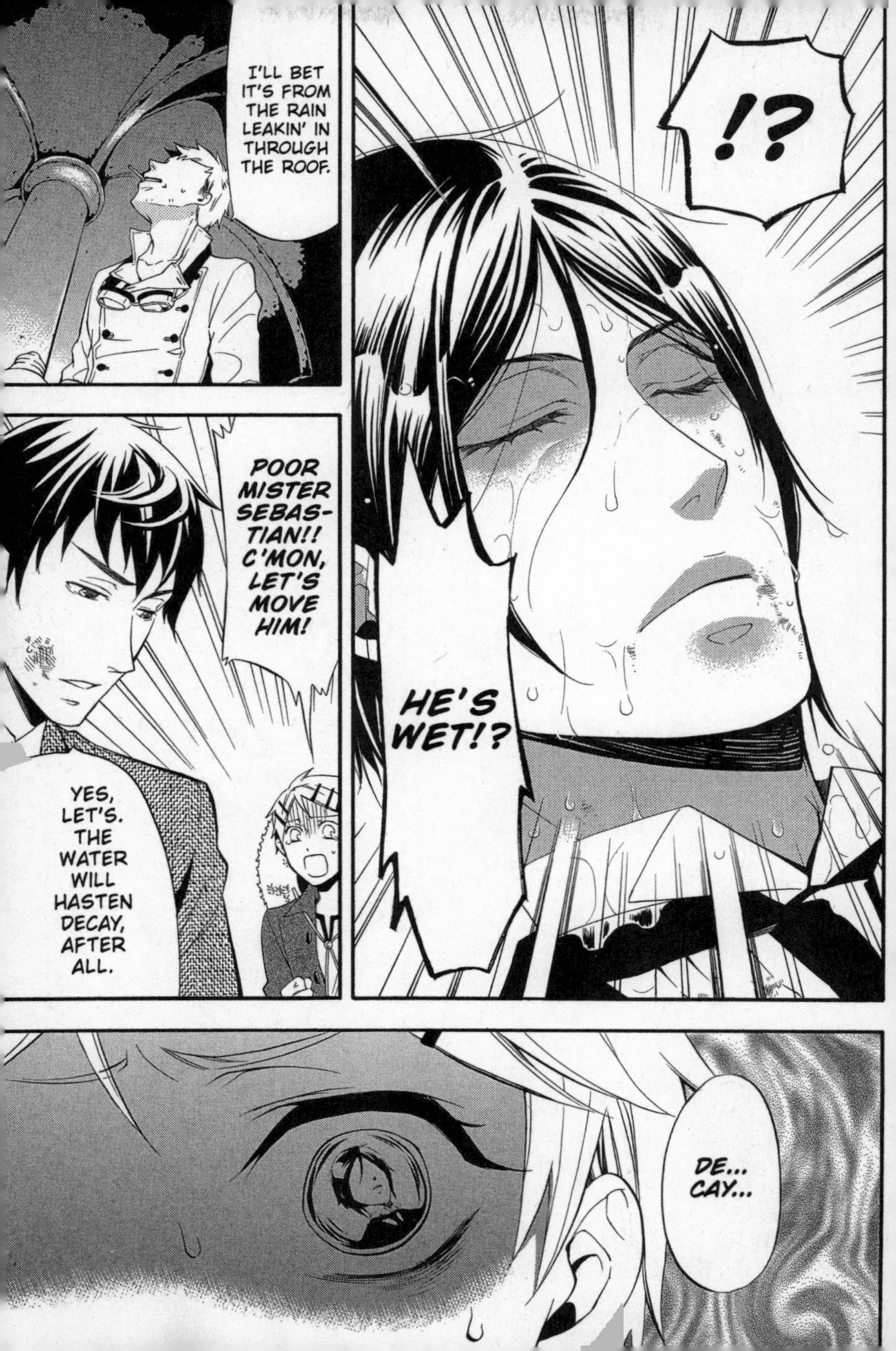
!?
HE'S WET!?
I'LL BET IT'S FROM THE RAIN LEAKIN' IN THROUGH THE ROOF.
POOR MISTER SEBASTIAN!! C'MON, LET'S MOVE HIM!
YES, LET'S. THE WATER WILL HASTEN DECAY, AFTER ALL.
DE... CAY...

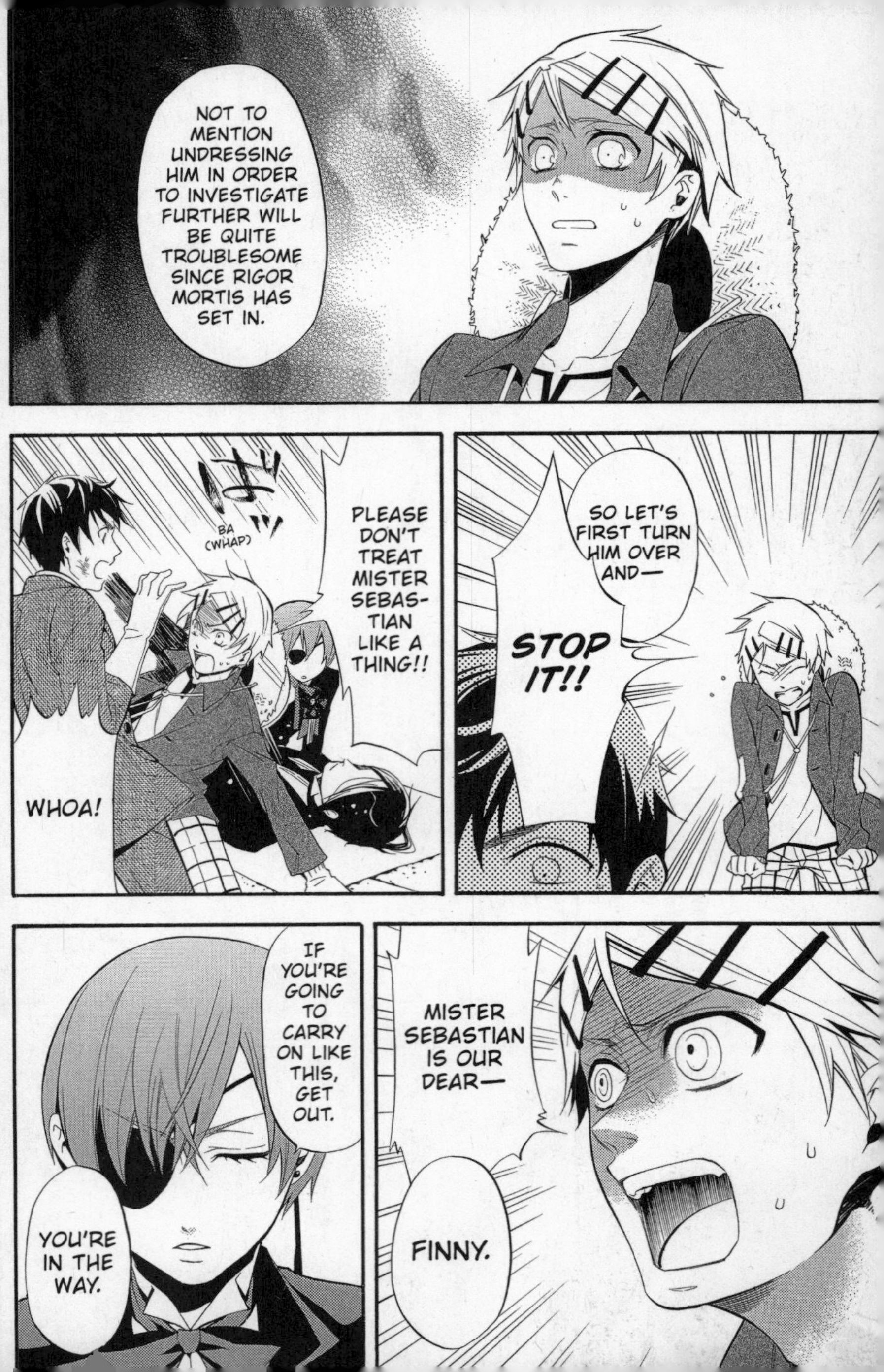
NOT TO MENTION UNDRESSING HIM IN ORDER TO INVESTIGATE FURTHER WILL BE QUITE TROUBLESOME SINCE RIGOR MORTIS HAS SET IN.
SO LET'S FIRST TURN HIM OVER AND—
STOP IT!!
PLEASE DON'T TREAT MISTER SEBAS-TIAN LIKE A THING!!
BA (WHAP)
WHOA!
MISTER SEBASTIAN IS OUR DEAR—
FINNY.
IF YOU'RE GOING TO CARRY ON LIKE THIS, GET OUT.
YOU'RE IN THE WAY.

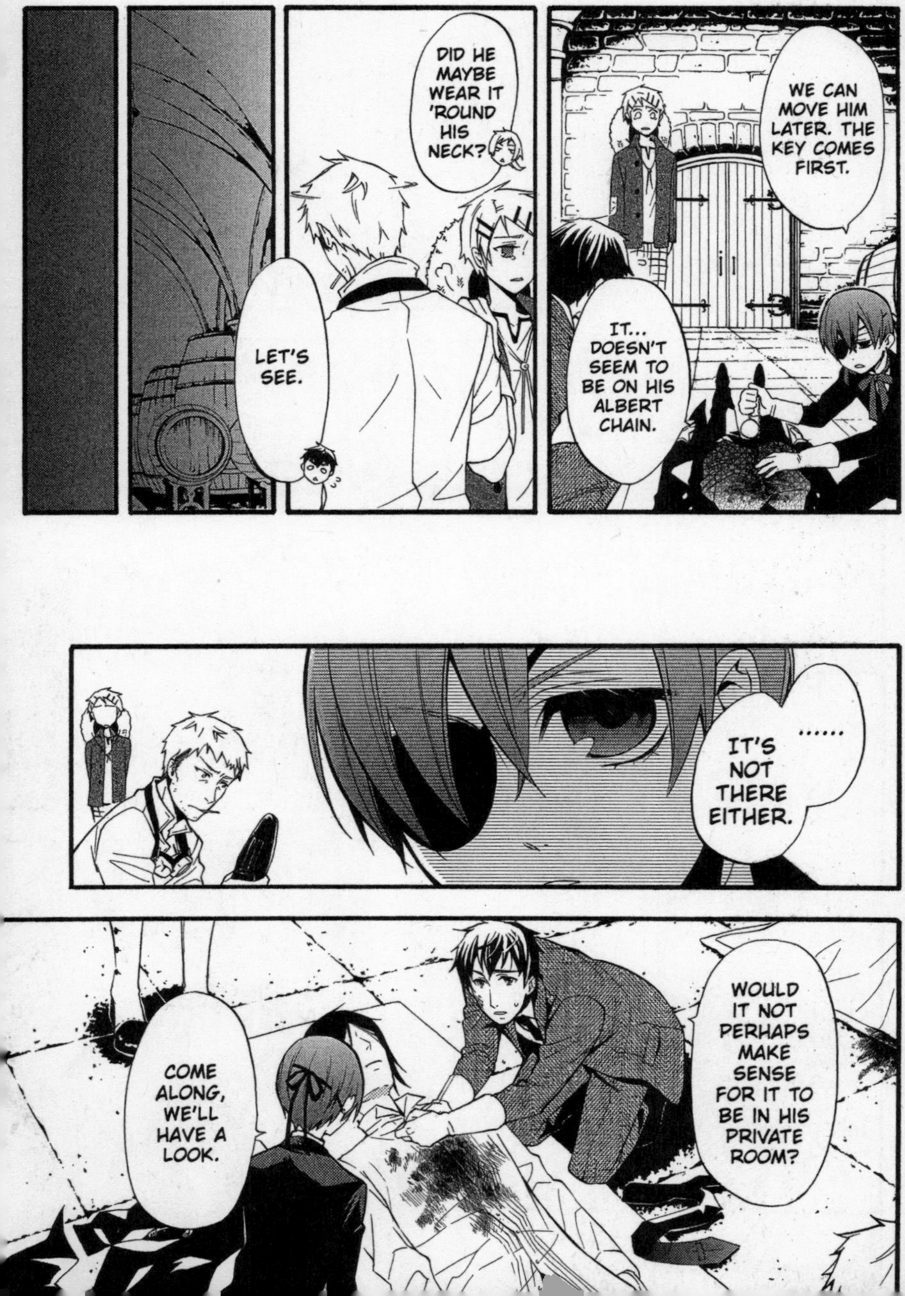
WE CAN MOVE HIM LATER. THE KEY COMES FIRST.
IT... DOESN'T SEEM TO BE ON HIS ALBERT CHAIN.
DID HE MAYBE WEAR IT 'ROUND HIS NECK?
LET'S SEE.
......
IT'S NOT THERE EITHER.
WOULD IT NOT PERHAPS MAKE SENSE FOR IT TO BE IN HIS PRIVATE ROOM?
COME ALONG, WE'LL HAVE A LOOK.

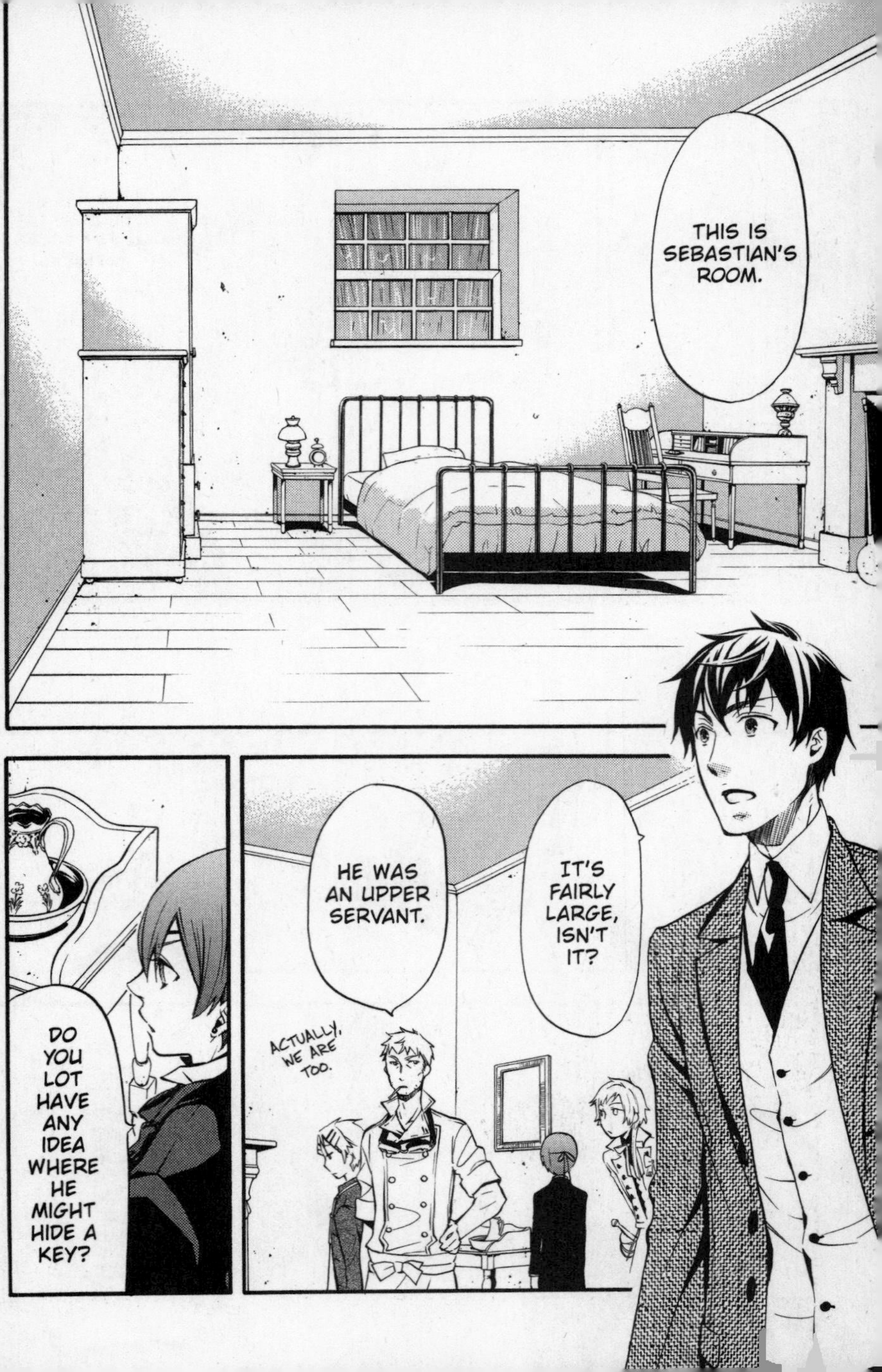
THIS IS SEBASTIAN'S ROOM.
IT'S FAIRLY LARGE, ISN'T IT?
HE WAS AN UPPER SERVANT.
ACTUALLY, WE ARE TOO.
DO YOU LOT HAVE ANY IDEA WHERE HE MIGHT HIDE A KEY?

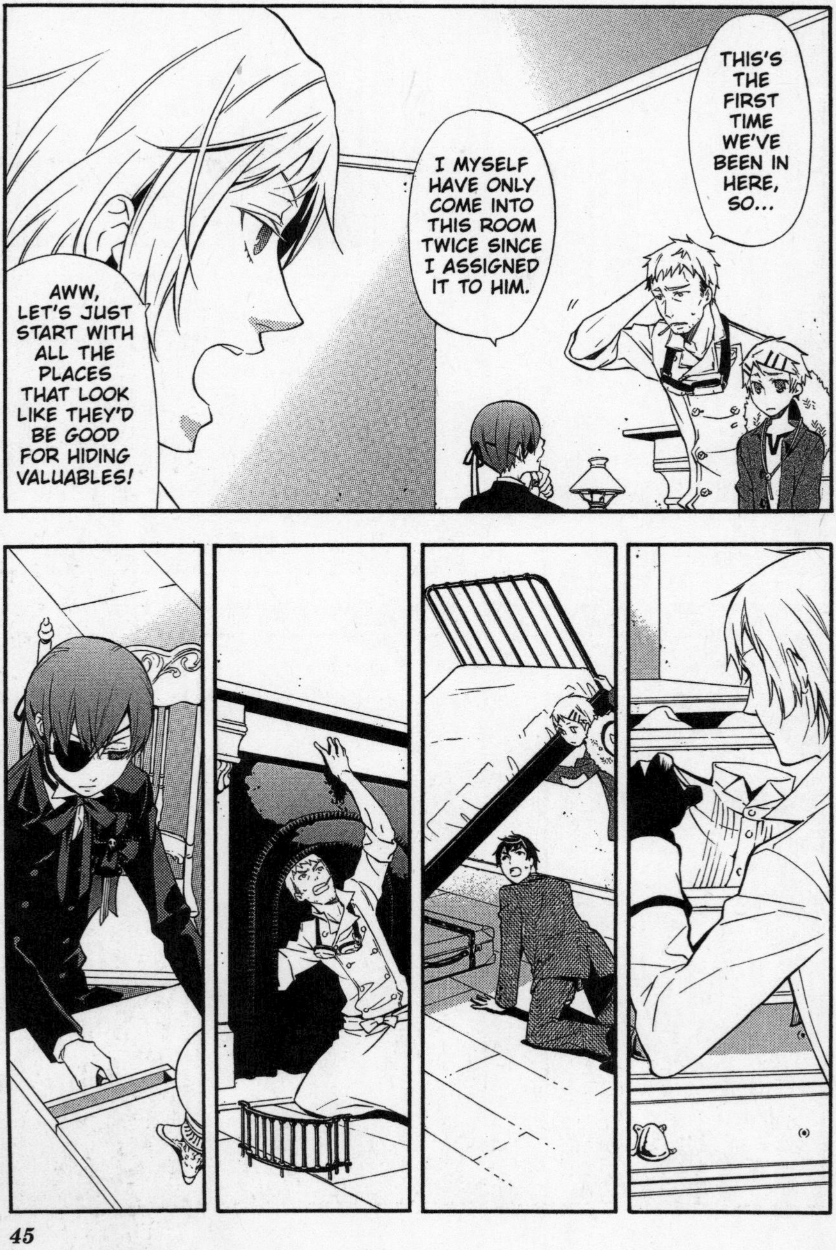
THIS'S THE FIRST TIME WE'VE BEEN IN HERE, SO...
I MYSELF HAVE ONLY COME INTO THIS ROOM TWICE SINCE I ASSIGNED IT TO HIM.
AWW, LET'S JUST START WITH ALL THE PLACES THAT LOOK LIKE THEY'D BE GOOD FOR HIDING VALUABLES!

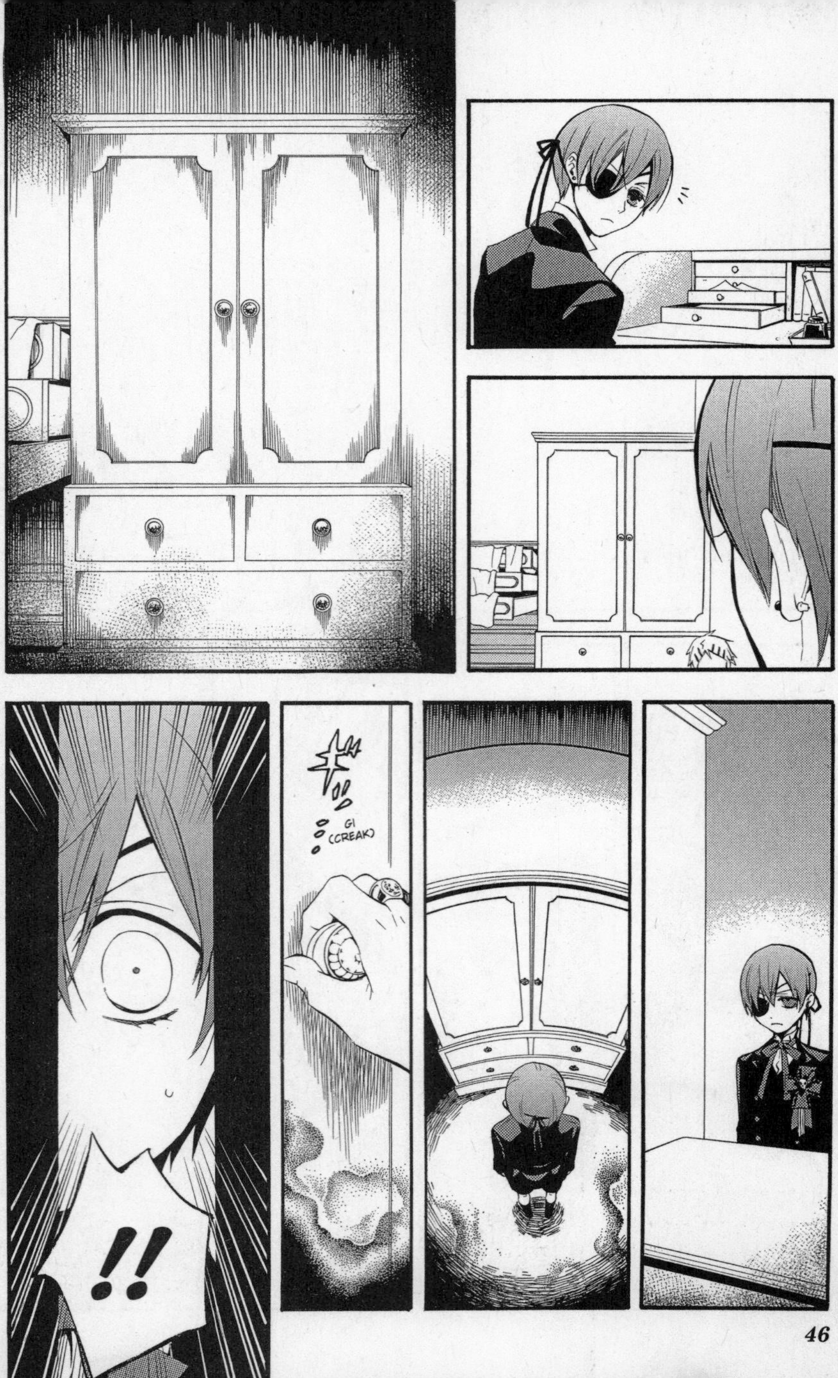
GI
(CREAK)
!!

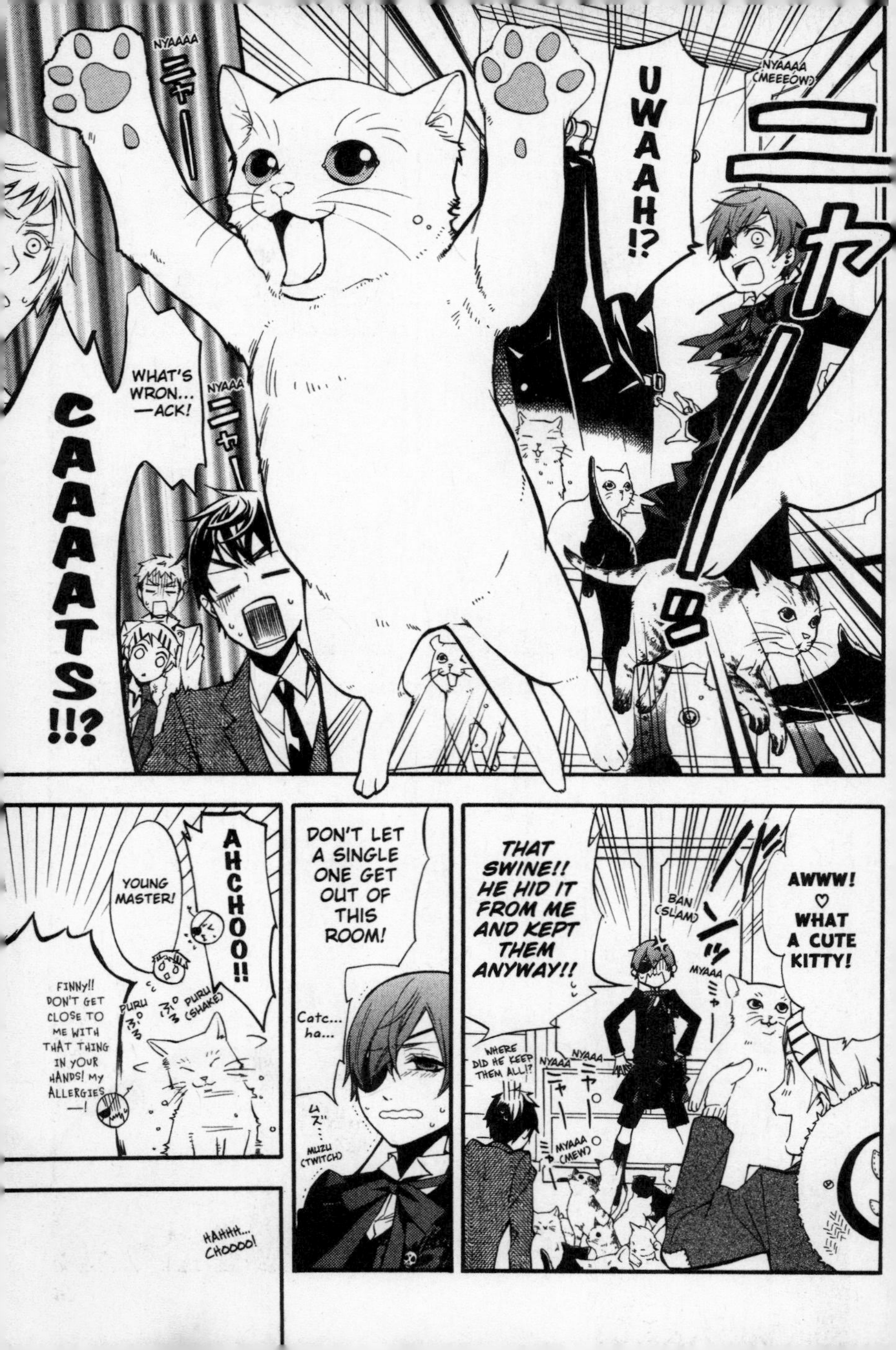

NYAAAA (MEEEOW)
ニャー
UWAAAH!?
NYAAAA
ニャー
WHAT'S WRON... —ACK!
NYAAA
ニャー
CAAAATS!!?
AWWW! ♡ WHAT A CUTE KITTY!
BAN (SLAM)
THAT SWINE!! HE HID IT FROM ME AND KEPT THEM ANYWAY!!
MYAAA
ミャー
NYAAA
ニャー
NYAAA
ニャー
WHERE DID HE KEEP THEM ALL!?
MYAAA (MEW)
DON'T LET A SINGLE ONE GET OUT OF THIS ROOM!
Catc... ha...
MUZU (TWITCH)
AHCHOO!!
YOUNG MASTER!
PURU PURU (SHAKE)
FINNY!! DON'T GET CLOSE TO ME WITH THAT THING IN YOUR HANDS! MY ALLERGIES —!
HAHHH... CHOOOO!

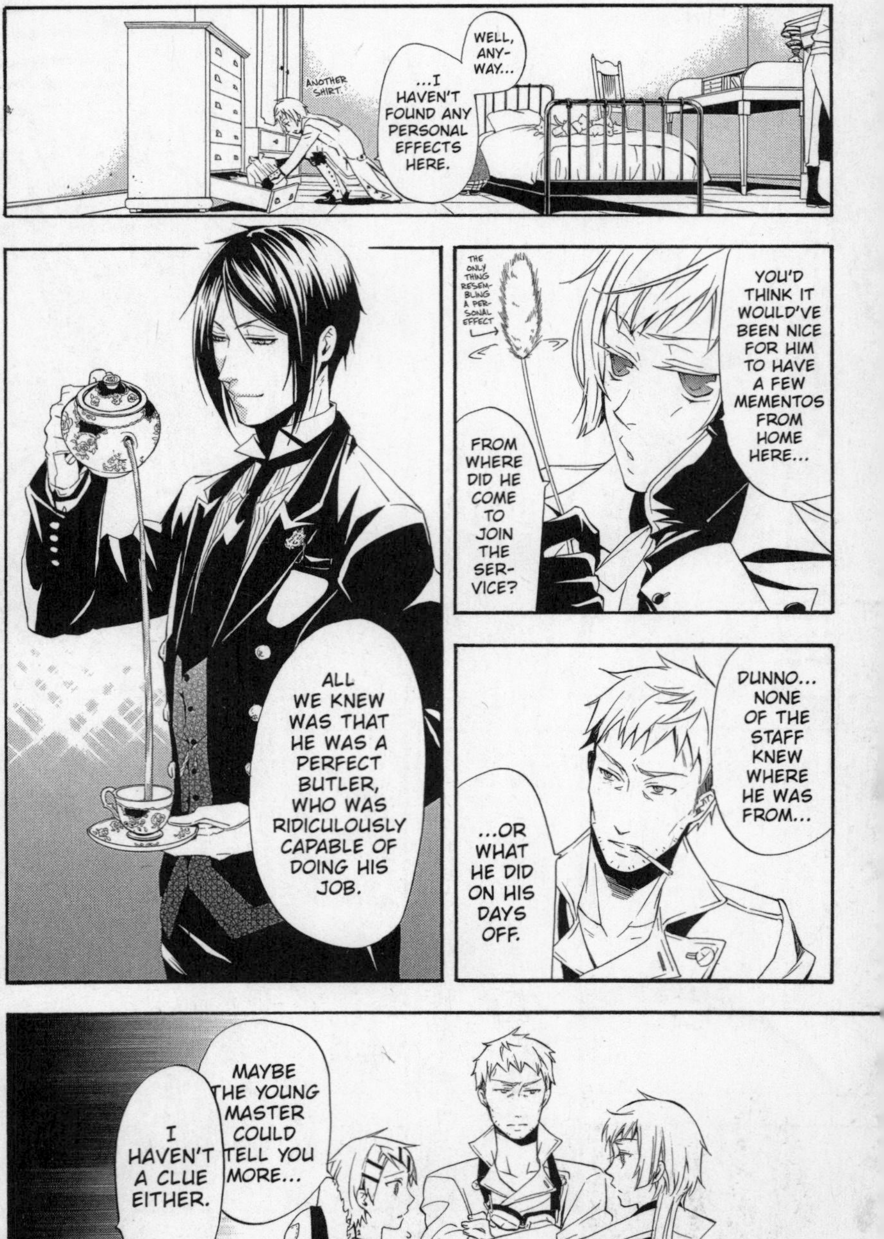
WELL, ANYWAY...
...I HAVEN'T FOUND ANY PERSONAL EFFECTS HERE.
ANOTHER SHIRT.
YOU'D THINK IT WOULD'VE BEEN NICE FOR HIM TO HAVE A FEW MEMENTOS FROM HOME HERE...
FROM WHERE DID HE COME TO JOIN THE SERVICE?
THE ONLY THING RESEMBLING A PERSONAL EFFECT
DUNNO... NONE OF THE STAFF KNEW WHERE HE WAS FROM...
...OR WHAT HE DID ON HIS DAYS OFF.
ALL WE KNEW WAS THAT HE WAS A PERFECT BUTLER, WHO WAS RIDICULOUSLY CAPABLE OF DOING HIS JOB.
MAYBE THE YOUNG MASTER COULD TELL YOU MORE...
I HAVEN'T A CLUE EITHER.

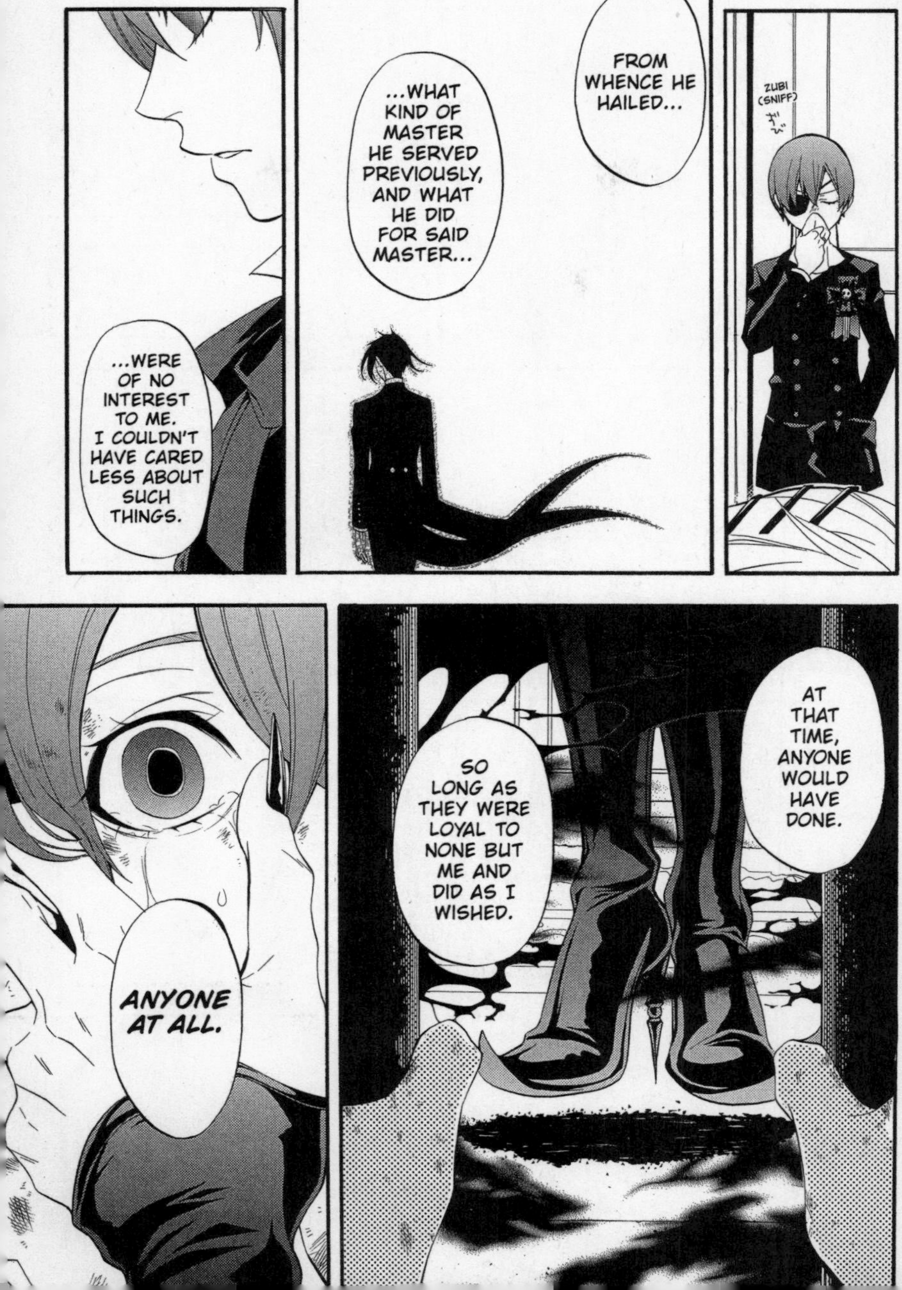
ZUBI (SNIFF)
FROM WHENCE HE HAILED...
...WHAT KIND OF MASTER HE SERVED PREVIOUSLY, AND WHAT HE DID FOR SAID MASTER...
...WERE OF NO INTEREST TO ME. I COULDN'T HAVE CARED LESS ABOUT SUCH THINGS.
AT THAT TIME, ANYONE WOULD HAVE DONE.
SO LONG AS THEY WERE LOYAL TO NONE BUT ME AND DID AS I WISHED.
ANYONE AT ALL.

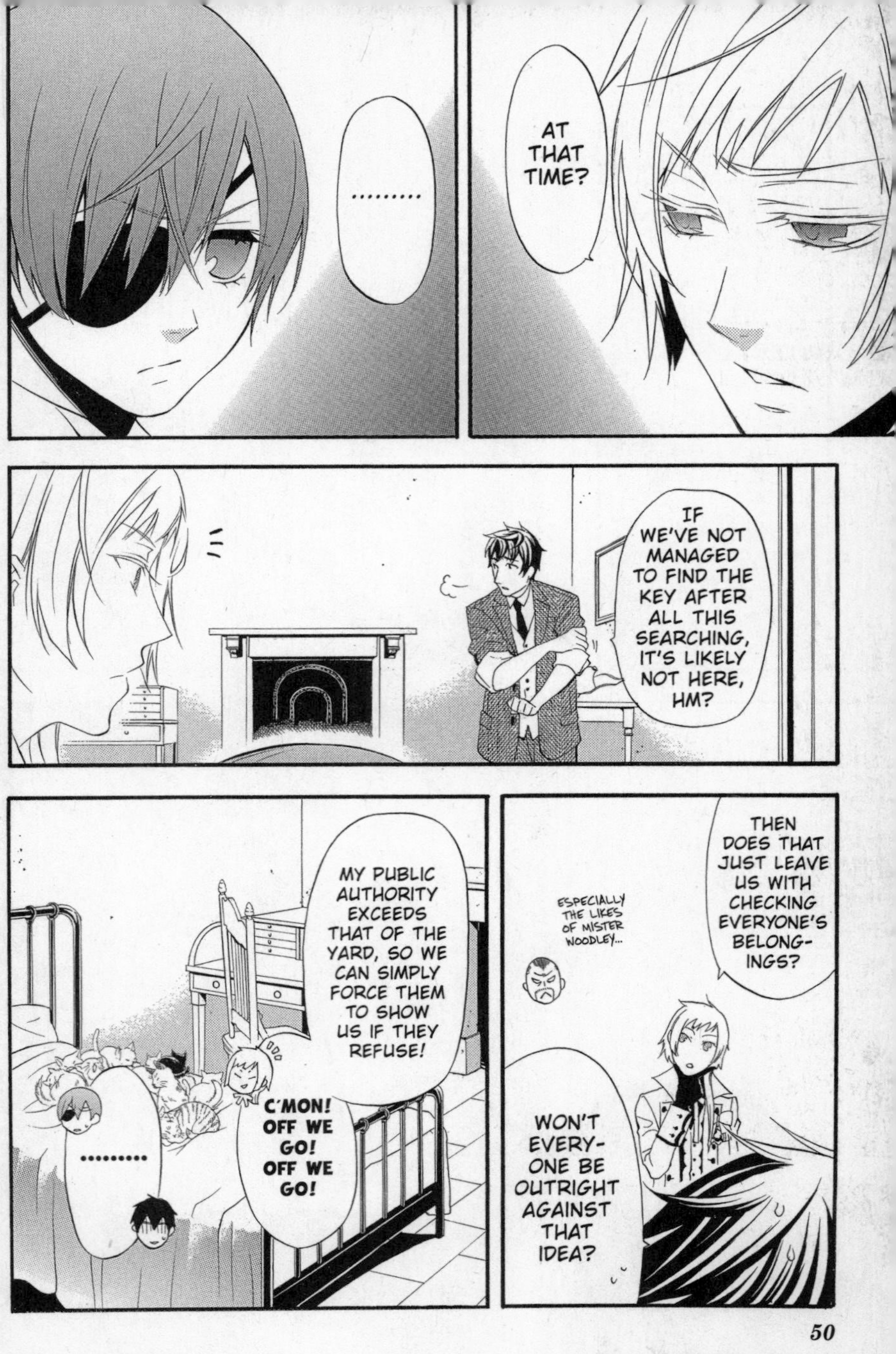
AT THAT TIME?
....
IF WE'VE NOT MANAGED TO FIND THE KEY AFTER ALL THIS SEARCHING, IT'S LIKELY NOT HERE, HM?
THEN DOES THAT JUST LEAVE US WITH CHECKING EVERYONE'S BELONG-INGS?
ESPECIALLY THE LIKES OF MISTER WOODLEY...
WON'T EVERY-ONE BE OUTRIGHT AGAINST THAT IDEA?
MY PUBLIC AUTHORITY EXCEEDS THAT OF THE YARD, SO WE CAN SIMPLY FORCE THEM TO SHOW US IF THEY REFUSE!
C'MON! OFF WE GO! OFF WE GO!
....

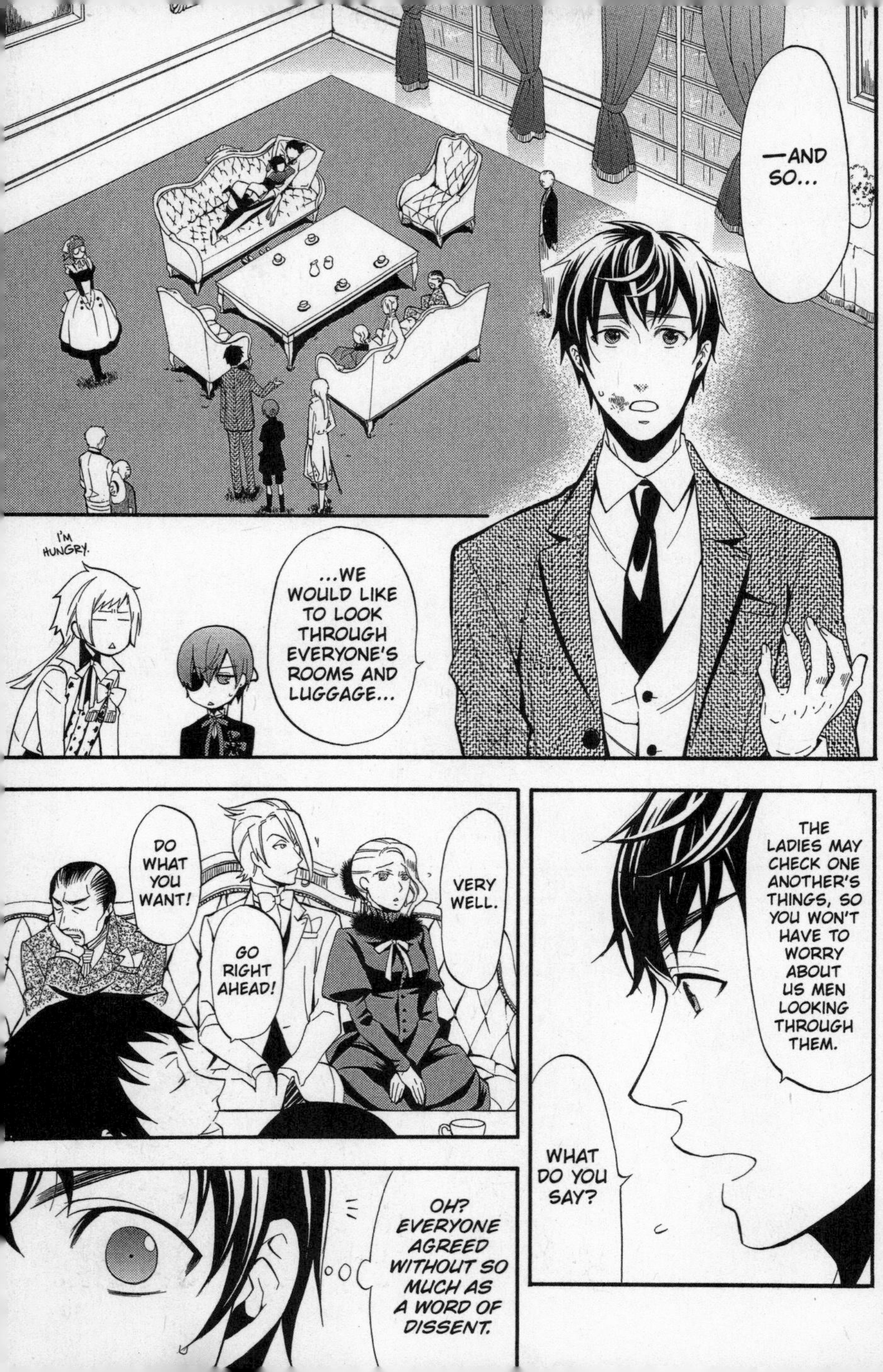
—AND SO...
...WE WOULD LIKE TO LOOK THROUGH EVERYONE'S ROOMS AND LUGGAGE...
I'M HUNGRY.
THE LADIES MAY CHECK ONE ANOTHER'S THINGS, SO YOU WON'T HAVE TO WORRY ABOUT US MEN LOOKING THROUGH THEM.
WHAT DO YOU SAY?
VERY WELL.
DO WHAT YOU WANT!
GO RIGHT AHEAD!
OH? EVERYONE AGREED WITHOUT SO MUCH AS A WORD OF DISSENT.

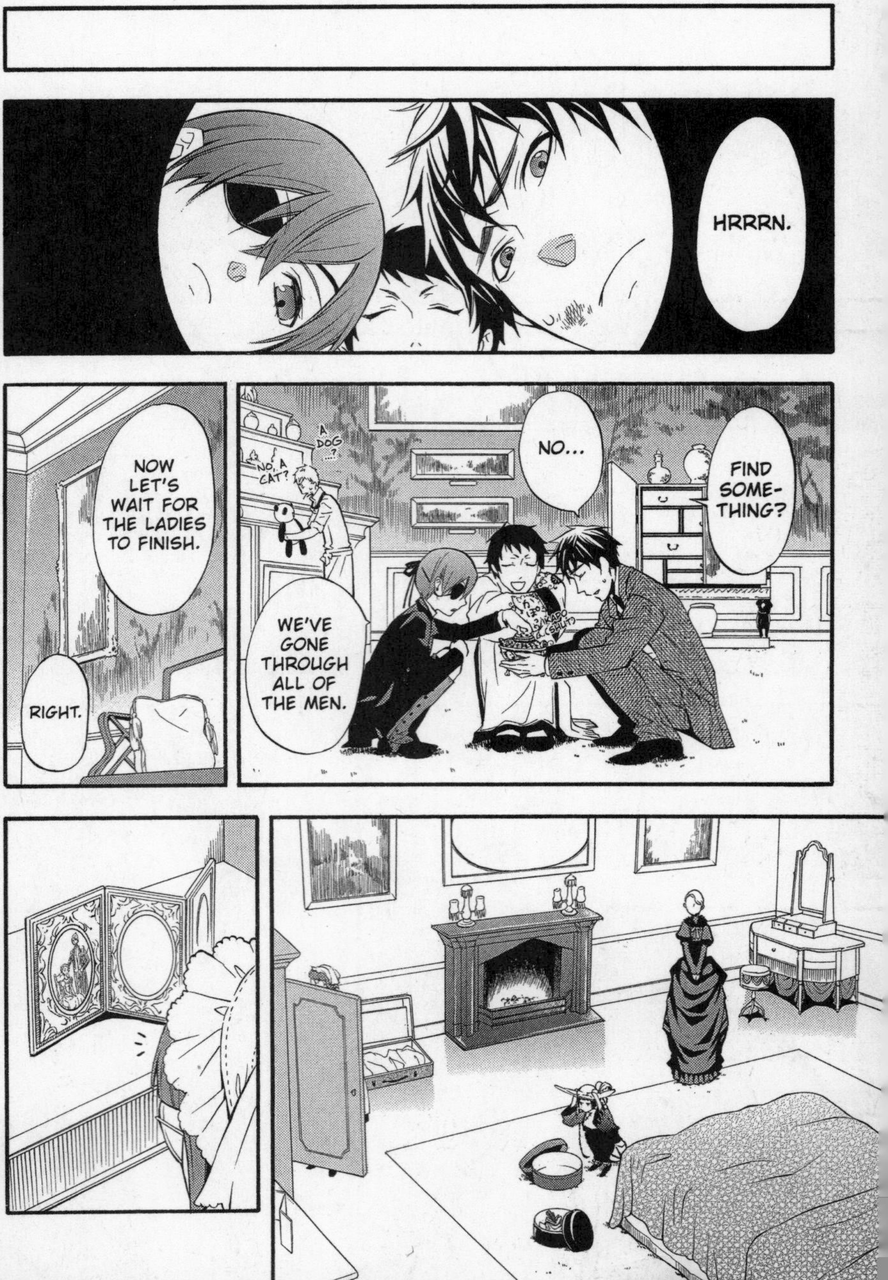
HRRRN.
FIND SOMETHING?
NO...
A DOG...?
NO, A CAT?
WE'VE GONE THROUGH ALL OF THE MEN.
NOW LET'S WAIT FOR THE LADIES TO FINISH.
RIGHT.

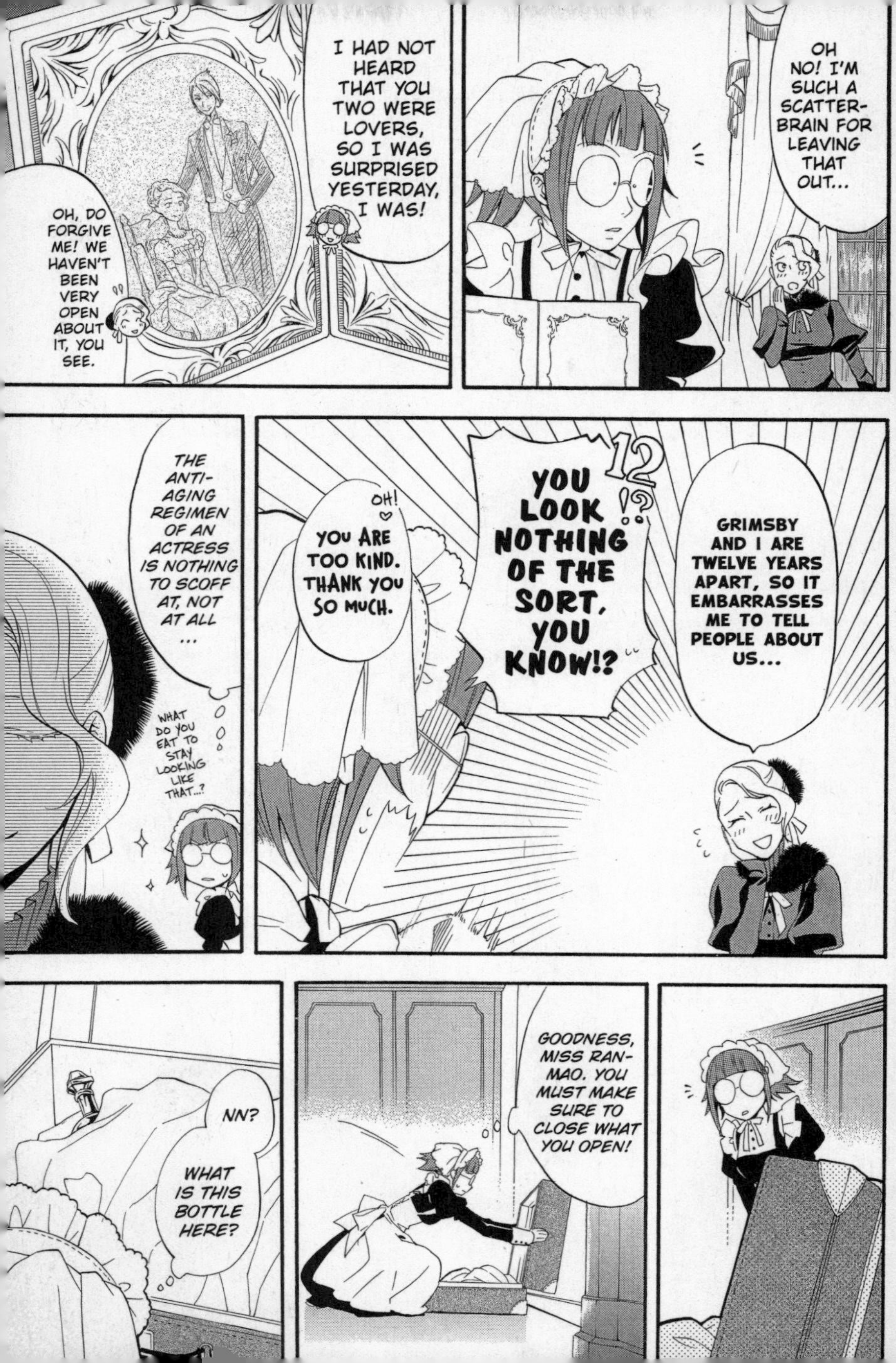
OH NO! I'M SUCH A SCATTER-BRAIN FOR LEAVING THAT OUT...
I HAD NOT HEARD THAT YOU TWO WERE LOVERS, SO I WAS SURPRISED YESTERDAY, I WAS!
OH, DO FORGIVE ME! WE HAVEN'T BEEN VERY OPEN ABOUT IT, YOU SEE.
GRIMSBY AND I ARE TWELVE YEARS APART, SO IT EMBARRASSES ME TO TELL PEOPLE ABOUT US...
12!?
YOU LOOK NOTHING OF THE SORT, YOU KNOW!?
OH! ♡
YOU ARE TOO KIND. THANK YOU SO MUCH.
THE ANTI-AGING REGIMEN OF AN ACTRESS IS NOTHING TO SCOFF AT, NOT AT ALL...
WHAT DO YOU EAT TO STAY LOOKING LIKE THAT...?
GOODNESS, MISS RAN-MAO. YOU MUST MAKE SURE TO CLOSE WHAT YOU OPEN!
NN?
WHAT IS THIS BOTTLE HERE?

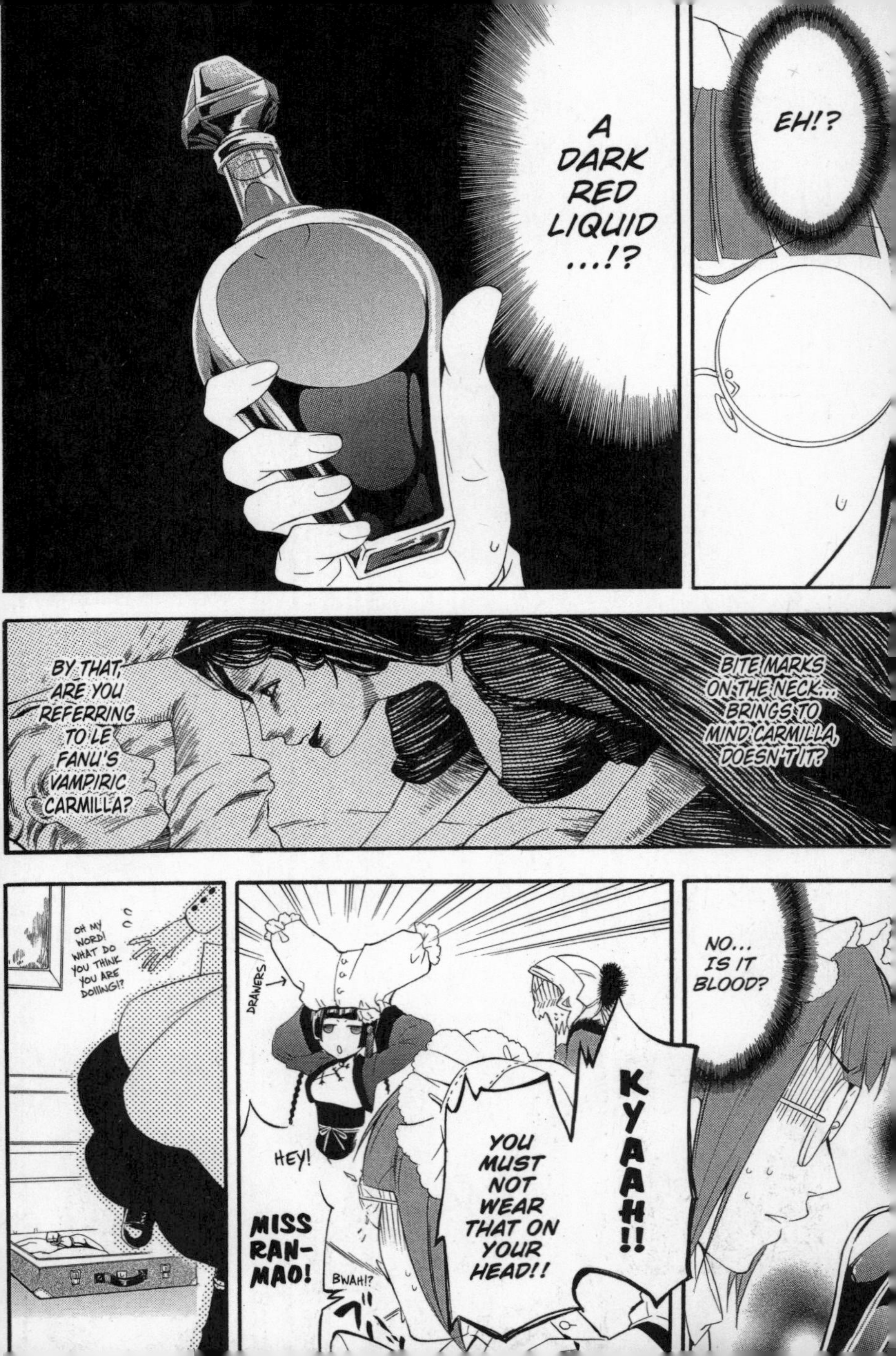
EH!?
A DARK RED LIQUID ...!?
BITE MARKS ON THE NECK... BRINGS TO MIND CARMILLA, DOESN'T IT?
BY THAT, ARE YOU REFERRING TO LE FANU'S VAMPIRIC CARMILLA?
NO... IS IT BLOOD?
KYAAH!!
YOU MUST NOT WEAR THAT ON YOUR HEAD!!
DRAWERS
HEY!
MISS RAN-MAO!
BWAH!?
OH MY WORD! WHAT DO YOU THINK YOU ARE DOIIING!?

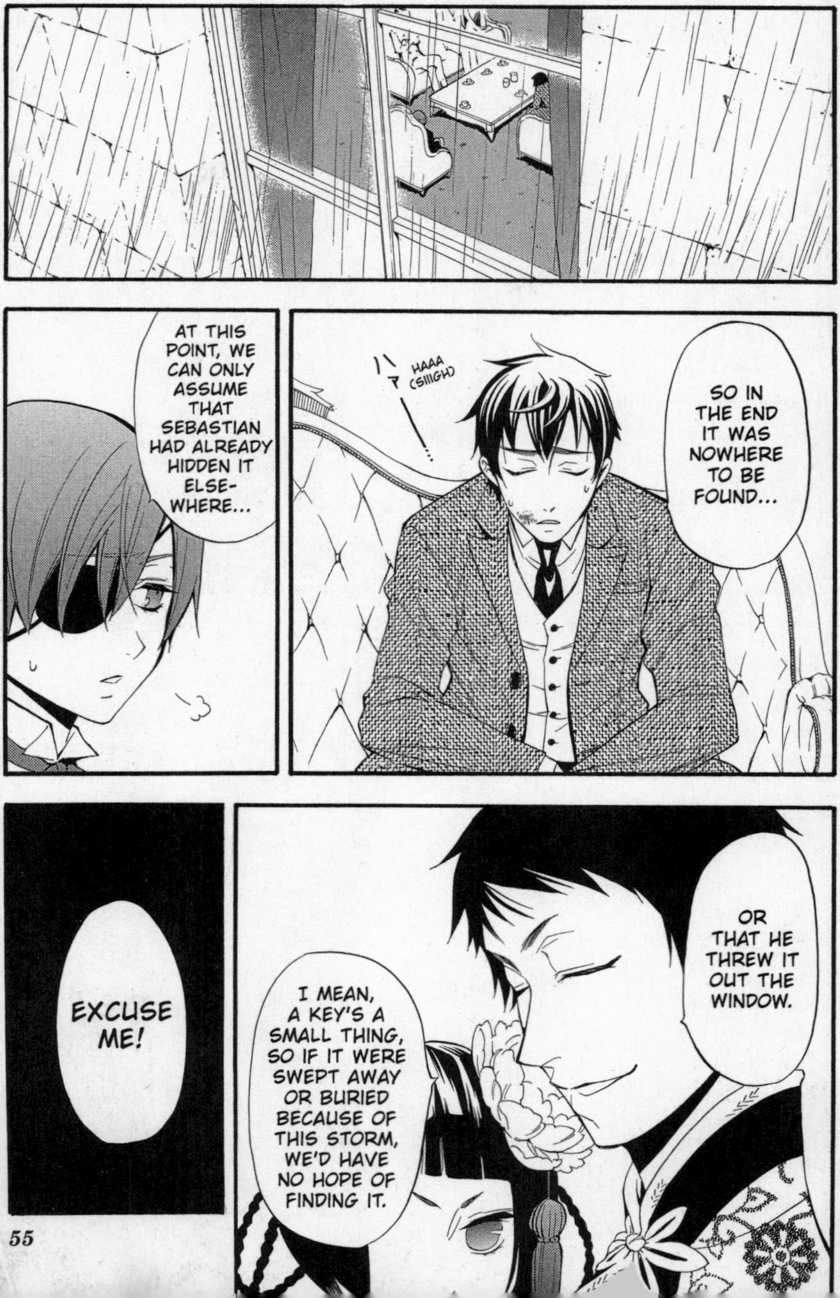
SO IN THE END IT WAS NOWHERE TO BE FOUND...
HAAA (SIIIGH)
AT THIS POINT, WE CAN ONLY ASSUME THAT SEBASTIAN HAD ALREADY HIDDEN IT ELSE-WHERE...
OR THAT HE THREW IT OUT THE WINDOW.
I MEAN, A KEY'S A SMALL THING, SO IF IT WERE SWEPT AWAY OR BURIED BECAUSE OF THIS STORM, WE'D HAVE NO HOPE OF FINDING IT.
EXCUSE ME!

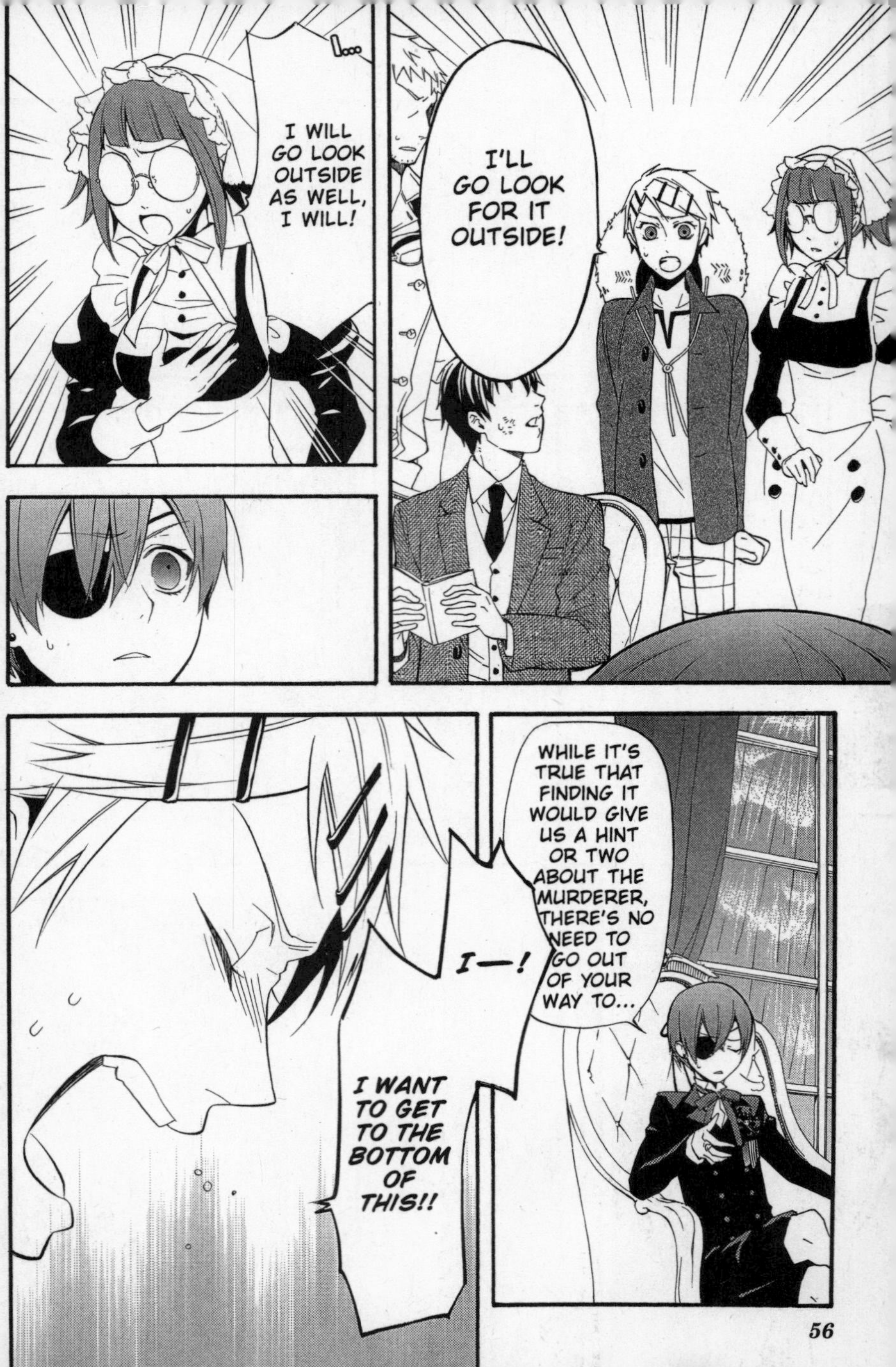
I'LL GO LOOK FOR IT OUTSIDE!
I...
I WILL GO LOOK OUTSIDE AS WELL, I WILL!
WHILE IT'S TRUE THAT FINDING IT WOULD GIVE US A HINT OR TWO ABOUT THE MURDERER, THERE'S NO NEED TO GO OUT OF YOUR WAY TO...
I—!
I WANT TO GET TO THE BOTTOM OF THIS!!

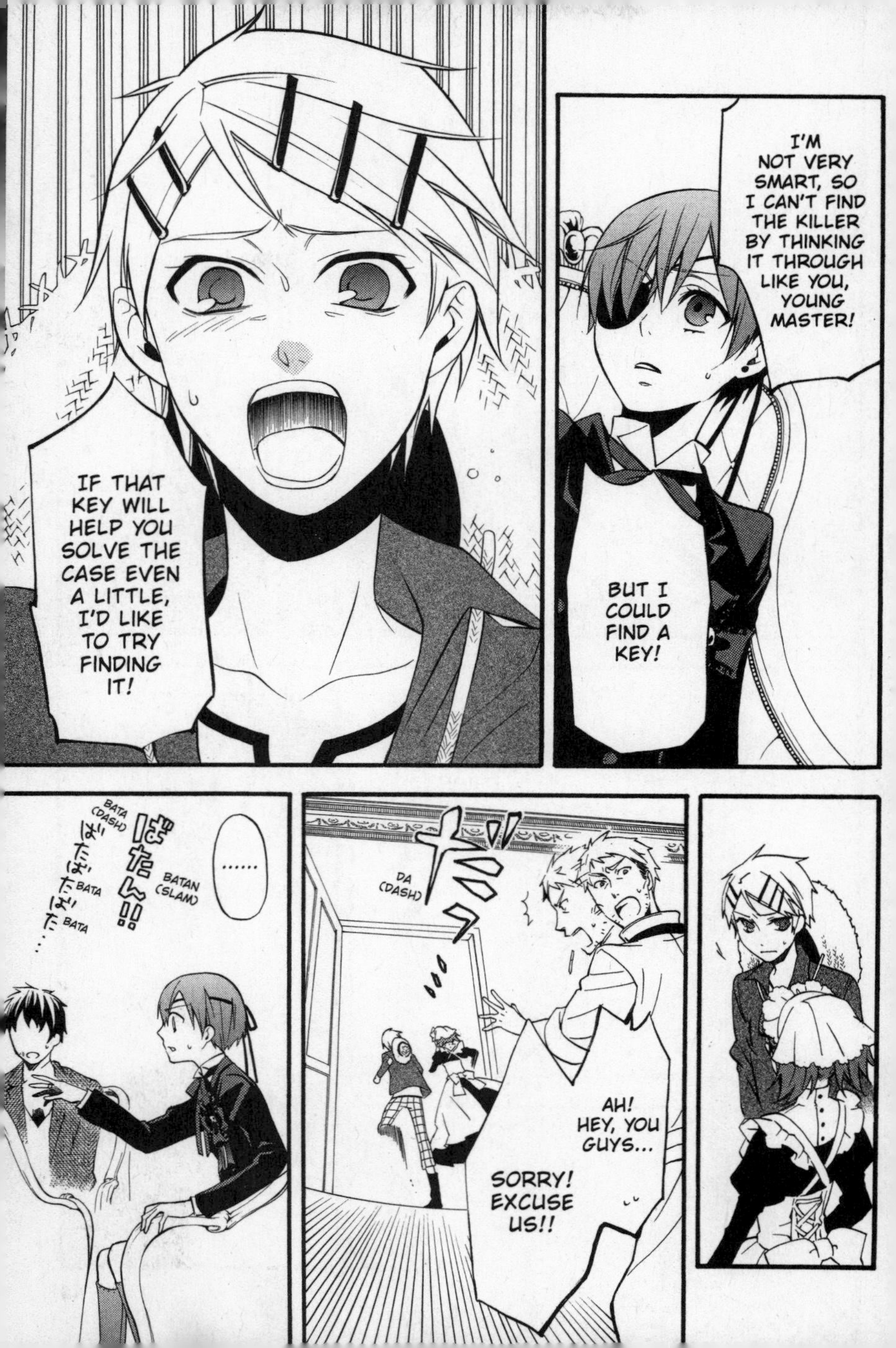
I'M NOT VERY SMART, SO I CAN'T FIND THE KILLER BY THINKING IT THROUGH LIKE YOU, YOUNG MASTER!
BUT I COULD FIND A KEY!
IF THAT KEY WILL HELP YOU SOLVE THE CASE EVEN A LITTLE, I'D LIKE TO TRY FINDING IT!
ダッ
DA (DASH)
AH! HEY, YOU GUYS...
SORRY! EXCUSE US!!
......
ばたん!!
BATAN (SLAM)
ばたばたばた…
BATA (DASH) BATA BATA

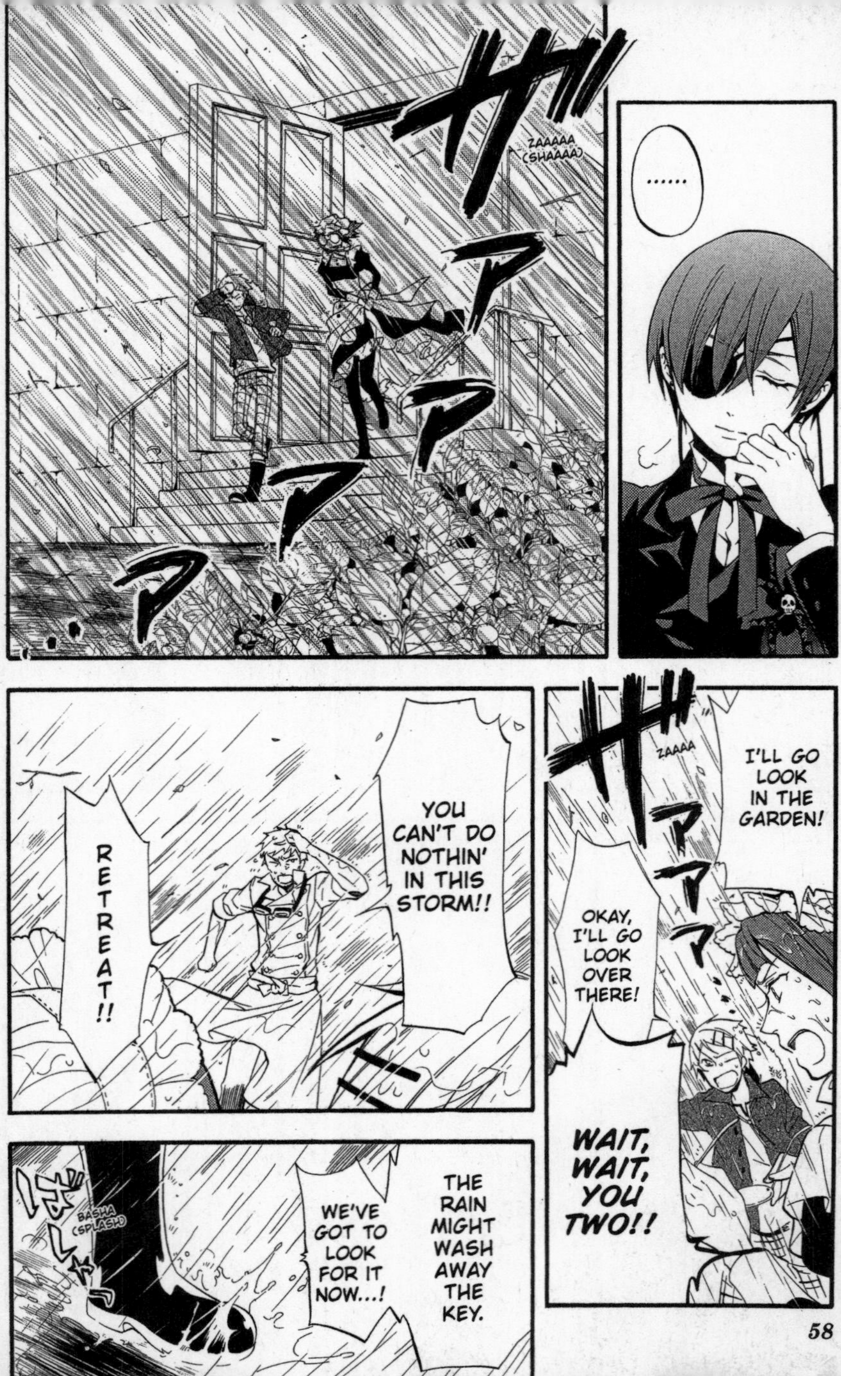
......
ZAAAAA (SHAAAA)
ZAAAA
I'LL GO LOOK IN THE GARDEN!
OKAY, I'LL GO LOOK OVER THERE!
WAIT, WAIT, YOU TWO!!
YOU CAN'T DO NOTHIN' IN THIS STORM!!
RETREAT!!
THE RAIN MIGHT WASH AWAY THE KEY.
WE'VE GOT TO LOOK FOR IT NOW...!
BASHA (SPLASH)

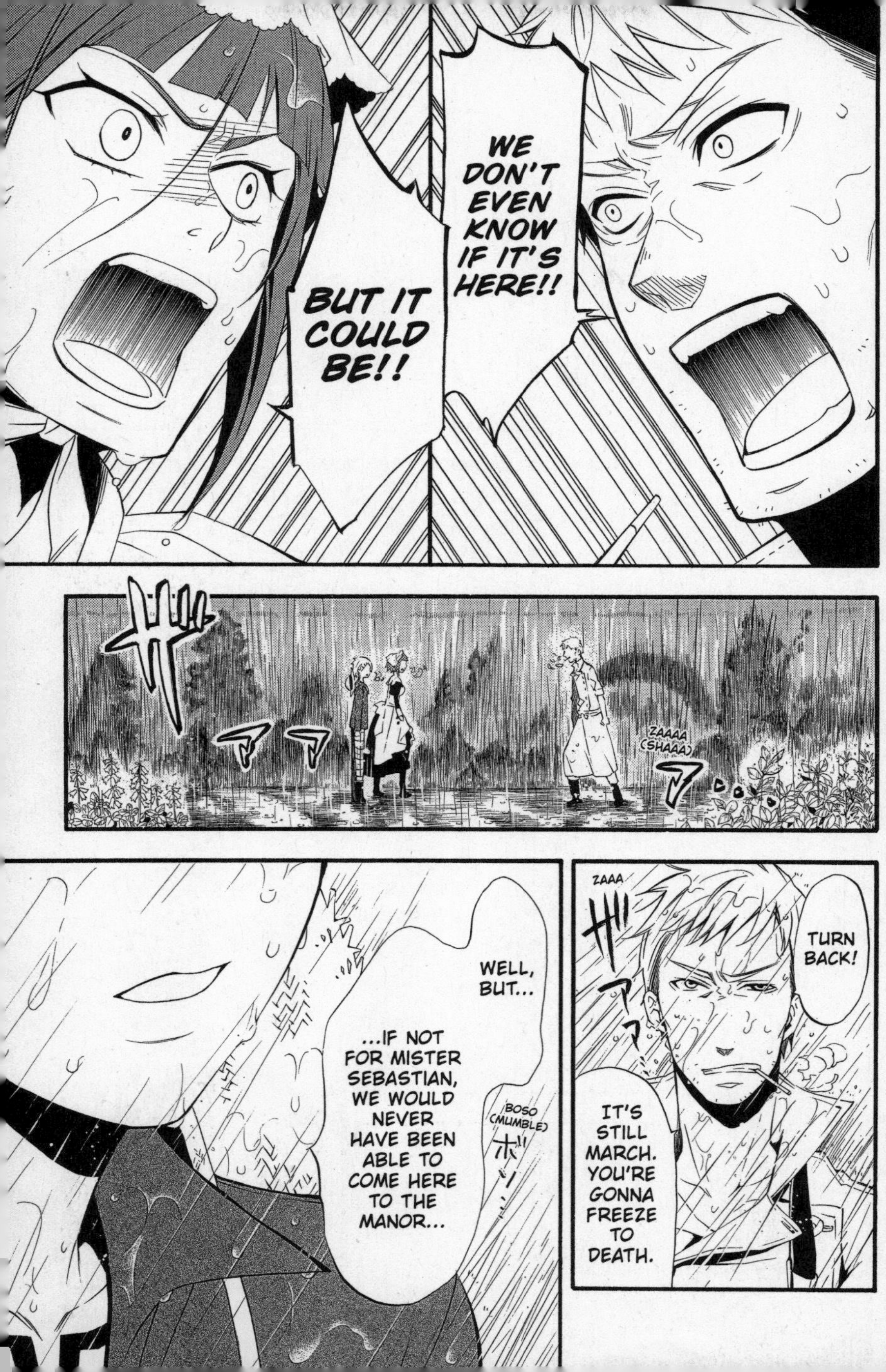
WE DON'T EVEN KNOW IF IT'S HERE!!
BUT IT COULD BE!!
ZAAAA (SHAAA)
ZAAA
TURN BACK!
IT'S STILL MARCH. YOU'RE GONNA FREEZE TO DEATH.
WELL, BUT...
...IF NOT FOR MISTER SEBASTIAN, WE WOULD NEVER HAVE BEEN ABLE TO COME HERE TO THE MANOR...
BOSO (MUMBLE)

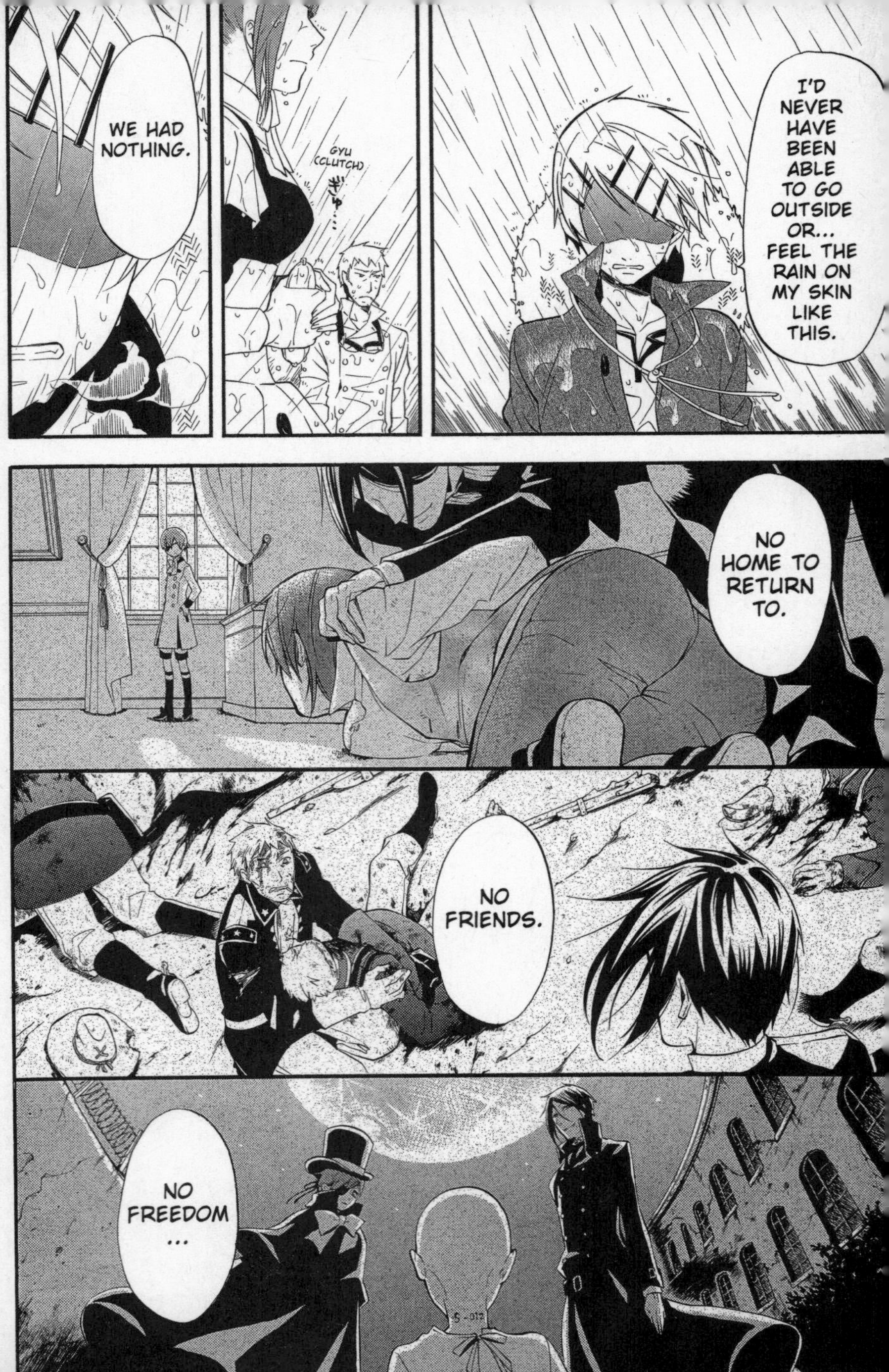
I'D NEVER HAVE BEEN ABLE TO GO OUTSIDE OR... FEEL THE RAIN ON MY SKIN LIKE THIS.
GYU (CLUTCH)
WE HAD NOTHING.
NO HOME TO RETURN TO.
NO FRIENDS.
NO FREEDOM ...

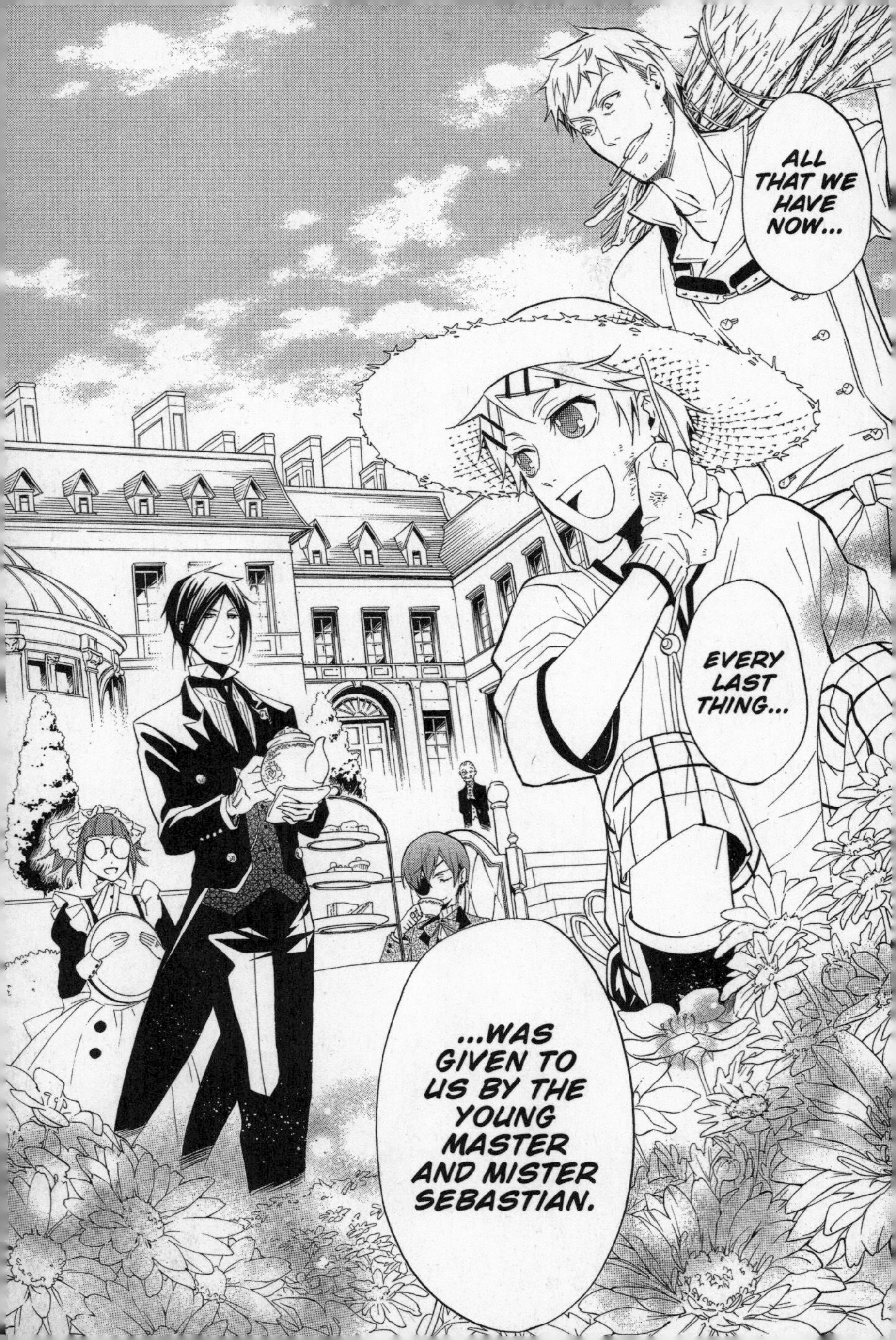
ALL THAT WE HAVE NOW...
EVERY LAST THING...
...WAS GIVEN TO US BY THE YOUNG MASTER AND MISTER SEBASTIAN.

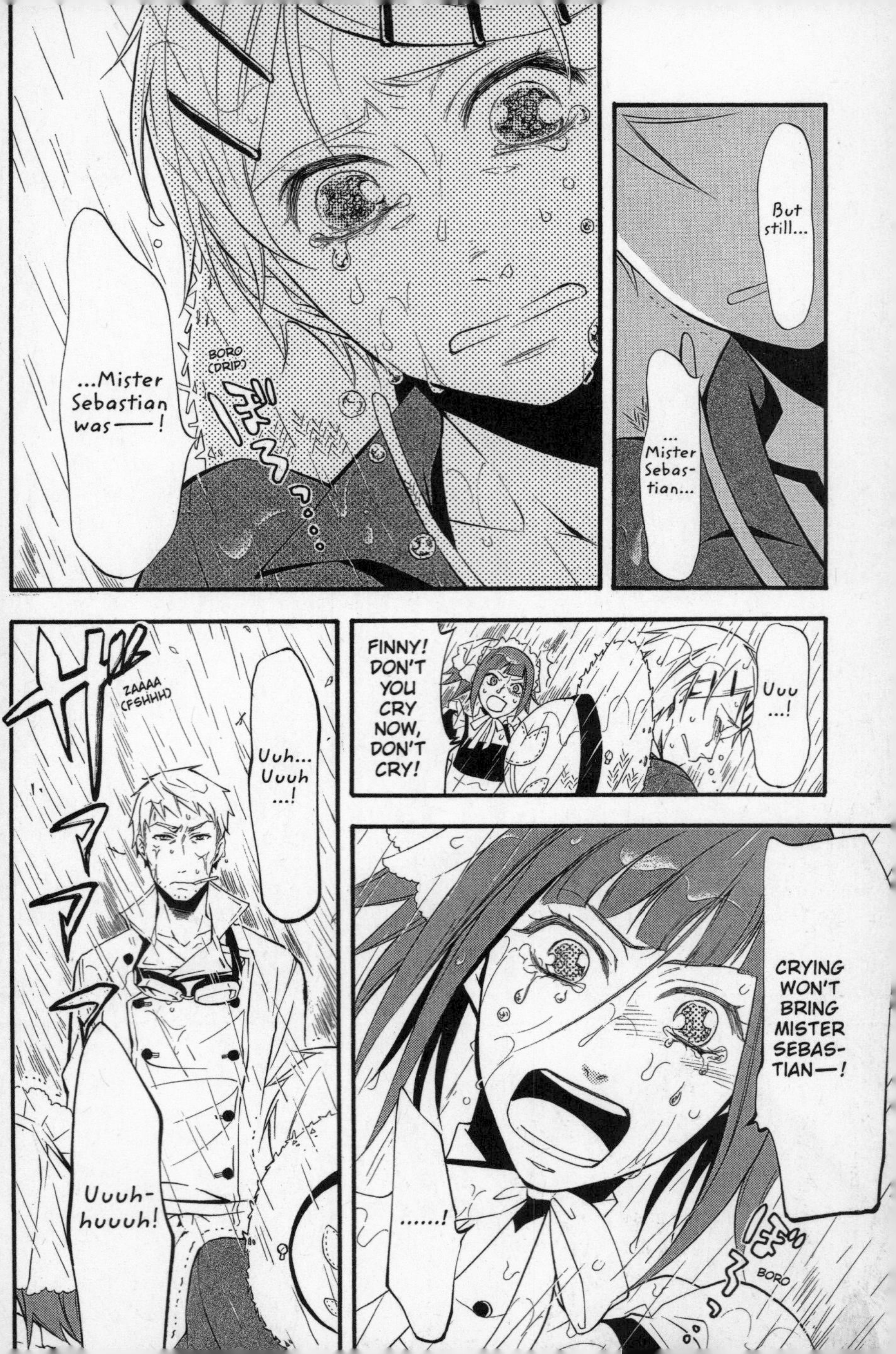

But still...
...Mister Sebas-tian...
...Mister Sebastian was—!
BORO (DRIP)
Uuu...!
FINNY! DON'T YOU CRY NOW, DON'T CRY!
CRYING WON'T BRING MISTER SEBAS-TIAN—!
......!
BORO
ZAAAA (FSHHH)
Uuh... Uuuh...!
Uuuh-huuuh!

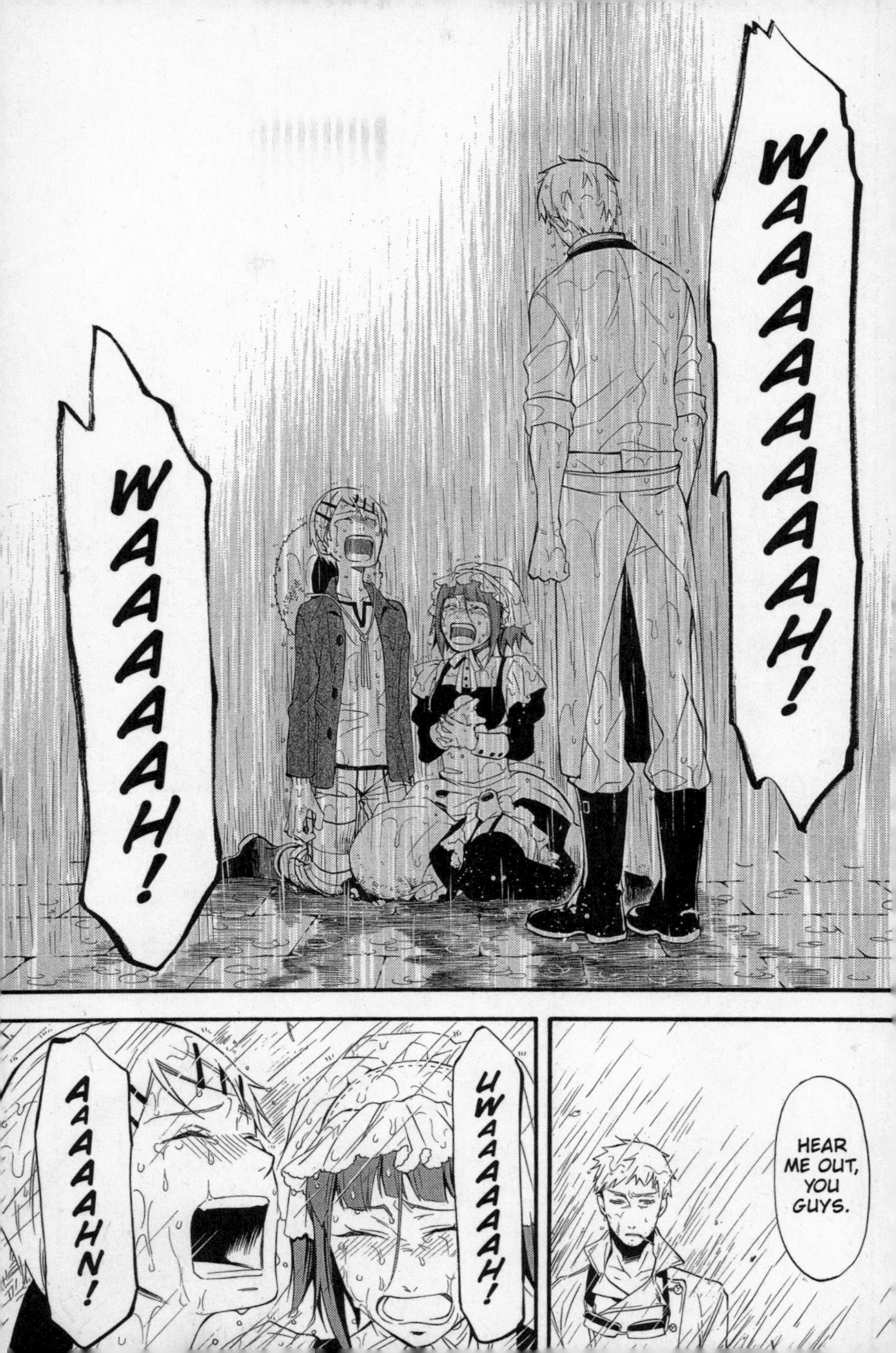
WAAAAAAAAH!
WAAAAAH!
HEAR ME OUT, YOU GUYS.
UWAAAAAAAAH!
AAAAAAHN!

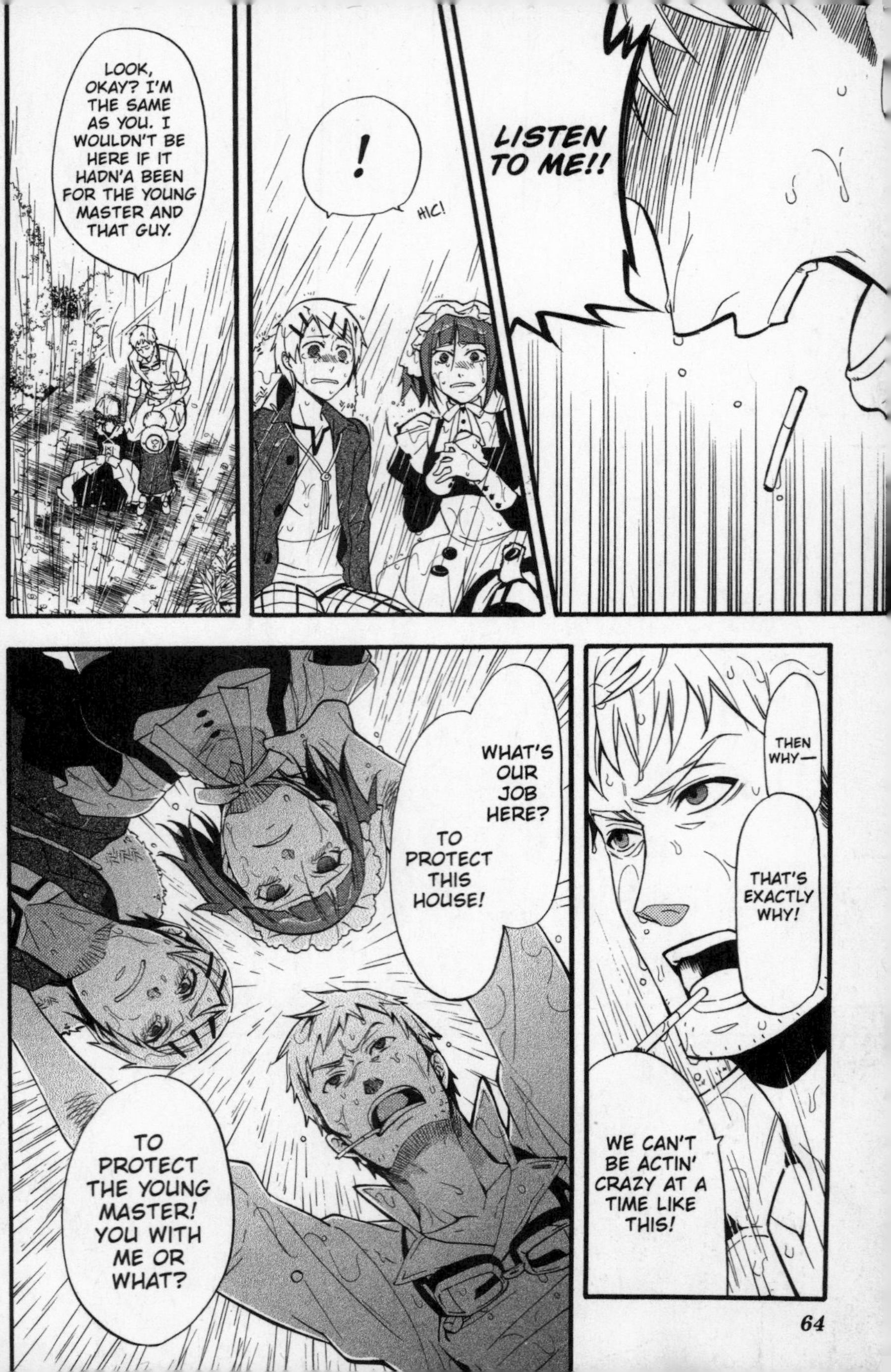
LISTEN TO ME!!
!
HIC!
LOOK, OKAY? I'M THE SAME AS YOU. I WOULDN'T BE HERE IF IT HADN'A BEEN FOR THE YOUNG MASTER AND THAT GUY.
THEN WHY—
THAT'S EXACTLY WHY!
WE CAN'T BE ACTIN' CRAZY AT A TIME LIKE THIS!
WHAT'S OUR JOB HERE?
TO PROTECT THIS HOUSE!
TO PROTECT THE YOUNG MASTER! YOU WITH ME OR WHAT?

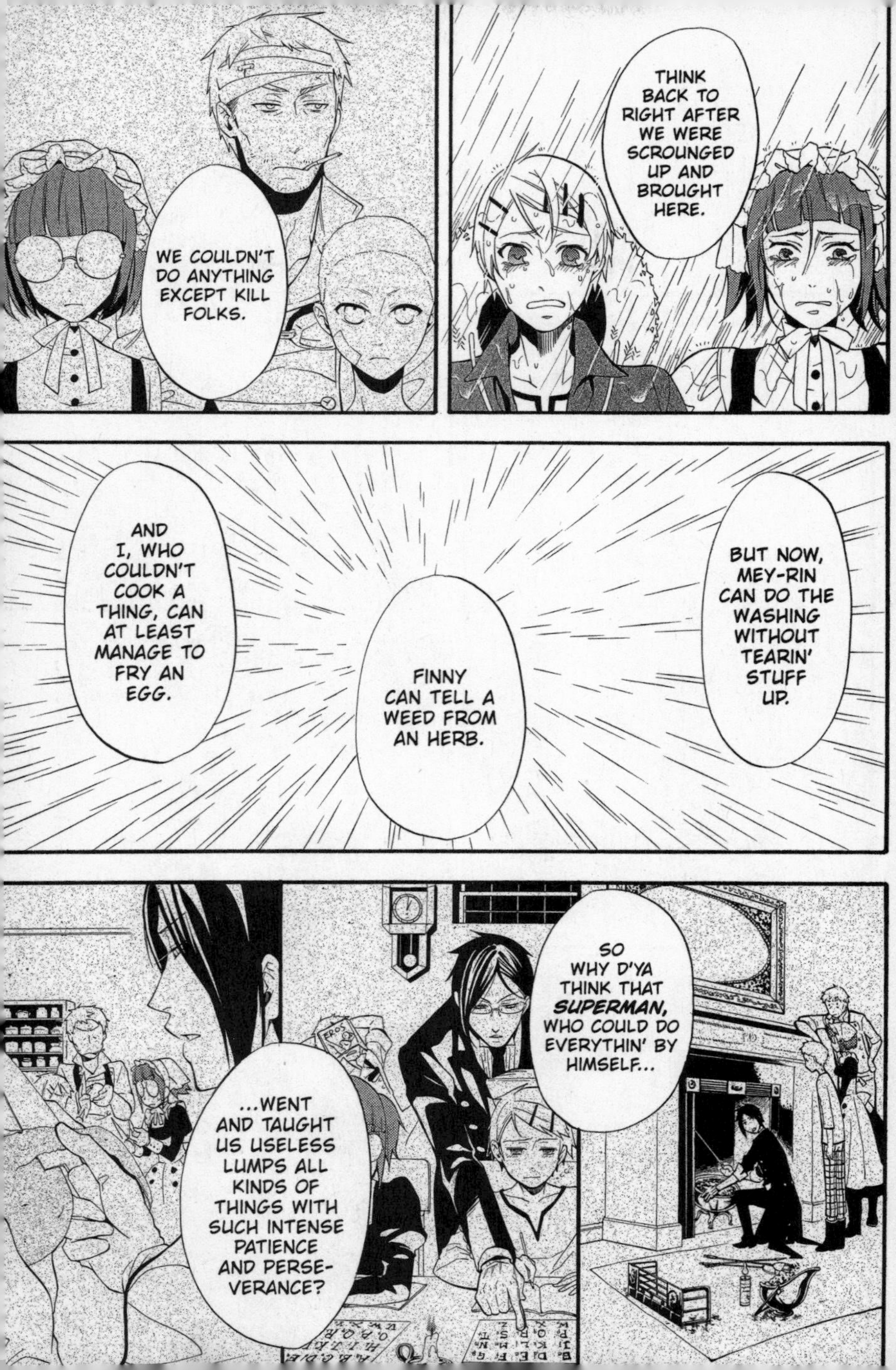
THINK BACK TO RIGHT AFTER WE WERE SCROUNGED UP AND BROUGHT HERE.
WE COULDN'T DO ANYTHING EXCEPT KILL FOLKS.
BUT NOW, MEY-RIN CAN DO THE WASHING WITHOUT TEARIN' STUFF UP.
FINNY CAN TELL A WEED FROM AN HERB.
AND I, WHO COULDN'T COOK A THING, CAN AT LEAST MANAGE TO FRY AN EGG.
SO WHY D'YA THINK THAT *SUPERMAN,* WHO COULD DO EVERYTHIN' BY HIMSELF...
...WENT AND TAUGHT US USELESS LUMPS ALL KINDS OF THINGS WITH SUCH INTENSE PATIENCE AND PERSE-VERANCE?

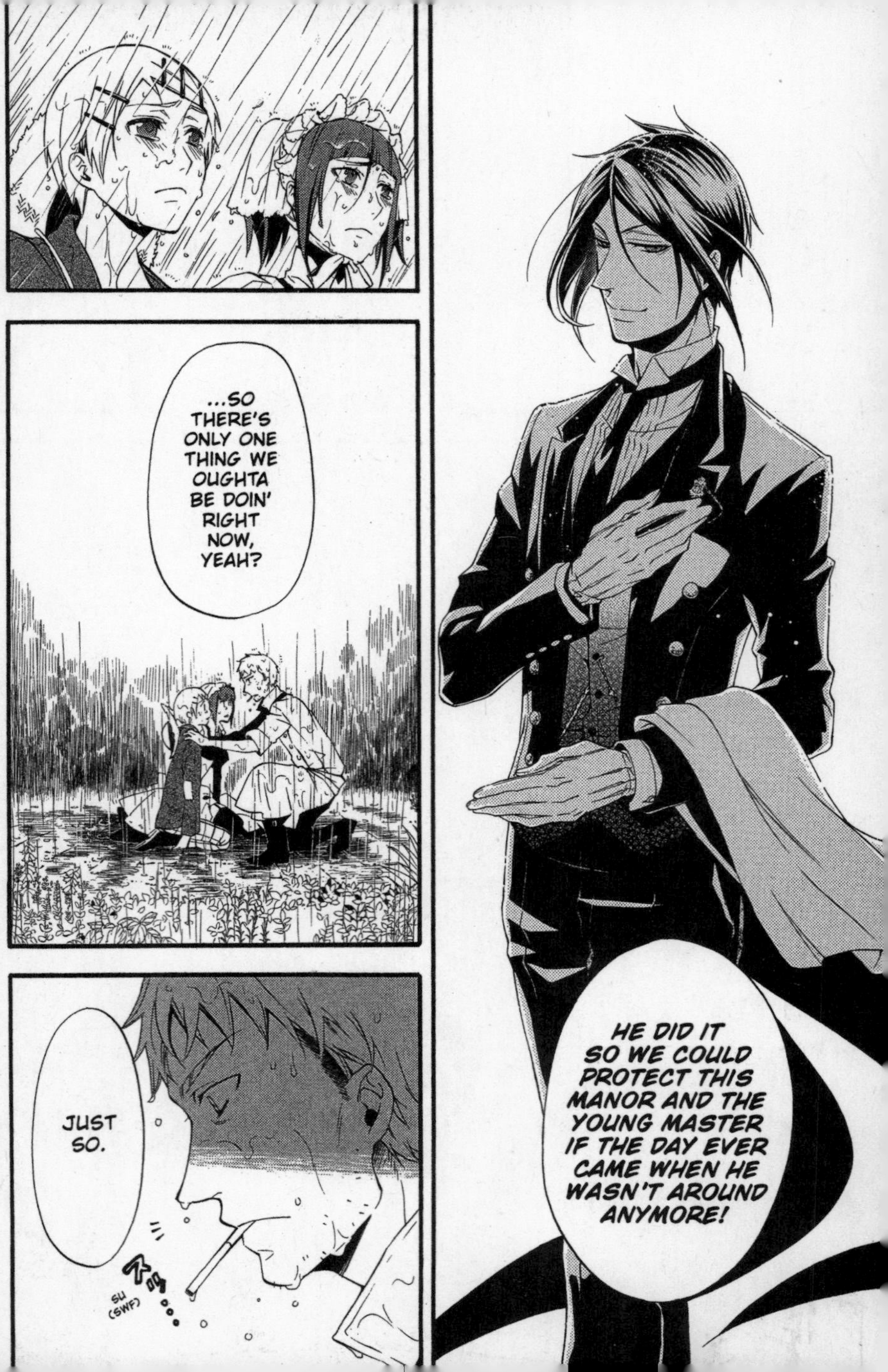
HE DID IT SO WE COULD PROTECT THIS MANOR AND THE YOUNG MASTER IF THE DAY EVER CAME WHEN HE WASN'T AROUND ANYMORE!
...SO THERE'S ONLY ONE THING WE OUGHTA BE DOIN' RIGHT NOW, YEAH?
JUST SO.
SU (SWF)

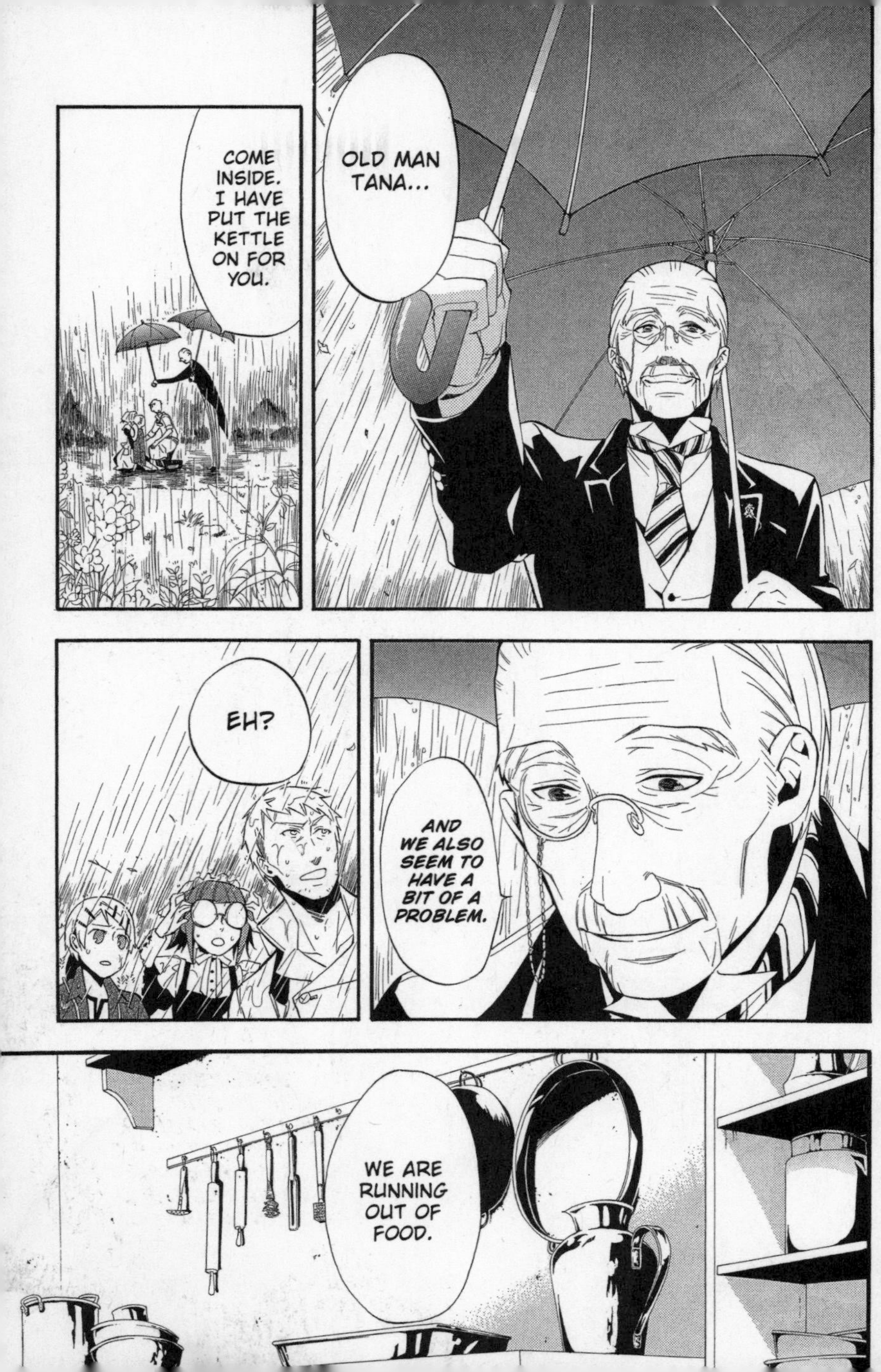
OLD MAN TANA...
COME INSIDE. I HAVE PUT THE KETTLE ON FOR YOU.
AND WE ALSO SEEM TO HAVE A BIT OF A PROBLEM.
EH?
WE ARE RUNNING OUT OF FOOD.

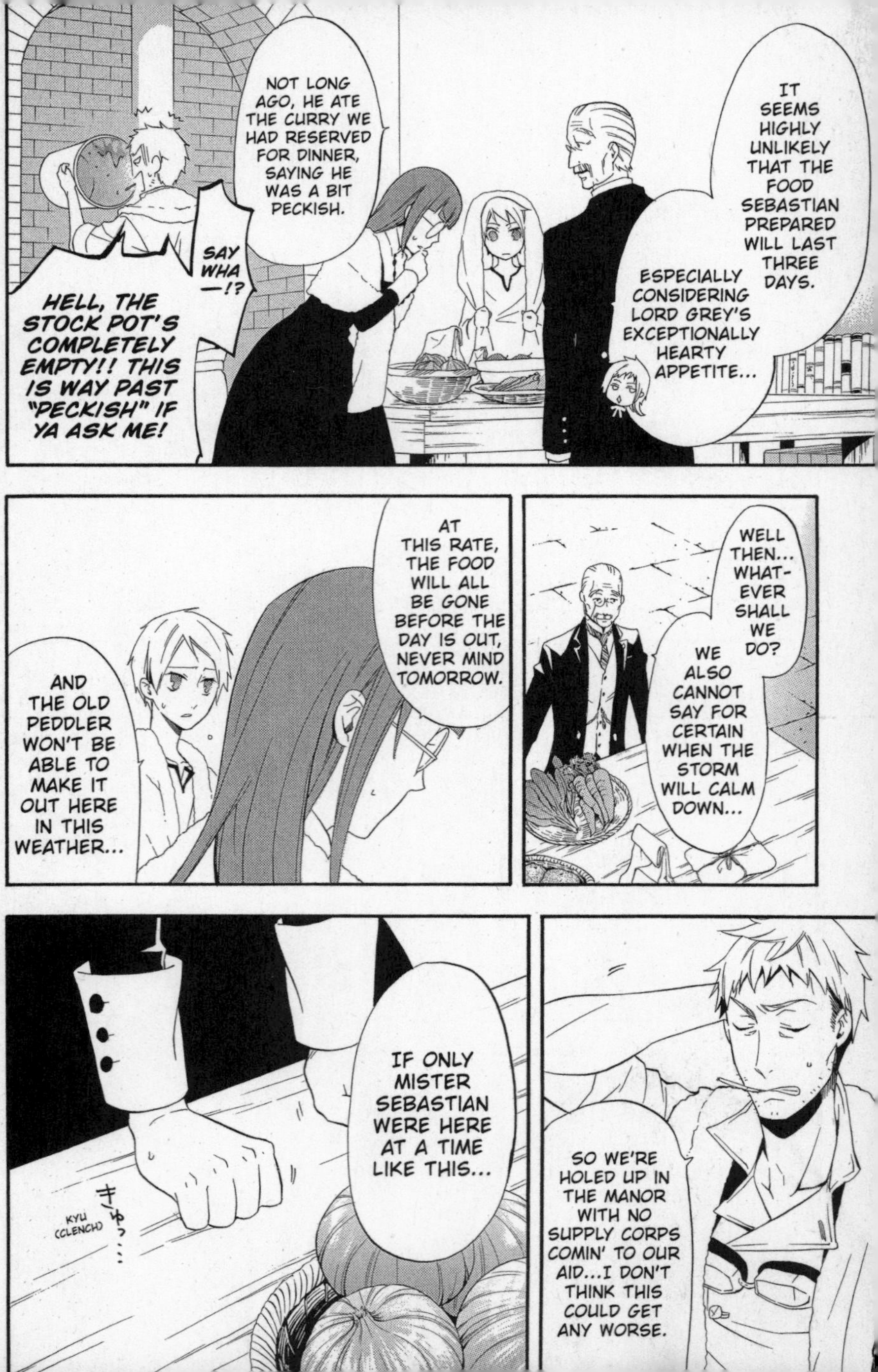
IT SEEMS HIGHLY UNLIKELY THAT THE FOOD SEBASTIAN PREPARED WILL LAST THREE DAYS.
ESPECIALLY CONSIDERING LORD GREY'S EXCEPTIONALLY HEARTY APPETITE...
NOT LONG AGO, HE ATE THE CURRY WE HAD RESERVED FOR DINNER, SAYING HE WAS A BIT PECKISH.
SAY WHA—!?
HELL, THE STOCK POT'S COMPLETELY EMPTY!! THIS IS WAY PAST "PECKISH" IF YA ASK ME!
WELL THEN... WHATEVER SHALL WE DO?
WE ALSO CANNOT SAY FOR CERTAIN WHEN THE STORM WILL CALM DOWN...
AT THIS RATE, THE FOOD WILL ALL BE GONE BEFORE THE DAY IS OUT, NEVER MIND TOMORROW.
AND THE OLD PEDDLER WON'T BE ABLE TO MAKE IT OUT HERE IN THIS WEATHER...
SO WE'RE HOLED UP IN THE MANOR WITH NO SUPPLY CORPS COMIN' TO OUR AID...I DON'T THINK THIS COULD GET ANY WORSE.
IF ONLY MISTER SEBASTIAN WERE HERE AT A TIME LIKE THIS...
キュっ...
KYU (CLENCH)

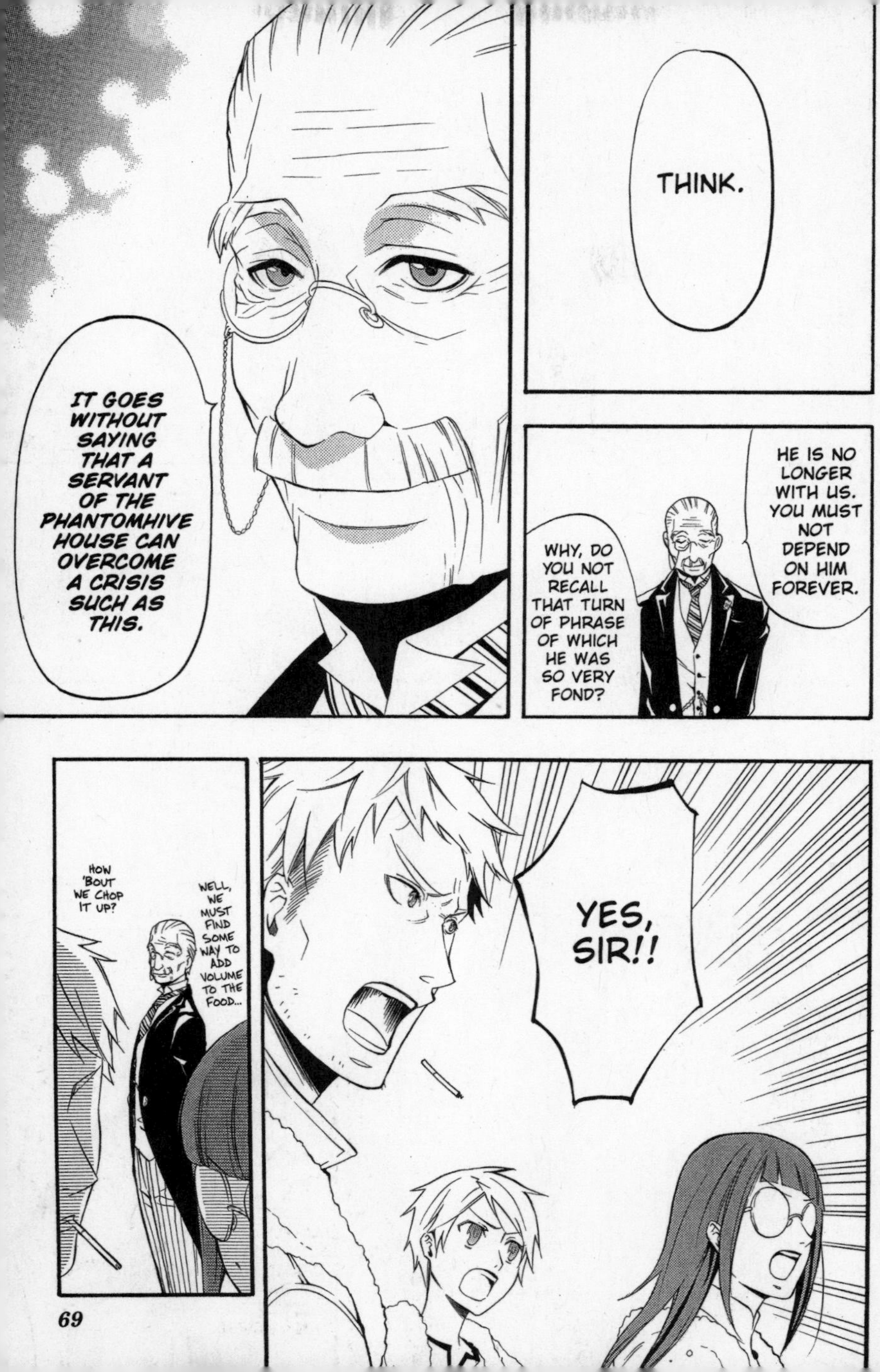

THINK.
HE IS NO LONGER WITH US. YOU MUST NOT DEPEND ON HIM FOREVER.
WHY, DO YOU NOT RECALL THAT TURN OF PHRASE OF WHICH HE WAS SO VERY FOND?
IT GOES WITHOUT SAYING THAT A SERVANT OF THE PHANTOMHIVE HOUSE CAN OVERCOME A CRISIS SUCH AS THIS.
YES, SIR!!
WELL, WE MUST FIND SOME WAY TO ADD VOLUME TO THE FOOD...
HOW 'BOUT WE CHOP IT UP?

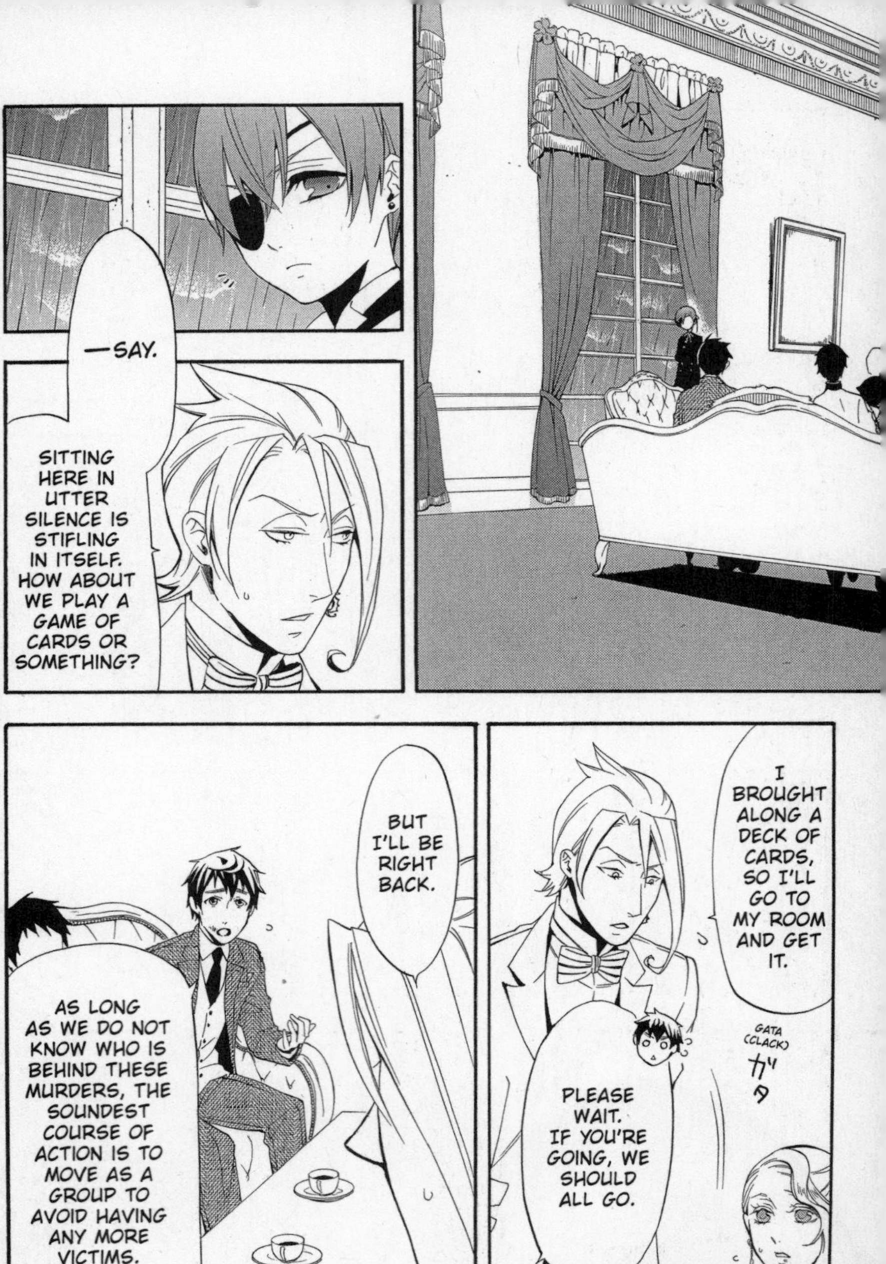
—SAY.
SITTING HERE IN UTTER SILENCE IS STIFLING IN ITSELF. HOW ABOUT WE PLAY A GAME OF CARDS OR SOMETHING?
I BROUGHT ALONG A DECK OF CARDS, SO I'LL GO TO MY ROOM AND GET IT.
GATA (CLACK)
ガタ
PLEASE WAIT. IF YOU'RE GOING, WE SHOULD ALL GO.
BUT I'LL BE RIGHT BACK.
AS LONG AS WE DO NOT KNOW WHO IS BEHIND THESE MURDERS, THE SOUNDEST COURSE OF ACTION IS TO MOVE AS A GROUP TO AVOID HAVING ANY MORE VICTIMS.

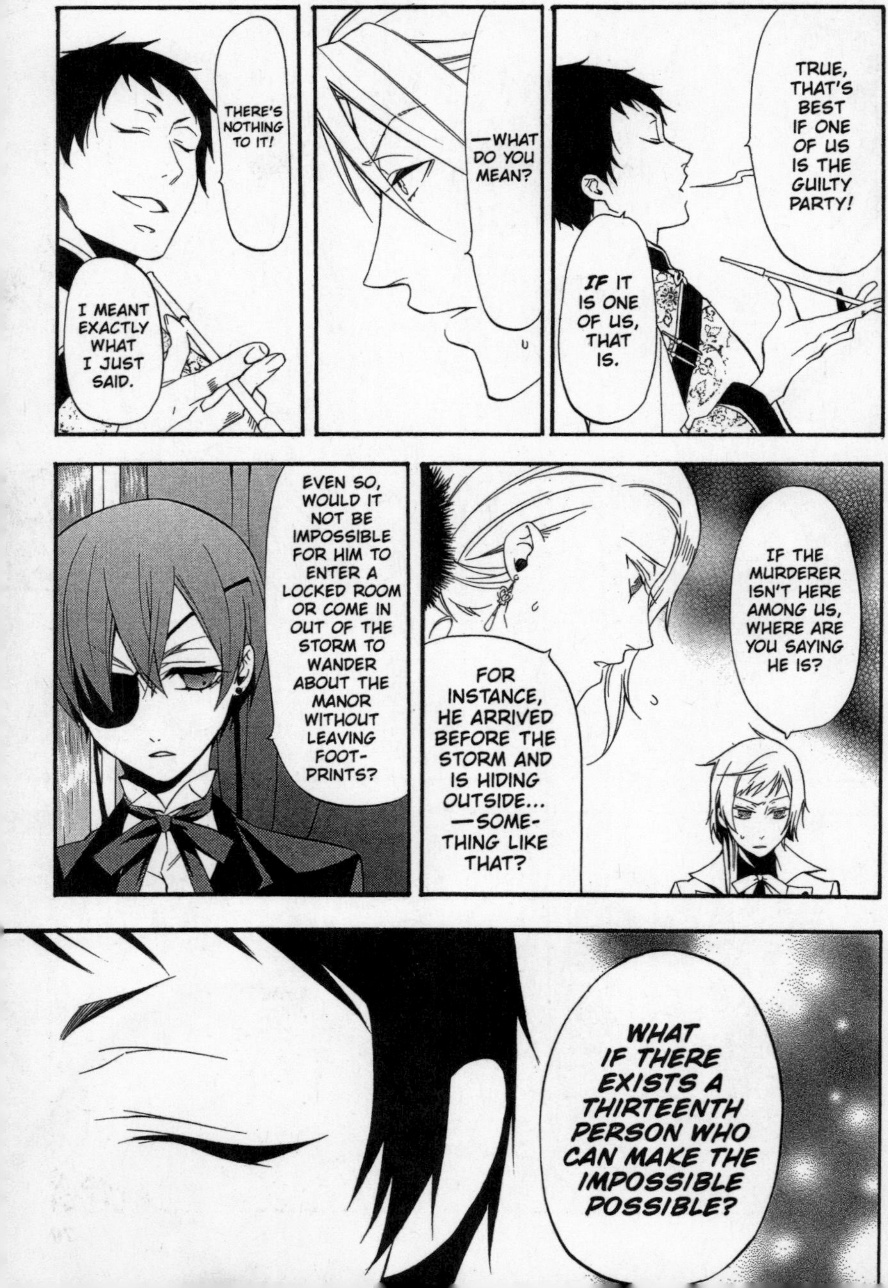
TRUE, THAT'S BEST IF ONE OF US IS THE GUILTY PARTY!
IF IT IS ONE OF US, THAT IS.
—WHAT DO YOU MEAN?
THERE'S NOTHING TO IT!
I MEANT EXACTLY WHAT I JUST SAID.
IF THE MURDERER ISN'T HERE AMONG US, WHERE ARE YOU SAYING HE IS?
FOR INSTANCE, HE ARRIVED BEFORE THE STORM AND IS HIDING OUTSIDE... —SOMETHING LIKE THAT?
EVEN SO, WOULD IT NOT BE IMPOSSIBLE FOR HIM TO ENTER A LOCKED ROOM OR COME IN OUT OF THE STORM TO WANDER ABOUT THE MANOR WITHOUT LEAVING FOOTPRINTS?
WHAT IF THERE EXISTS A THIRTEENTH PERSON WHO CAN MAKE THE IMPOSSIBLE POSSIBLE?

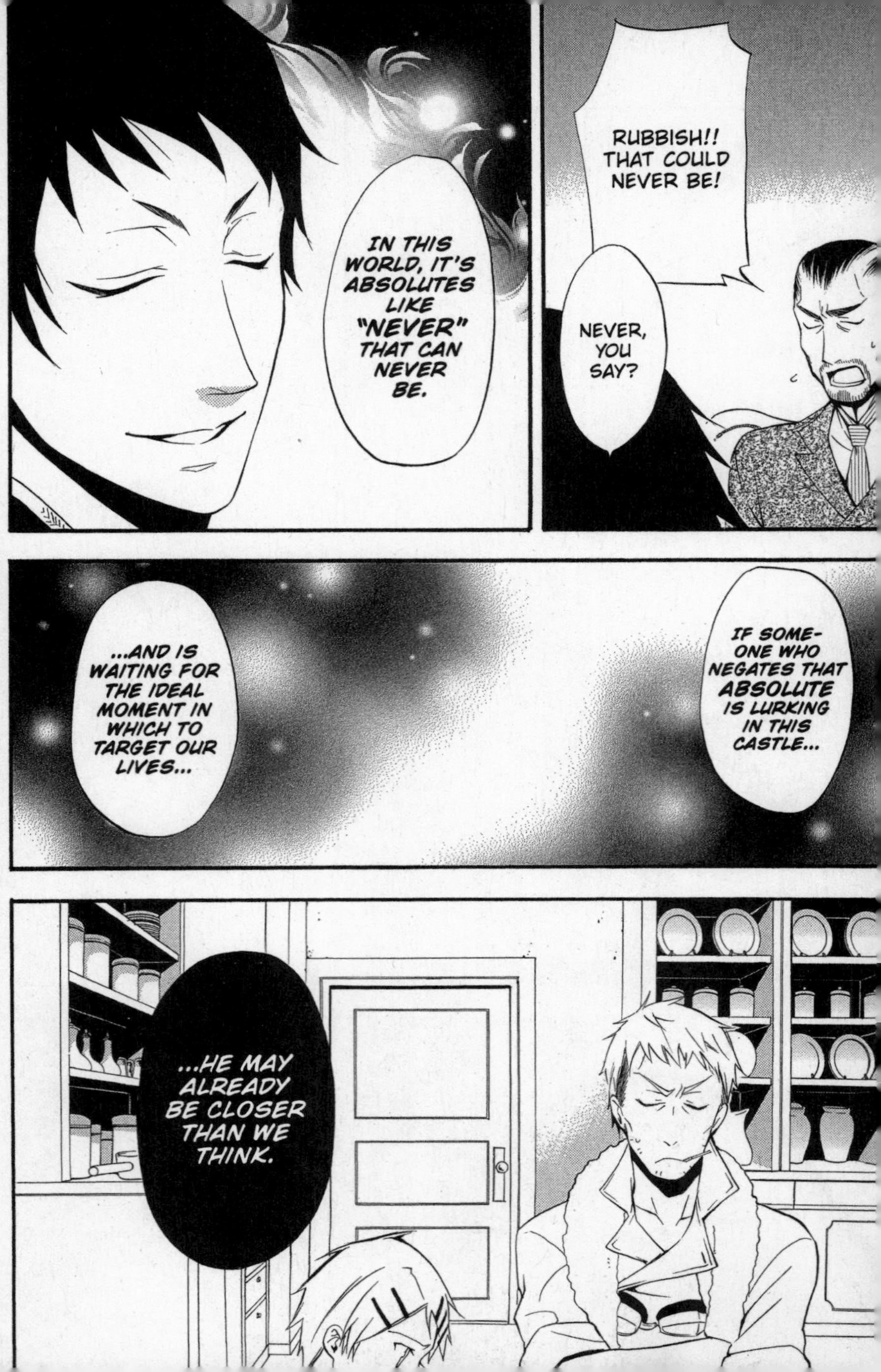
RUBBISH!! THAT COULD NEVER BE!
NEVER, YOU SAY?
IN THIS WORLD, IT'S ABSOLUTES LIKE "NEVER" THAT CAN NEVER BE.
IF SOME-ONE WHO NEGATES THAT ABSOLUTE IS LURKING IN THIS CASTLE...
...AND IS WAITING FOR THE IDEAL MOMENT IN WHICH TO TARGET OUR LIVES...
...HE MAY ALREADY BE CLOSER THAN WE THINK.

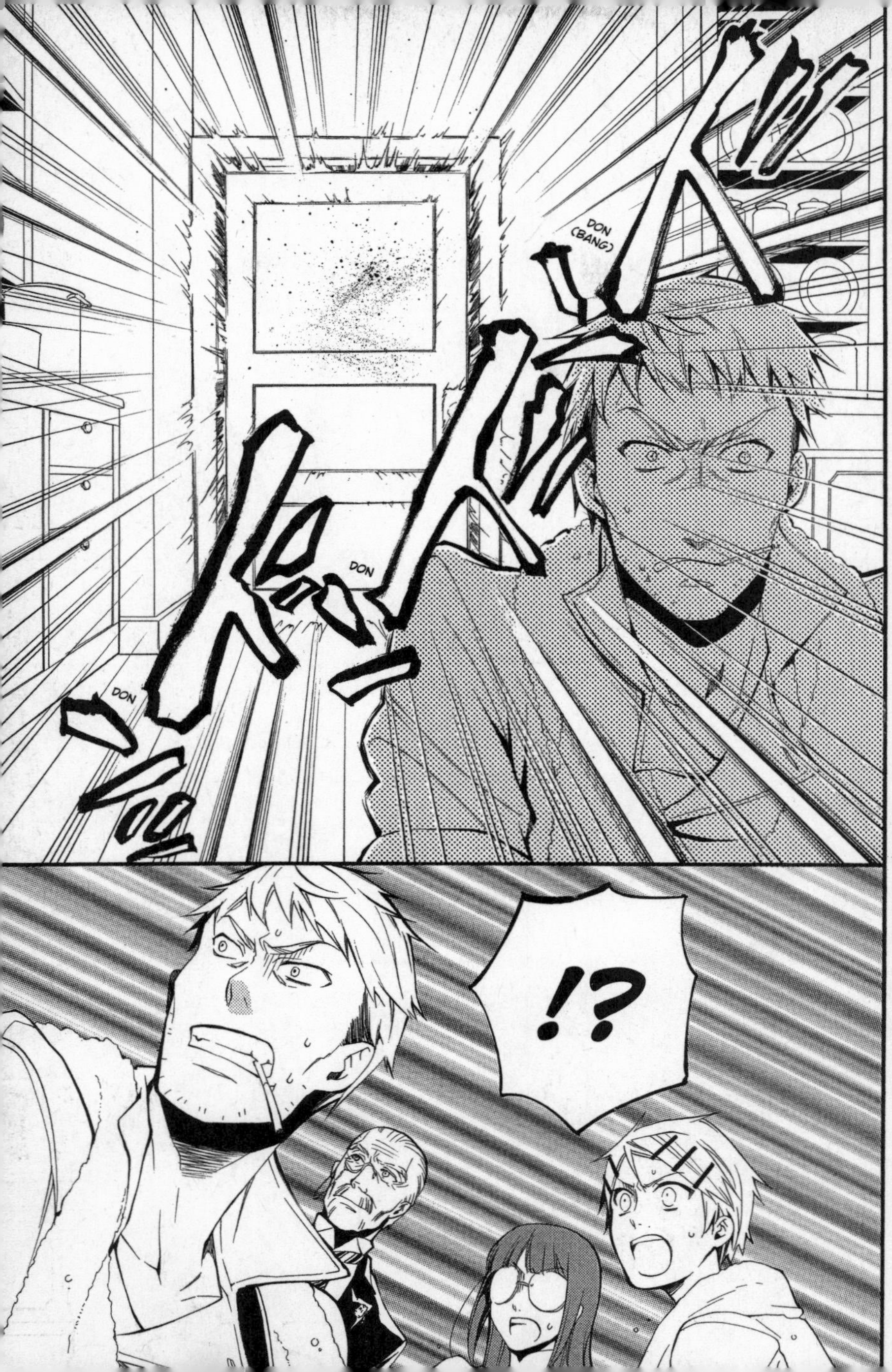
DON (BANG)
DON
DON
!?

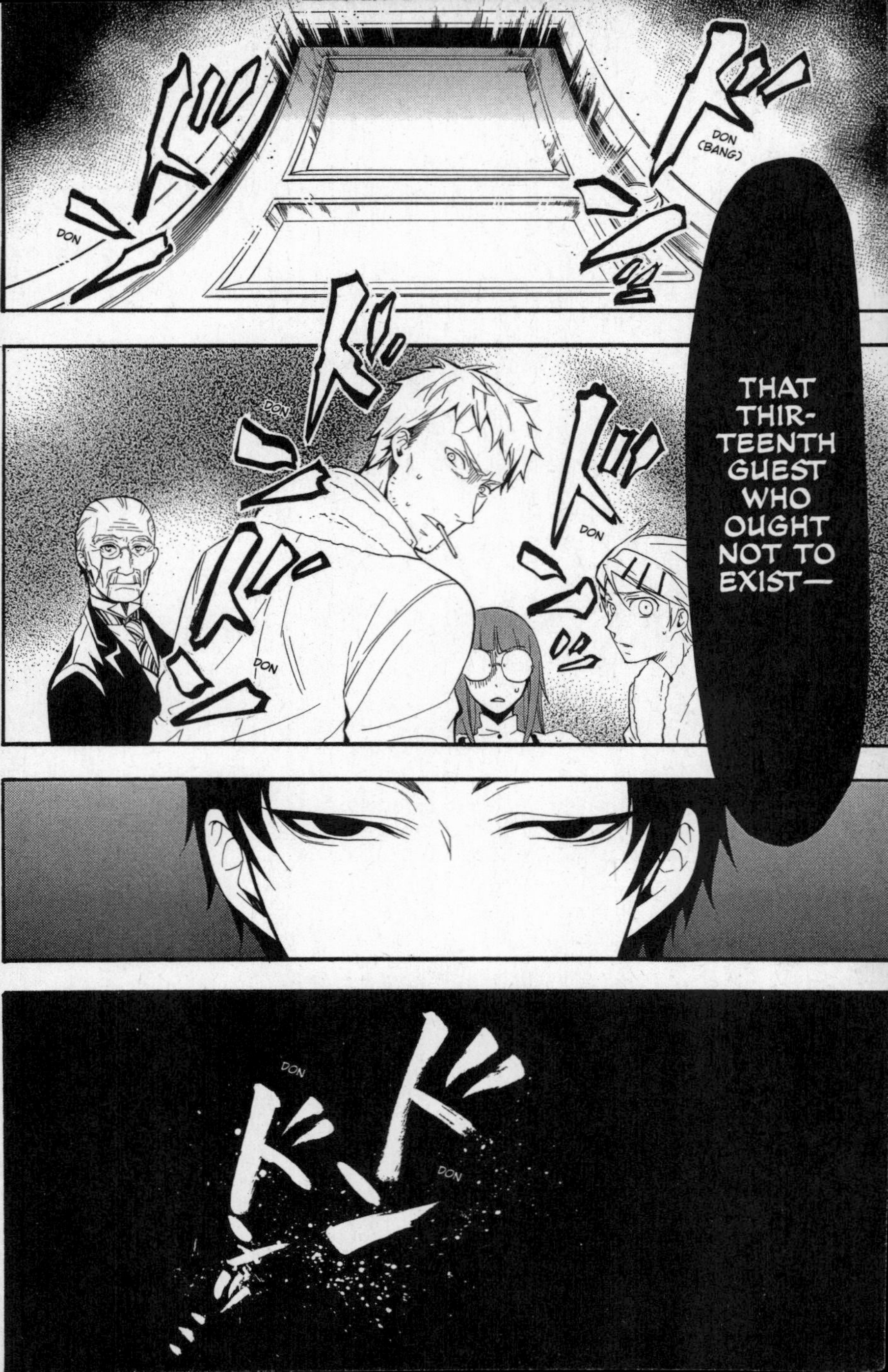
DON (BANG)
DON
THAT THIRTEENTH GUEST WHO OUGHT NOT TO EXIST—
DON
DON
DON
DON
DON

Black Butler

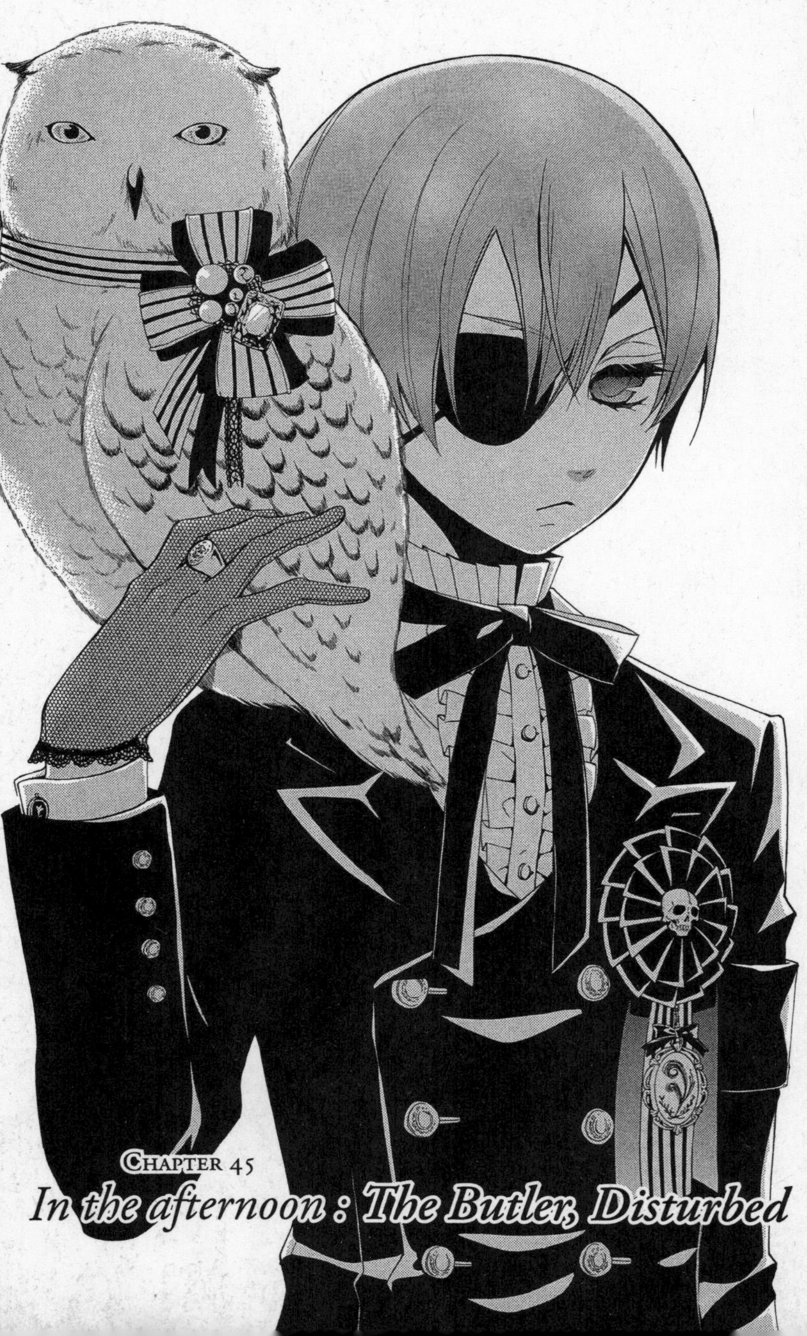

Chapter 45
In the afternoon : The Butler, Disturbed

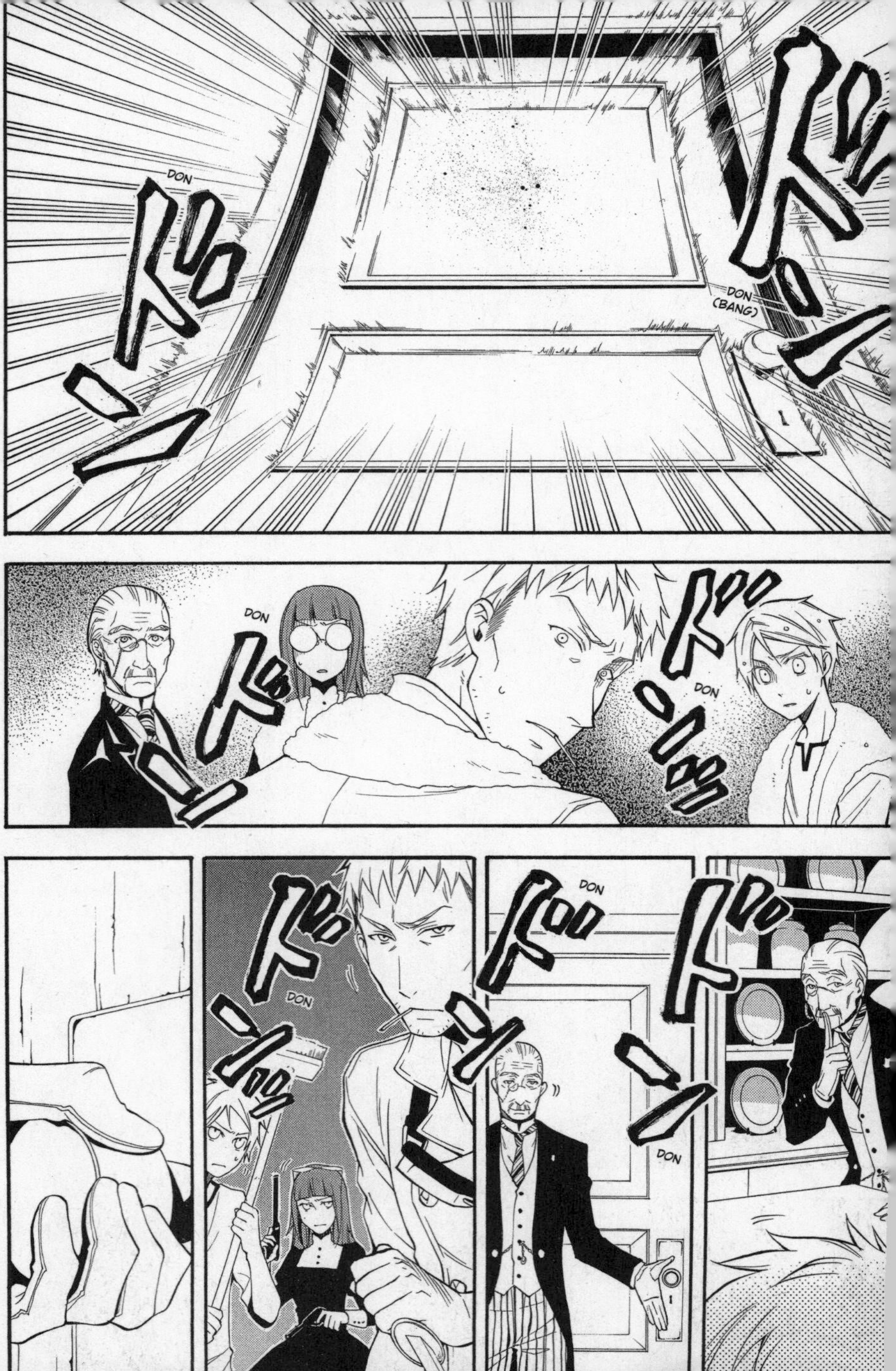
DON
(BANG)
DON
DON
DON
DON
DON
DON

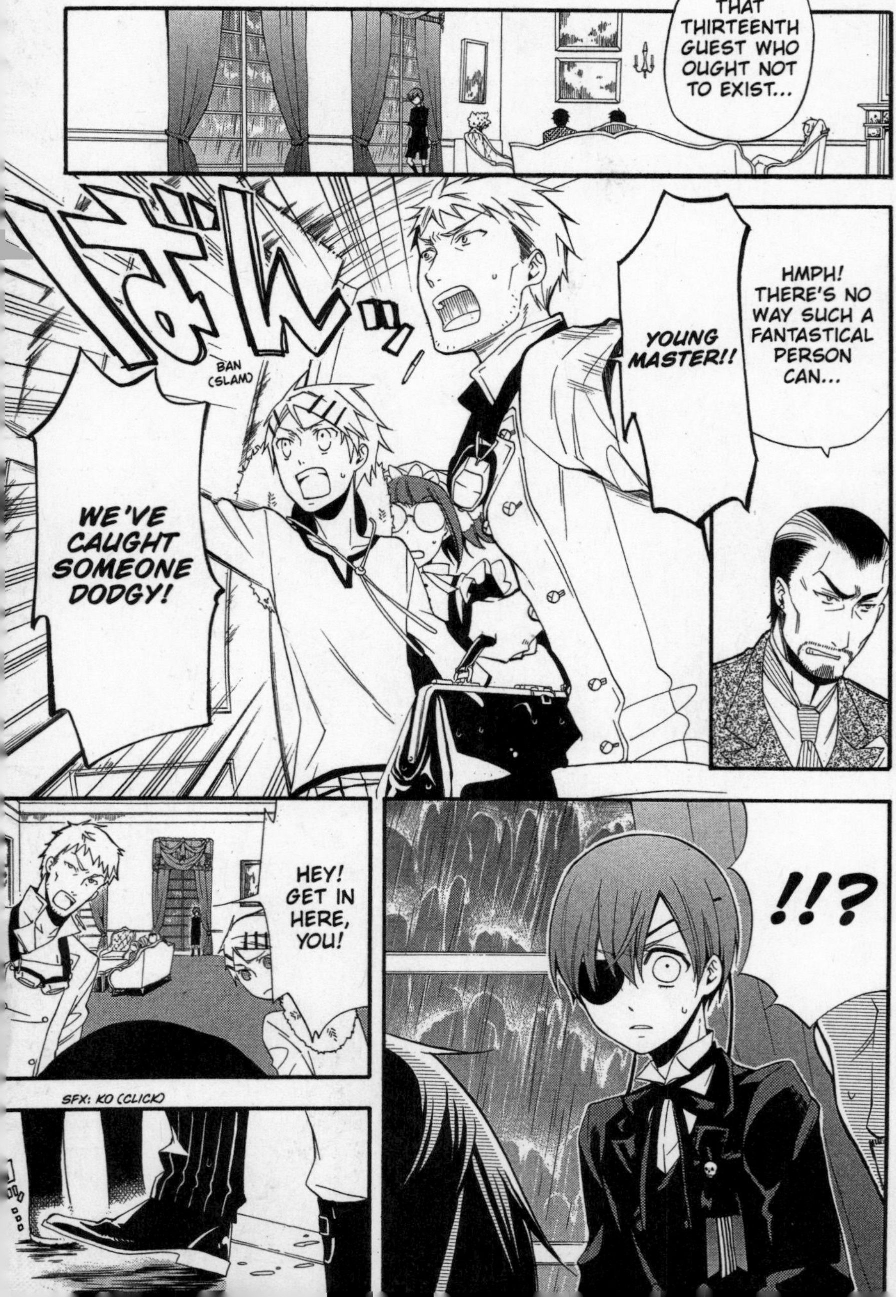
THAT THIRTEENTH GUEST WHO OUGHT NOT TO EXIST...
HMPH! THERE'S NO WAY SUCH A FANTASTICAL PERSON CAN...
YOUNG MASTER!!
BAN (SLAM)
WE'VE CAUGHT SOMEONE DODGY!
!!?
HEY! GET IN HERE, YOU!
SFX: KO (CLICK)

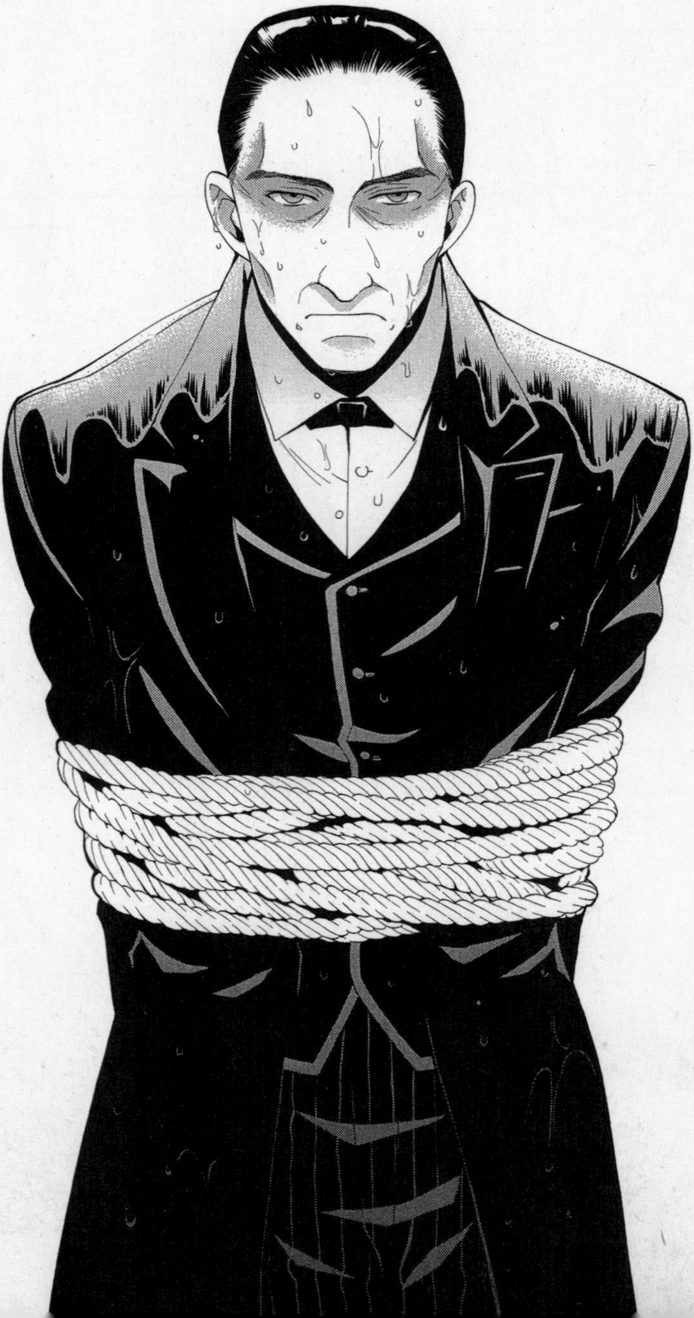

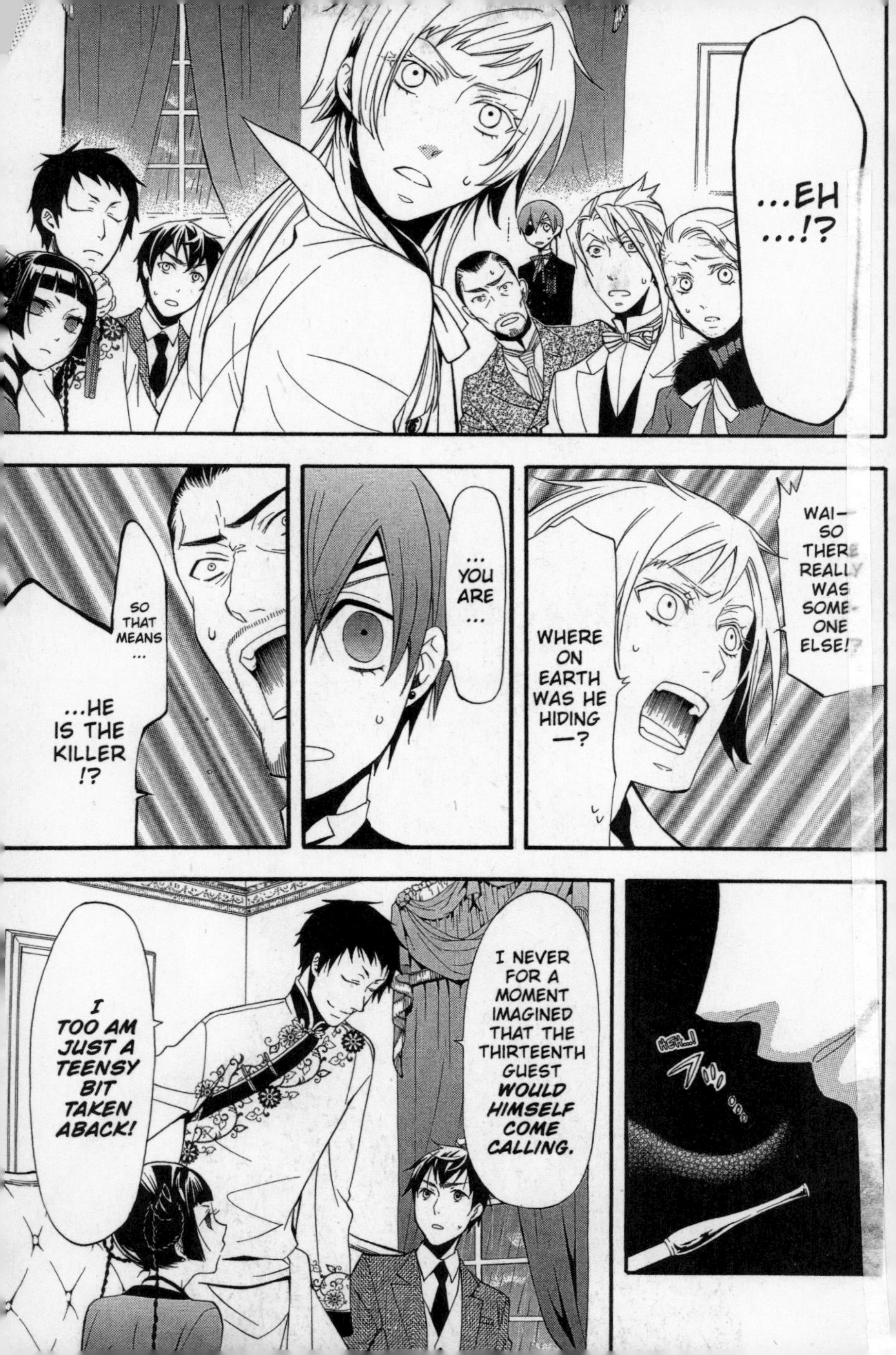
...EH ...!?
WAI— SO THERE REALLY WAS SOME-ONE ELSE!?
WHERE ON EARTH WAS HE HIDING —?
... YOU ARE ...
SO THAT MEANS ...
...HE IS THE KILLER !?
HEH...!
I NEVER FOR A MOMENT IMAGINED THAT THE THIRTEENTH GUEST WOULD HIMSELF COME CALLING.
I TOO AM JUST A TEENSY BIT TAKEN ABACK!

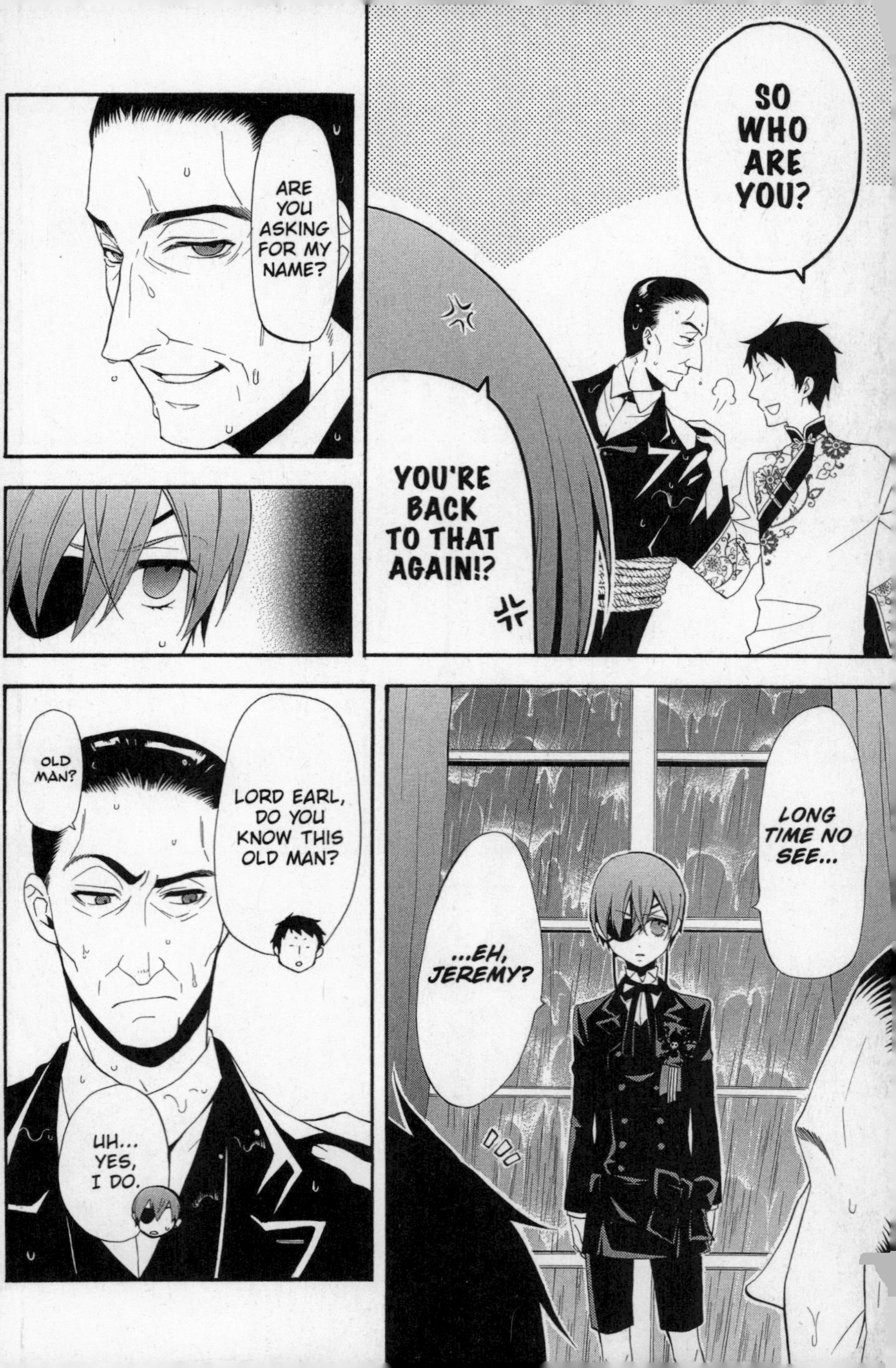
SO WHO ARE YOU?
YOU'RE BACK TO THAT AGAIN!?
ARE YOU ASKING FOR MY NAME?
LONG TIME NO SEE...
...EH, JEREMY?
LORD EARL, DO YOU KNOW THIS OLD MAN?
OLD MAN?
UH... YES, I DO.

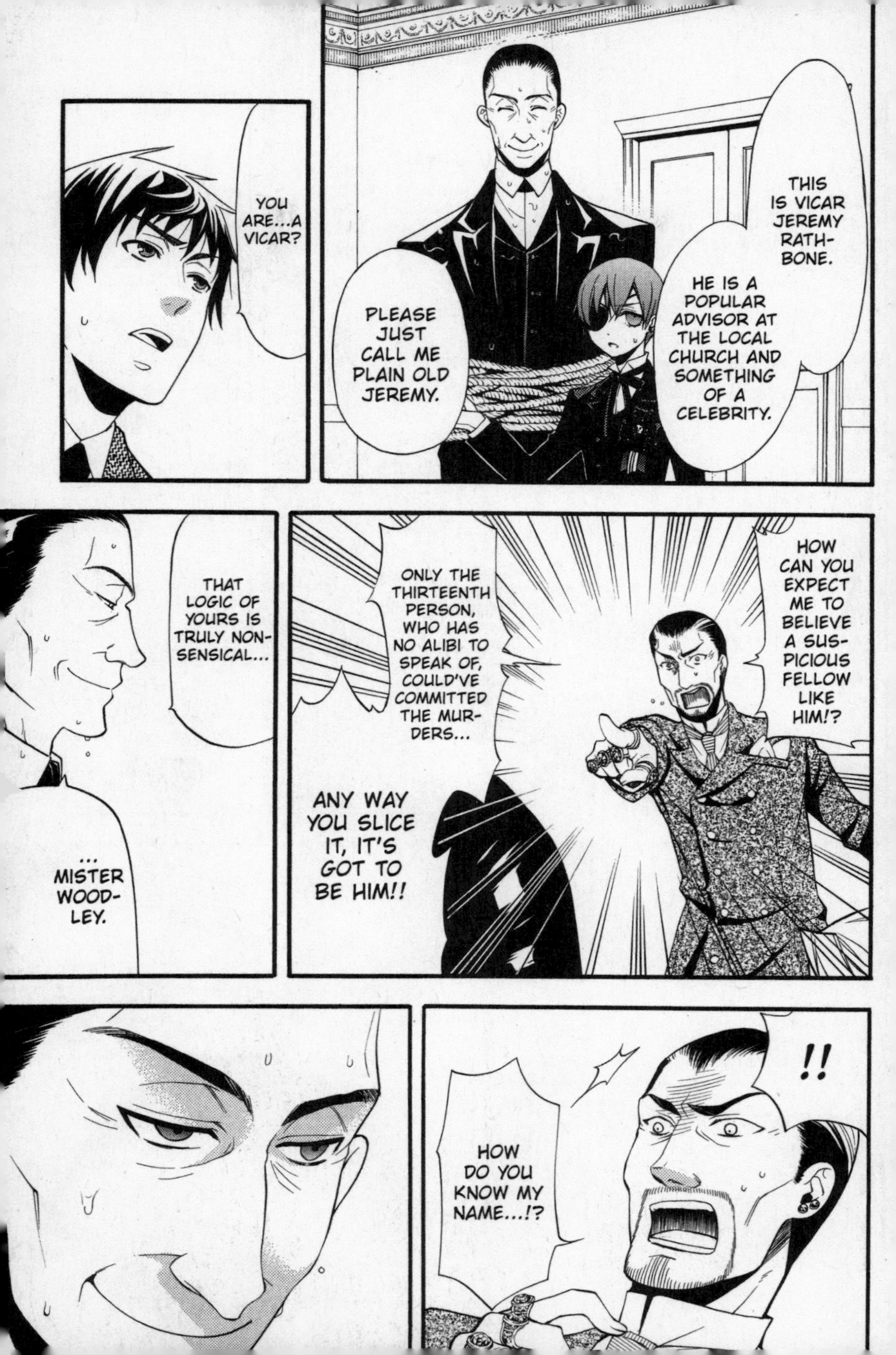
THIS IS VICAR JEREMY RATH-BONE.
HE IS A POPULAR ADVISOR AT THE LOCAL CHURCH AND SOMETHING OF A CELEBRITY.
PLEASE JUST CALL ME PLAIN OLD JEREMY.
YOU ARE...A VICAR?
HOW CAN YOU EXPECT ME TO BELIEVE A SUS-PICIOUS FELLOW LIKE HIM!?
ONLY THE THIRTEENTH PERSON, WHO HAS NO ALIBI TO SPEAK OF, COULD'VE COMMITTED THE MUR-DERS...
ANY WAY YOU SLICE IT, IT'S GOT TO BE HIM!!
THAT LOGIC OF YOURS IS TRULY NON-SENSICAL...
...MISTER WOOD-LEY.
!!
HOW DO YOU KNOW MY NAME...!?

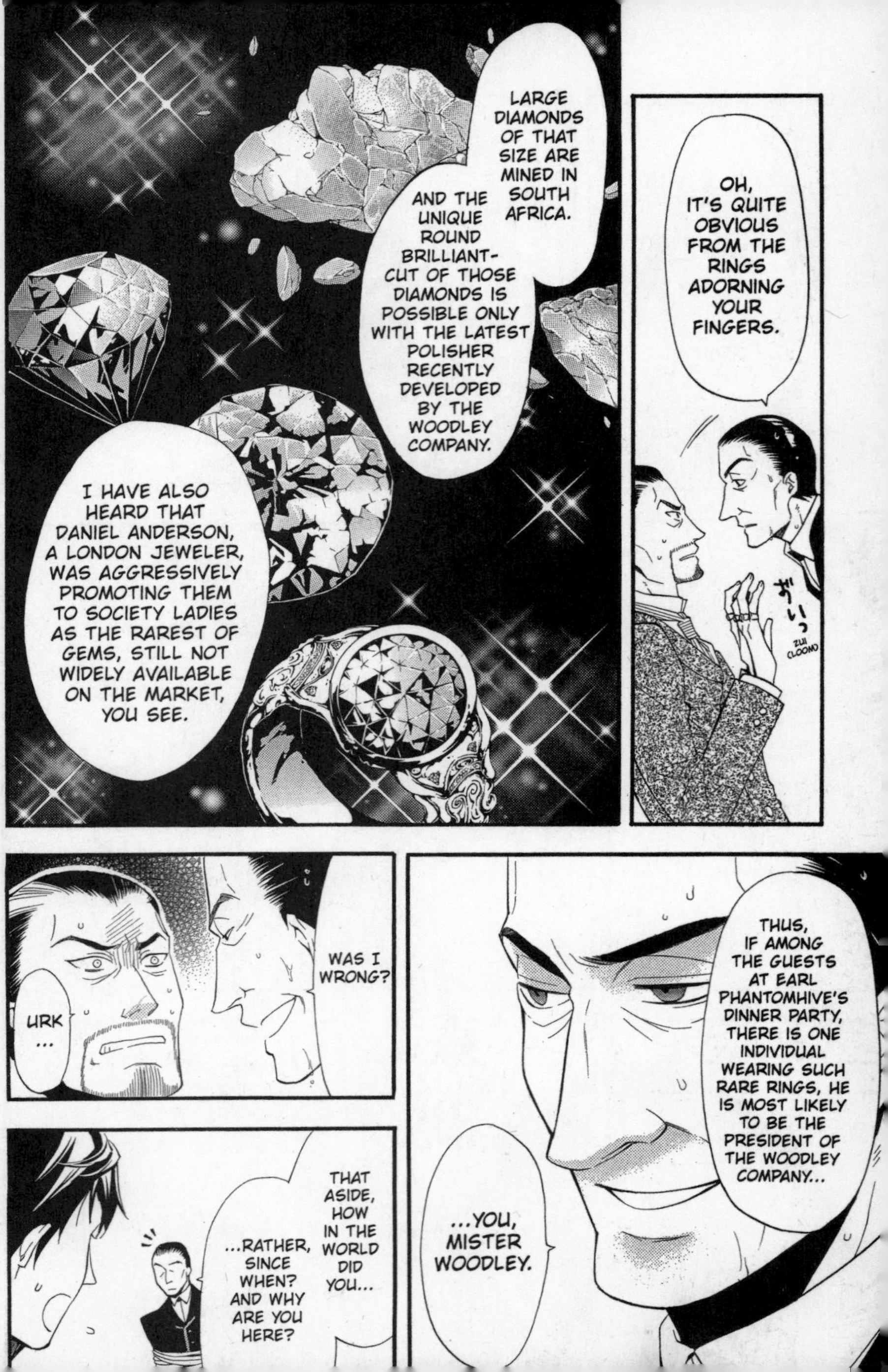
OH, IT'S QUITE OBVIOUS FROM THE RINGS ADORNING YOUR FINGERS.
ずいっ
ZUI (LOOM)
LARGE DIAMONDS OF THAT SIZE ARE MINED IN SOUTH AFRICA.
AND THE UNIQUE ROUND BRILLIANT-CUT OF THOSE DIAMONDS IS POSSIBLE ONLY WITH THE LATEST POLISHER RECENTLY DEVELOPED BY THE WOODLEY COMPANY.
I HAVE ALSO HEARD THAT DANIEL ANDERSON, A LONDON JEWELER, WAS AGGRESSIVELY PROMOTING THEM TO SOCIETY LADIES AS THE RAREST OF GEMS, STILL NOT WIDELY AVAILABLE ON THE MARKET, YOU SEE.
THUS, IF AMONG THE GUESTS AT EARL PHANTOMHIVE'S DINNER PARTY, THERE IS ONE INDIVIDUAL WEARING SUCH RARE RINGS, HE IS MOST LIKELY TO BE THE PRESIDENT OF THE WOODLEY COMPANY...
...YOU, MISTER WOODLEY.
WAS I WRONG?
URK ...
THAT ASIDE, HOW IN THE WORLD DID YOU...
...RATHER, SINCE WHEN? AND WHY ARE YOU HERE?

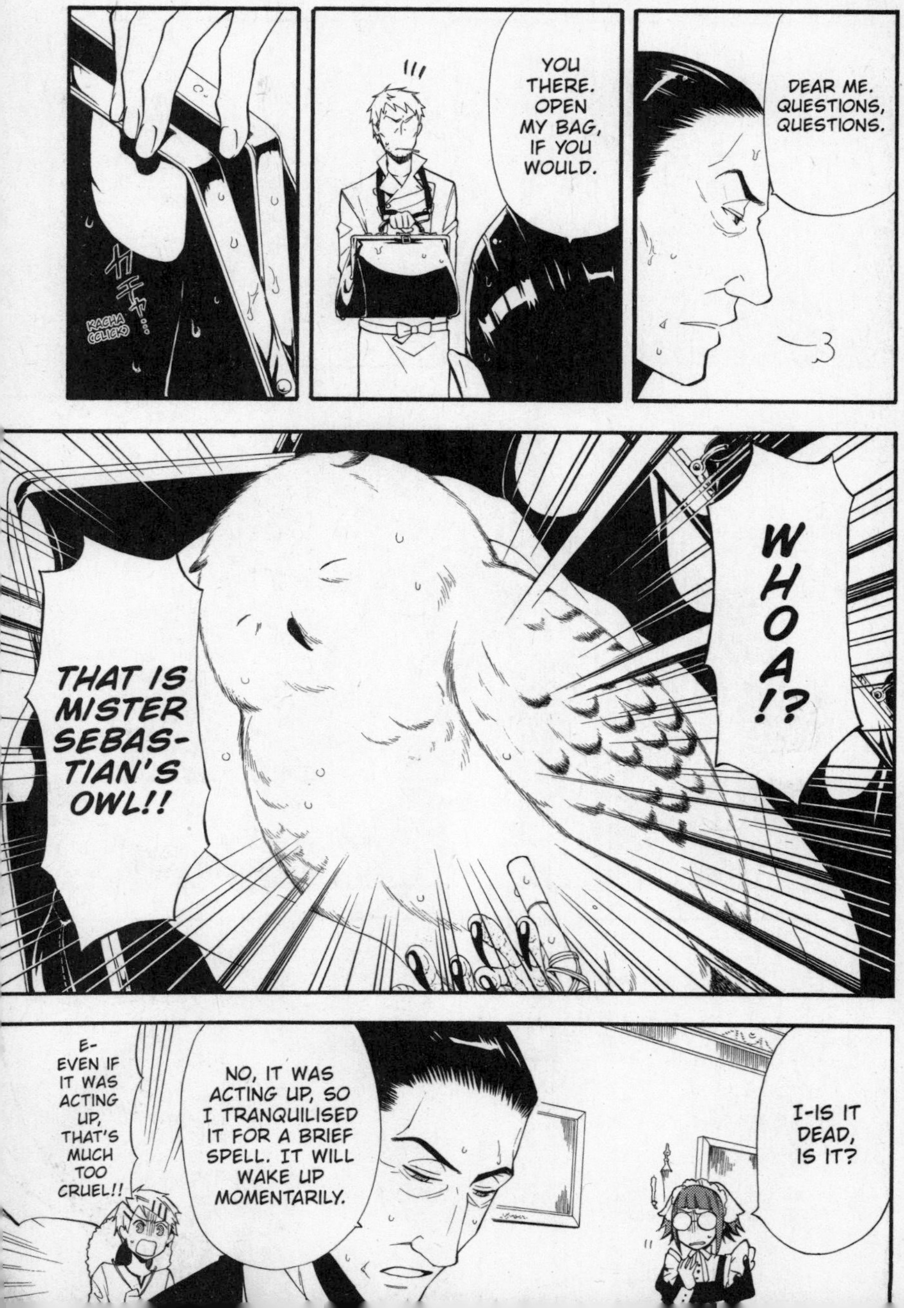
DEAR ME. QUESTIONS, QUESTIONS.
YOU THERE. OPEN MY BAG, IF YOU WOULD.
KACHA (CLICK)
WHOA!?
THAT IS MISTER SEBAS-TIAN'S OWL!!
I-IS IT DEAD, IS IT?
NO, IT WAS ACTING UP, SO I TRANQUILISED IT FOR A BRIEF SPELL. IT WILL WAKE UP MOMENTARILY.
E-EVEN IF IT WAS ACTING UP, THAT'S MUCH TOO CRUEL!!

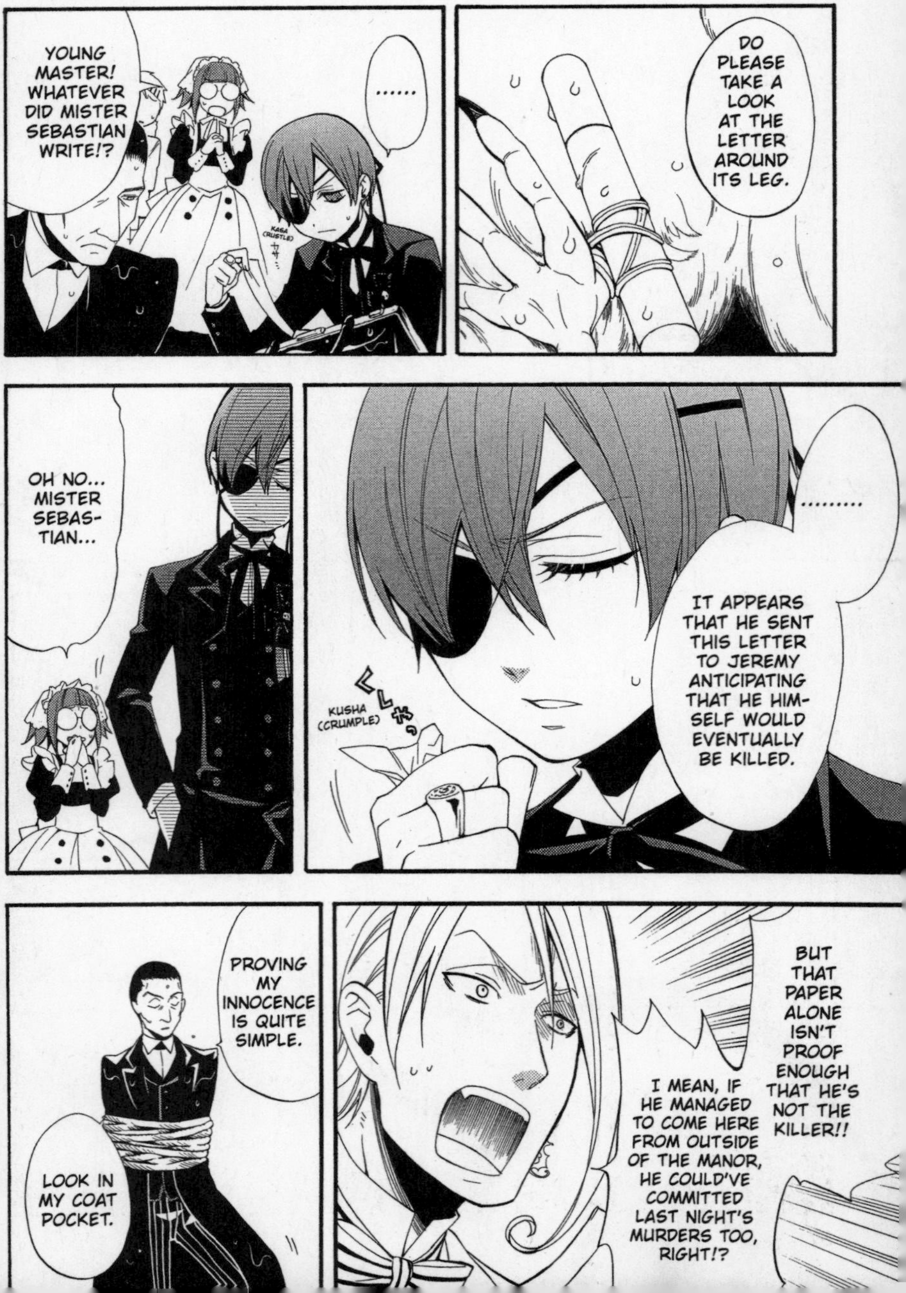
DO PLEASE TAKE A LOOK AT THE LETTER AROUND ITS LEG.
......
YOUNG MASTER! WHATEVER DID MISTER SEBASTIAN WRITE!?
KASA (RUSTLE)
....
IT APPEARS THAT HE SENT THIS LETTER TO JEREMY ANTICIPATING THAT HE HIMSELF WOULD EVENTUALLY BE KILLED.
KUSHA (CRUMPLE)
OH NO... MISTER SEBAS-TIAN...
BUT THAT PAPER ALONE ISN'T PROOF ENOUGH THAT HE'S NOT THE KILLER!!
I MEAN, IF HE MANAGED TO COME HERE FROM OUTSIDE OF THE MANOR, HE COULD'VE COMMITTED LAST NIGHT'S MURDERS TOO, RIGHT!?
PROVING MY INNOCENCE IS QUITE SIMPLE.
LOOK IN MY COAT POCKET.

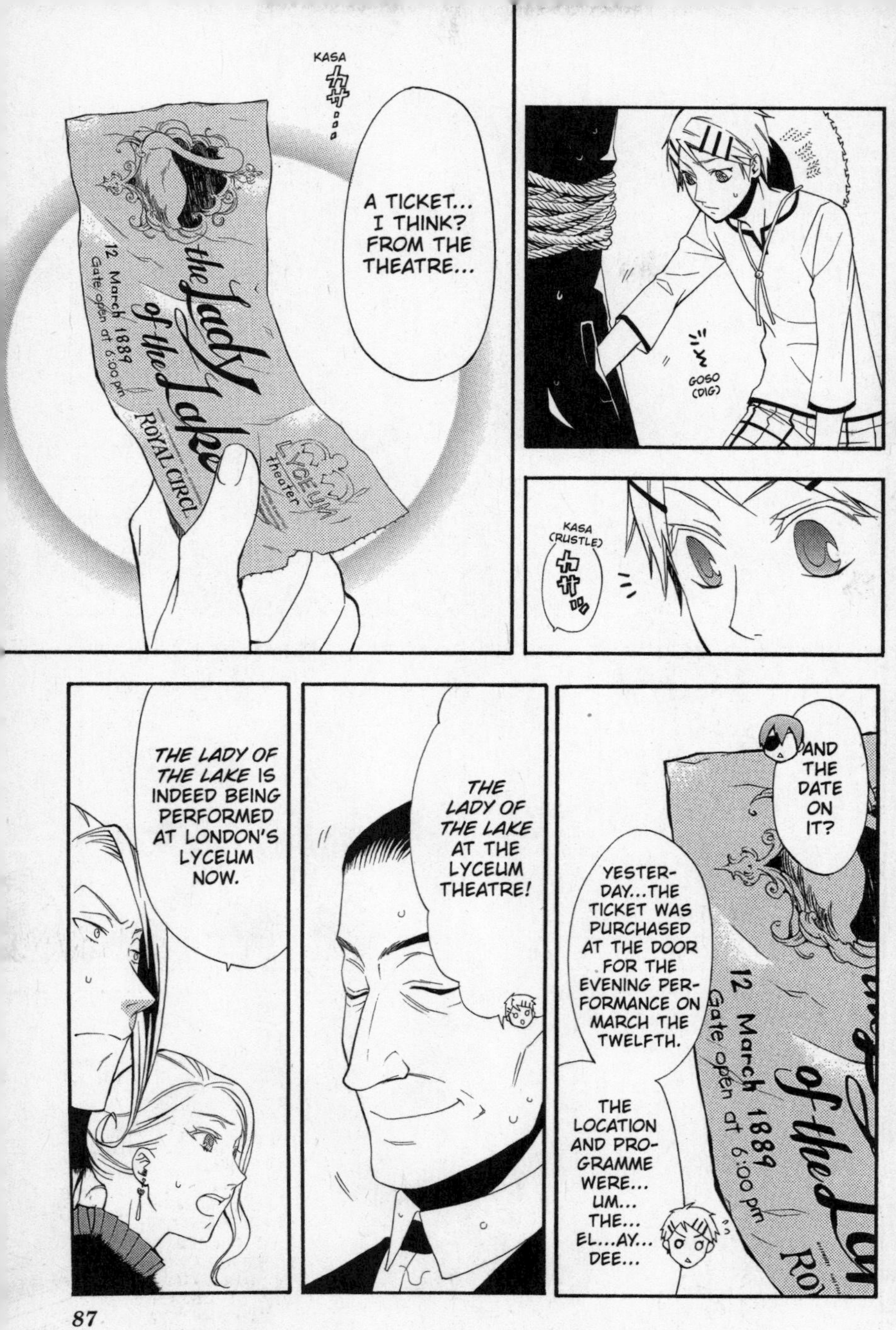
ゴソ
GOSO (DIG)
KASA (RUSTLE)
カサッ
KASA
カサ...
A TICKET... I THINK? FROM THE THEATRE...
the Lady of the Lake
12 March 1889 Gate open at 6:00 pm
ROYAL CIRCL
LYCEUM theater
AND THE DATE ON IT?
YESTER-DAY...THE TICKET WAS PURCHASED AT THE DOOR FOR THE EVENING PER-FORMANCE ON MARCH THE TWELFTH.
THE LOCATION AND PRO-GRAMME WERE... UM... THE... EL...AY... DEE...
12 March 1889 Gate open at 6:00 pm
THE LADY OF THE LAKE AT THE LYCEUM THEATRE!
THE LADY OF THE LAKE IS INDEED BEING PERFORMED AT LONDON'S LYCEUM NOW.

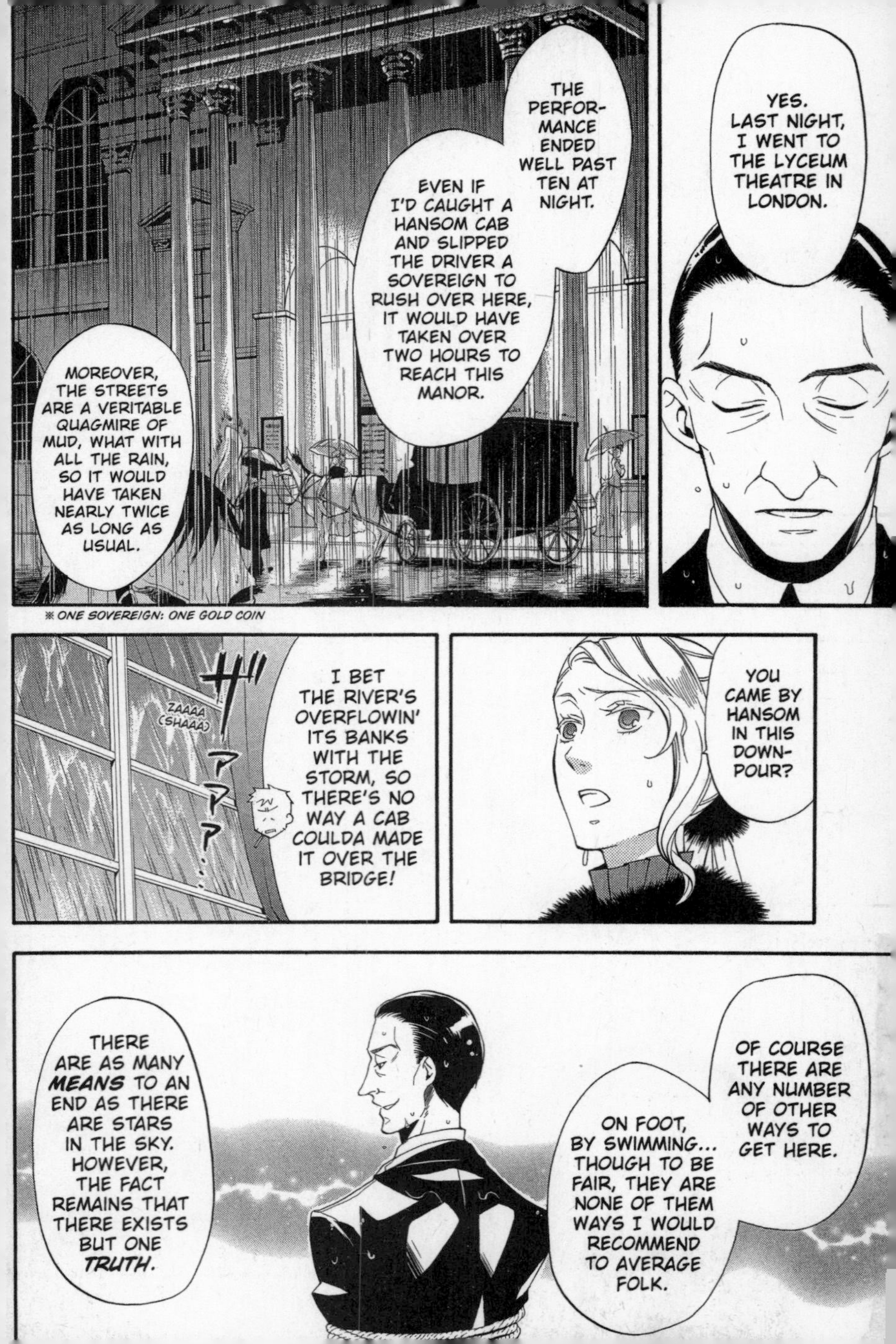
YES. LAST NIGHT, I WENT TO THE LYCEUM THEATRE IN LONDON.
THE PERFORMANCE ENDED WELL PAST TEN AT NIGHT.
EVEN IF I'D CAUGHT A HANSOM CAB AND SLIPPED THE DRIVER A SOVEREIGN TO RUSH OVER HERE, IT WOULD HAVE TAKEN OVER TWO HOURS TO REACH THIS MANOR.
MOREOVER, THE STREETS ARE A VERITABLE QUAGMIRE OF MUD, WHAT WITH ALL THE RAIN, SO IT WOULD HAVE TAKEN NEARLY TWICE AS LONG AS USUAL.
YOU CAME BY HANSOM IN THIS DOWNPOUR?
ザァァァ...
ZAAAA (SHAAA)
I BET THE RIVER'S OVERFLOWIN' ITS BANKS WITH THE STORM, SO THERE'S NO WAY A CAB COULDA MADE IT OVER THE BRIDGE!
OF COURSE THERE ARE ANY NUMBER OF OTHER WAYS TO GET HERE.
ON FOOT, BY SWIMMING... THOUGH TO BE FAIR, THEY ARE NONE OF THEM WAYS I WOULD RECOMMEND TO AVERAGE FOLK.
THERE ARE AS MANY MEANS TO AN END AS THERE ARE STARS IN THE SKY. HOWEVER, THE FACT REMAINS THAT THERE EXISTS BUT ONE TRUTH.
※ ONE SOVEREIGN: ONE GOLD COIN

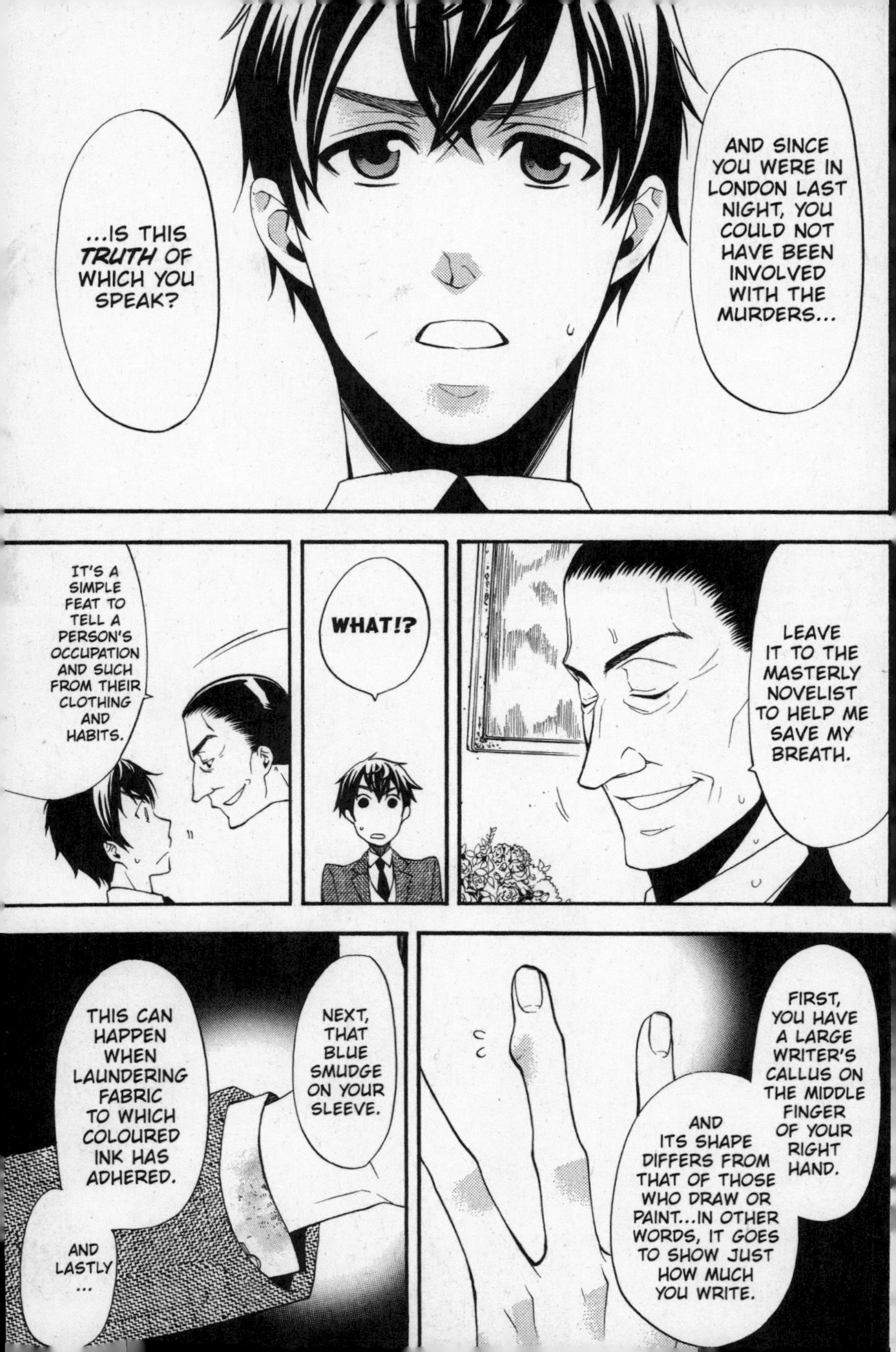
AND SINCE YOU WERE IN LONDON LAST NIGHT, YOU COULD NOT HAVE BEEN INVOLVED WITH THE MURDERS...
...IS THIS *TRUTH* OF WHICH YOU SPEAK?
LEAVE IT TO THE MASTERLY NOVELIST TO HELP ME SAVE MY BREATH.
WHAT!?
IT'S A SIMPLE FEAT TO TELL A PERSON'S OCCUPATION AND SUCH FROM THEIR CLOTHING AND HABITS.
FIRST, YOU HAVE A LARGE WRITER'S CALLUS ON THE MIDDLE FINGER OF YOUR RIGHT HAND.
AND ITS SHAPE DIFFERS FROM THAT OF THOSE WHO DRAW OR PAINT...IN OTHER WORDS, IT GOES TO SHOW JUST HOW MUCH YOU WRITE.
NEXT, THAT BLUE SMUDGE ON YOUR SLEEVE.
THIS CAN HAPPEN WHEN LAUNDERING FABRIC TO WHICH COLOURED INK HAS ADHERED.
AND LASTLY...

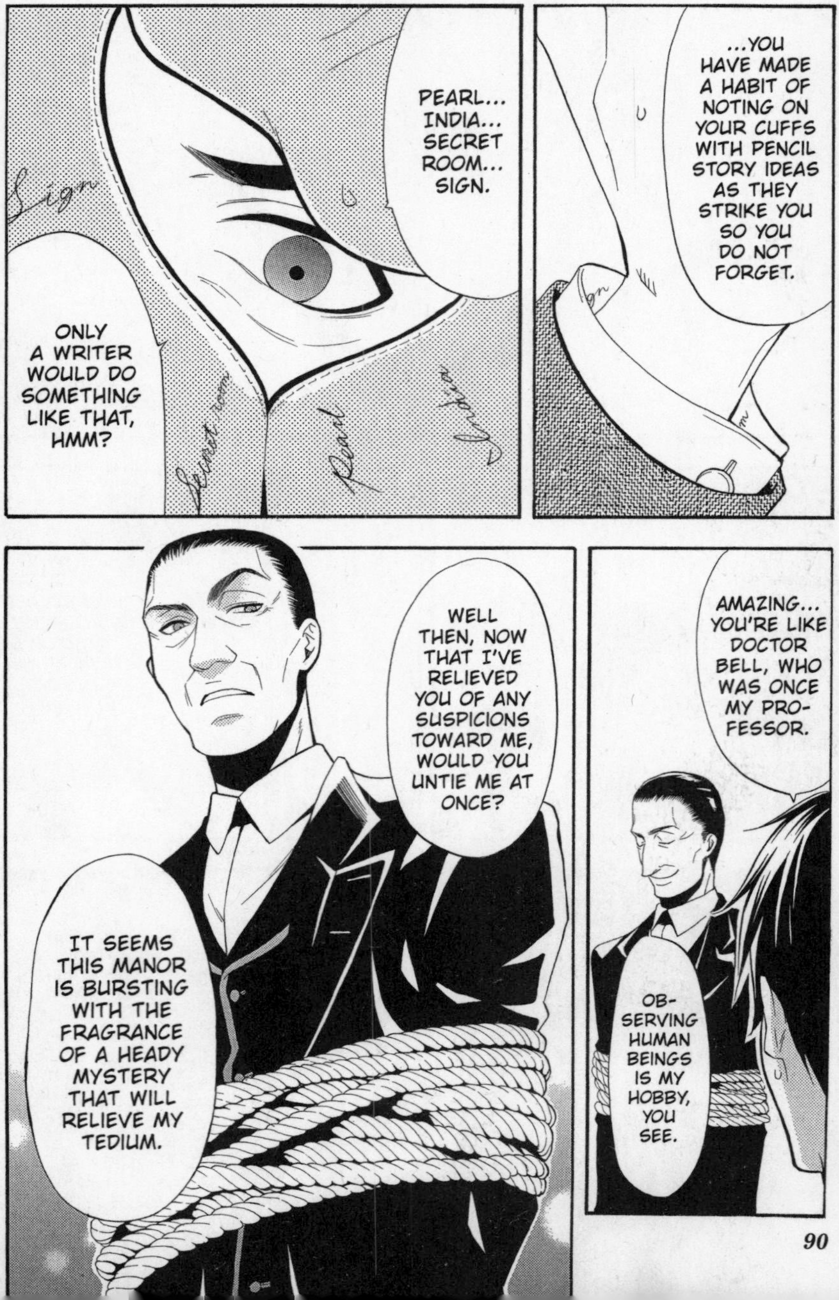

...YOU HAVE MADE A HABIT OF NOTING ON YOUR CUFFS WITH PENCIL STORY IDEAS AS THEY STRIKE YOU SO YOU DO NOT FORGET.
PEARL... INDIA... SECRET ROOM... SIGN.
Sign
ONLY A WRITER WOULD DO SOMETHING LIKE THAT, HMM?
AMAZING... YOU'RE LIKE DOCTOR BELL, WHO WAS ONCE MY PRO-FESSOR.
OB-SERVING HUMAN BEINGS IS MY HOBBY, YOU SEE.
WELL THEN, NOW THAT I'VE RELIEVED YOU OF ANY SUSPICIONS TOWARD ME, WOULD YOU UNTIE ME AT ONCE?
IT SEEMS THIS MANOR IS BURSTING WITH THE FRAGRANCE OF A HEADY MYSTERY THAT WILL RELIEVE MY TEDIUM.

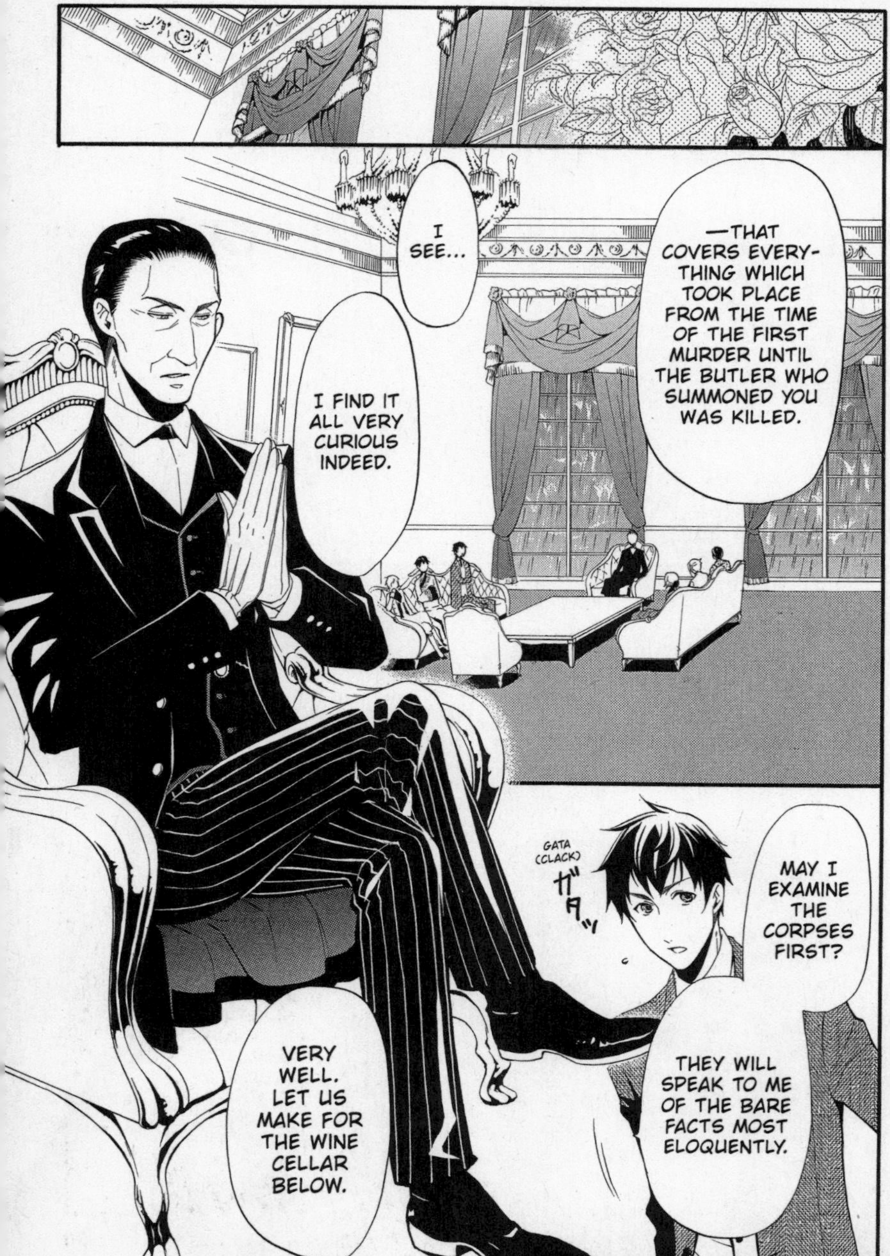
—THAT COVERS EVERYTHING WHICH TOOK PLACE FROM THE TIME OF THE FIRST MURDER UNTIL THE BUTLER WHO SUMMONED YOU WAS KILLED.
I SEE...
I FIND IT ALL VERY CURIOUS INDEED.
GATA (CLACK)
ガタッ
MAY I EXAMINE THE CORPSES FIRST?
THEY WILL SPEAK TO ME OF THE BARE FACTS MOST ELOQUENTLY.
VERY WELL. LET US MAKE FOR THE WINE CELLAR BELOW.

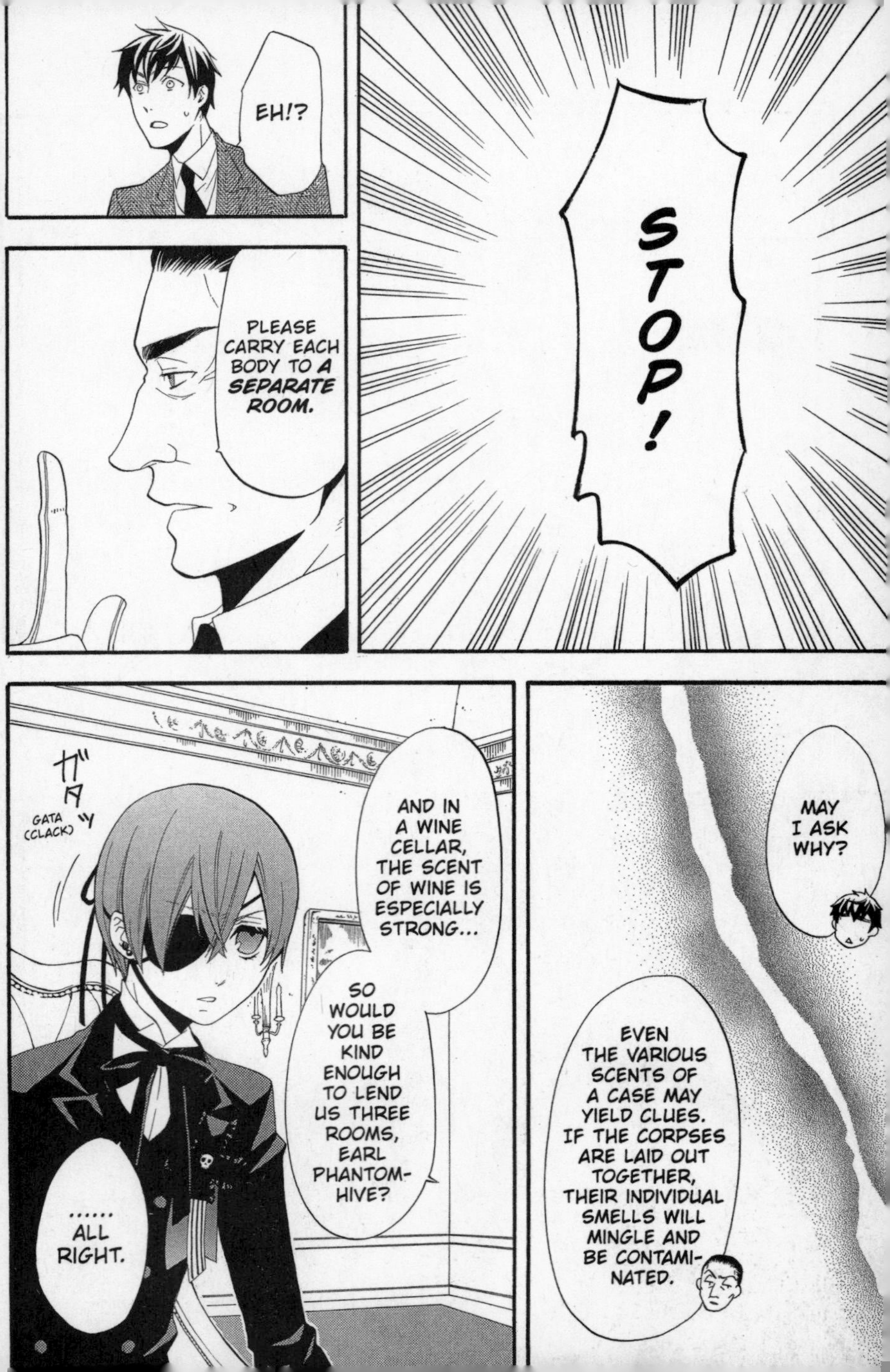
STOP!
EH!?
PLEASE CARRY EACH BODY TO A SEPARATE ROOM.
MAY I ASK WHY?
EVEN THE VARIOUS SCENTS OF A CASE MAY YIELD CLUES. IF THE CORPSES ARE LAID OUT TOGETHER, THEIR INDIVIDUAL SMELLS WILL MINGLE AND BE CONTAMI-NATED.
AND IN A WINE CELLAR, THE SCENT OF WINE IS ESPECIALLY STRONG...
SO WOULD YOU BE KIND ENOUGH TO LEND US THREE ROOMS, EARL PHANTOM-HIVE?
ガタッ
GATA (CLACK)
...... ALL RIGHT.

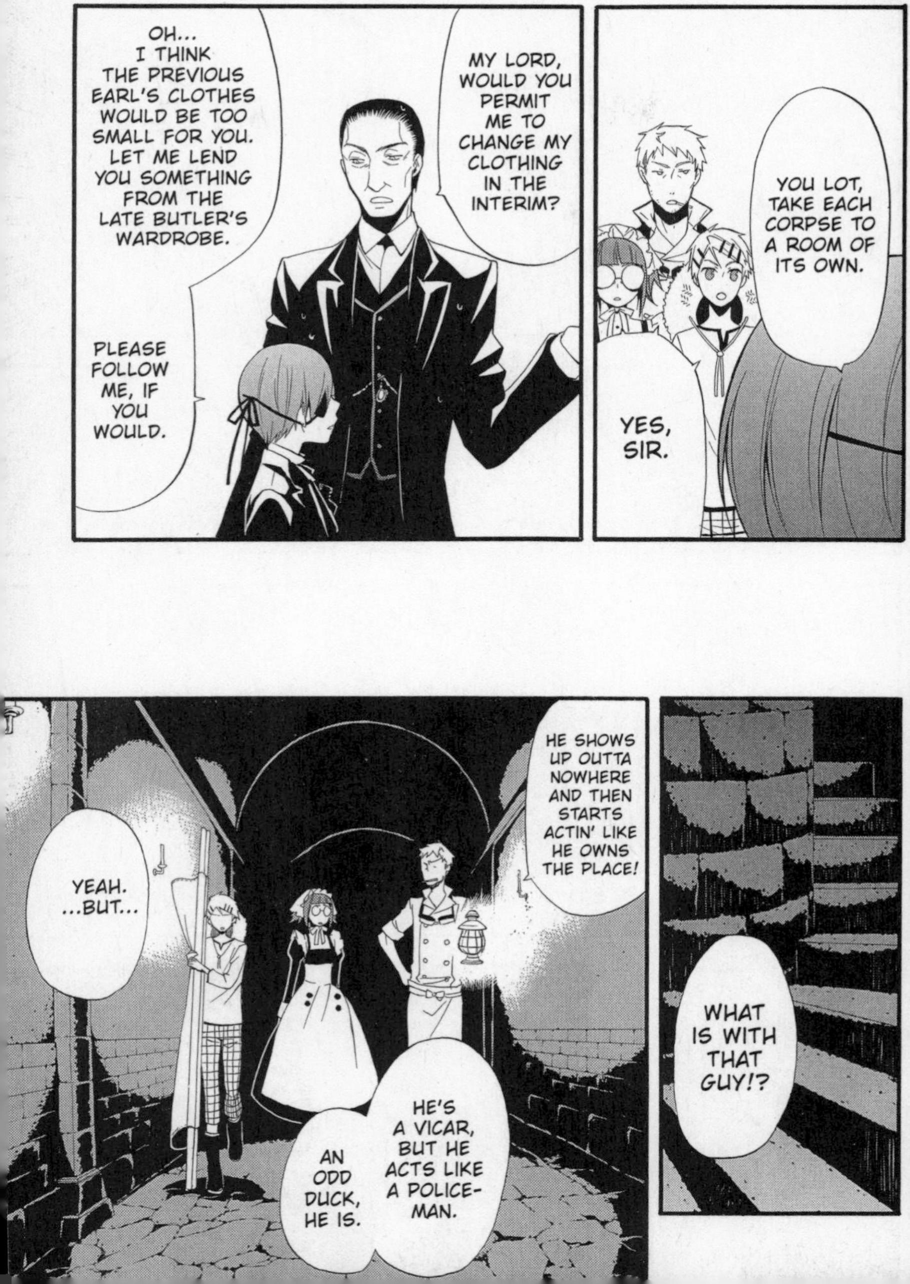
YOU LOT, TAKE EACH CORPSE TO A ROOM OF ITS OWN.
YES, SIR.
MY LORD, WOULD YOU PERMIT ME TO CHANGE MY CLOTHING IN THE INTERIM?
OH... I THINK THE PREVIOUS EARL'S CLOTHES WOULD BE TOO SMALL FOR YOU. LET ME LEND YOU SOMETHING FROM THE LATE BUTLER'S WARDROBE.
PLEASE FOLLOW ME, IF YOU WOULD.
WHAT IS WITH THAT GUY!?
HE SHOWS UP OUTTA NOWHERE AND THEN STARTS ACTIN' LIKE HE OWNS THE PLACE!
YEAH. ...BUT...
HE'S A VICAR, BUT HE ACTS LIKE A POLICE-MAN.
AN ODD DUCK, HE IS.

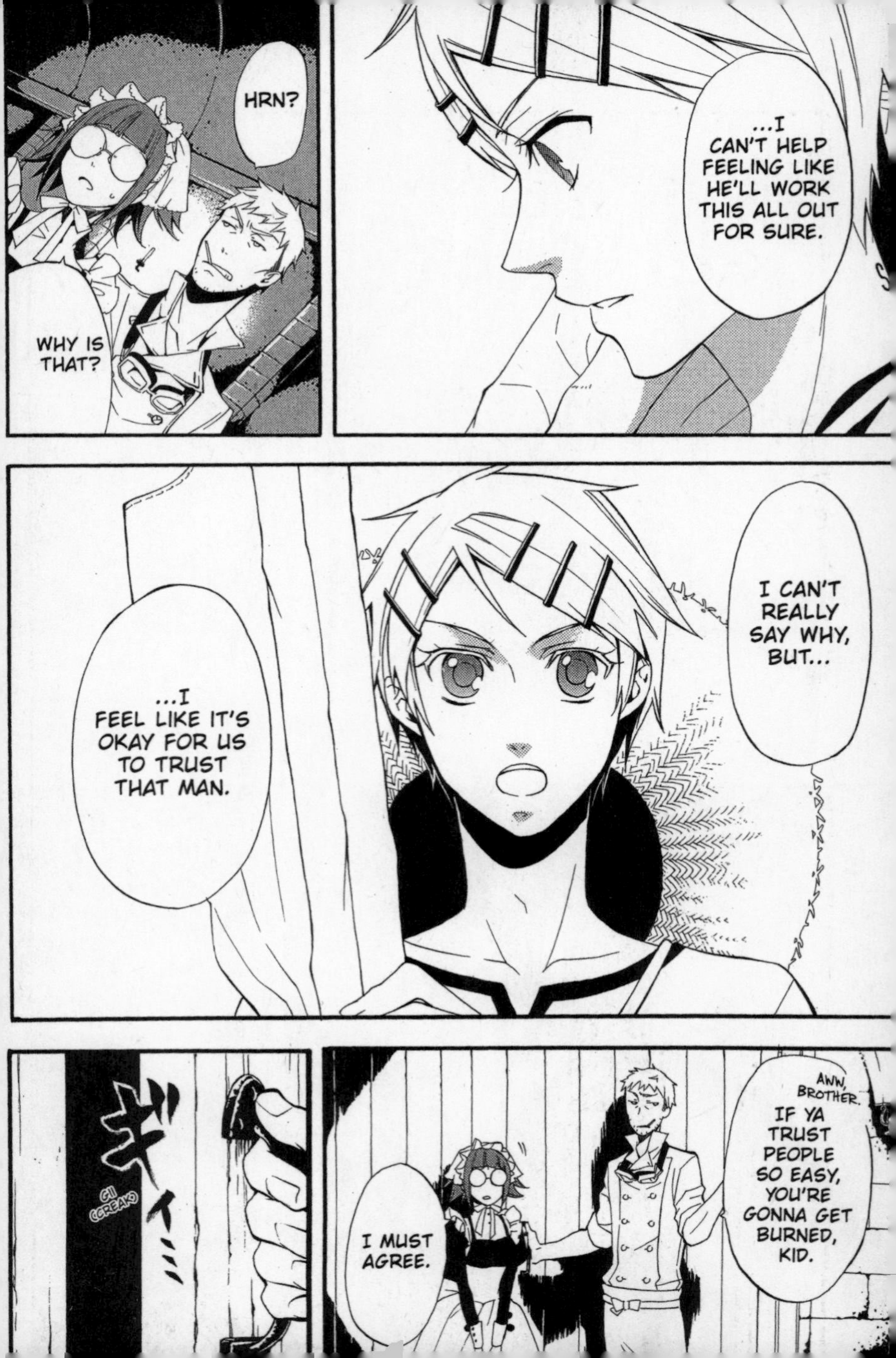
...I CAN'T HELP FEELING LIKE HE'LL WORK THIS ALL OUT FOR SURE.
HRN?
WHY IS THAT?
I CAN'T REALLY SAY WHY, BUT...
...I FEEL LIKE IT'S OKAY FOR US TO TRUST THAT MAN.
AWW, BROTHER.
IF YA TRUST PEOPLE SO EASY, YOU'RE GONNA GET BURNED, KID.
I MUST AGREE.
GI (CREAK)

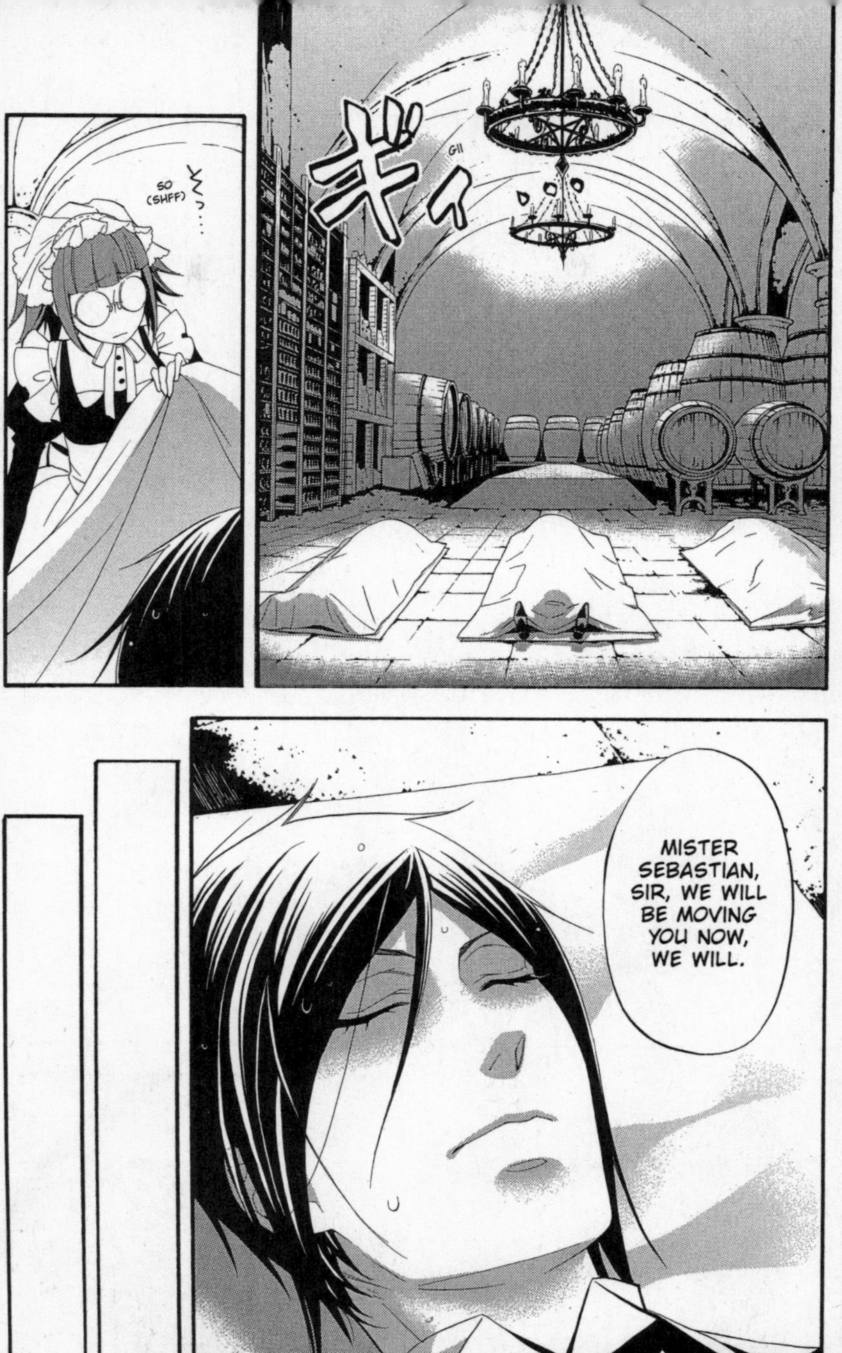
ギィ
GII
SO (SHFF)
MISTER SEBASTIAN, SIR, WE WILL BE MOVING YOU NOW, WE WILL.

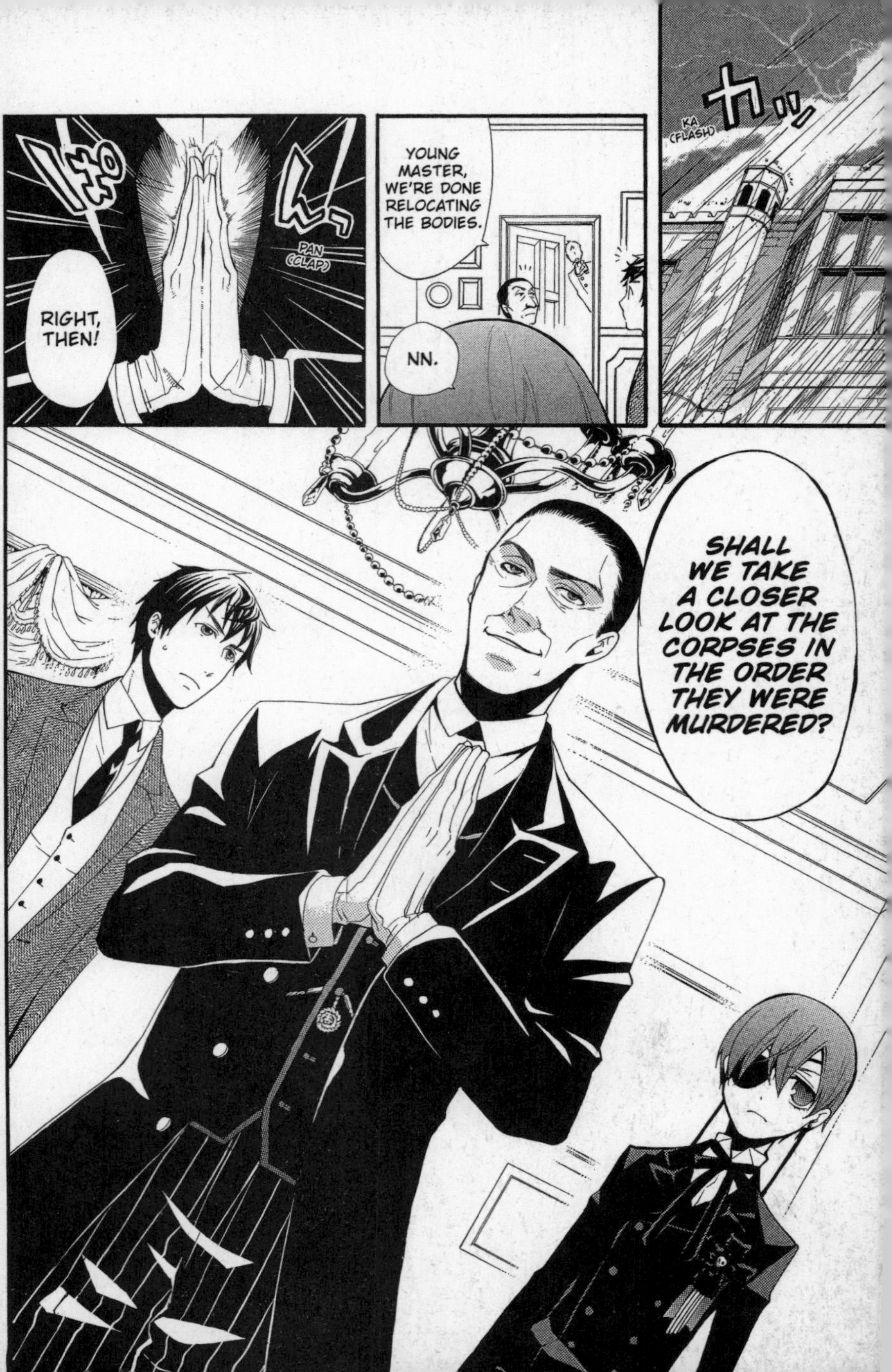
KA (FLASH)
YOUNG MASTER, WE'RE DONE RELOCATING THE BODIES.
NN.
PAN (CLAP)
RIGHT, THEN!
SHALL WE TAKE A CLOSER LOOK AT THE CORPSES IN THE ORDER THEY WERE MURDERED?

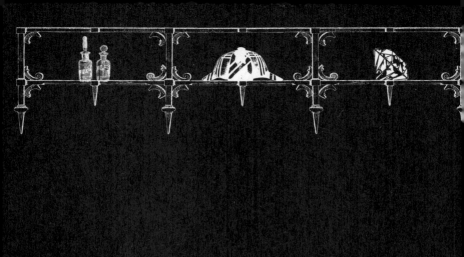

Black Butler

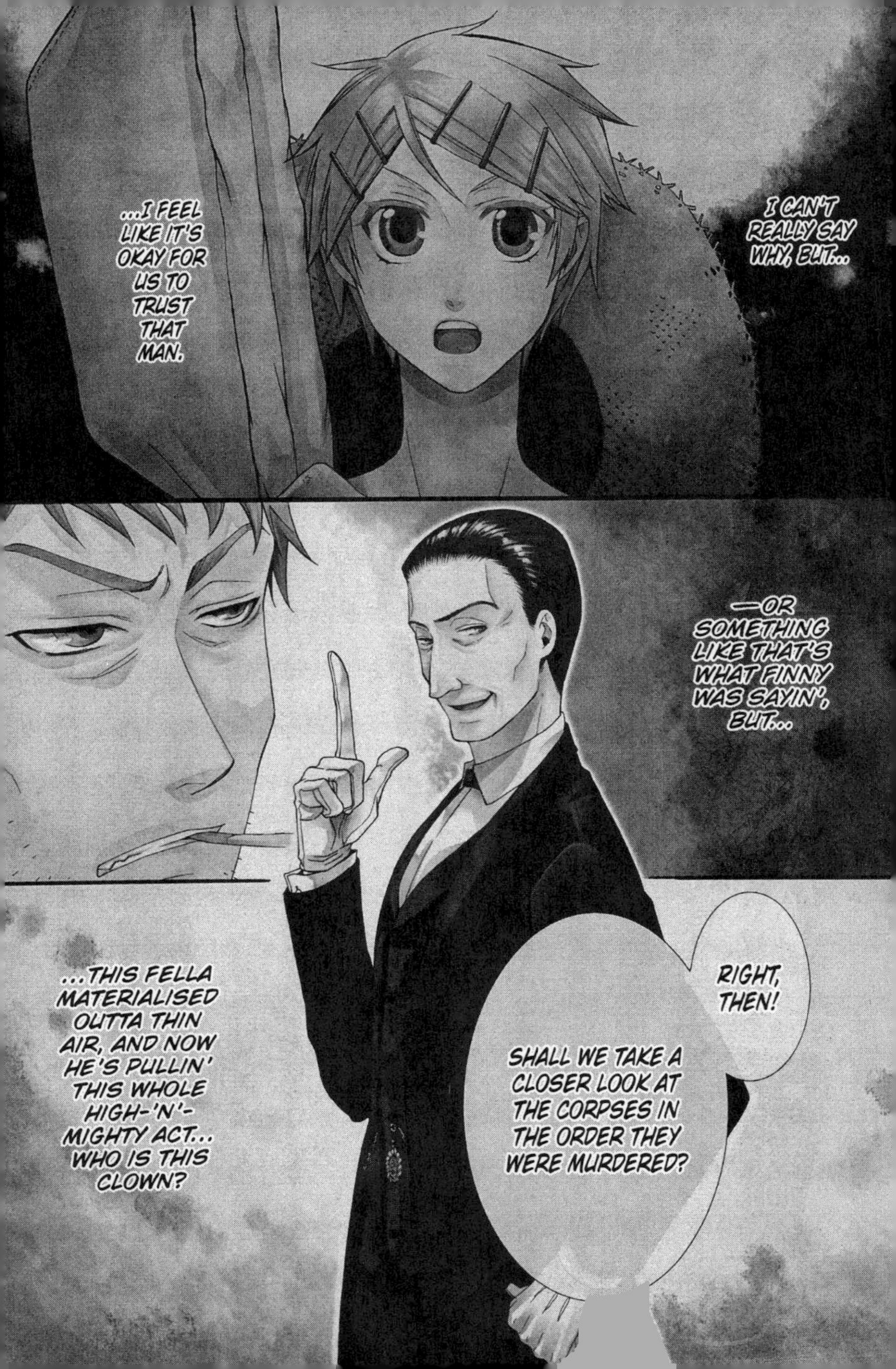
I CAN'T REALLY SAY WHY, BUT...
...I FEEL LIKE IT'S OKAY FOR US TO TRUST THAT MAN.
—OR SOMETHING LIKE THAT'S WHAT FINNY WAS SAYIN', BUT...
RIGHT, THEN!
SHALL WE TAKE A CLOSER LOOK AT THE CORPSES IN THE ORDER THEY WERE MURDERED?
...THIS FELLA MATERIALISED OUTTA THIN AIR, AND NOW HE'S PULLIN' THIS WHOLE HIGH-'N'-MIGHTY ACT... WHO IS THIS CLOWN?

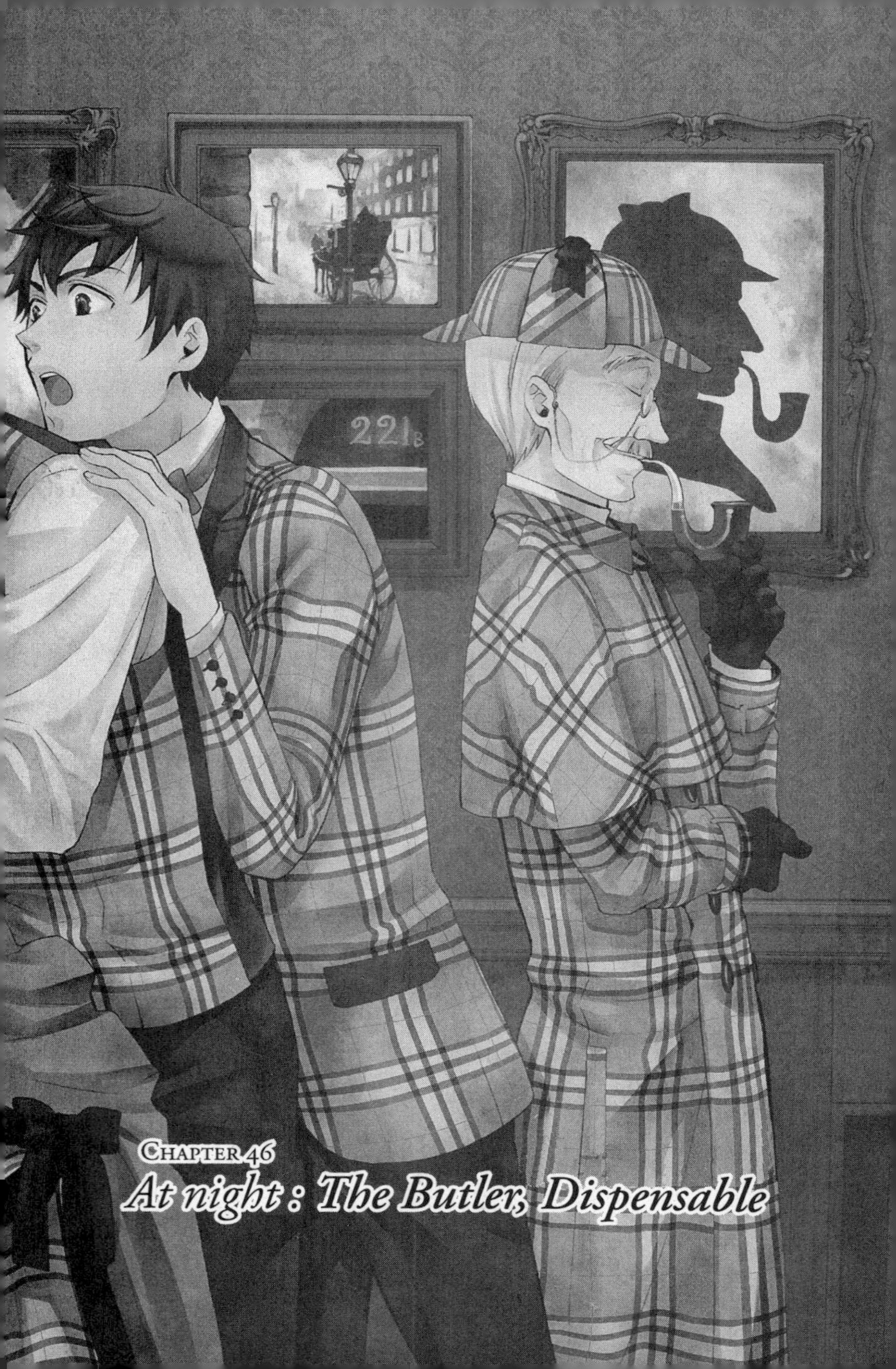
221B

Chapter 46
At night : The Butler, Dispensable

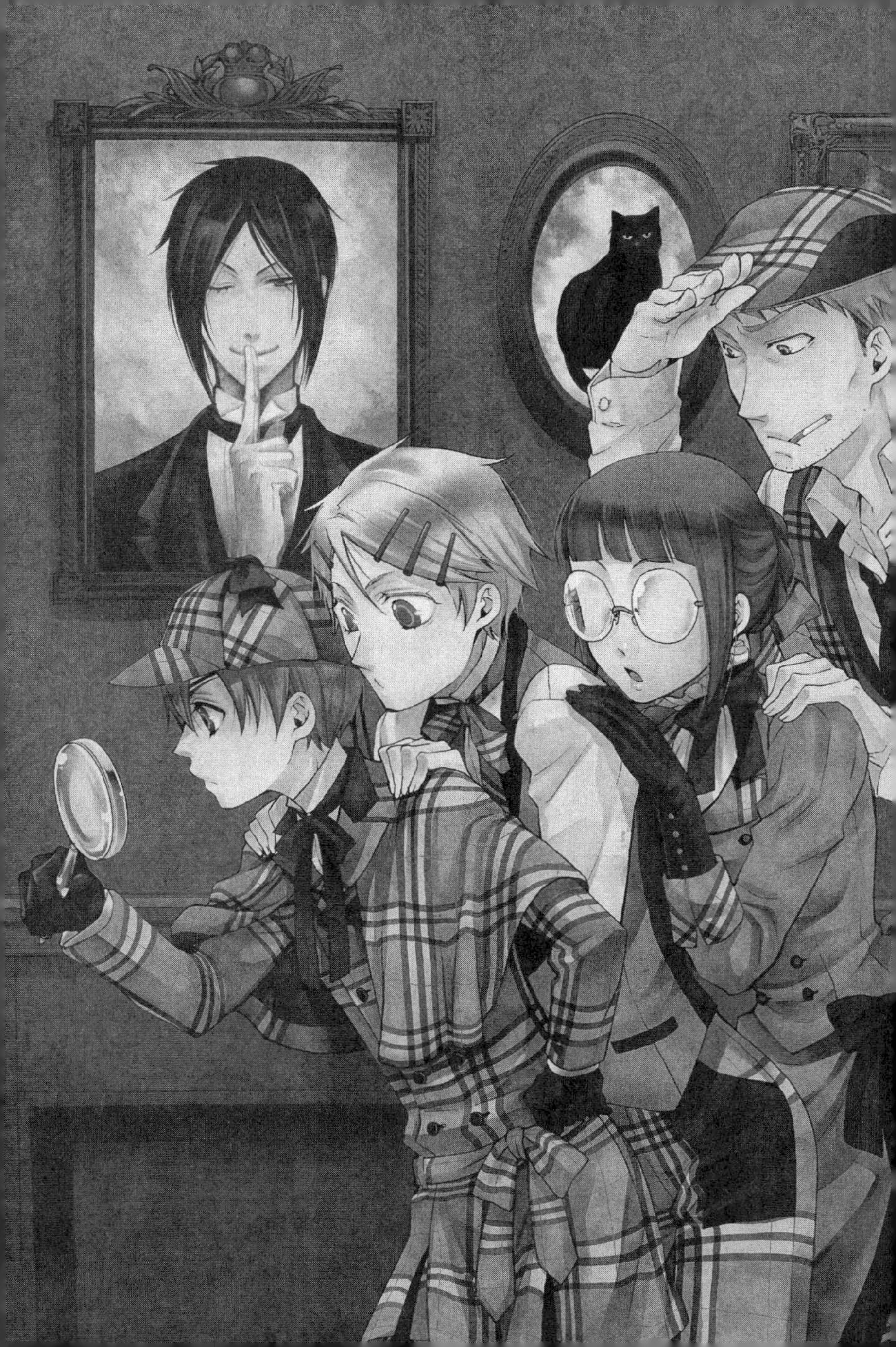

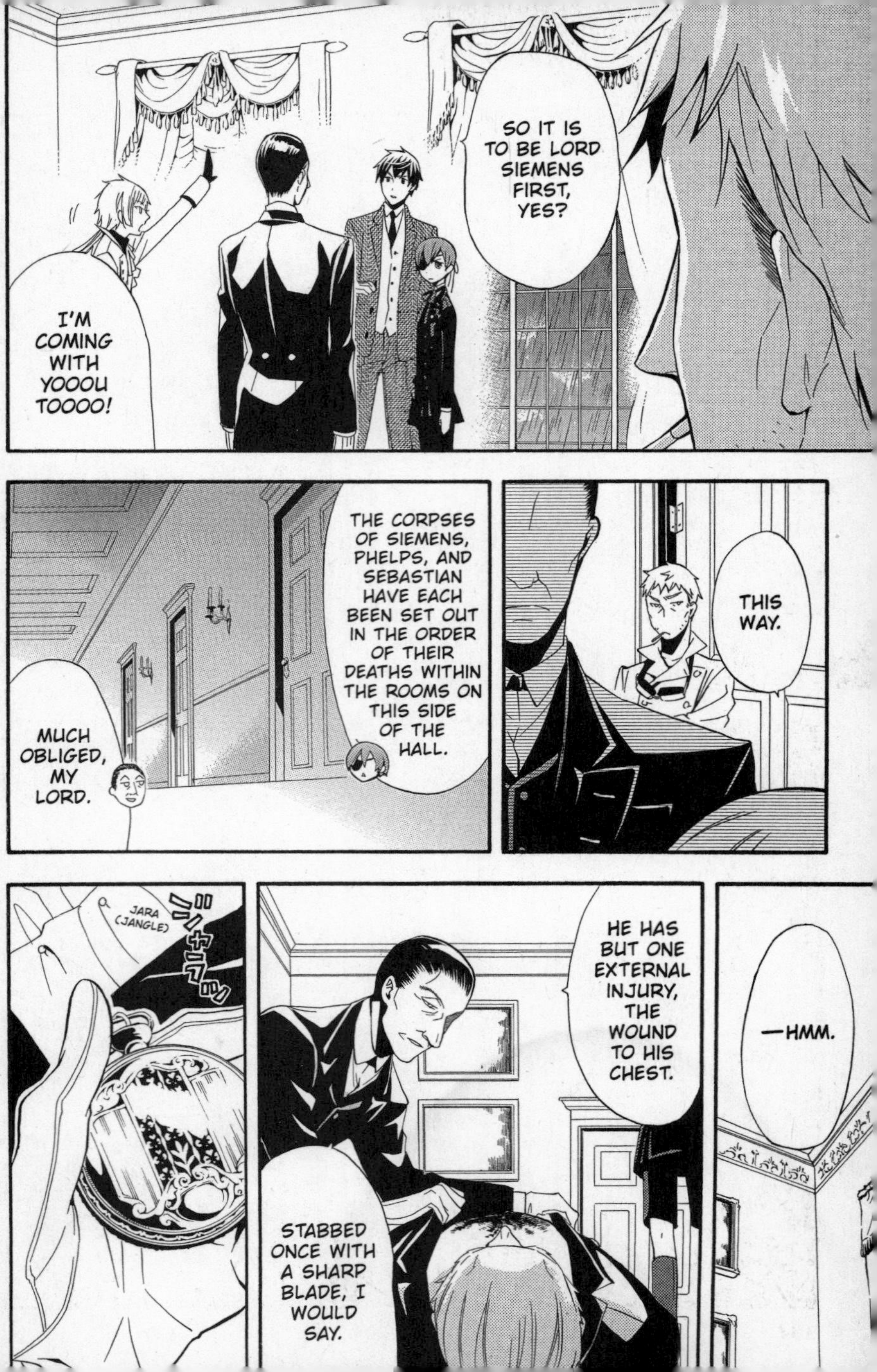
SO IT IS TO BE LORD SIEMENS FIRST, YES?
I'M COMING WITH YOOOU TOOOO!
THIS WAY.
THE CORPSES OF SIEMENS, PHELPS, AND SEBASTIAN HAVE EACH BEEN SET OUT IN THE ORDER OF THEIR DEATHS WITHIN THE ROOMS ON THIS SIDE OF THE HALL.
MUCH OBLIGED, MY LORD.
—HMM.
HE HAS BUT ONE EXTERNAL INJURY, THE WOUND TO HIS CHEST.
STABBED ONCE WITH A SHARP BLADE, I WOULD SAY.
JARA (JANGLE)

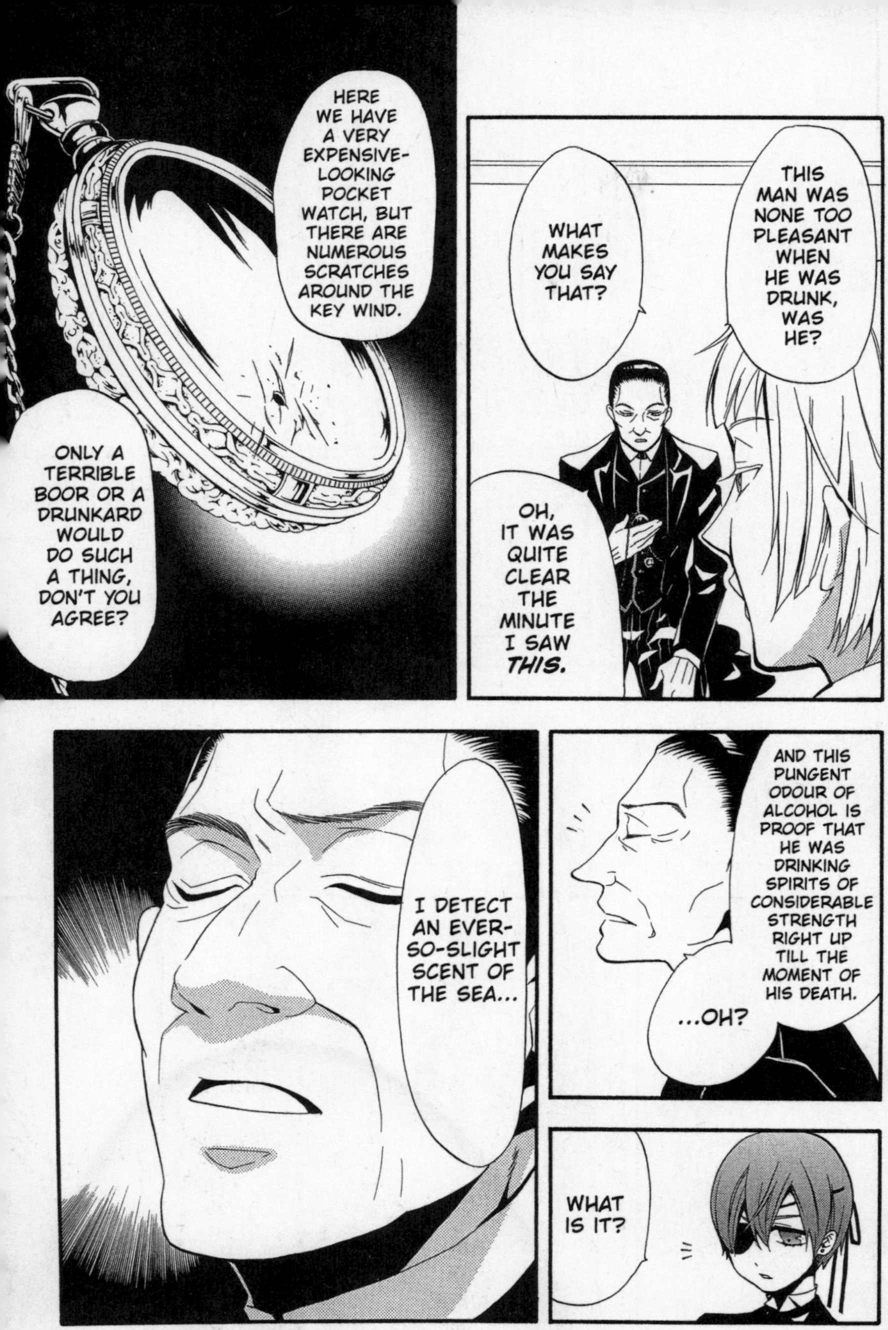
THIS MAN WAS NONE TOO PLEASANT WHEN HE WAS DRUNK, WAS HE?
WHAT MAKES YOU SAY THAT?
OH, IT WAS QUITE CLEAR THE MINUTE I SAW *THIS.*
HERE WE HAVE A VERY EXPENSIVE-LOOKING POCKET WATCH, BUT THERE ARE NUMEROUS SCRATCHES AROUND THE KEY WIND.
ONLY A TERRIBLE BOOR OR A DRUNKARD WOULD DO SUCH A THING, DON'T YOU AGREE?
AND THIS PUNGENT ODOUR OF ALCOHOL IS PROOF THAT HE WAS DRINKING SPIRITS OF CONSIDERABLE STRENGTH RIGHT UP TILL THE MOMENT OF HIS DEATH.
...OH?
WHAT IS IT?
I DETECT AN EVER-SO-SLIGHT SCENT OF THE SEA...

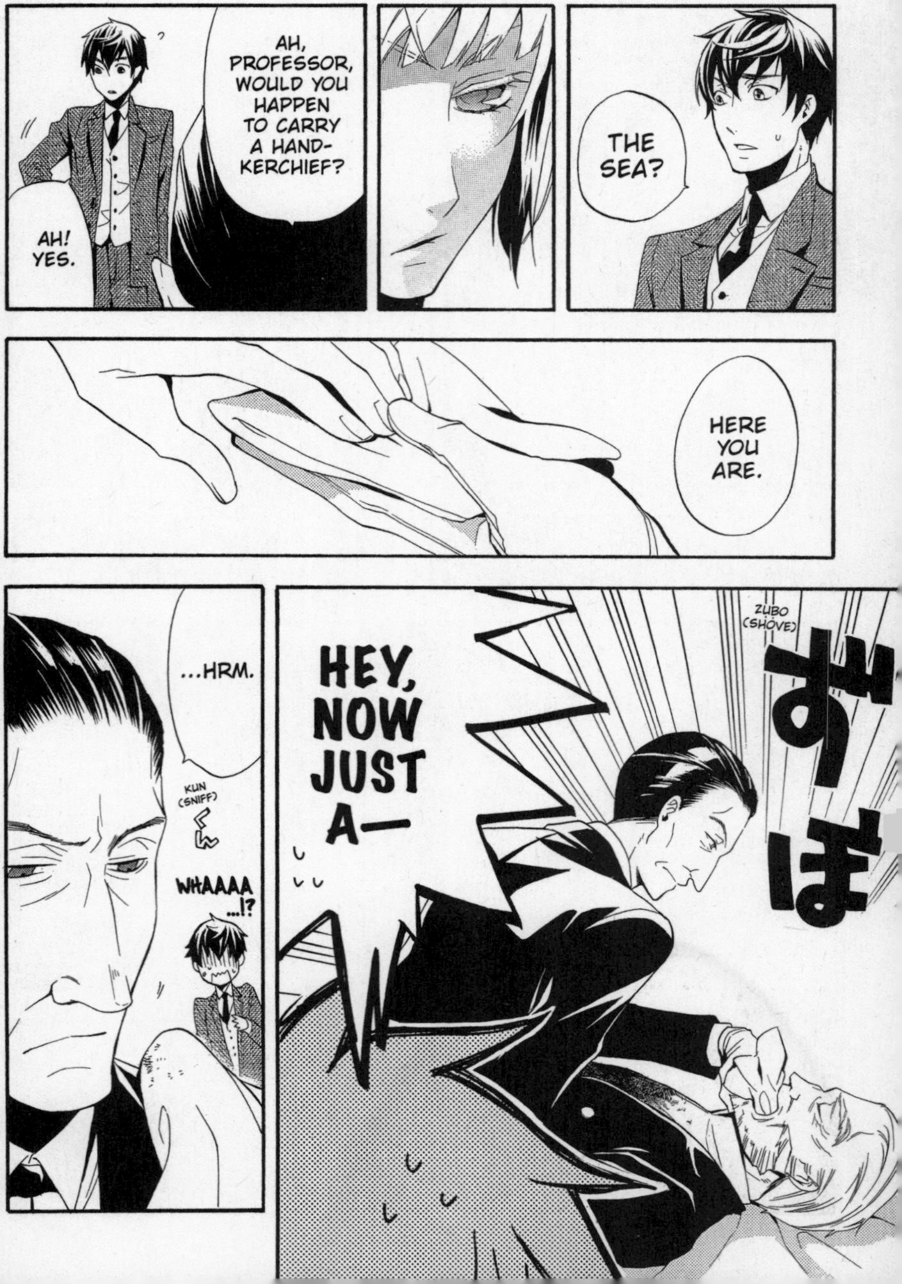
THE SEA?
AH, PROFESSOR, WOULD YOU HAPPEN TO CARRY A HAND-KERCHIEF?
AH! YES.
HERE YOU ARE.
ZUBO (SHOVE)
ずぼ
HEY, NOW JUST A—
...HRM.
KUN (SNIFF)
くん
WHAAAA ...!?

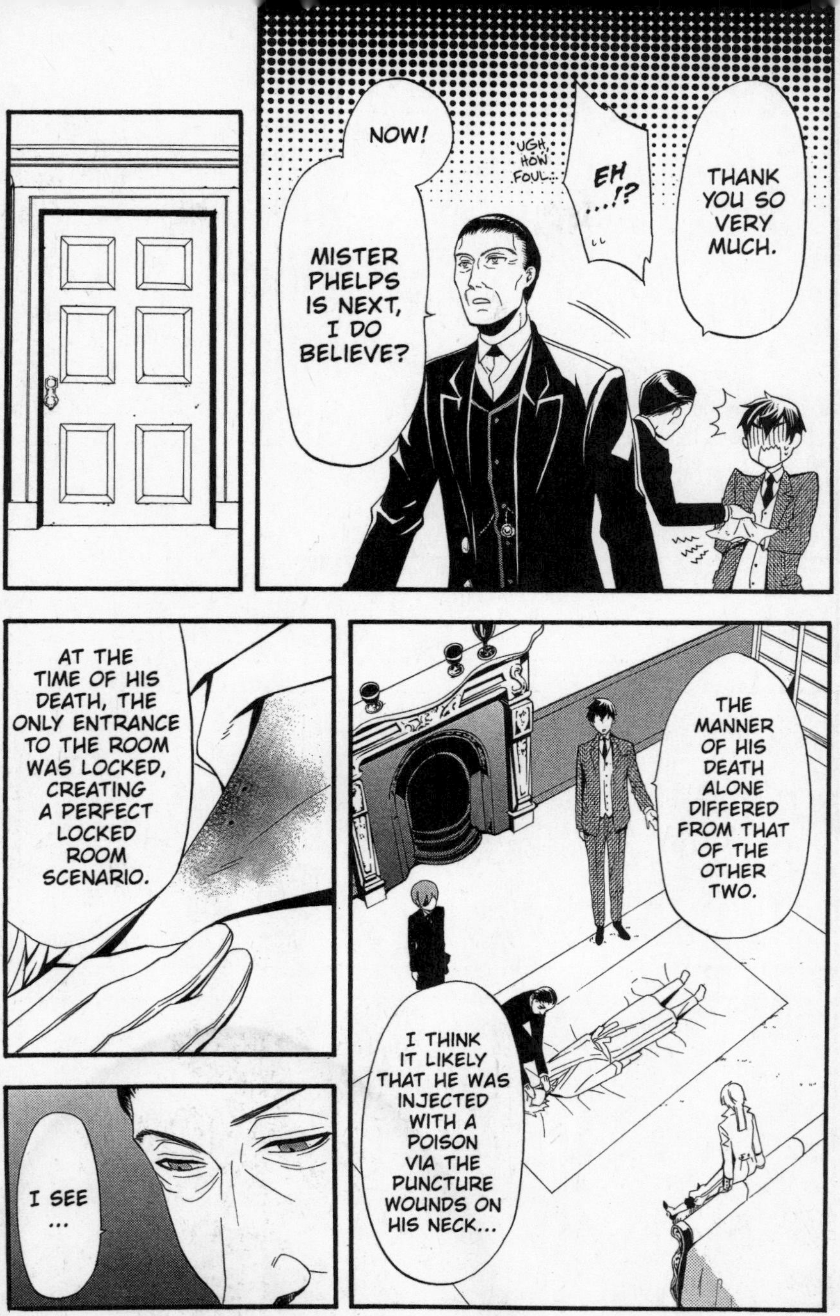
THANK YOU SO VERY MUCH.
EH ...!?
UGH, HOW FOUL...
NOW!
MISTER PHELPS IS NEXT, I DO BELIEVE?
THE MANNER OF HIS DEATH ALONE DIFFERED FROM THAT OF THE OTHER TWO.
I THINK IT LIKELY THAT HE WAS INJECTED WITH A POISON VIA THE PUNCTURE WOUNDS ON HIS NECK...
AT THE TIME OF HIS DEATH, THE ONLY ENTRANCE TO THE ROOM WAS LOCKED, CREATING A PERFECT LOCKED ROOM SCENARIO.
I SEE ...

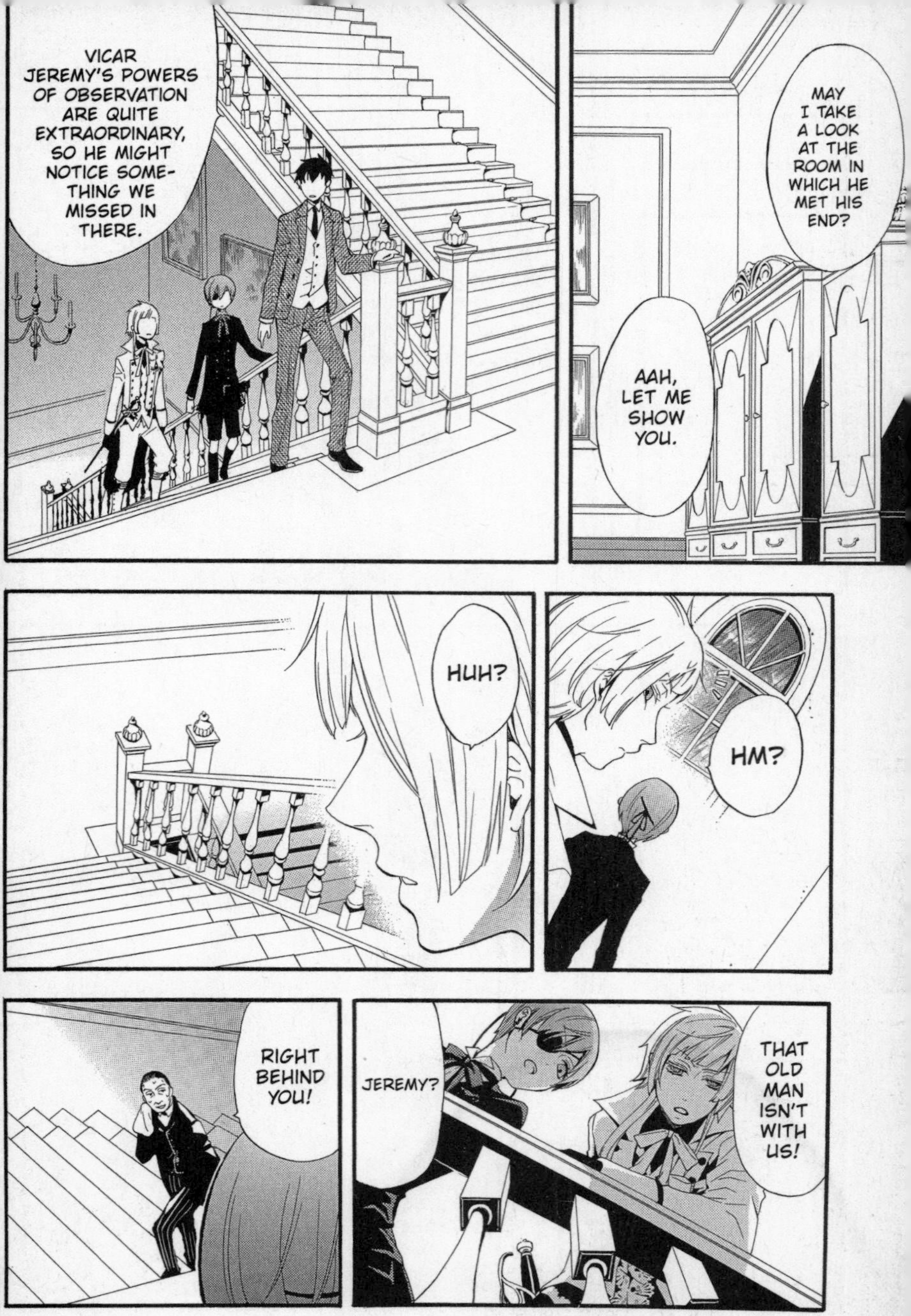
MAY I TAKE A LOOK AT THE ROOM IN WHICH HE MET HIS END?
AAH, LET ME SHOW YOU.
VICAR JEREMY'S POWERS OF OBSERVATION ARE QUITE EXTRAORDINARY, SO HE MIGHT NOTICE SOME-THING WE MISSED IN THERE.
HM?
HUH?
THAT OLD MAN ISN'T WITH US!
JEREMY?
RIGHT BEHIND YOU!

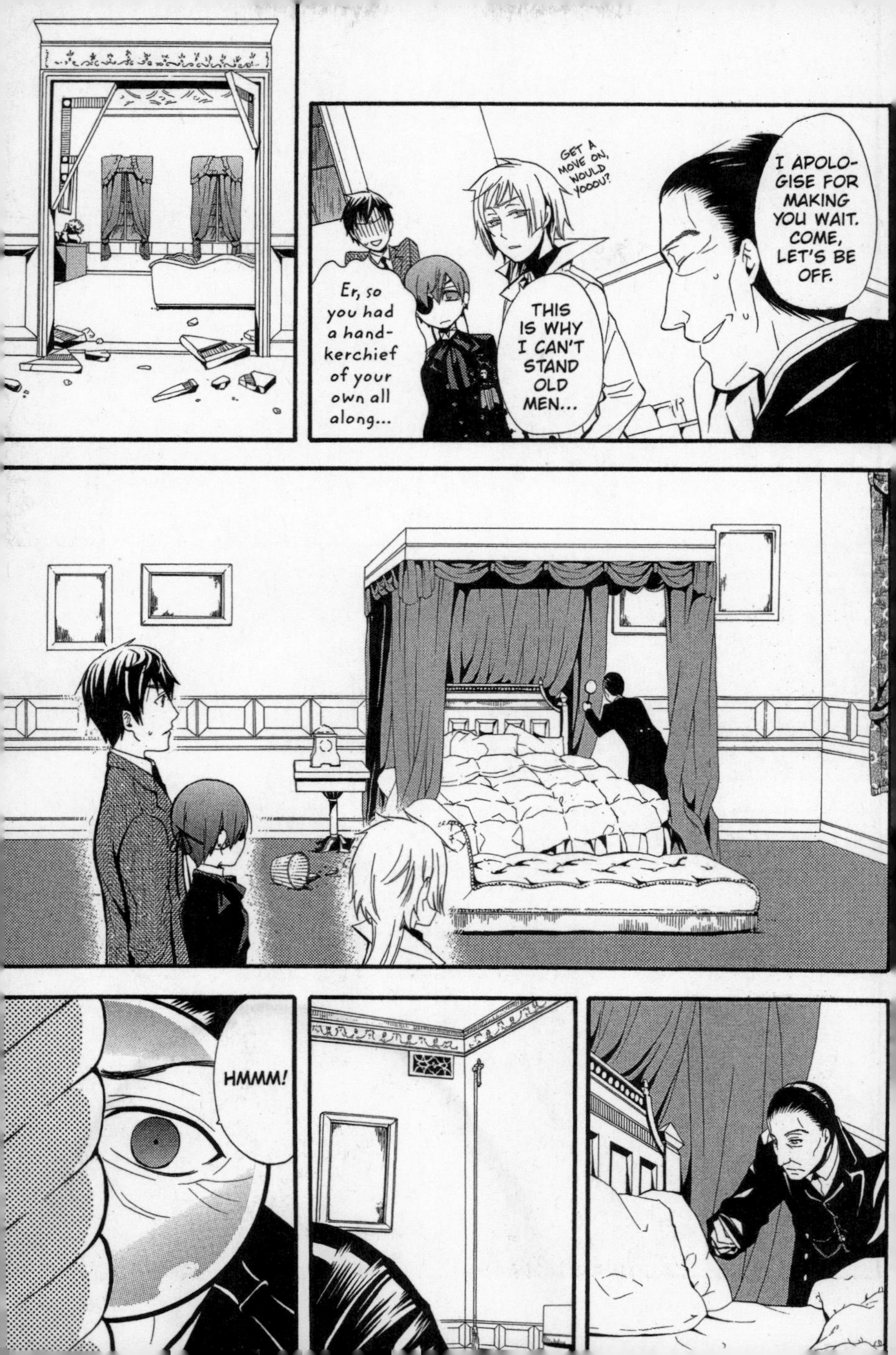
I APOLOGISE FOR MAKING YOU WAIT. COME, LET'S BE OFF.
GET A MOVE ON, WOULD YOOOU?
THIS IS WHY I CAN'T STAND OLD MEN...
Er, so you had a handkerchief of your own all along...
HMMM!

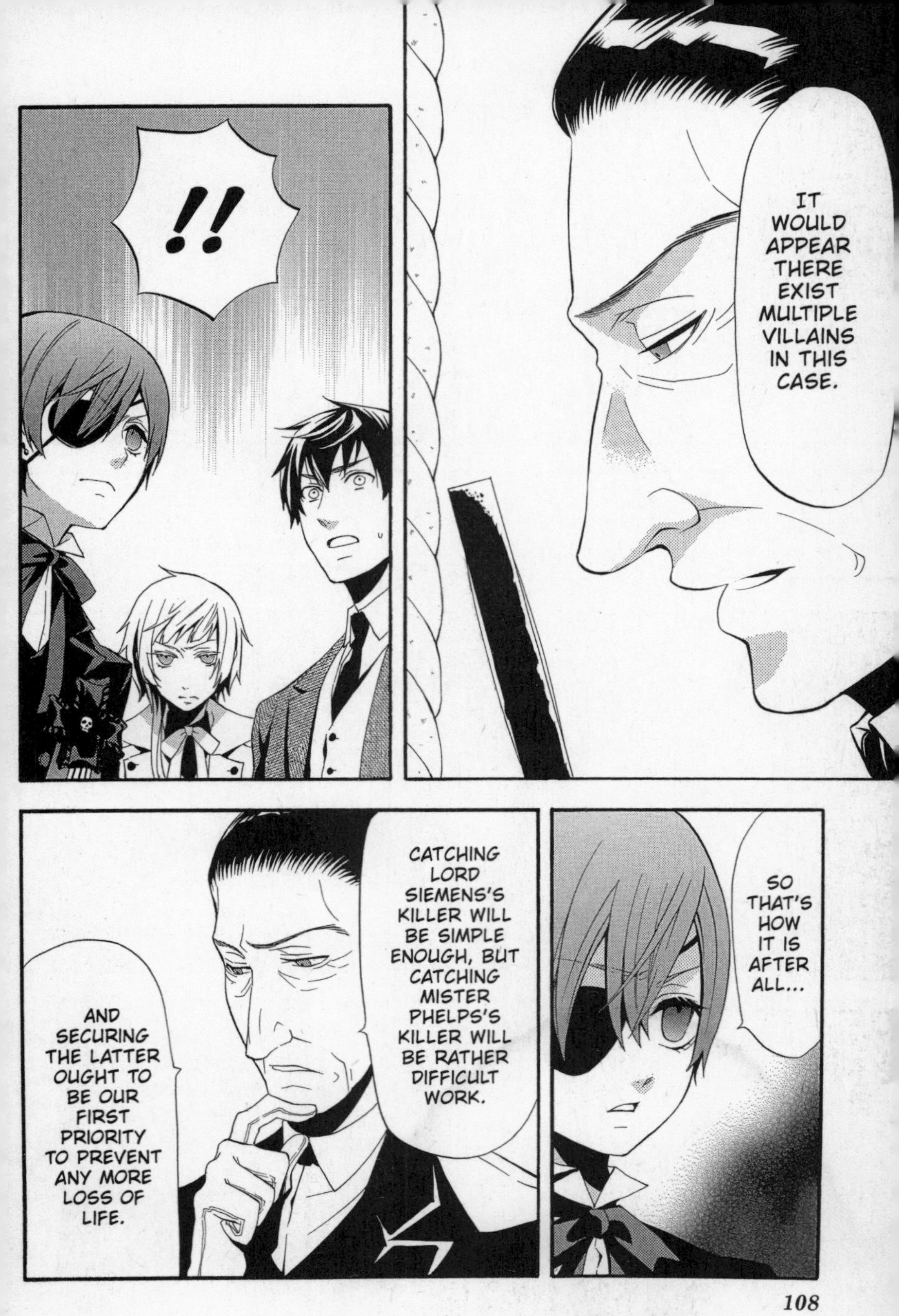

IT WOULD APPEAR THERE EXIST MULTIPLE VILLAINS IN THIS CASE.
!!
SO THAT'S HOW IT IS AFTER ALL...
CATCHING LORD SIEMENS'S KILLER WILL BE SIMPLE ENOUGH, BUT CATCHING MISTER PHELPS'S KILLER WILL BE RATHER DIFFICULT WORK.
AND SECURING THE LATTER OUGHT TO BE OUR FIRST PRIORITY TO PREVENT ANY MORE LOSS OF LIFE.

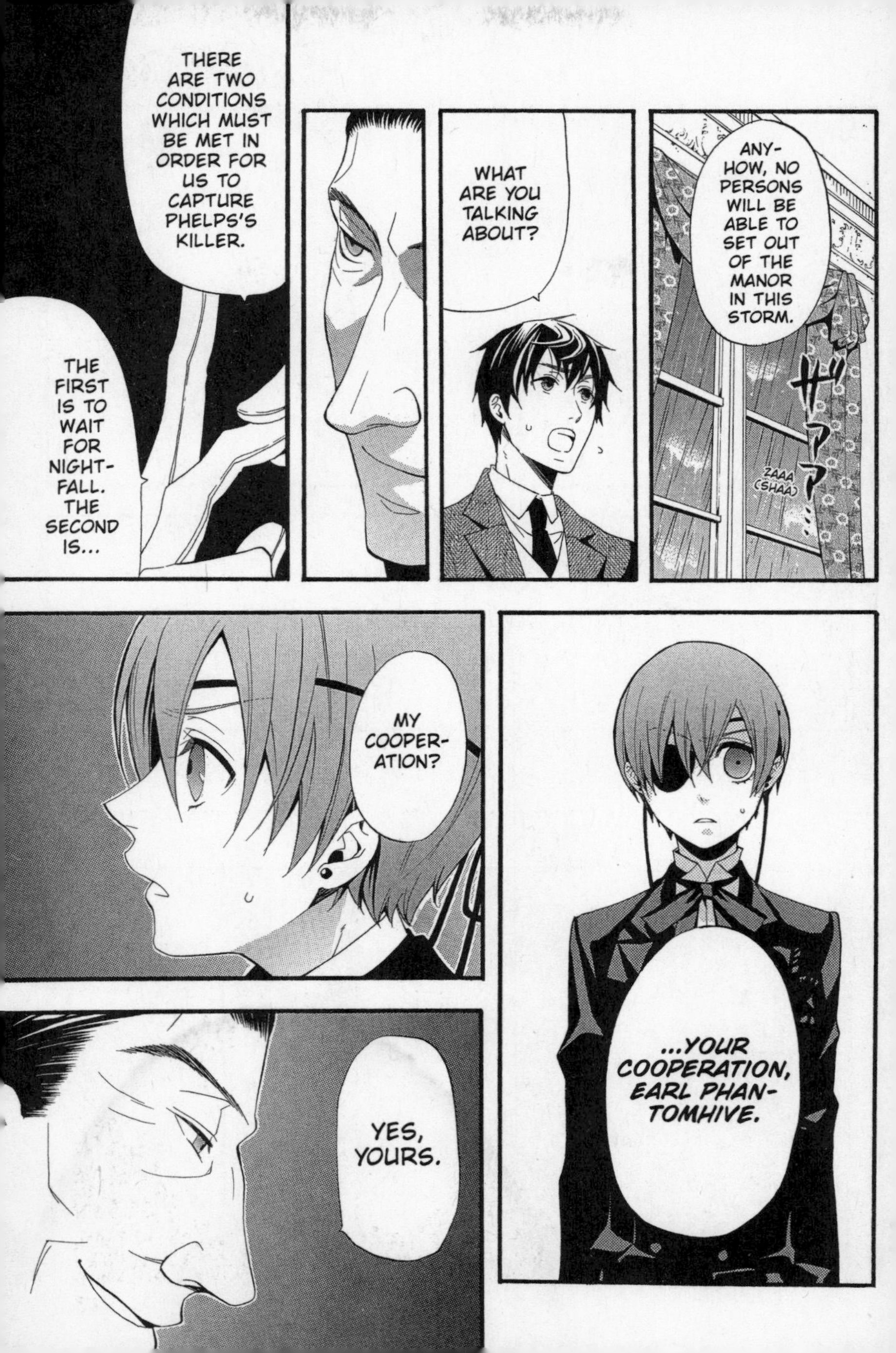

ANY-HOW, NO PERSONS WILL BE ABLE TO SET OUT OF THE MANOR IN THIS STORM.
ZAAA (SHAA)
WHAT ARE YOU TALKING ABOUT?
THERE ARE TWO CONDITIONS WHICH MUST BE MET IN ORDER FOR US TO CAPTURE PHELPS'S KILLER.
THE FIRST IS TO WAIT FOR NIGHT-FALL. THE SECOND IS...
...YOUR COOPERATION, EARL PHAN-TOMHIVE.
MY COOPER-ATION?
YES, YOURS.

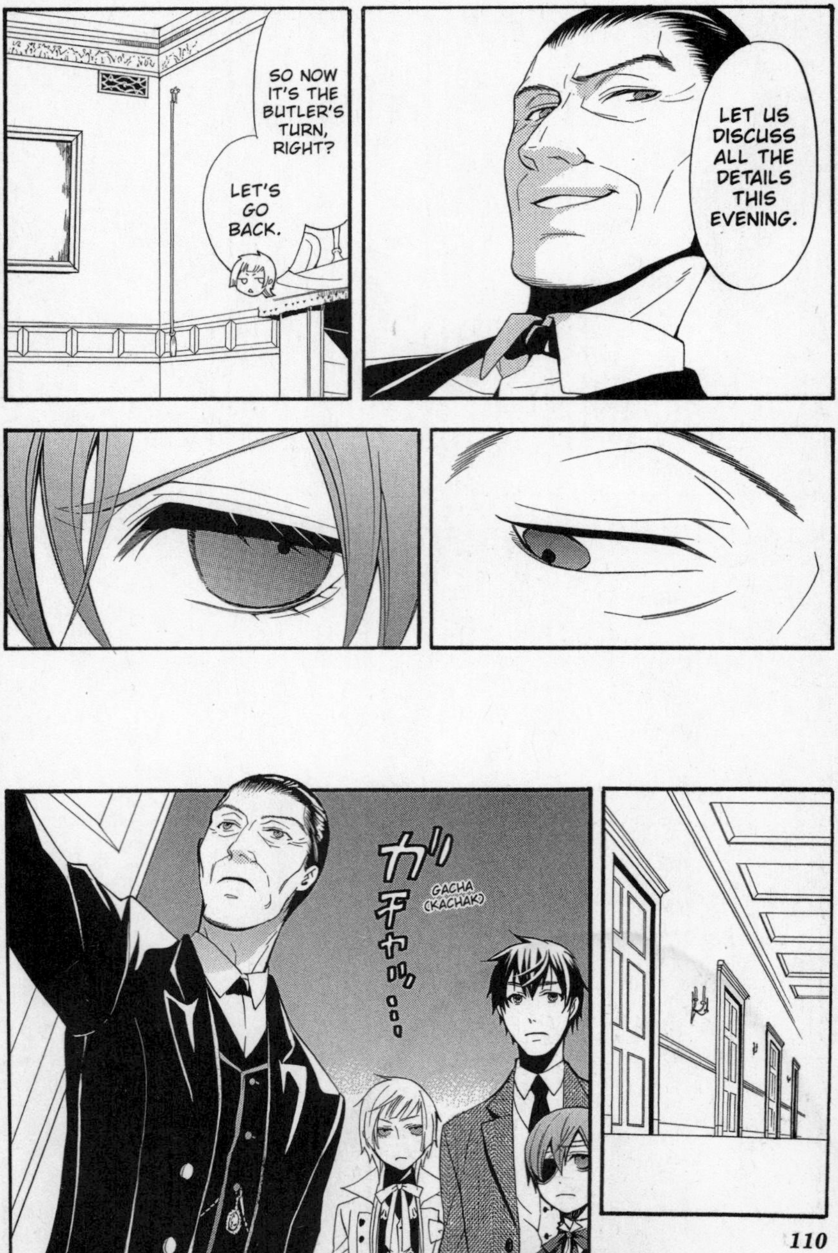
LET US DISCUSS ALL THE DETAILS THIS EVENING.
SO NOW IT'S THE BUTLER'S TURN, RIGHT?
LET'S GO BACK.
カチャッ...
GACHA (KACHAK)

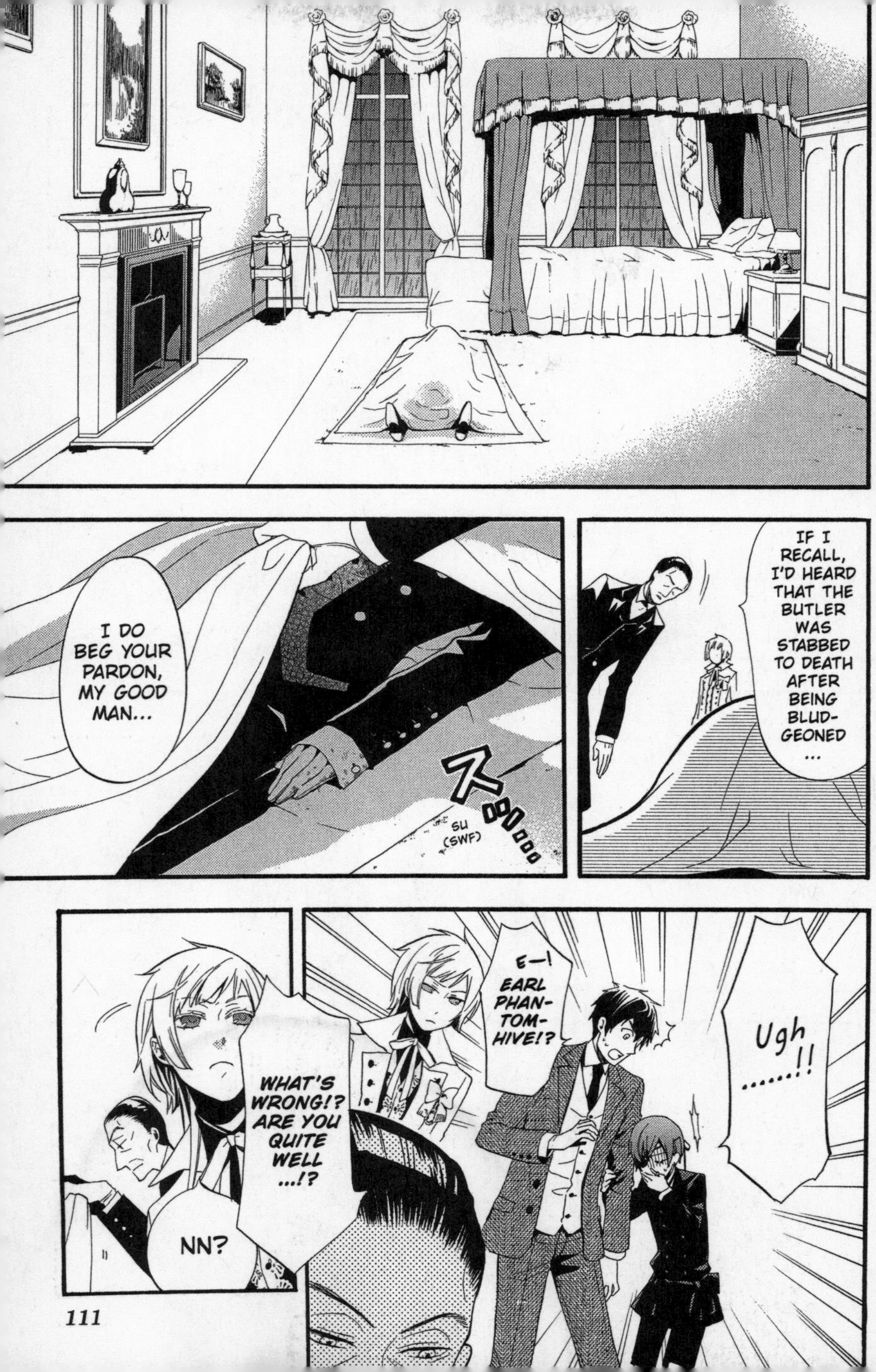
IF I RECALL, I'D HEARD THAT THE BUTLER WAS STABBED TO DEATH AFTER BEING BLUDGEONED...
I DO BEG YOUR PARDON, MY GOOD MAN...
SU (SWF)
Ugh ......!!
E—! EARL PHANTOMHIVE!?
WHAT'S WRONG!? ARE YOU QUITE WELL...!?
NN?

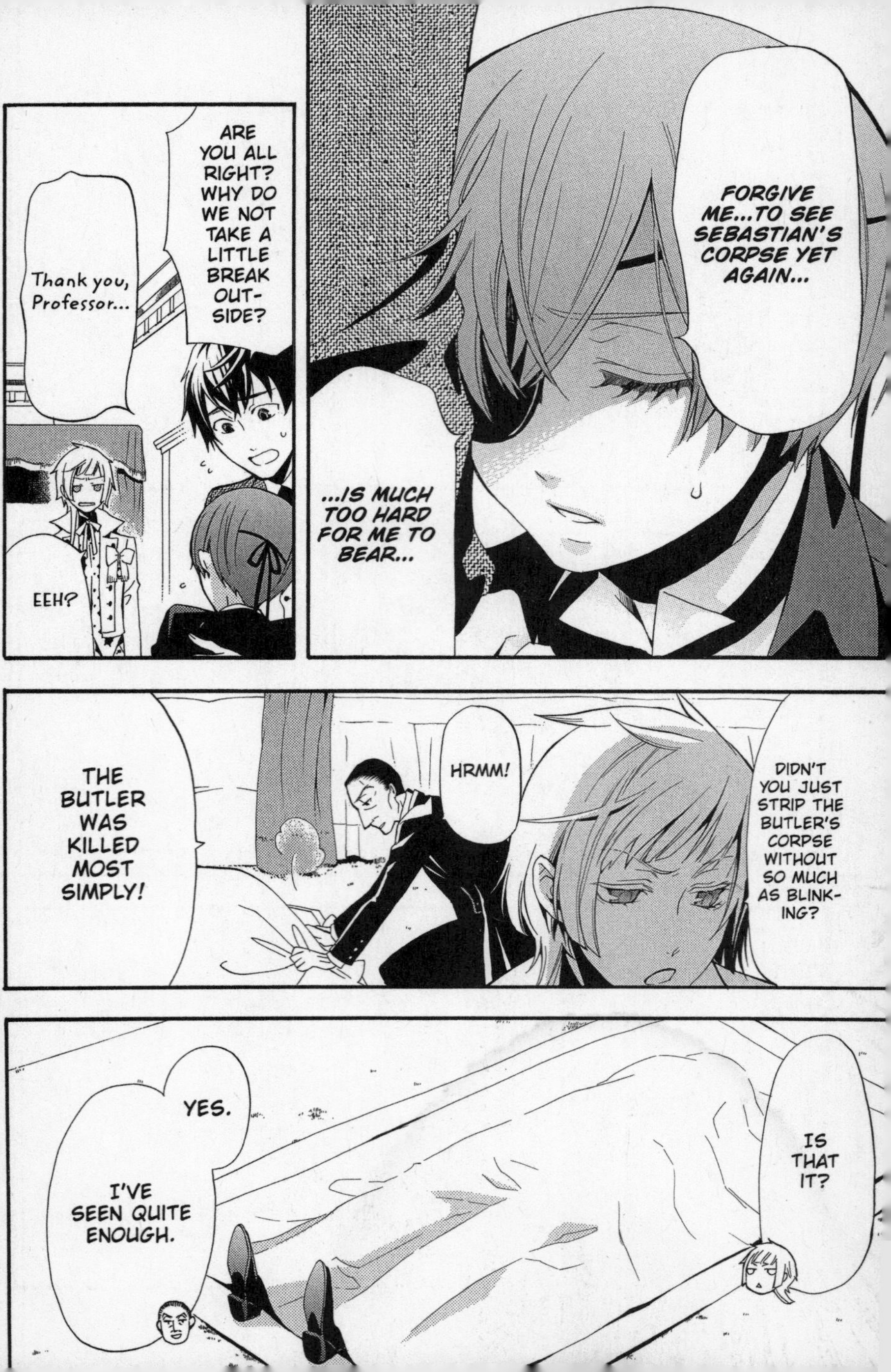
FORGIVE ME...TO SEE SEBASTIAN'S CORPSE YET AGAIN...
...IS MUCH TOO HARD FOR ME TO BEAR...
ARE YOU ALL RIGHT? WHY DO WE NOT TAKE A LITTLE BREAK OUT-SIDE?
Thank you, Professor...
EEH?
DIDN'T YOU JUST STRIP THE BUTLER'S CORPSE WITHOUT SO MUCH AS BLINK-ING?
HRMM!
THE BUTLER WAS KILLED MOST SIMPLY!
IS THAT IT?
YES.
I'VE SEEN QUITE ENOUGH.

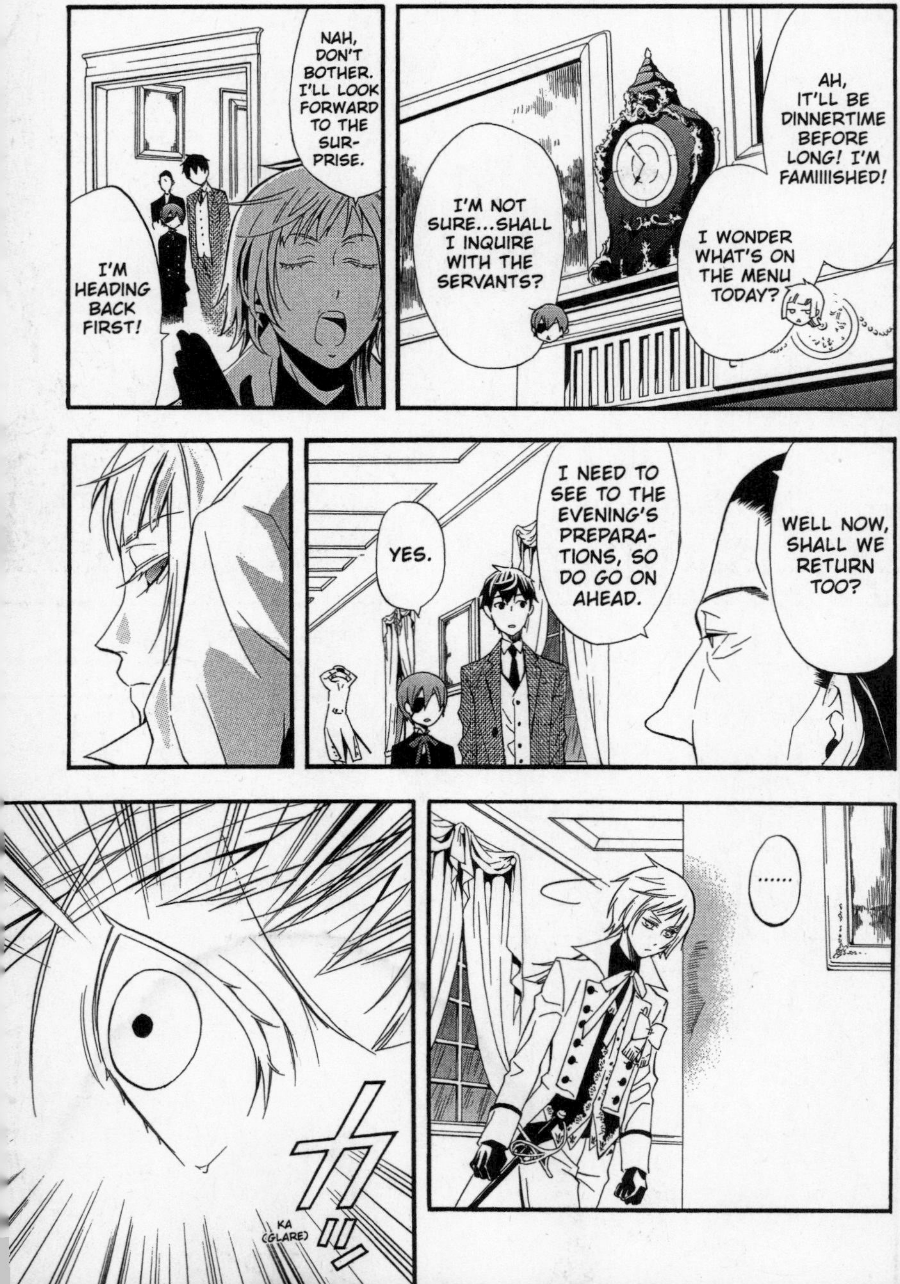
AH, IT'LL BE DINNERTIME BEFORE LONG! I'M FAMIIIIISHED!
I WONDER WHAT'S ON THE MENU TODAY?
I'M NOT SURE...SHALL I INQUIRE WITH THE SERVANTS?
NAH, DON'T BOTHER. I'LL LOOK FORWARD TO THE SUR-PRISE.
I'M HEADING BACK FIRST!
WELL NOW, SHALL WE RETURN TOO?
I NEED TO SEE TO THE EVENING'S PREPARATIONS, SO DO GO ON AHEAD.
YES.
......
KA (GLARE)

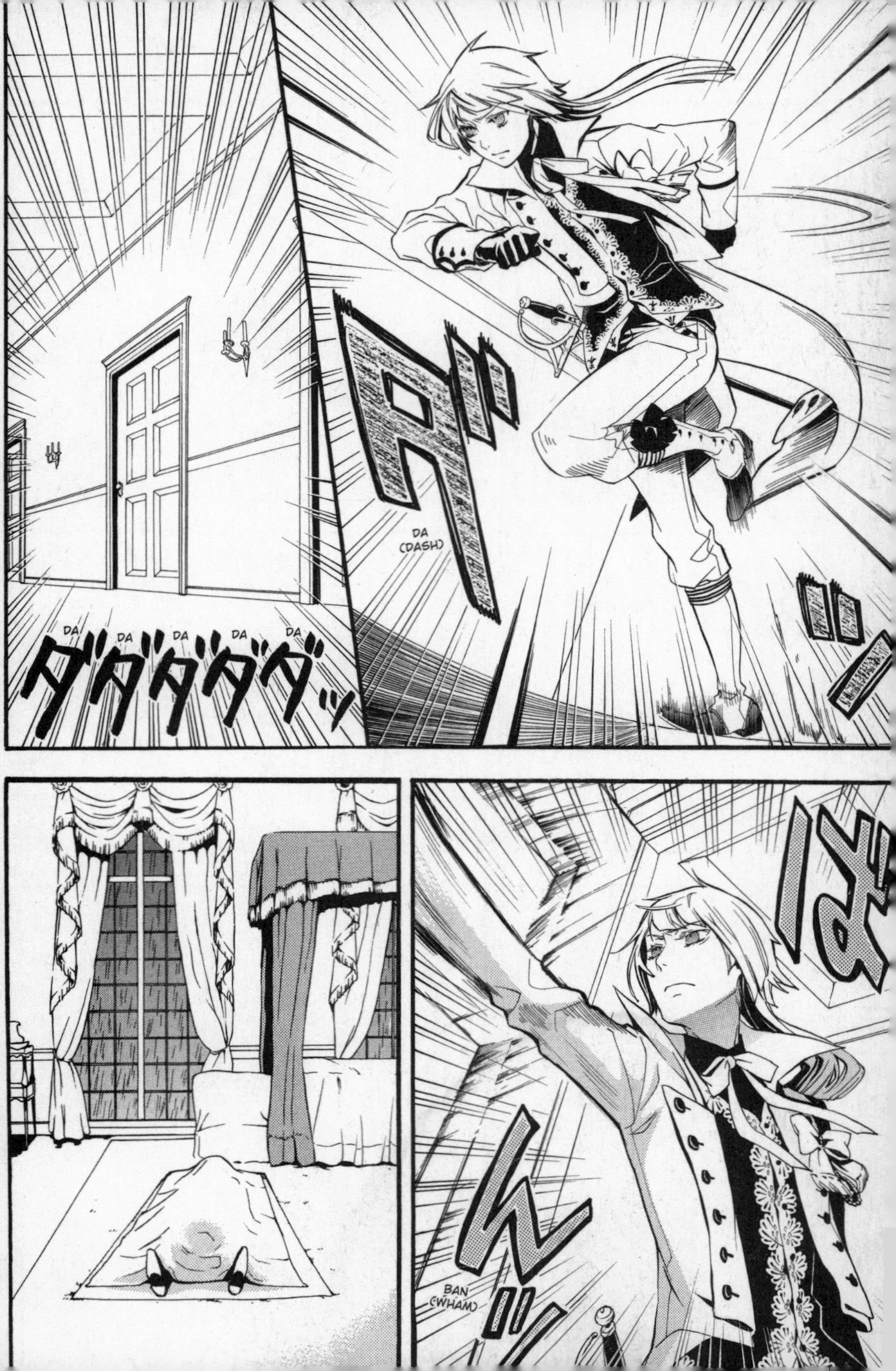
ダッ
DA (DASH)
DA DA DA DA DA
ダダダダダッ
ばんッ
BAN (WHAM)

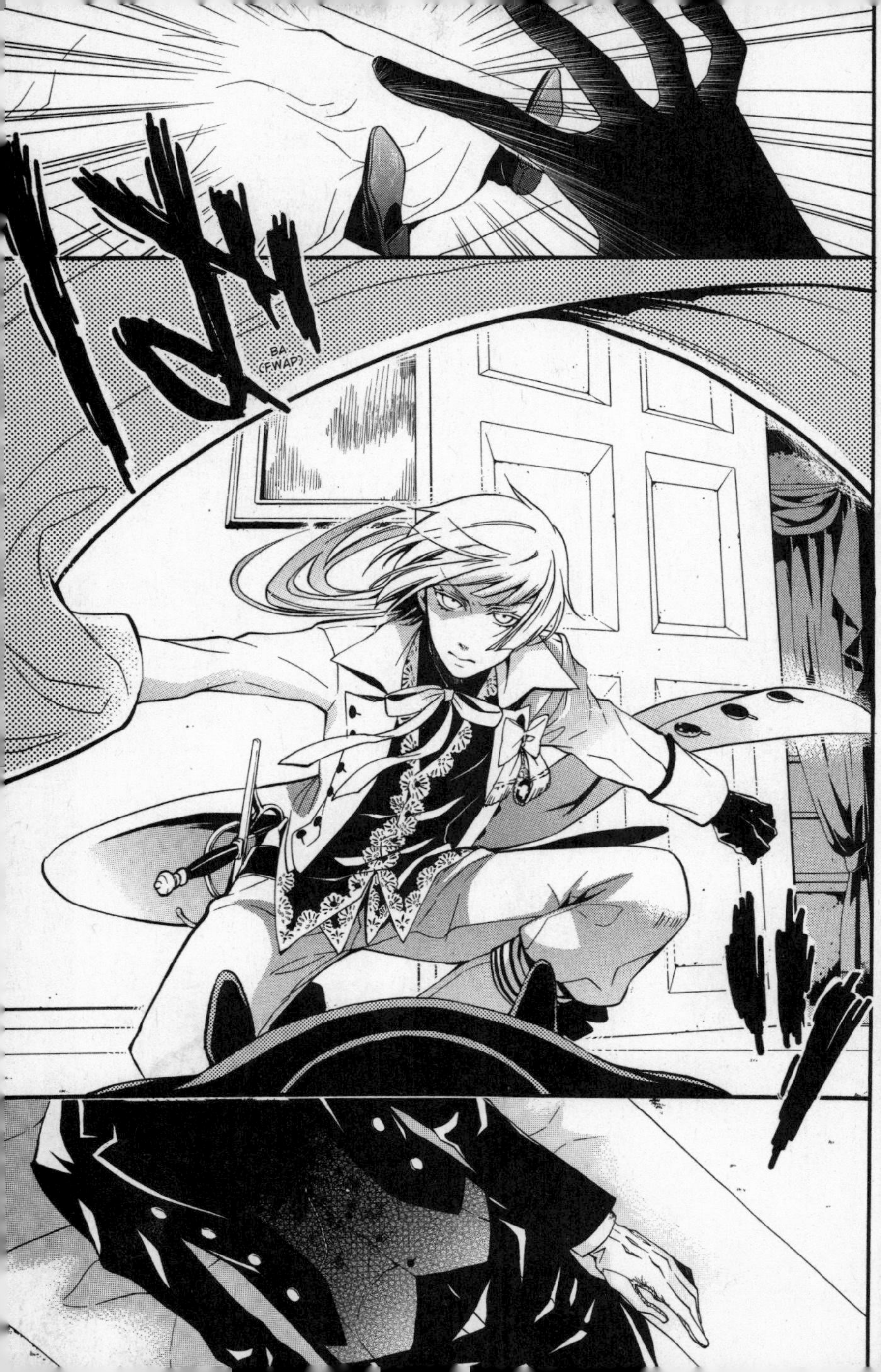
BA
(FWAP)

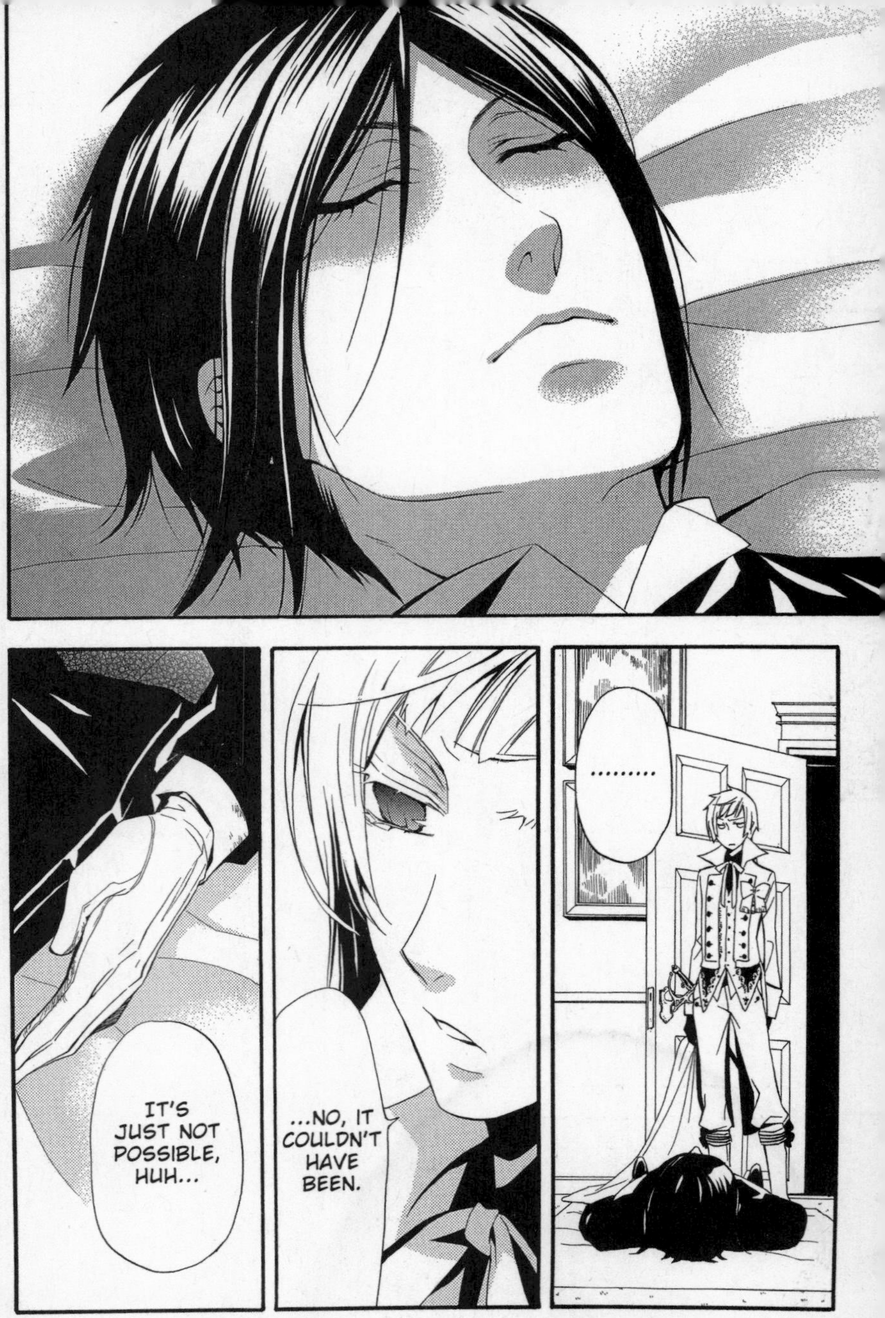
....
...NO, IT COULDN'T HAVE BEEN.
IT'S JUST NOT POSSIBLE, HUH...

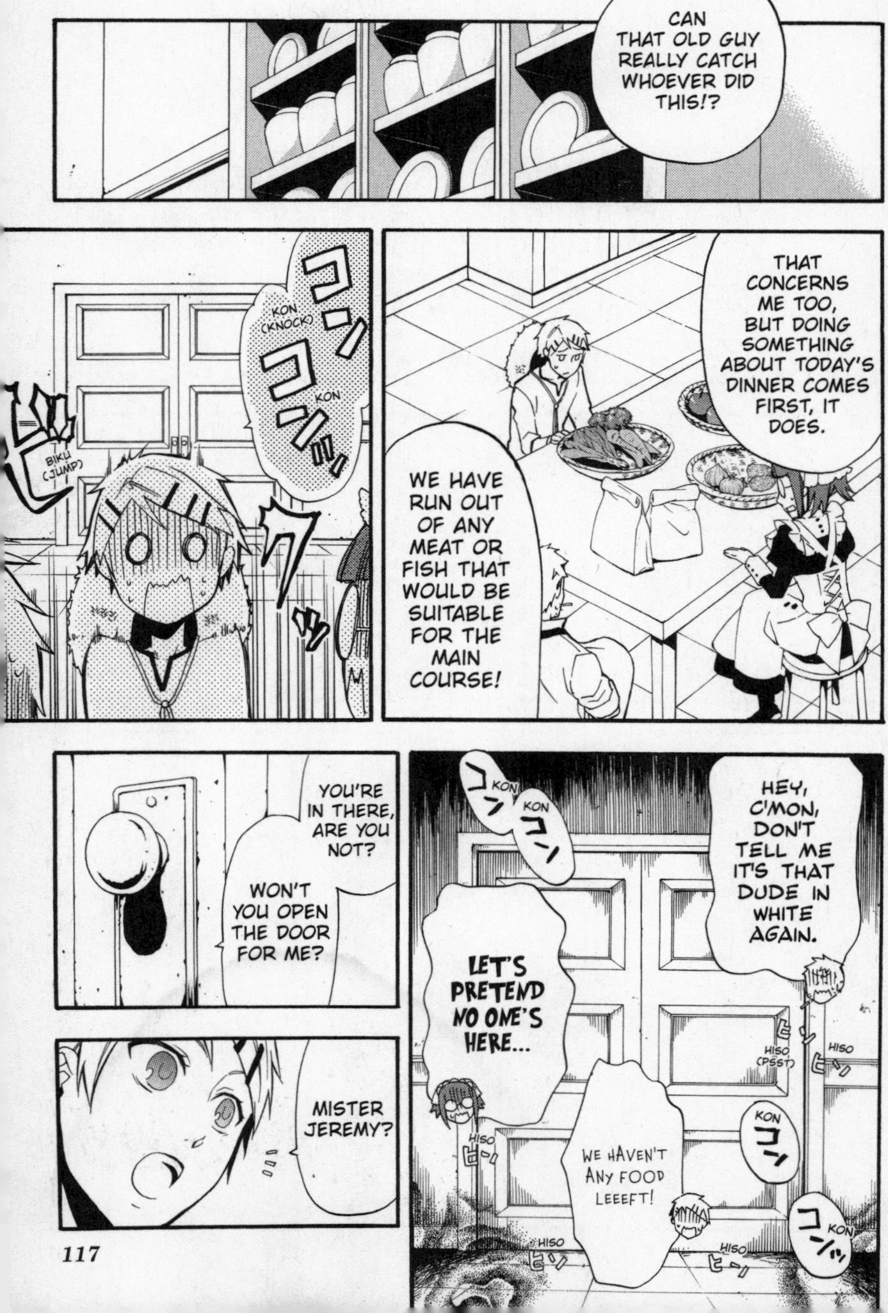
CAN THAT OLD GUY REALLY CATCH WHOEVER DID THIS!?
THAT CONCERNS ME TOO, BUT DOING SOMETHING ABOUT TODAY'S DINNER COMES FIRST, IT DOES.
WE HAVE RUN OUT OF ANY MEAT OR FISH THAT WOULD BE SUITABLE FOR THE MAIN COURSE!
KON (KNOCK)
KON
BIKU (JUMP)
KON
KON
HEY, C'MON, DON'T TELL ME IT'S THAT DUDE IN WHITE AGAIN.
LET'S PRETEND NO ONE'S HERE...
HISO (PSST)
HISO
HISO
KON
WE HAVEN'T ANY FOOD LEEEFT!
KON
HISO
HISO
YOU'RE IN THERE, ARE YOU NOT?
WON'T YOU OPEN THE DOOR FOR ME?
MISTER JEREMY?

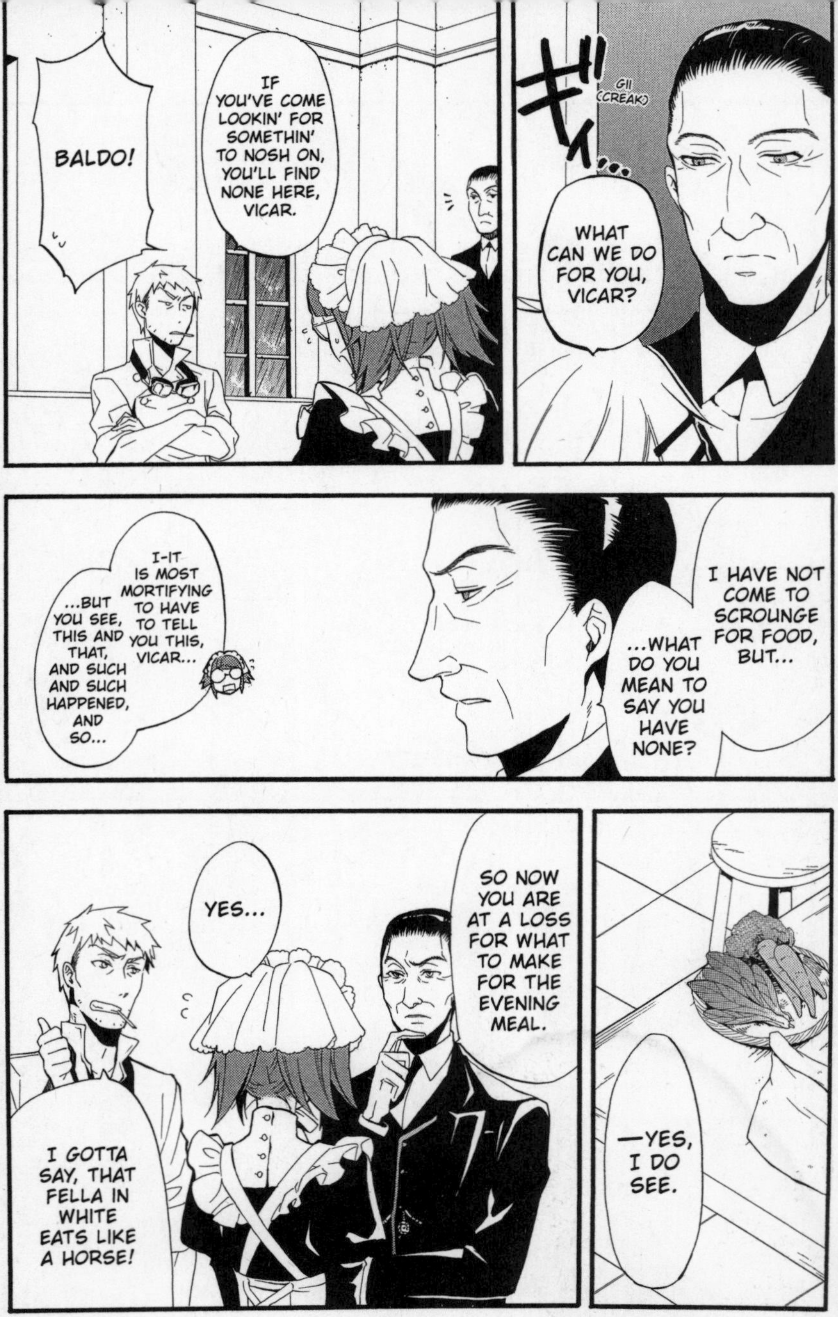
ギィ…
GII (CREAK)
WHAT CAN WE DO FOR YOU, VICAR?
IF YOU'VE COME LOOKIN' FOR SOMETHIN' TO NOSH ON, YOU'LL FIND NONE HERE, VICAR.
BALDO!
I HAVE NOT COME TO SCROUNGE FOR FOOD, BUT...
...WHAT DO YOU MEAN TO SAY YOU HAVE NONE?
I-IT IS MOST MORTIFYING TO HAVE TO TELL YOU THIS, VICAR...
...BUT YOU SEE, THIS AND THAT, AND SUCH AND SUCH HAPPENED, AND SO...
—YES, I DO SEE.
SO NOW YOU ARE AT A LOSS FOR WHAT TO MAKE FOR THE EVENING MEAL.
YES...
I GOTTA SAY, THAT FELLA IN WHITE EATS LIKE A HORSE!

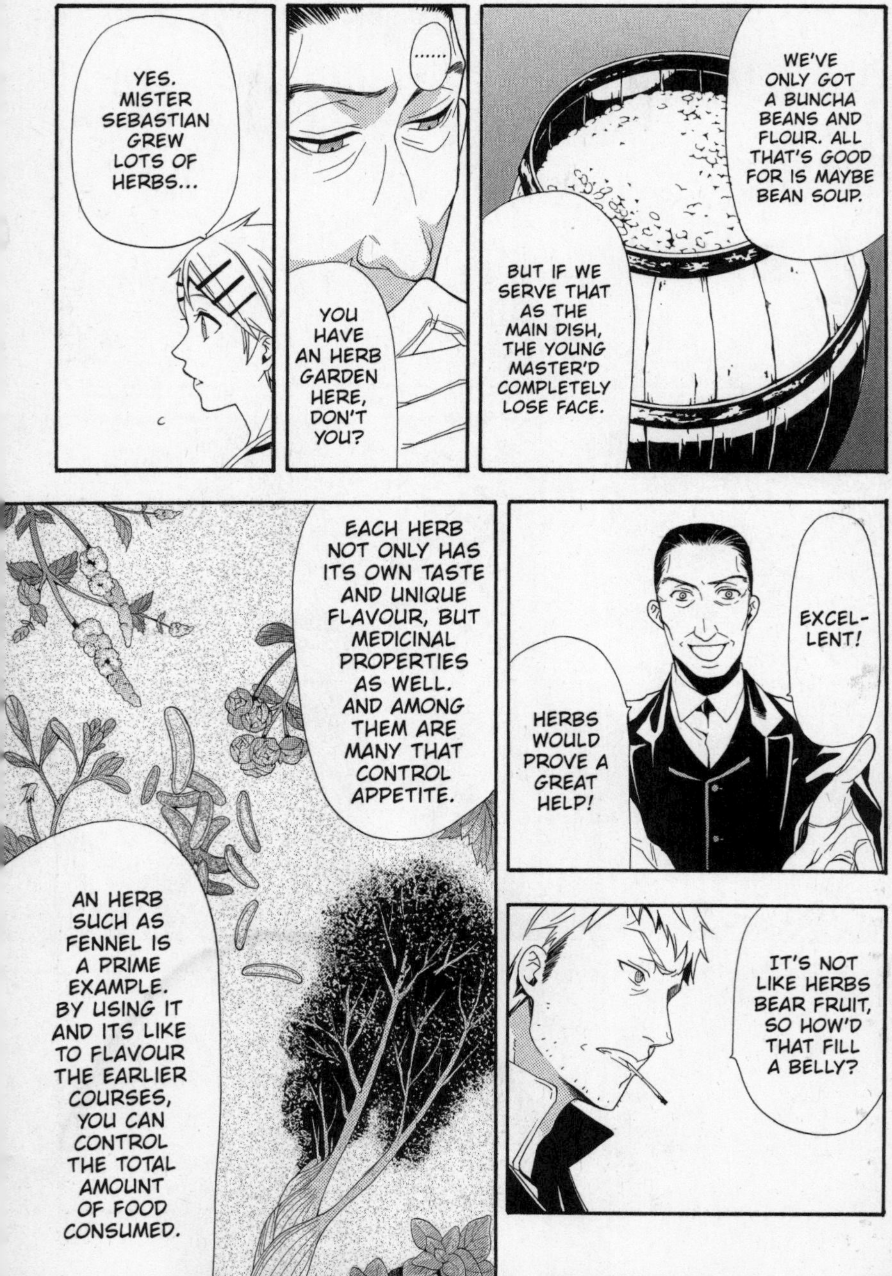
WE'VE ONLY GOT A BUNCHA BEANS AND FLOUR. ALL THAT'S GOOD FOR IS MAYBE BEAN SOUP.
BUT IF WE SERVE THAT AS THE MAIN DISH, THE YOUNG MASTER'D COMPLETELY LOSE FACE.
......
YOU HAVE AN HERB GARDEN HERE, DON'T YOU?
YES. MISTER SEBASTIAN GREW LOTS OF HERBS...
EXCEL-LENT!
HERBS WOULD PROVE A GREAT HELP!
IT'S NOT LIKE HERBS BEAR FRUIT, SO HOW'D THAT FILL A BELLY?
EACH HERB NOT ONLY HAS ITS OWN TASTE AND UNIQUE FLAVOUR, BUT MEDICINAL PROPERTIES AS WELL. AND AMONG THEM ARE MANY THAT CONTROL APPETITE.
AN HERB SUCH AS FENNEL IS A PRIME EXAMPLE. BY USING IT AND ITS LIKE TO FLAVOUR THE EARLIER COURSES, YOU CAN CONTROL THE TOTAL AMOUNT OF FOOD CONSUMED.

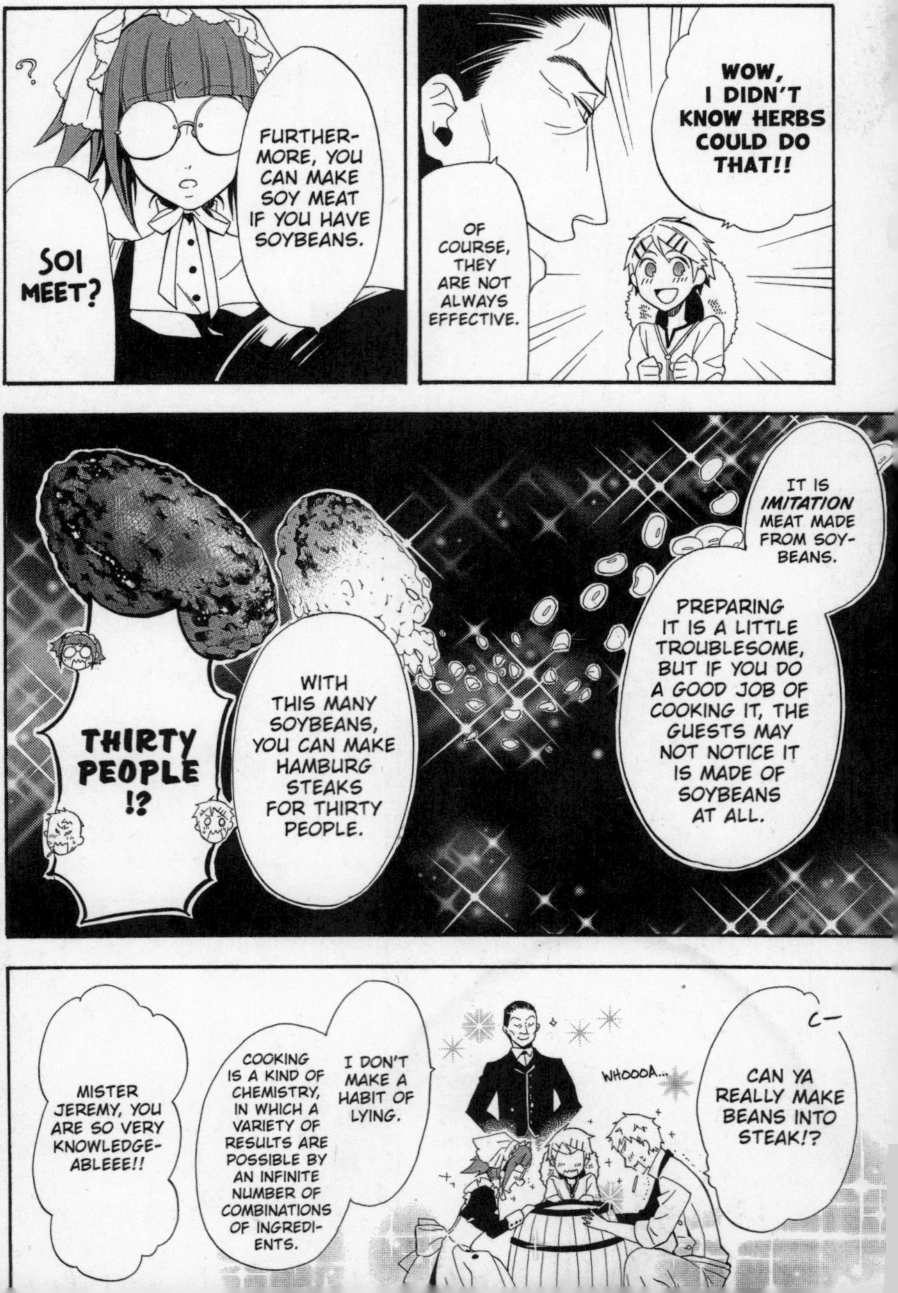
WOW, I DIDN'T KNOW HERBS COULD DO THAT!!
OF COURSE, THEY ARE NOT ALWAYS EFFECTIVE.
FURTHER-MORE, YOU CAN MAKE SOY MEAT IF YOU HAVE SOYBEANS.
SOI MEET?
?
IT IS *IMITATION* MEAT MADE FROM SOY-BEANS.
PREPARING IT IS A LITTLE TROUBLESOME, BUT IF YOU DO A GOOD JOB OF COOKING IT, THE GUESTS MAY NOT NOTICE IT IS MADE OF SOYBEANS AT ALL.
WITH THIS MANY SOYBEANS, YOU CAN MAKE HAMBURG STEAKS FOR THIRTY PEOPLE.
THIRTY PEOPLE!?
C—
CAN YA REALLY MAKE BEANS INTO STEAK!?
WHOOOA...
I DON'T MAKE A HABIT OF LYING.
COOKING IS A KIND OF CHEMISTRY, IN WHICH A VARIETY OF RESULTS ARE POSSIBLE BY AN INFINITE NUMBER OF COMBINATIONS OF INGREDI-ENTS.
MISTER JEREMY, YOU ARE SO VERY KNOWLEDGE-ABLEEE!!

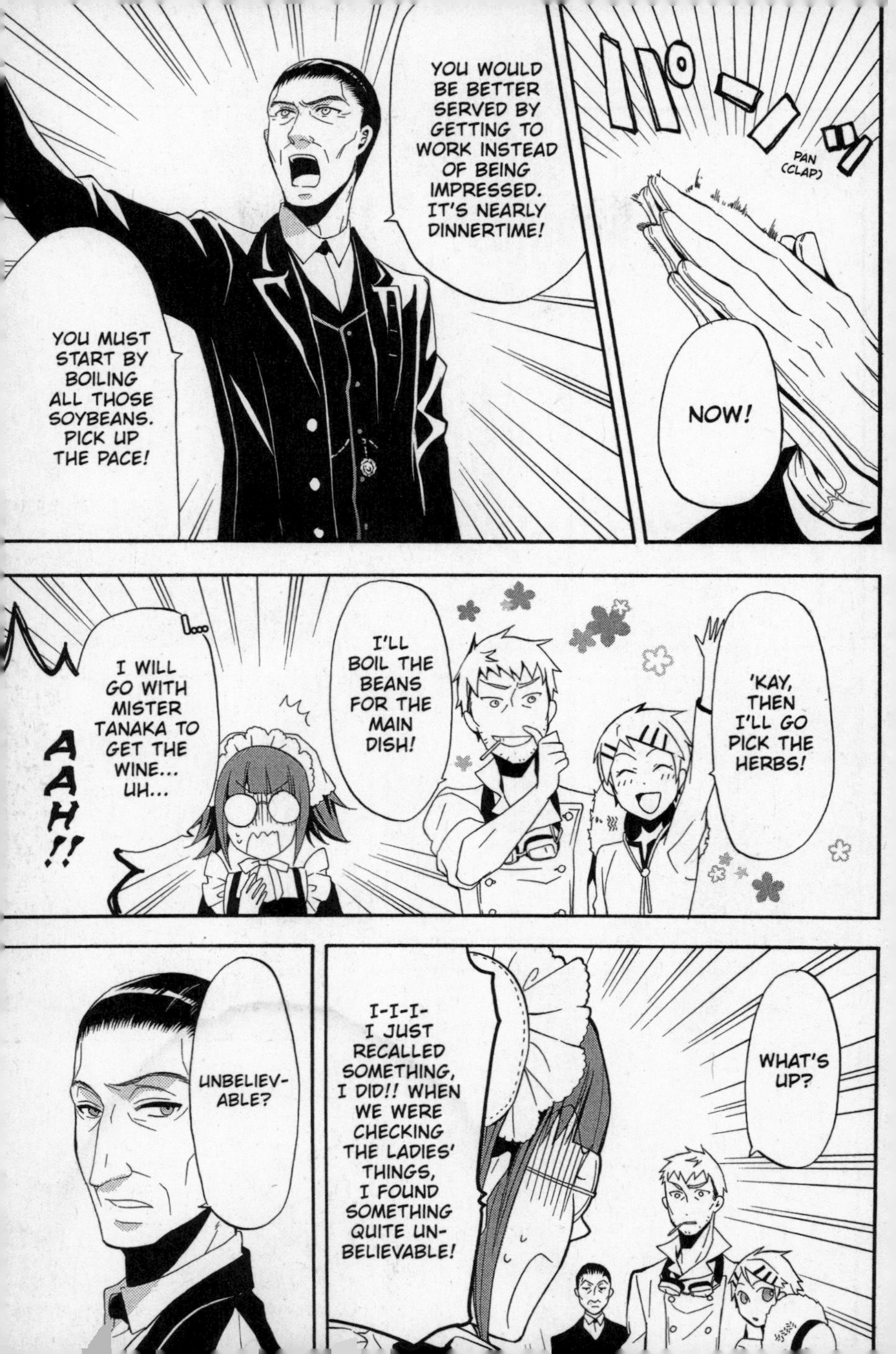
PAN (CLAP)
NOW!
YOU WOULD BE BETTER SERVED BY GETTING TO WORK INSTEAD OF BEING IMPRESSED. IT'S NEARLY DINNERTIME!
YOU MUST START BY BOILING ALL THOSE SOYBEANS. PICK UP THE PACE!
'KAY, THEN I'LL GO PICK THE HERBS!
I'LL BOIL THE BEANS FOR THE MAIN DISH!
I WILL GO WITH MISTER TANAKA TO GET THE WINE... UH...
AAH!!
WHAT'S UP?
I-I-I- I JUST RECALLED SOMETHING, I DID!! WHEN WE WERE CHECKING THE LADIES' THINGS, I FOUND SOMETHING QUITE UN-BELIEVABLE!
UNBELIEV-ABLE?

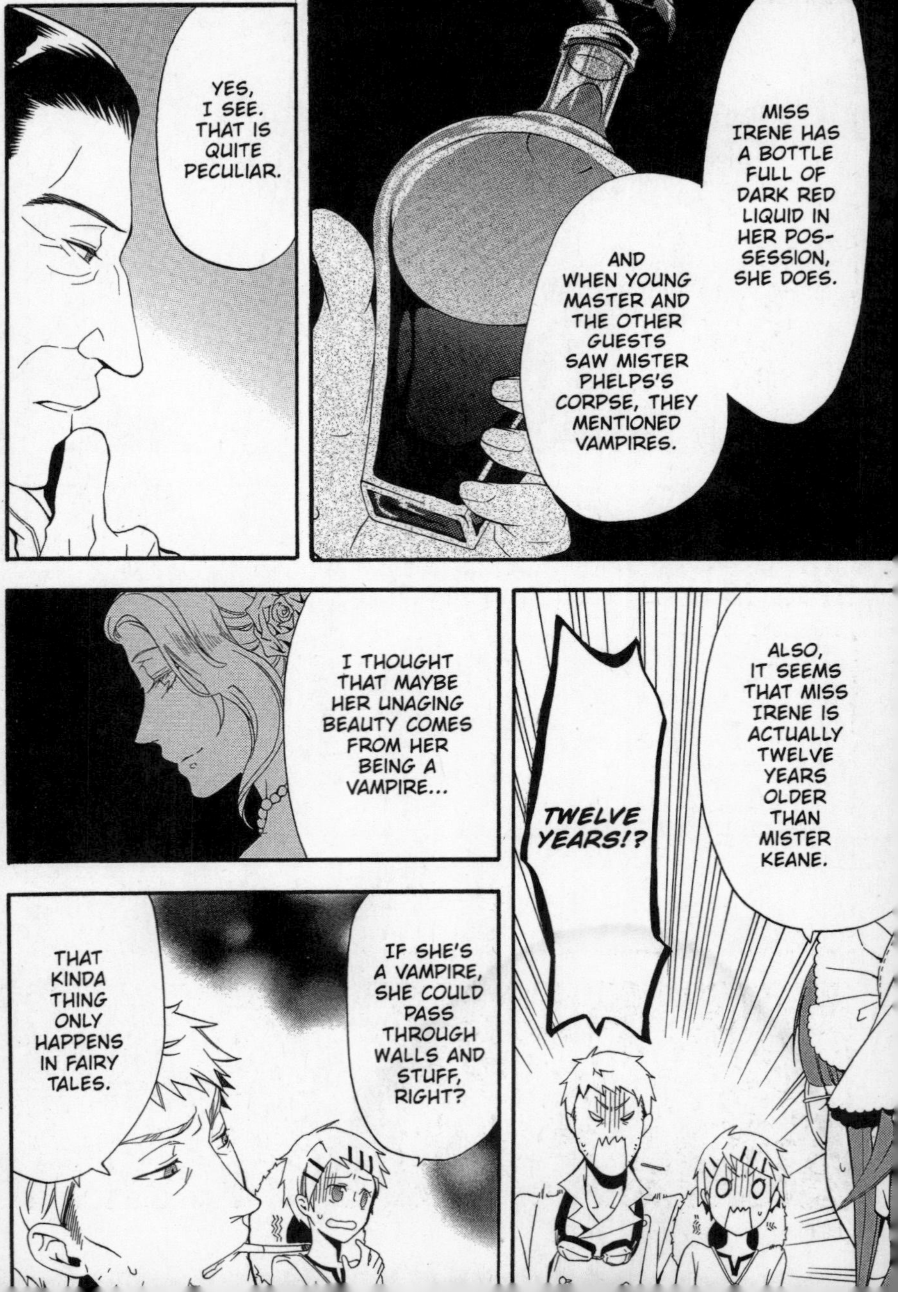
MISS IRENE HAS A BOTTLE FULL OF DARK RED LIQUID IN HER POS-SESSION, SHE DOES.
AND WHEN YOUNG MASTER AND THE OTHER GUESTS SAW MISTER PHELPS'S CORPSE, THEY MENTIONED VAMPIRES.
YES, I SEE. THAT IS QUITE PECULIAR.
ALSO, IT SEEMS THAT MISS IRENE IS ACTUALLY TWELVE YEARS OLDER THAN MISTER KEANE.
TWELVE YEARS!?
I THOUGHT THAT MAYBE HER UNAGING BEAUTY COMES FROM HER BEING A VAMPIRE...
IF SHE'S A VAMPIRE, SHE COULD PASS THROUGH WALLS AND STUFF, RIGHT?
THAT KINDA THING ONLY HAPPENS IN FAIRY TALES.

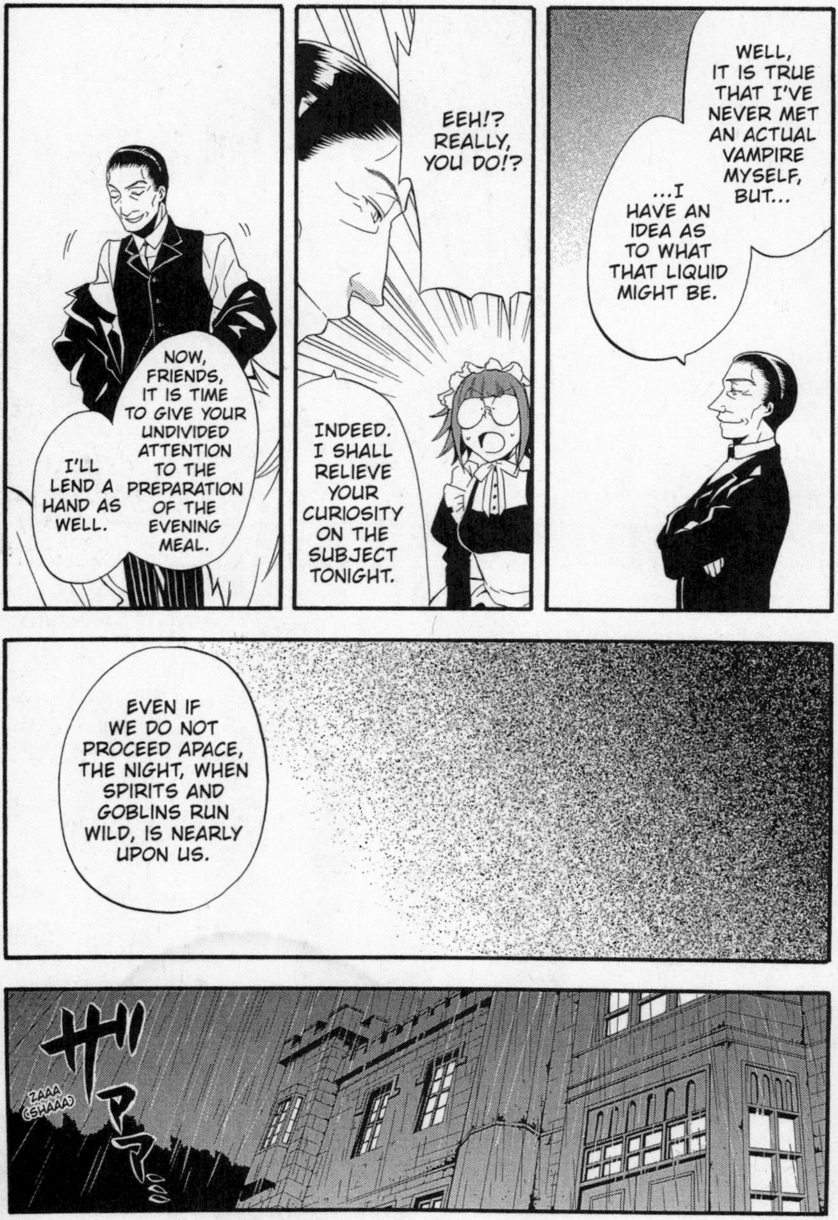
WELL, IT IS TRUE THAT I'VE NEVER MET AN ACTUAL VAMPIRE MYSELF, BUT...
...I HAVE AN IDEA AS TO WHAT THAT LIQUID MIGHT BE.
EEH!? REALLY, YOU DO!?
INDEED. I SHALL RELIEVE YOUR CURIOSITY ON THE SUBJECT TONIGHT.
NOW, FRIENDS, IT IS TIME TO GIVE YOUR UNDIVIDED ATTENTION TO THE PREPARATION OF THE EVENING MEAL.
I'LL LEND A HAND AS WELL.
EVEN IF WE DO NOT PROCEED APACE, THE NIGHT, WHEN SPIRITS AND GOBLINS RUN WILD, IS NEARLY UPON US.
ZAAA (SHAAA)

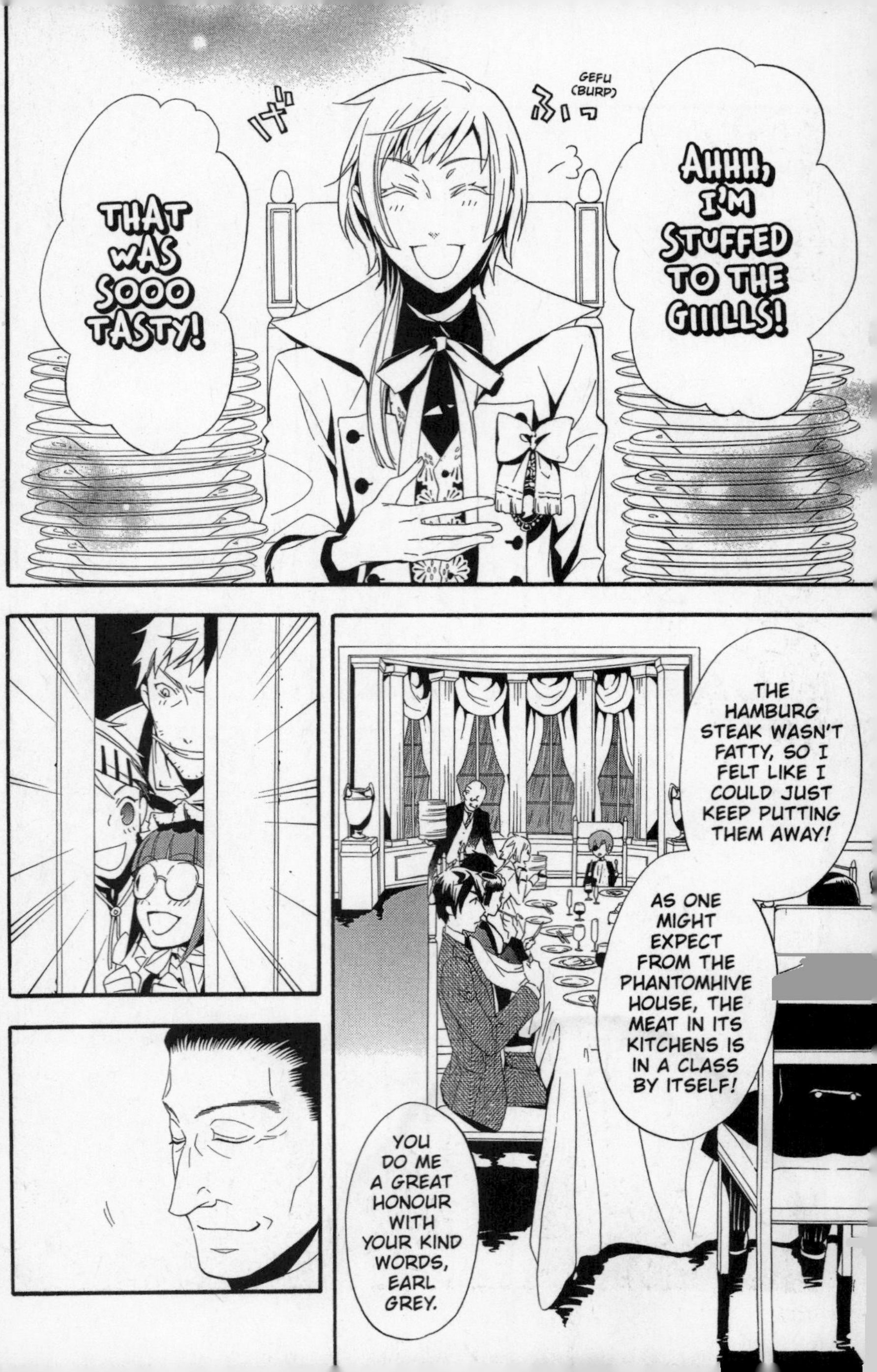
GEFU (BURP)
AHHH, I'M STUFFED TO THE GIIILLS!
THAT WAS SOOO TASTY!
THE HAMBURG STEAK WASN'T FATTY, SO I FELT LIKE I COULD JUST KEEP PUTTING THEM AWAY!
AS ONE MIGHT EXPECT FROM THE PHANTOMHIVE HOUSE, THE MEAT IN ITS KITCHENS IS IN A CLASS BY ITSELF!
YOU DO ME A GREAT HONOUR WITH YOUR KIND WORDS, EARL GREY.

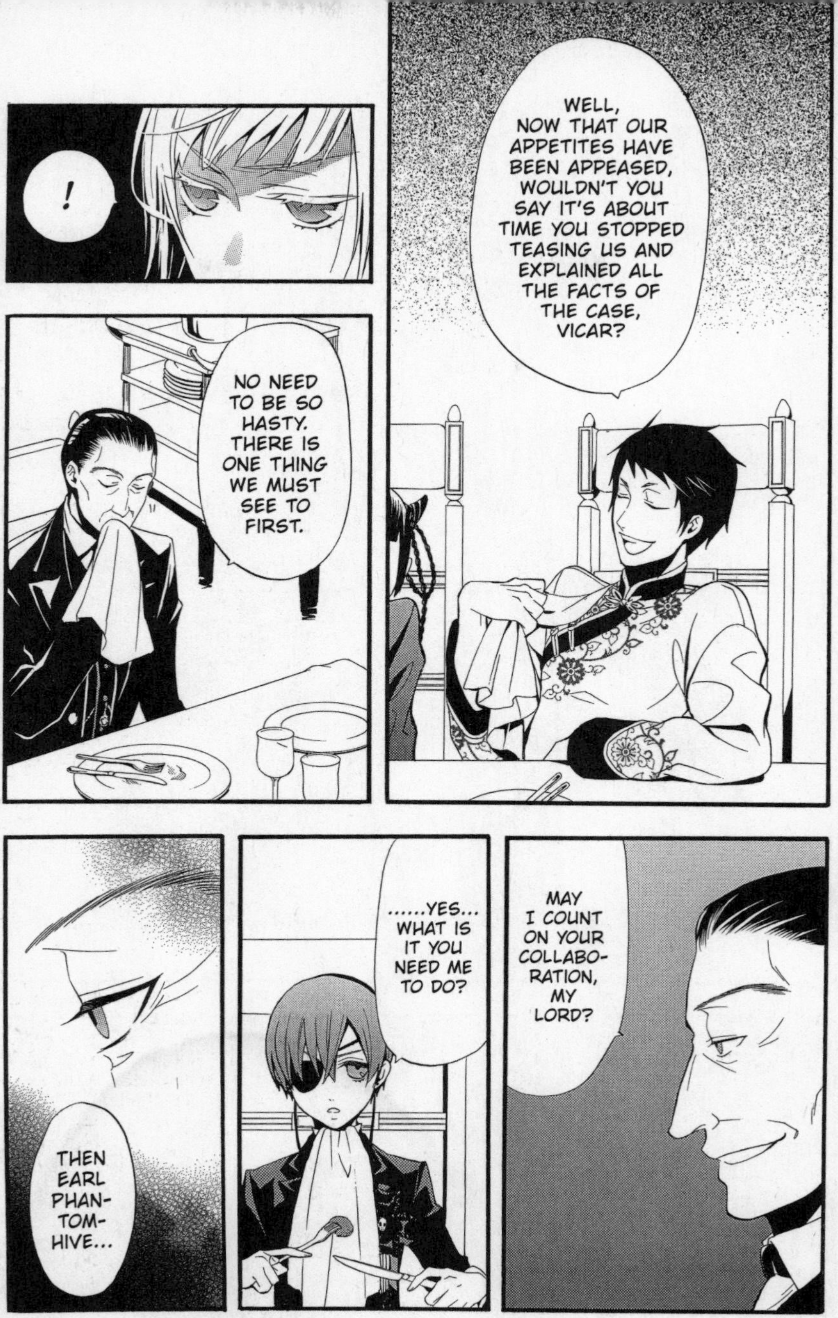
WELL, NOW THAT OUR APPETITES HAVE BEEN APPEASED, WOULDN'T YOU SAY IT'S ABOUT TIME YOU STOPPED TEASING US AND EXPLAINED ALL THE FACTS OF THE CASE, VICAR?
!
NO NEED TO BE SO HASTY. THERE IS ONE THING WE MUST SEE TO FIRST.
MAY I COUNT ON YOUR COLLABO-RATION, MY LORD?
......YES... WHAT IS IT YOU NEED ME TO DO?
THEN EARL PHAN-TOM-HIVE...

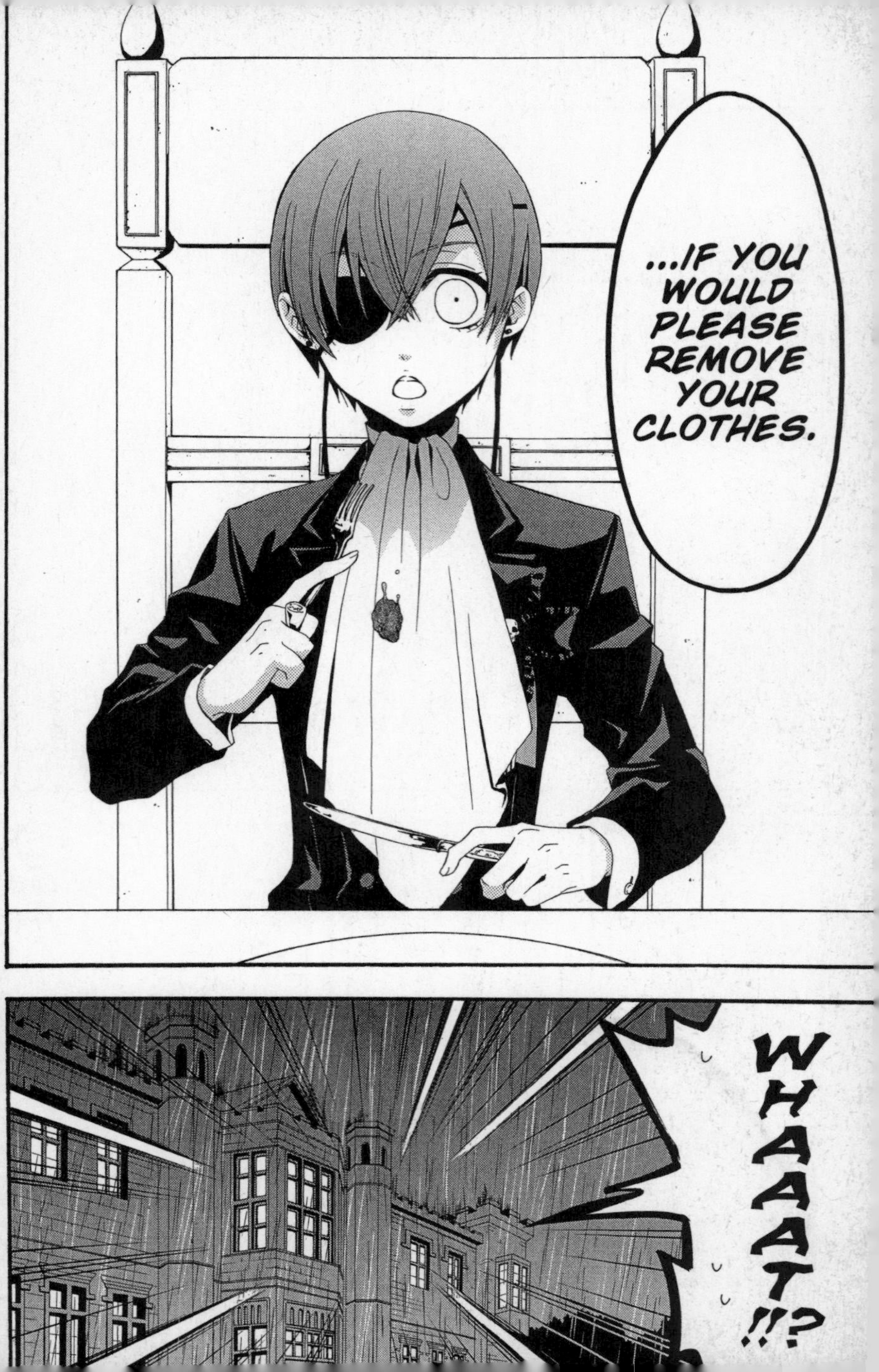
...IF YOU WOULD PLEASE REMOVE YOUR CLOTHES.
WHAAAT!!?

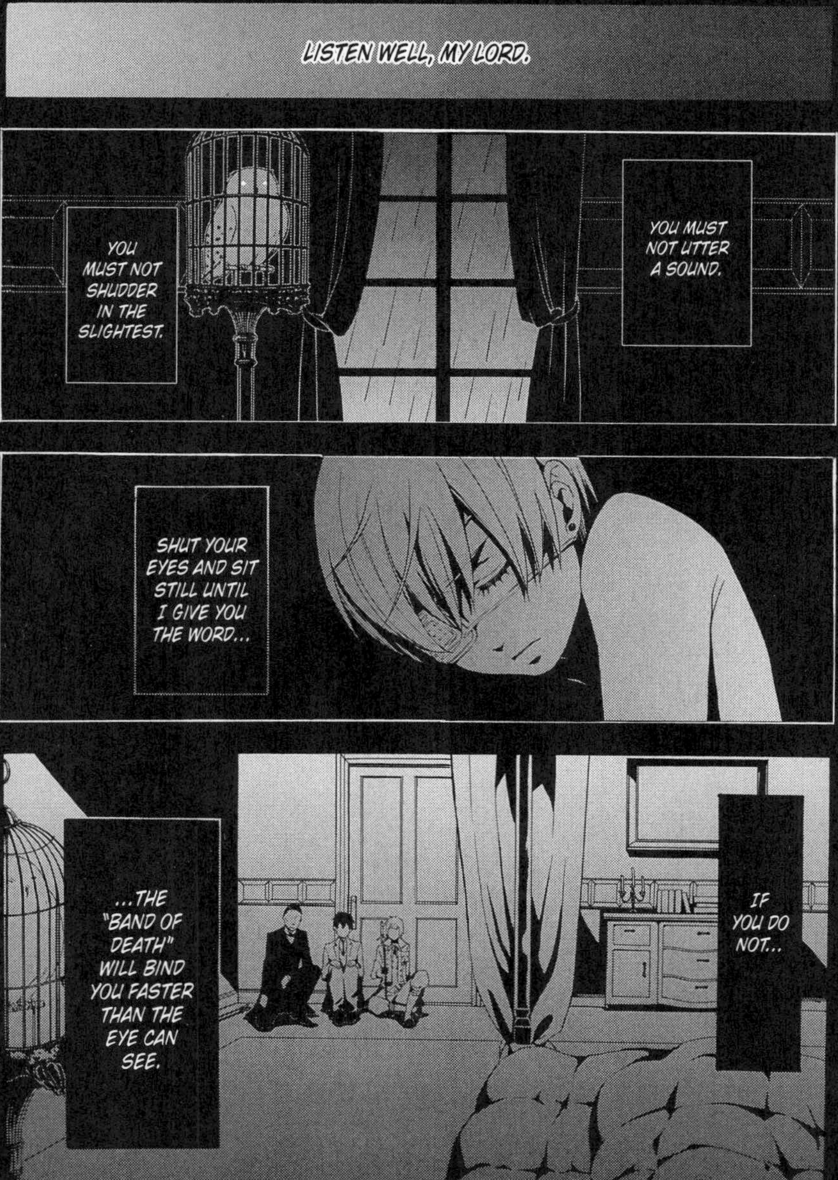
LISTEN WELL, MY LORD.
YOU MUST NOT UTTER A SOUND.
YOU MUST NOT SHUDDER IN THE SLIGHTEST.
SHUT YOUR EYES AND SIT STILL UNTIL I GIVE YOU THE WORD...
IF YOU DO NOT...
...THE "BAND OF DEATH" WILL BIND YOU FASTER THAN THE EYE CAN SEE.

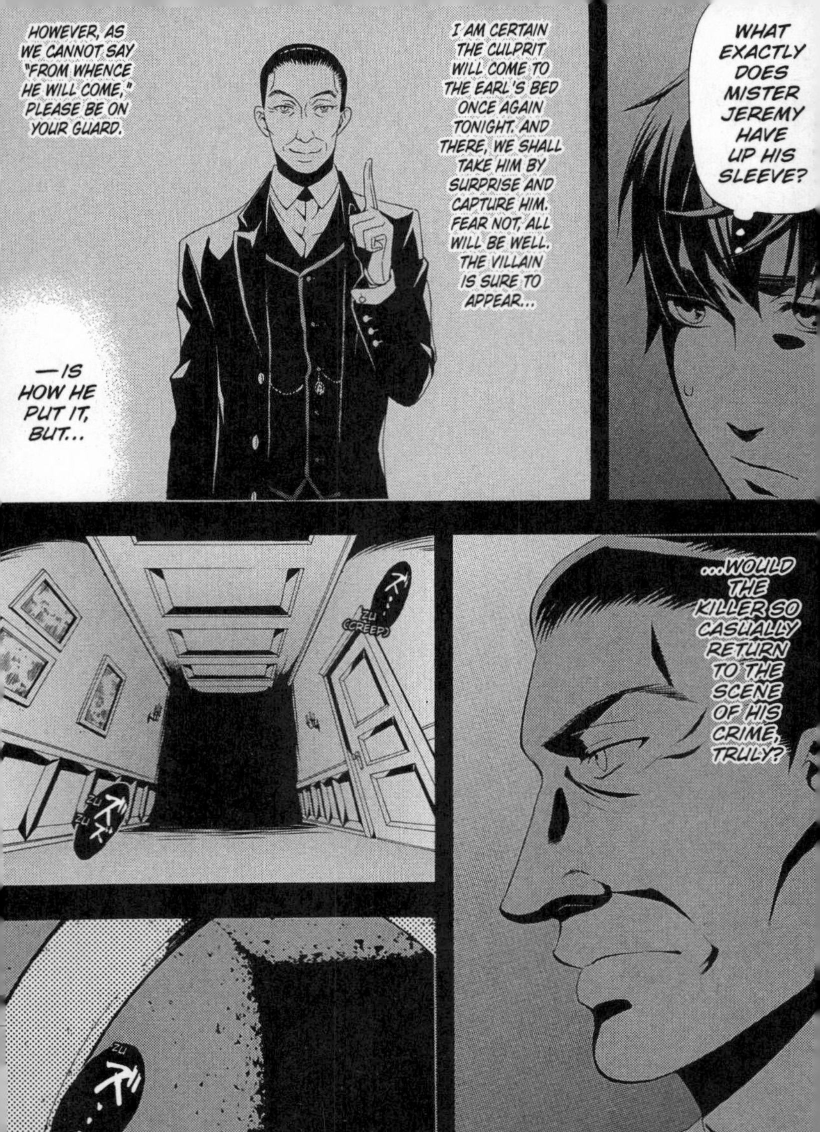
WHAT EXACTLY DOES MISTER JEREMY HAVE UP HIS SLEEVE?
I AM CERTAIN THE CULPRIT WILL COME TO THE EARL'S BED ONCE AGAIN TONIGHT. AND THERE, WE SHALL TAKE HIM BY SURPRISE AND CAPTURE HIM. FEAR NOT, ALL WILL BE WELL. THE VILLAIN IS SURE TO APPEAR...
HOWEVER, AS WE CANNOT SAY "FROM WHENCE HE WILL COME," PLEASE BE ON YOUR GUARD.
—IS HOW HE PUT IT, BUT...
...WOULD THE KILLER SO CASUALLY RETURN TO THE SCENE OF HIS CRIME, TRULY?
ZU (CREEP)
ZU
ZU
ZU

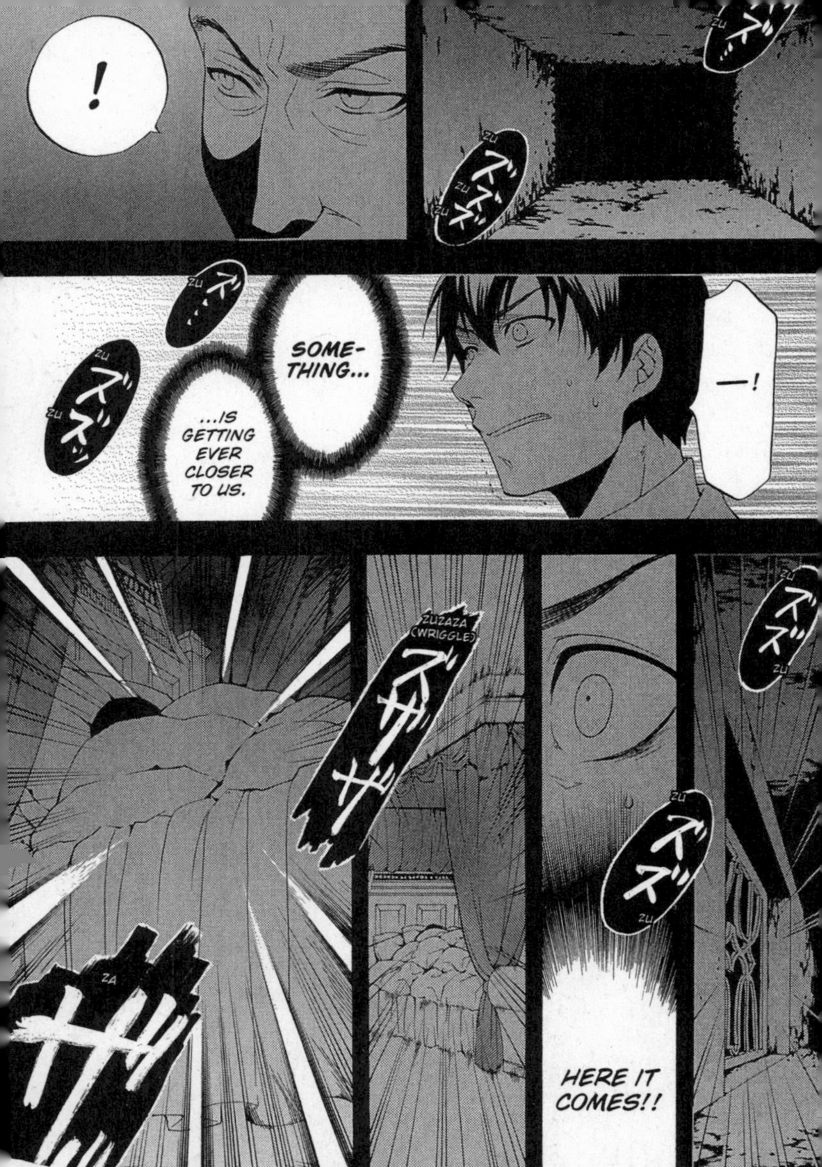
ZU
ZU ZU ZU
!
—!
SOME-THING...
...IS GETTING EVER CLOSER TO US.
ZU
ZU ZU
ZU ZU
ZU ZU
HERE IT COMES!!
ZUZAZA (WRIGGLE)
ZA

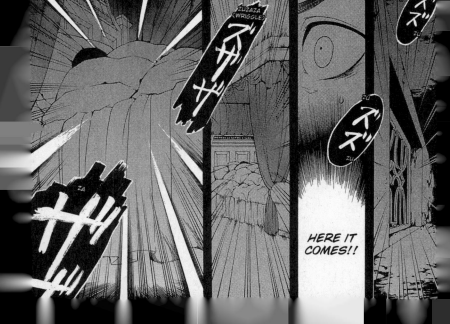

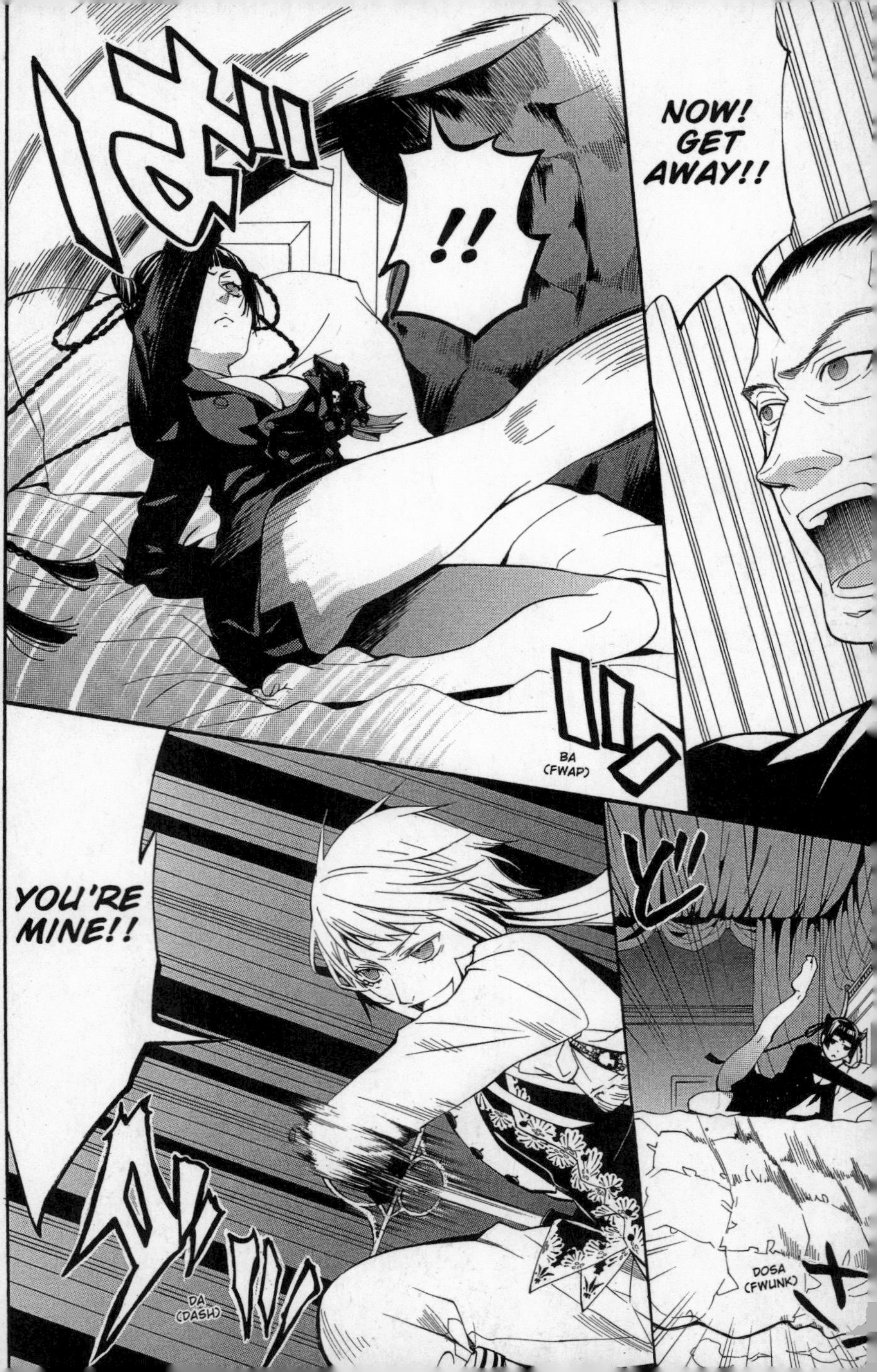
NOW! GET AWAY!!
!!
BA (FWAP)
DOSA (FWUNK)
YOU'RE MINE!!
DA (DASH)

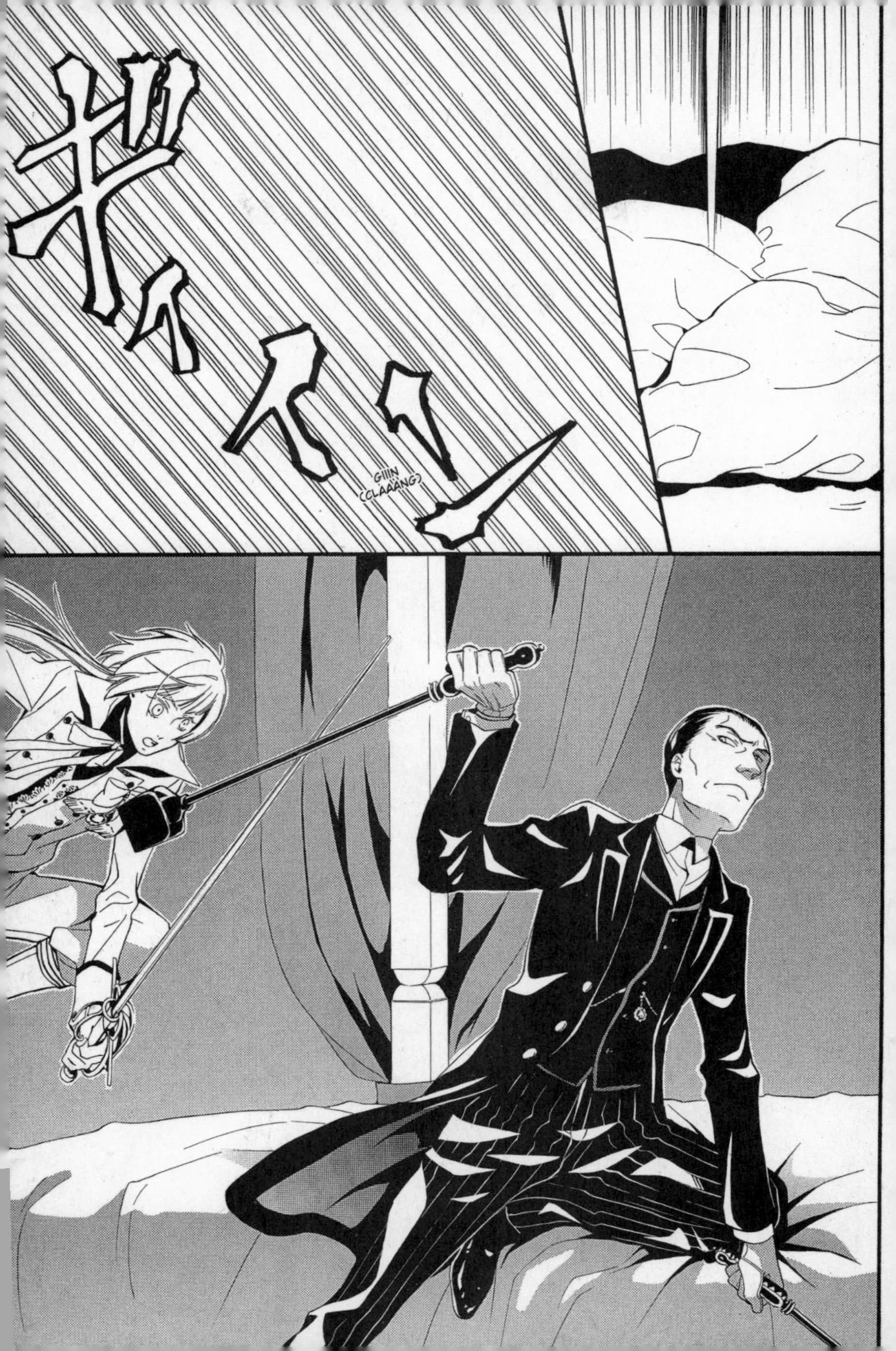
ギィィン
GIIIN (CLAAANG)

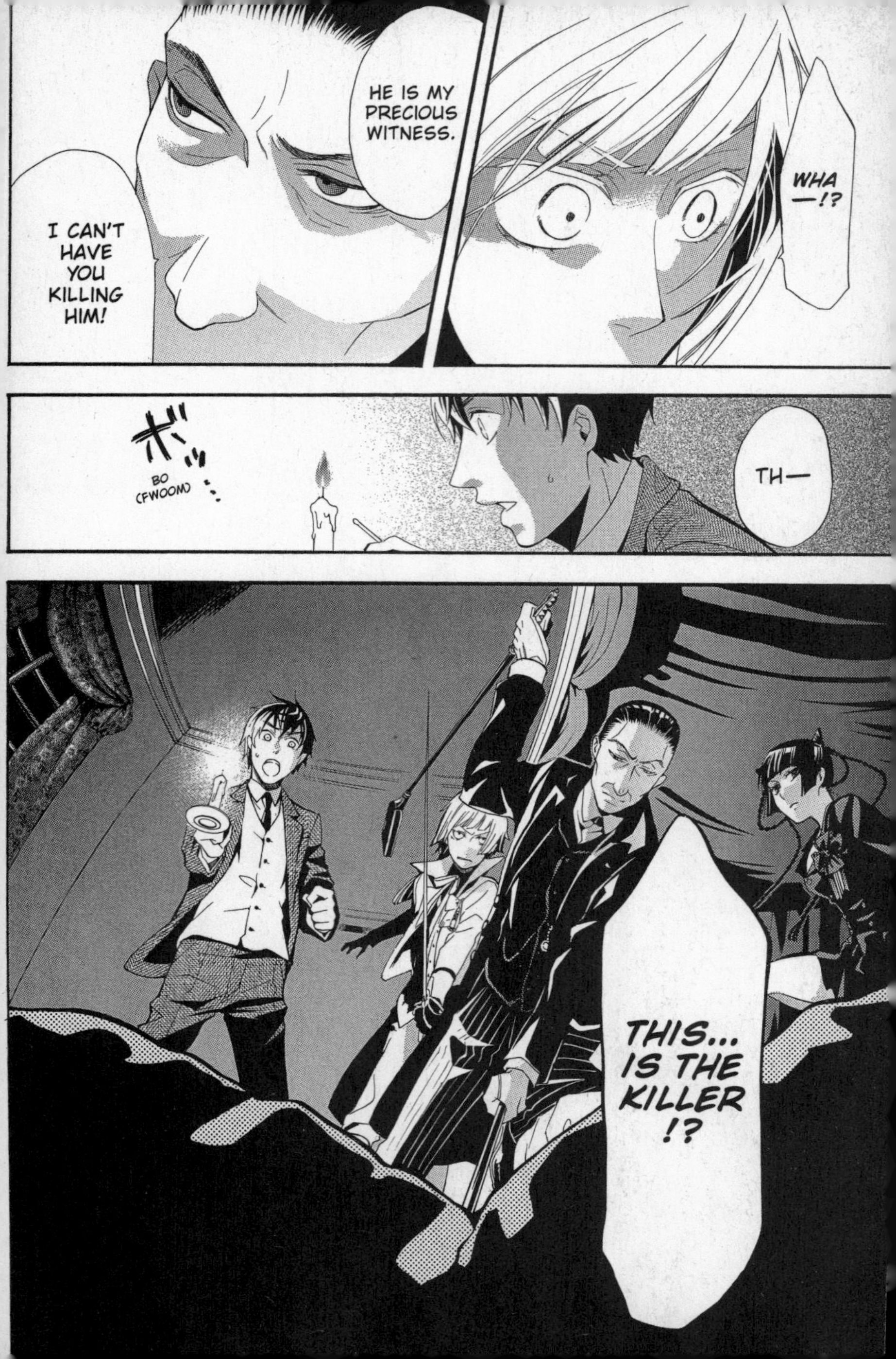
WHA—!?
HE IS MY PRECIOUS WITNESS.
I CAN'T HAVE YOU KILLING HIM!
TH—
ボッ
BO (FWOOM)
THIS... IS THE KILLER!?

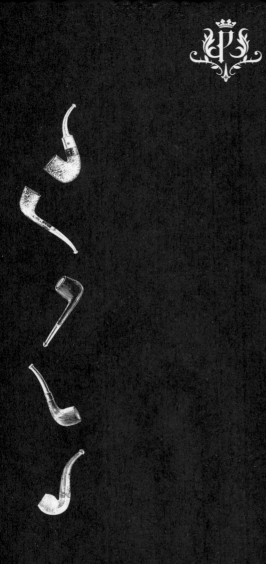

Black Butler

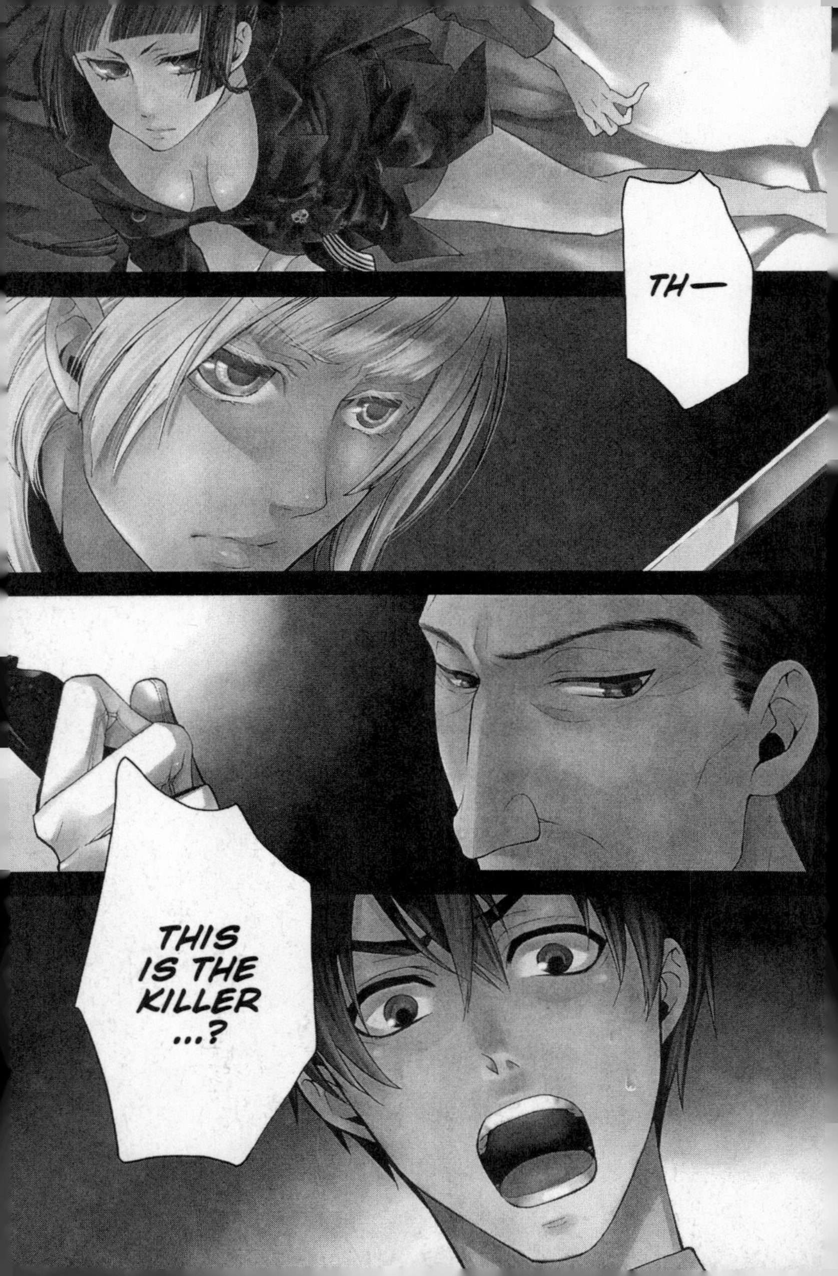
TH—
THIS IS THE KILLER ...?

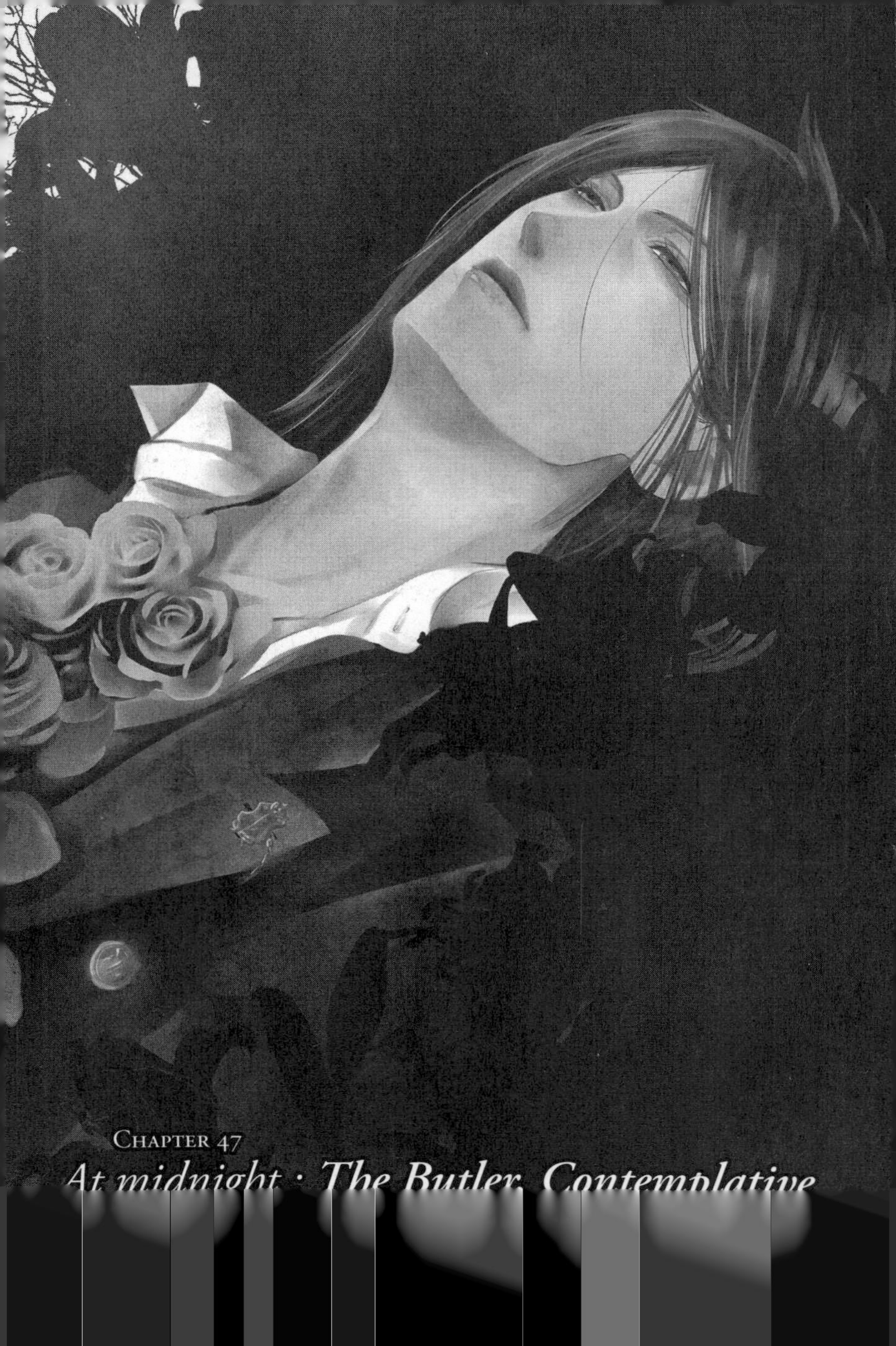

Chapter 47

At midnight : The Butler, Contemplative

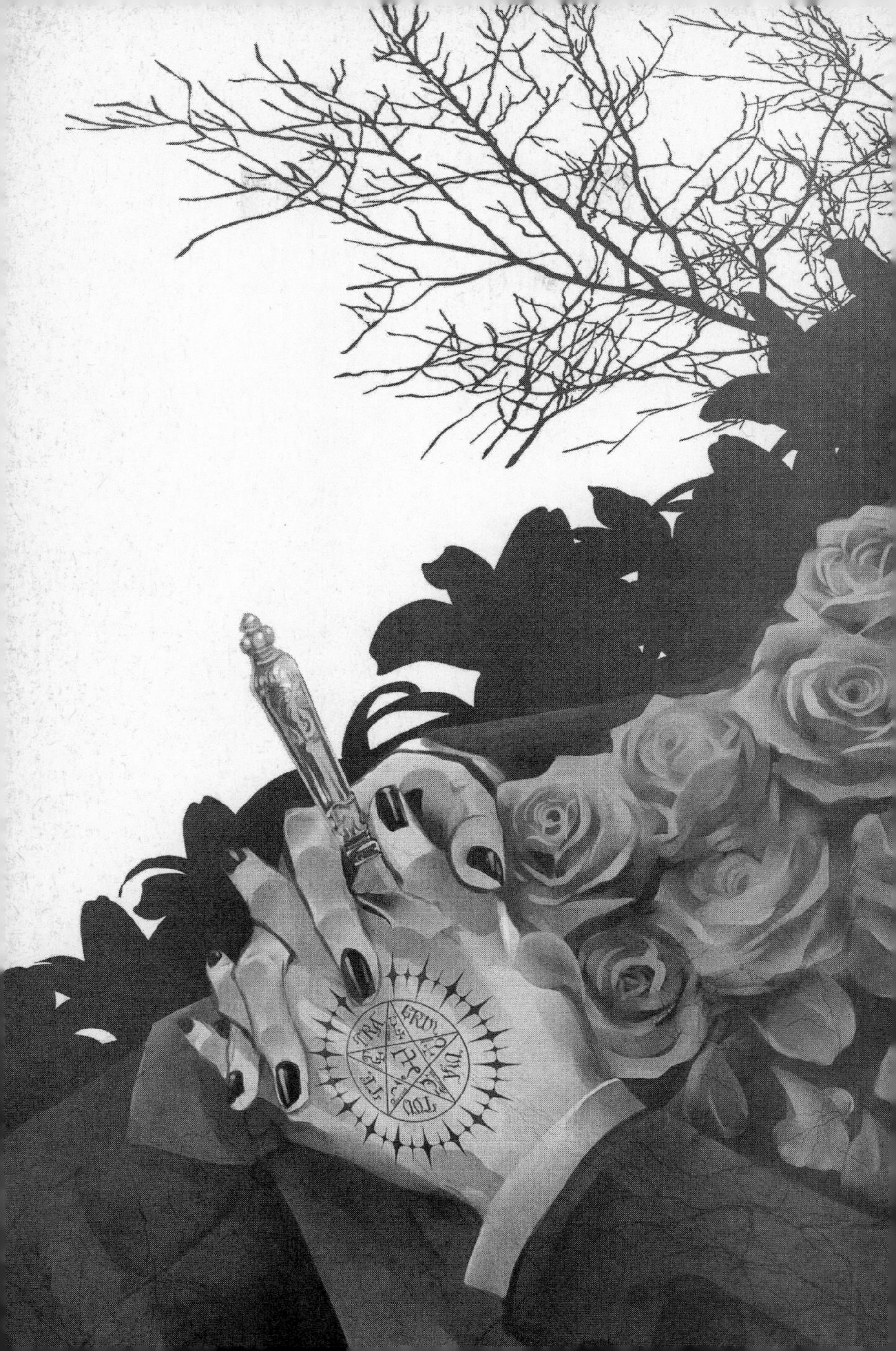

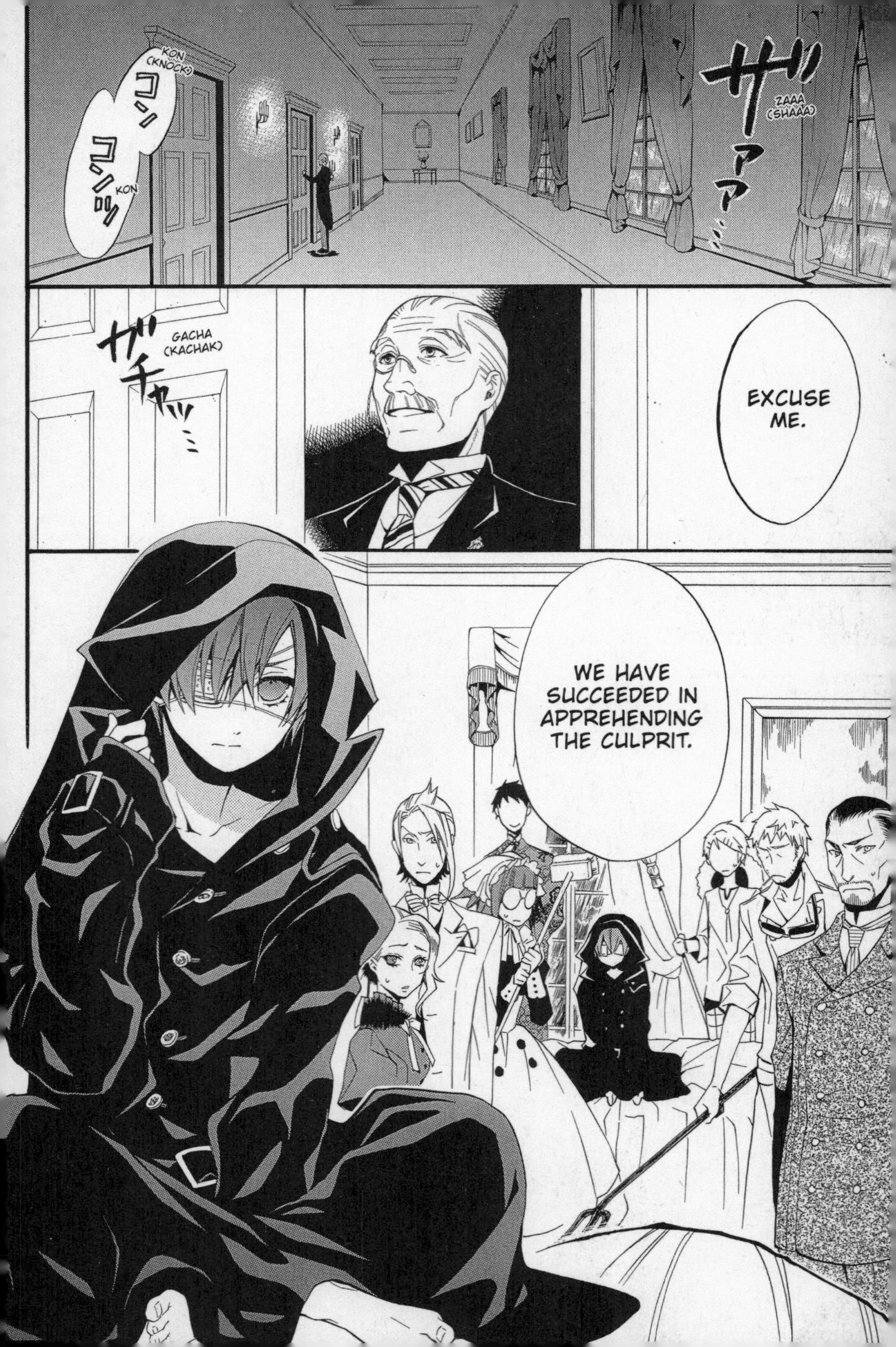
ザァァ…
ZAAA (SHAAA)
コン コンッ
KON (KNOCK) KON
EXCUSE ME.
ガチャッ…
GACHA (KACHAK)
WE HAVE SUCCEEDED IN APPREHENDING THE CULPRIT.

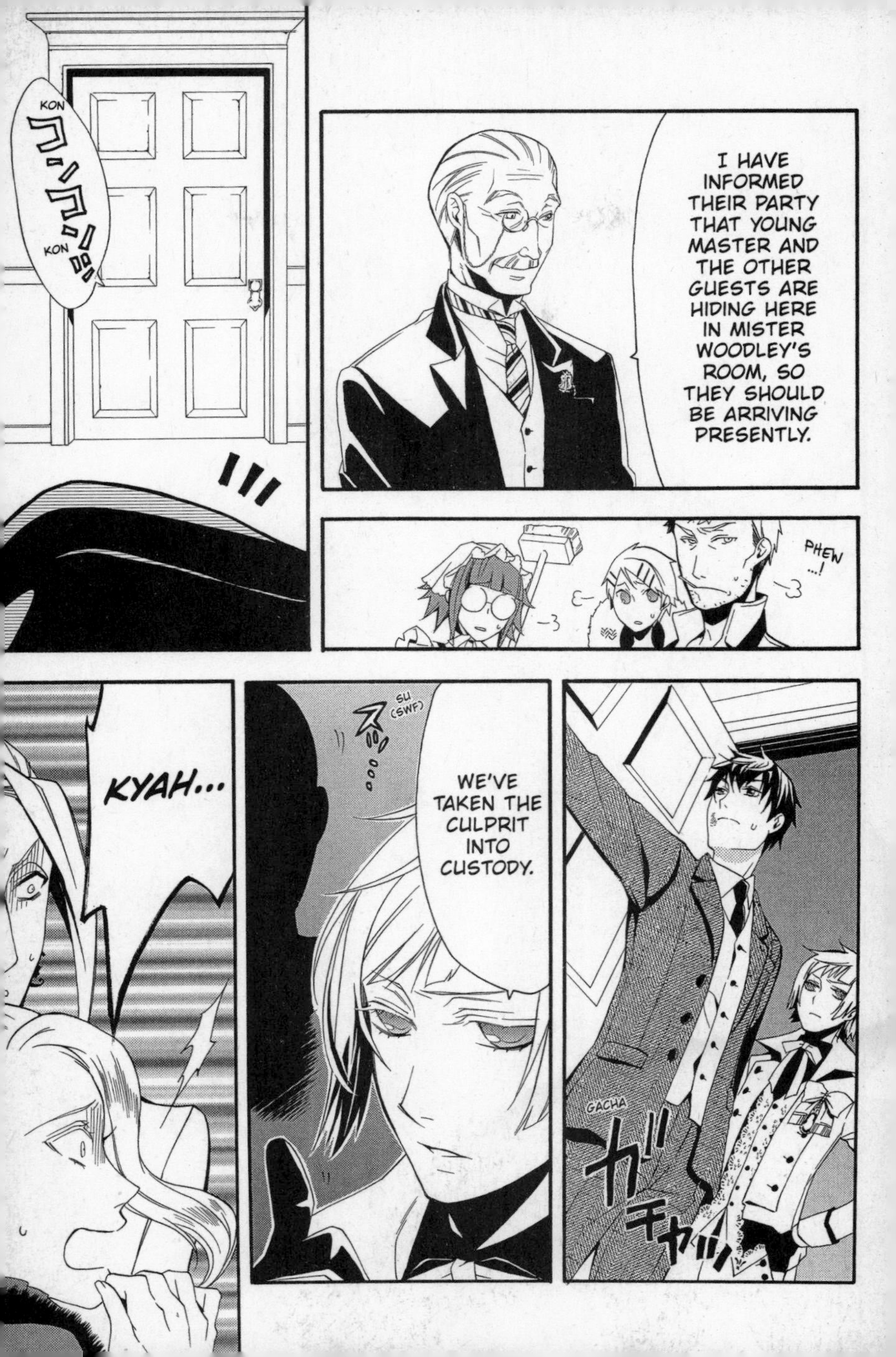
I HAVE INFORMED THEIR PARTY THAT YOUNG MASTER AND THE OTHER GUESTS ARE HIDING HERE IN MISTER WOODLEY'S ROOM, SO THEY SHOULD BE ARRIVING PRESENTLY.
PHEW ...!
KON
KON
GACHA
WE'VE TAKEN THE CULPRIT INTO CUSTODY.
SU (SWF)
KYAH...

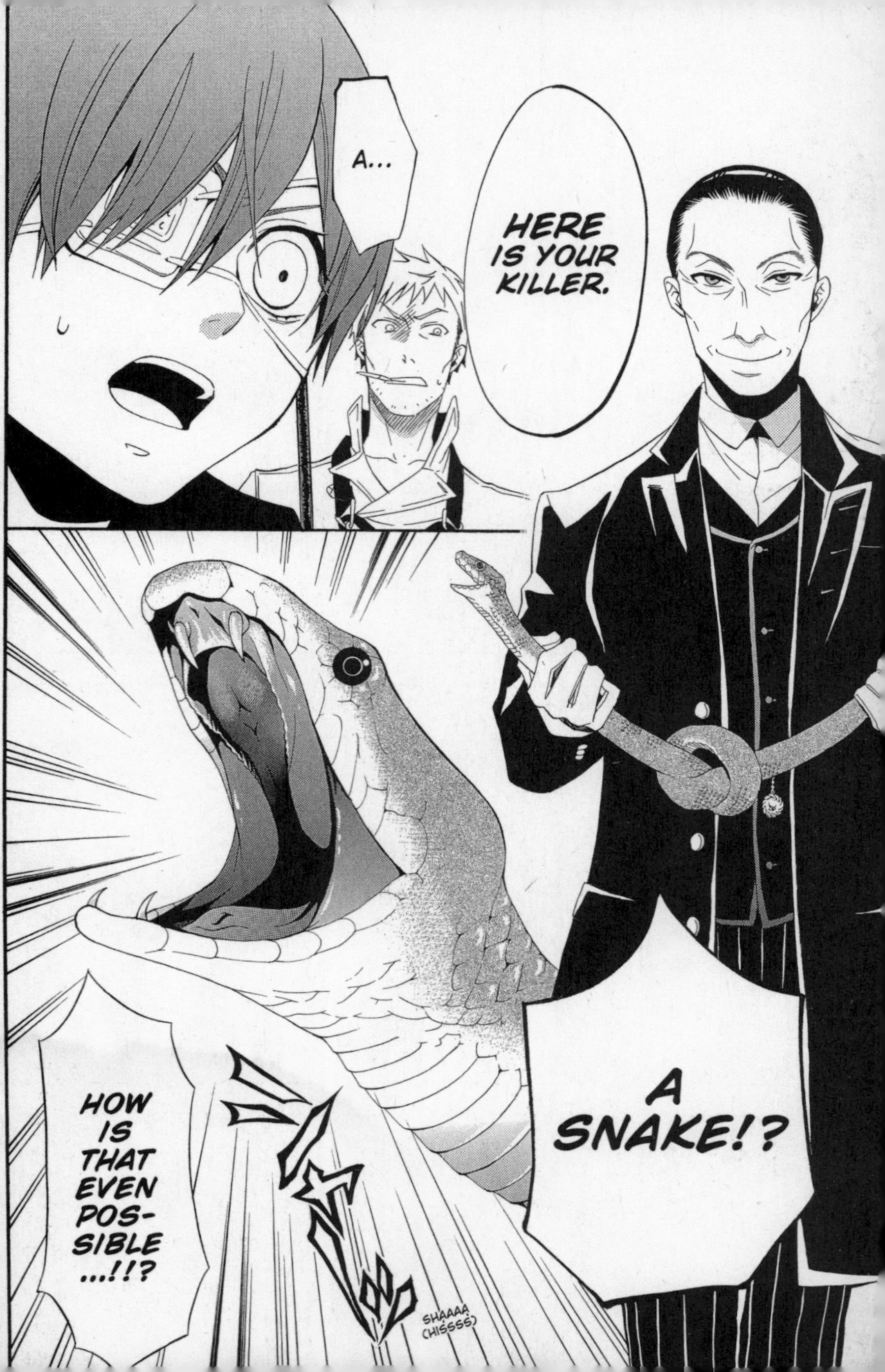
HERE IS YOUR KILLER.
A...
A SNAKE!?
HOW IS THAT EVEN POS-SIBLE ...!!?
SHAAAA (HISSSS)

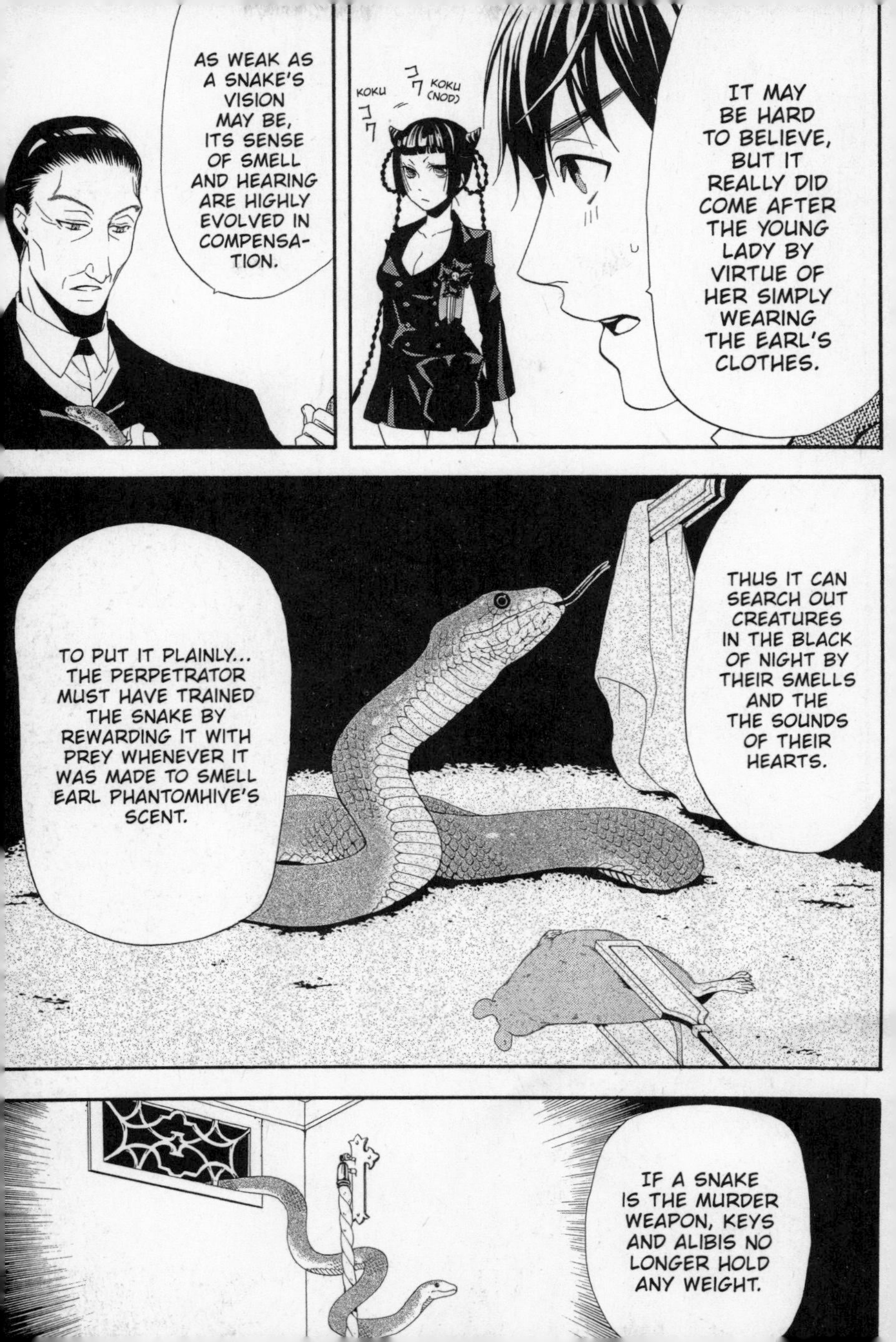

IT MAY BE HARD TO BELIEVE, BUT IT REALLY DID COME AFTER THE YOUNG LADY BY VIRTUE OF HER SIMPLY WEARING THE EARL'S CLOTHES.
KOKU (NOD)
KOKU
AS WEAK AS A SNAKE'S VISION MAY BE, ITS SENSE OF SMELL AND HEARING ARE HIGHLY EVOLVED IN COMPENSA-TION.
THUS IT CAN SEARCH OUT CREATURES IN THE BLACK OF NIGHT BY THEIR SMELLS AND THE THE SOUNDS OF THEIR HEARTS.
TO PUT IT PLAINLY... THE PERPETRATOR MUST HAVE TRAINED THE SNAKE BY REWARDING IT WITH PREY WHENEVER IT WAS MADE TO SMELL EARL PHANTOMHIVE'S SCENT.
IF A SNAKE IS THE MURDER WEAPON, KEYS AND ALIBIS NO LONGER HOLD ANY WEIGHT.

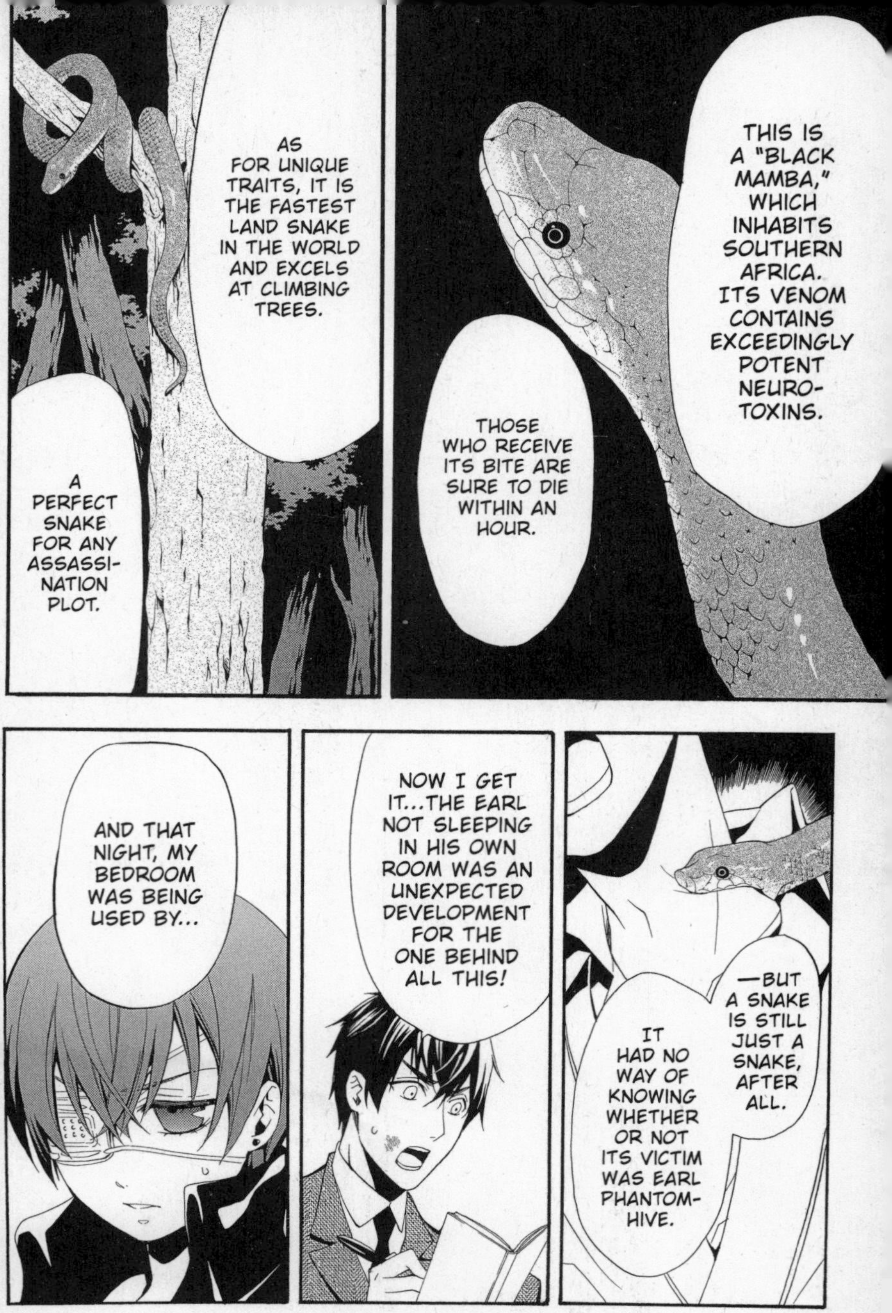
THIS IS A "BLACK MAMBA," WHICH INHABITS SOUTHERN AFRICA. ITS VENOM CONTAINS EXCEEDINGLY POTENT NEURO-TOXINS.
THOSE WHO RECEIVE ITS BITE ARE SURE TO DIE WITHIN AN HOUR.
AS FOR UNIQUE TRAITS, IT IS THE FASTEST LAND SNAKE IN THE WORLD AND EXCELS AT CLIMBING TREES.
A PERFECT SNAKE FOR ANY ASSASSI-NATION PLOT.
—BUT A SNAKE IS STILL JUST A SNAKE, AFTER ALL.
IT HAD NO WAY OF KNOWING WHETHER OR NOT ITS VICTIM WAS EARL PHANTOM-HIVE.
NOW I GET IT...THE EARL NOT SLEEPING IN HIS OWN ROOM WAS AN UNEXPECTED DEVELOPMENT FOR THE ONE BEHIND ALL THIS!
AND THAT NIGHT, MY BEDROOM WAS BEING USED BY...

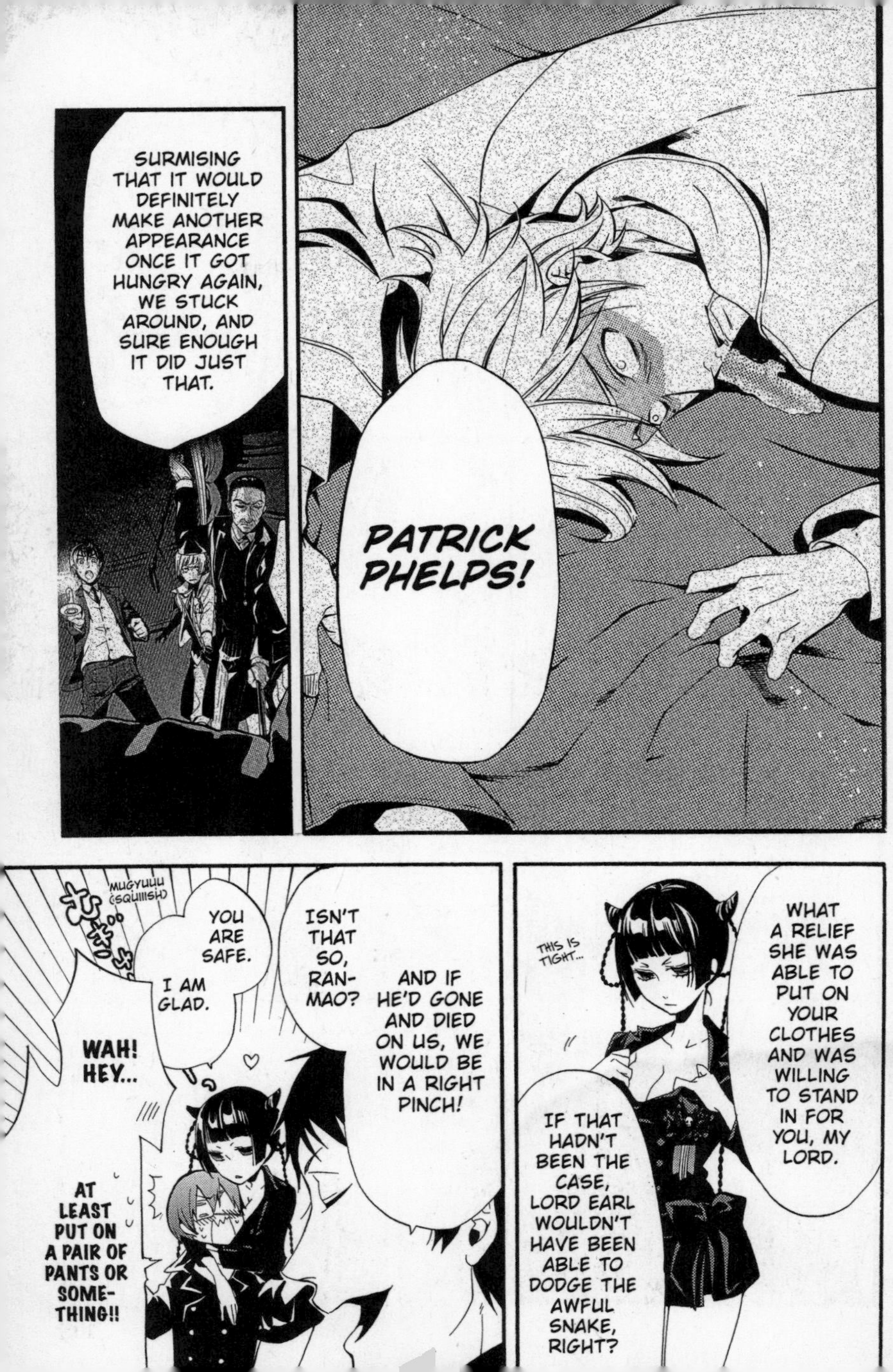
PATRICK PHELPS!
SURMISING THAT IT WOULD DEFINITELY MAKE ANOTHER APPEARANCE ONCE IT GOT HUNGRY AGAIN, WE STUCK AROUND, AND SURE ENOUGH IT DID JUST THAT.
WHAT A RELIEF SHE WAS ABLE TO PUT ON YOUR CLOTHES AND WAS WILLING TO STAND IN FOR YOU, MY LORD.
THIS IS TIGHT...
IF THAT HADN'T BEEN THE CASE, LORD EARL WOULDN'T HAVE BEEN ABLE TO DODGE THE AWFUL SNAKE, RIGHT?
ISN'T THAT SO, RAN-MAO?
AND IF HE'D GONE AND DIED ON US, WE WOULD BE IN A RIGHT PINCH!
YOU ARE SAFE.
I AM GLAD.
MUGYUUU (SQUIIISH)
WAH! HEY...
AT LEAST PUT ON A PAIR OF PANTS OR SOME-THING!!

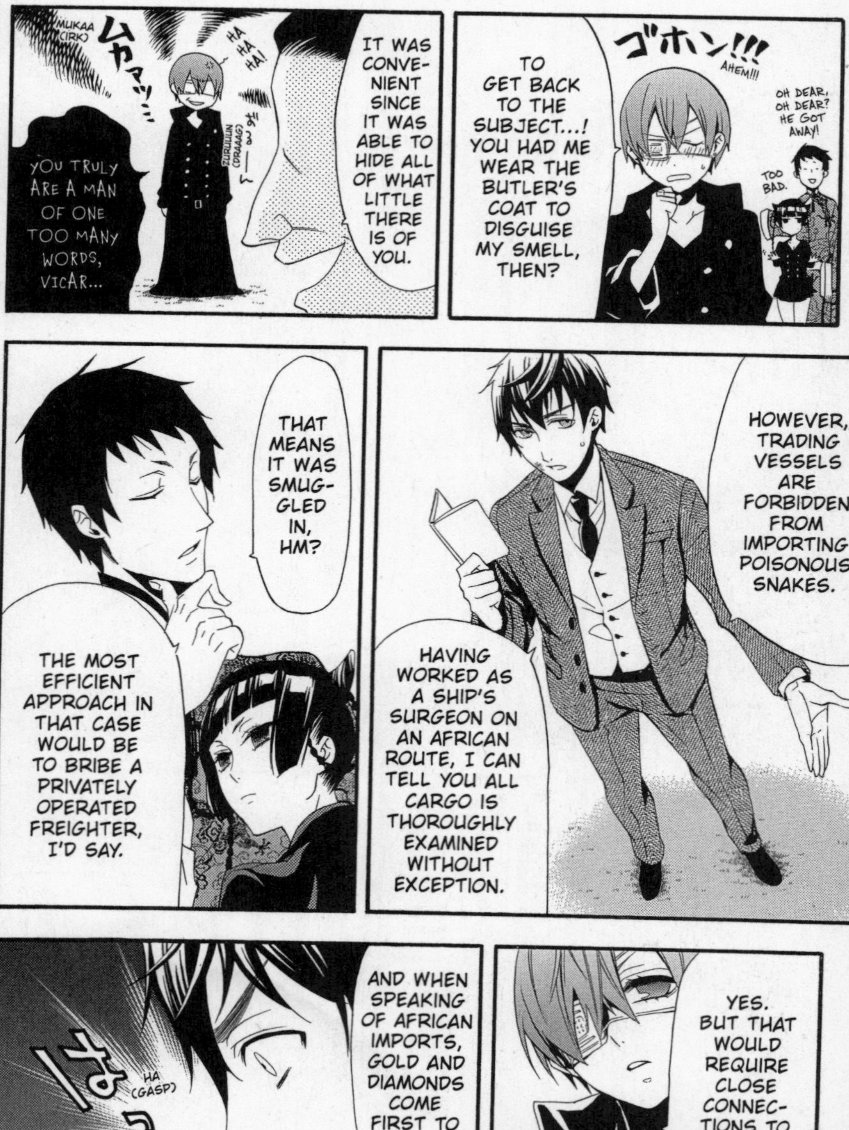
ゴホン!!!
AHEM!!!
OH DEAR, OH DEAR? HE GOT AWAY!
TOO BAD.
TO GET BACK TO THE SUBJECT...! YOU HAD ME WEAR THE BUTLER'S COAT TO DISGUISE MY SMELL, THEN?
IT WAS CONVENIENT SINCE IT WAS ABLE TO HIDE ALL OF WHAT LITTLE THERE IS OF YOU.
ずるーん
ZURUUUN (DRAAAG)
HA HA HA!
ムカァッ
MUKAA (IRK)
YOU TRULY ARE A MAN OF ONE TOO MANY WORDS, VICAR...
HOWEVER, TRADING VESSELS ARE FORBIDDEN FROM IMPORTING POISONOUS SNAKES.
HAVING WORKED AS A SHIP'S SURGEON ON AN AFRICAN ROUTE, I CAN TELL YOU ALL CARGO IS THOROUGHLY EXAMINED WITHOUT EXCEPTION.
THAT MEANS IT WAS SMUGGLED IN, HM?
THE MOST EFFICIENT APPROACH IN THAT CASE WOULD BE TO BRIBE A PRIVATELY OPERATED FREIGHTER, I'D SAY.
YES. BUT THAT WOULD REQUIRE CLOSE CONNECTIONS TO BUSINESSES IN AFRICA.
AND WHEN SPEAKING OF AFRICAN IMPORTS, GOLD AND DIAMONDS COME FIRST TO MIND...
はっ!
HA (GASP)

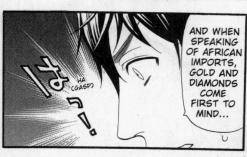

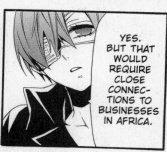

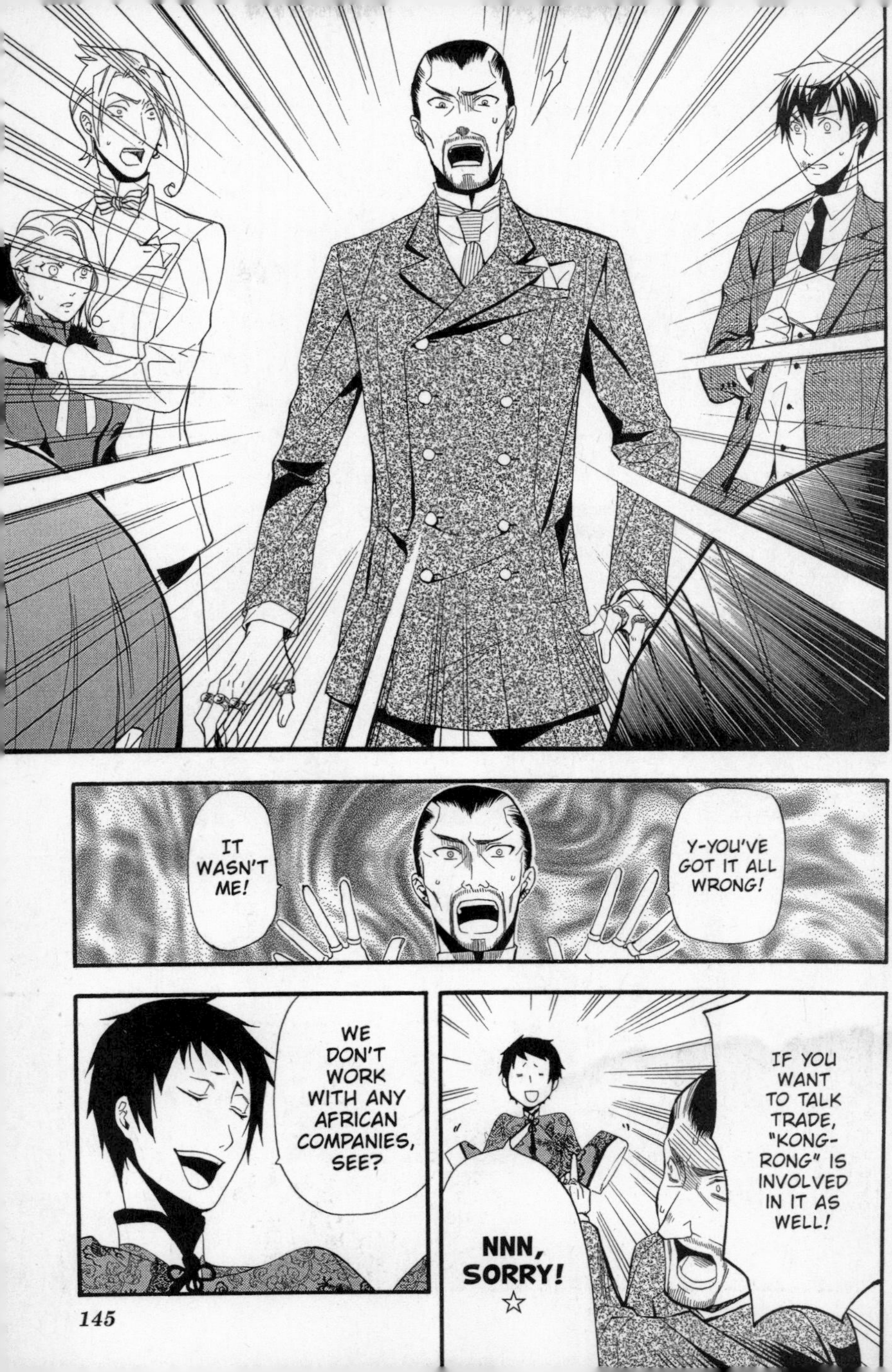
Y-YOU'VE GOT IT ALL WRONG!
IT WASN'T ME!
IF YOU WANT TO TALK TRADE, "KONG-RONG" IS INVOLVED IN IT AS WELL!
NNN, SORRY! ☆
WE DON'T WORK WITH ANY AFRICAN COMPANIES, SEE?

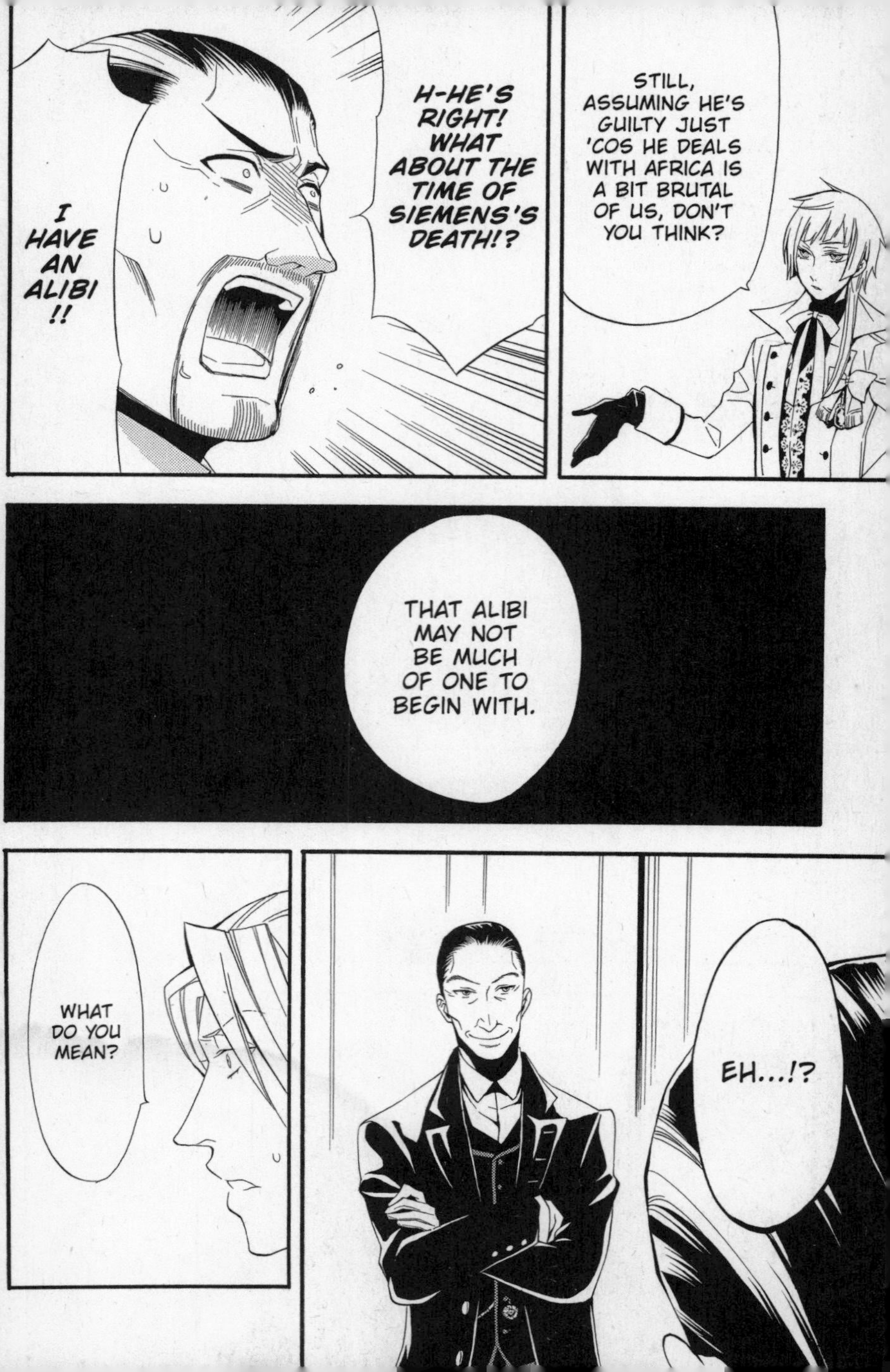
STILL, ASSUMING HE'S GUILTY JUST 'COS HE DEALS WITH AFRICA IS A BIT BRUTAL OF US, DON'T YOU THINK?
H-HE'S RIGHT! WHAT ABOUT THE TIME OF SIEMENS'S DEATH!?
I HAVE AN ALIBI!!
THAT ALIBI MAY NOT BE MUCH OF ONE TO BEGIN WITH.
EH...!?
WHAT DO YOU MEAN?

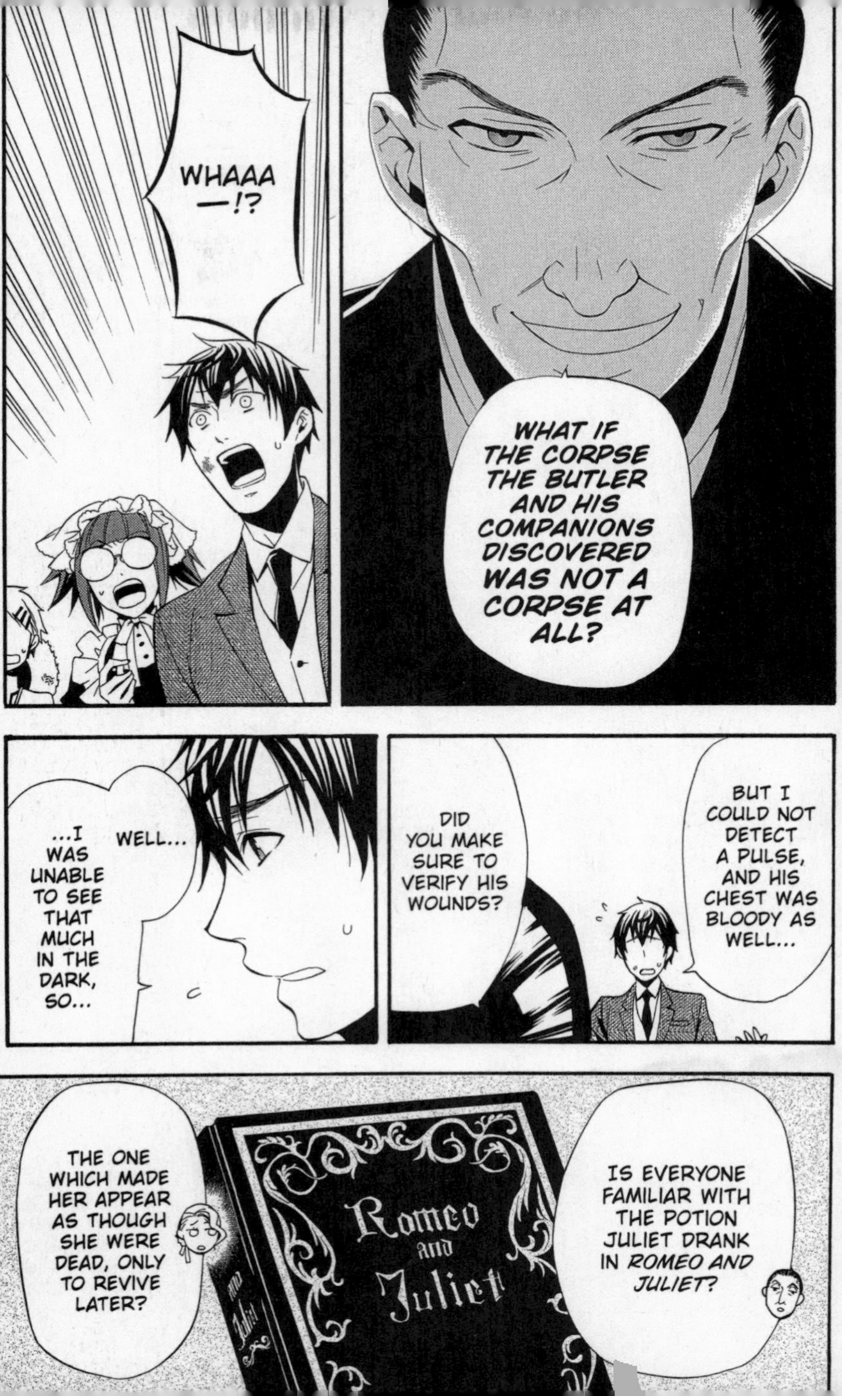
WHAT IF THE CORPSE THE BUTLER AND HIS COMPANIONS DISCOVERED WAS NOT A CORPSE AT ALL?
WHAAA—!?
BUT I COULD NOT DETECT A PULSE, AND HIS CHEST WAS BLOODY AS WELL...
DID YOU MAKE SURE TO VERIFY HIS WOUNDS?
WELL...
...I WAS UNABLE TO SEE THAT MUCH IN THE DARK, SO...
IS EVERYONE FAMILIAR WITH THE POTION JULIET DRANK IN *ROMEO AND JULIET*?
THE ONE WHICH MADE HER APPEAR AS THOUGH SHE WERE DEAD, ONLY TO REVIVE LATER?
Romeo and Juliet

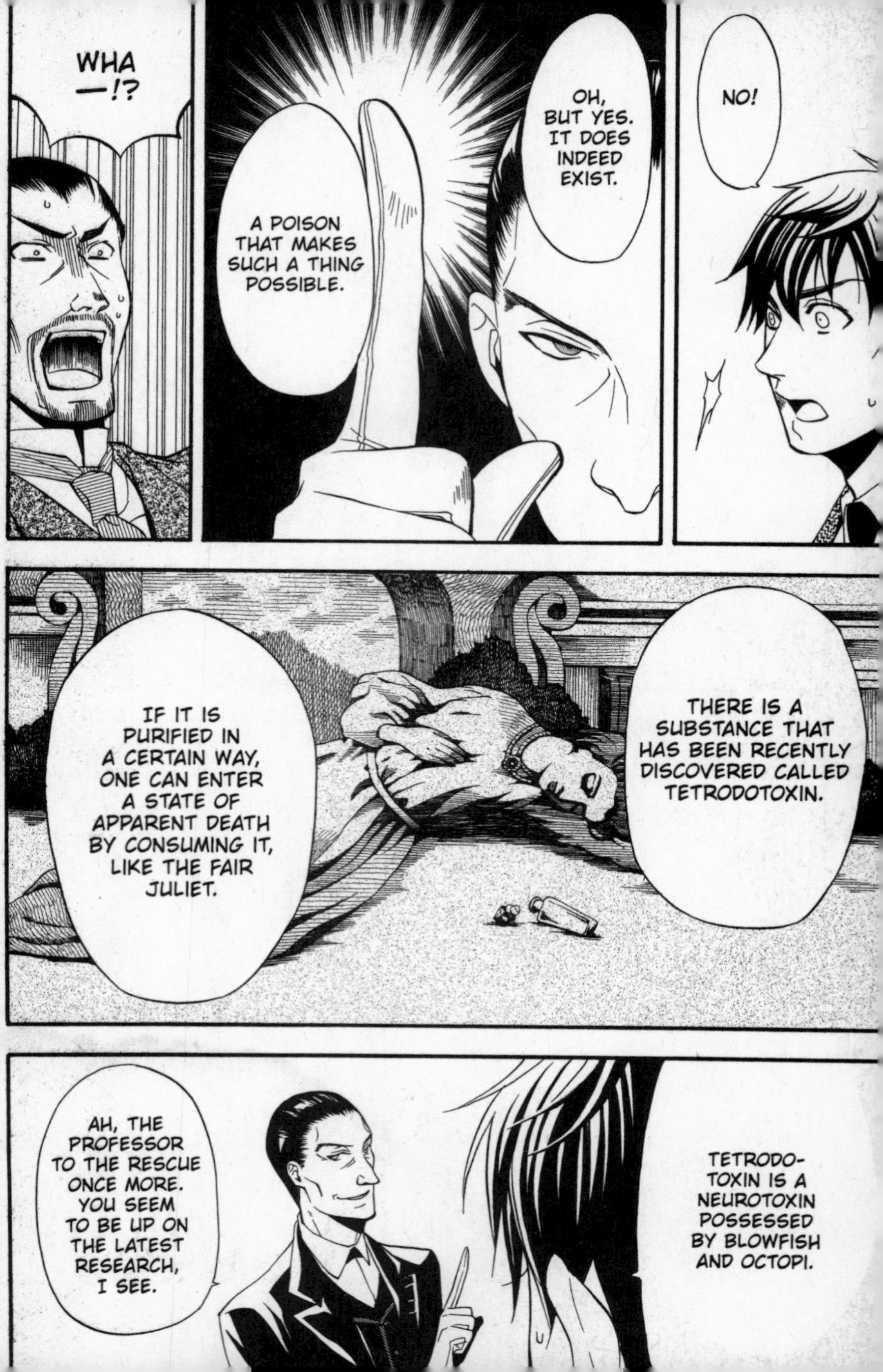
NO!
OH, BUT YES. IT DOES INDEED EXIST.
A POISON THAT MAKES SUCH A THING POSSIBLE.
WHA—!?
THERE IS A SUBSTANCE THAT HAS BEEN RECENTLY DISCOVERED CALLED TETRODOTOXIN.
IF IT IS PURIFIED IN A CERTAIN WAY, ONE CAN ENTER A STATE OF APPARENT DEATH BY CONSUMING IT, LIKE THE FAIR JULIET.
TETRODO-TOXIN IS A NEUROTOXIN POSSESSED BY BLOWFISH AND OCTOPI.
AH, THE PROFESSOR TO THE RESCUE ONCE MORE. YOU SEEM TO BE UP ON THE LATEST RESEARCH, I SEE.

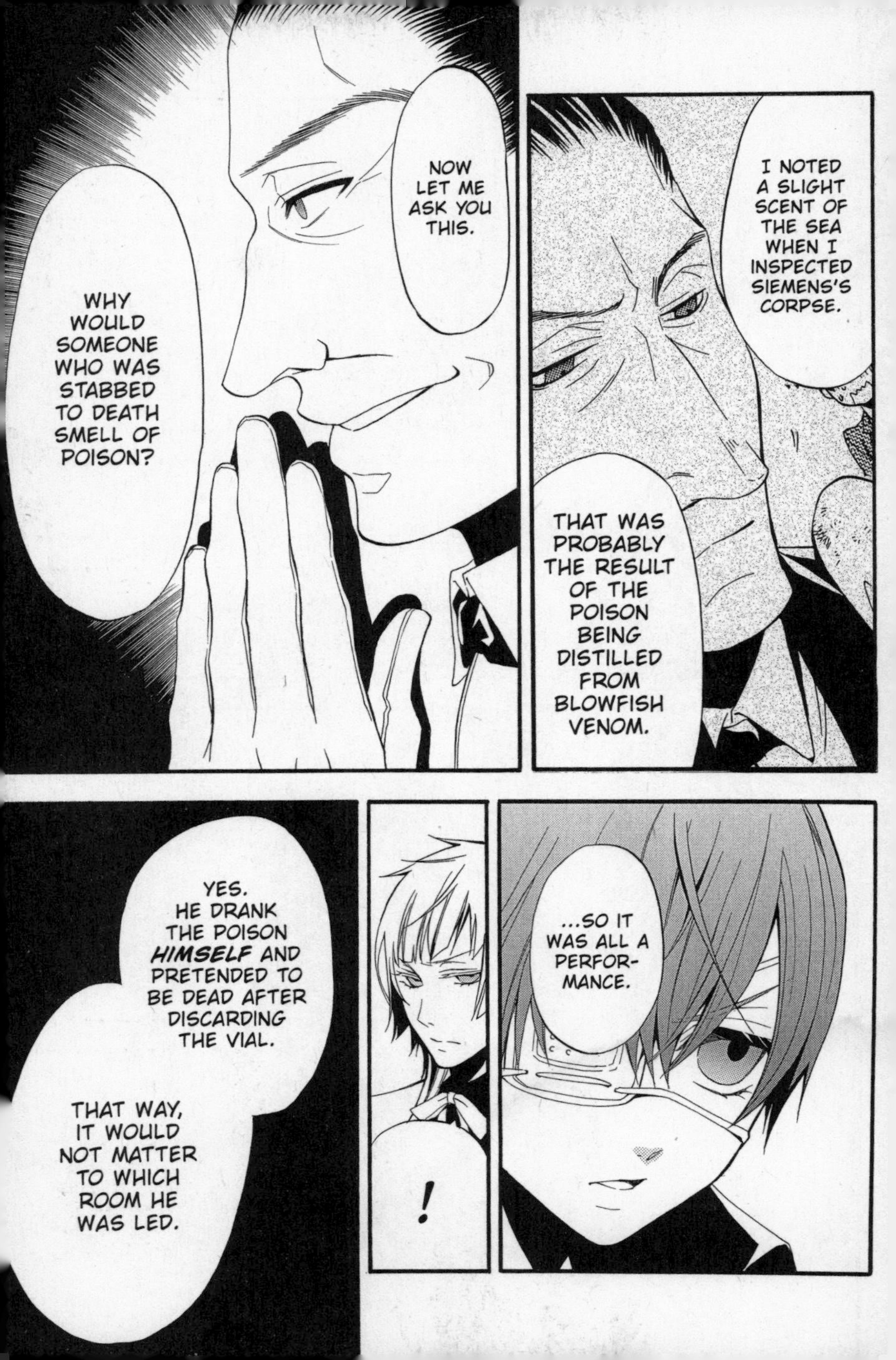
I NOTED A SLIGHT SCENT OF THE SEA WHEN I INSPECTED SIEMENS'S CORPSE.
THAT WAS PROBABLY THE RESULT OF THE POISON BEING DISTILLED FROM BLOWFISH VENOM.
NOW LET ME ASK YOU THIS.
WHY WOULD SOMEONE WHO WAS STABBED TO DEATH SMELL OF POISON?
...SO IT WAS ALL A PERFORMANCE.
!
YES. HE DRANK THE POISON *HIMSELF* AND PRETENDED TO BE DEAD AFTER DISCARDING THE VIAL.
THAT WAY, IT WOULD NOT MATTER TO WHICH ROOM HE WAS LED.

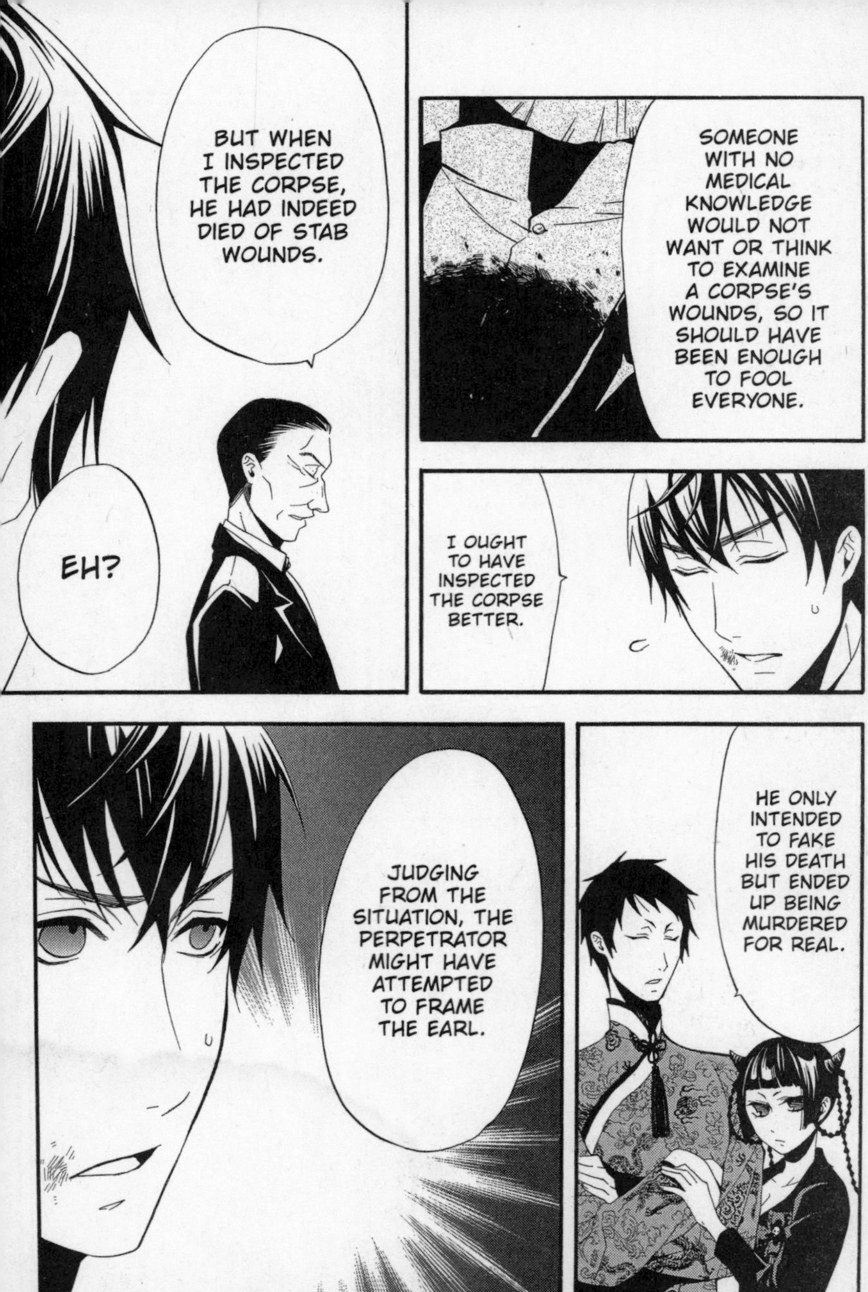
SOMEONE WITH NO MEDICAL KNOWLEDGE WOULD NOT WANT OR THINK TO EXAMINE A CORPSE'S WOUNDS, SO IT SHOULD HAVE BEEN ENOUGH TO FOOL EVERYONE.
I OUGHT TO HAVE INSPECTED THE CORPSE BETTER.
BUT WHEN I INSPECTED THE CORPSE, HE HAD INDEED DIED OF STAB WOUNDS.
EH?
HE ONLY INTENDED TO FAKE HIS DEATH BUT ENDED UP BEING MURDERED FOR REAL.
JUDGING FROM THE SITUATION, THE PERPETRATOR MIGHT HAVE ATTEMPTED TO FRAME THE EARL.

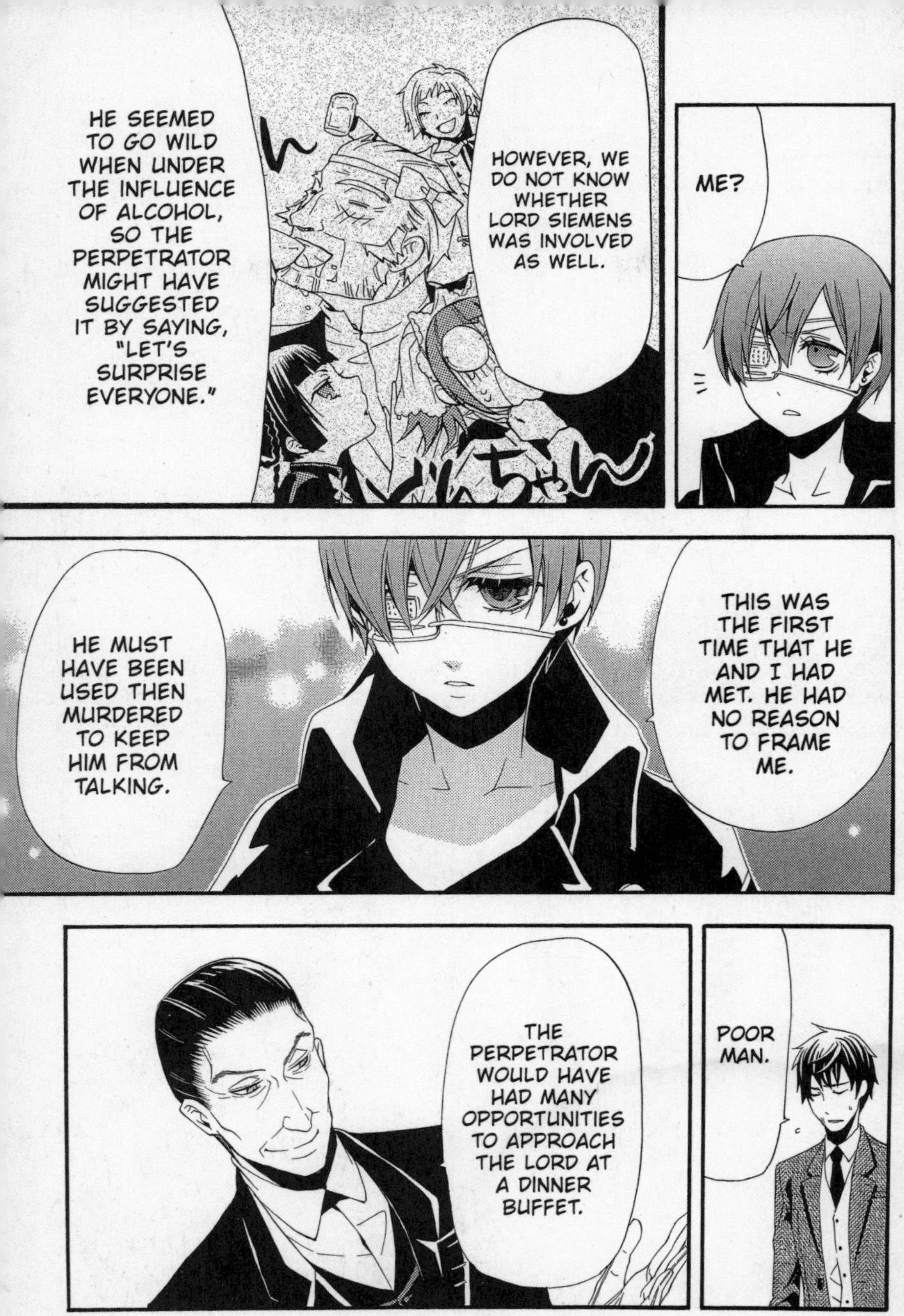
ME?
HOWEVER, WE DO NOT KNOW WHETHER LORD SIEMENS WAS INVOLVED AS WELL.
HE SEEMED TO GO WILD WHEN UNDER THE INFLUENCE OF ALCOHOL, SO THE PERPETRATOR MIGHT HAVE SUGGESTED IT BY SAYING, "LET'S SURPRISE EVERYONE."
THIS WAS THE FIRST TIME THAT HE AND I HAD MET. HE HAD NO REASON TO FRAME ME.
HE MUST HAVE BEEN USED THEN MURDERED TO KEEP HIM FROM TALKING.
POOR MAN.
THE PERPETRATOR WOULD HAVE HAD MANY OPPORTUNITIES TO APPROACH THE LORD AT A DINNER BUFFET.

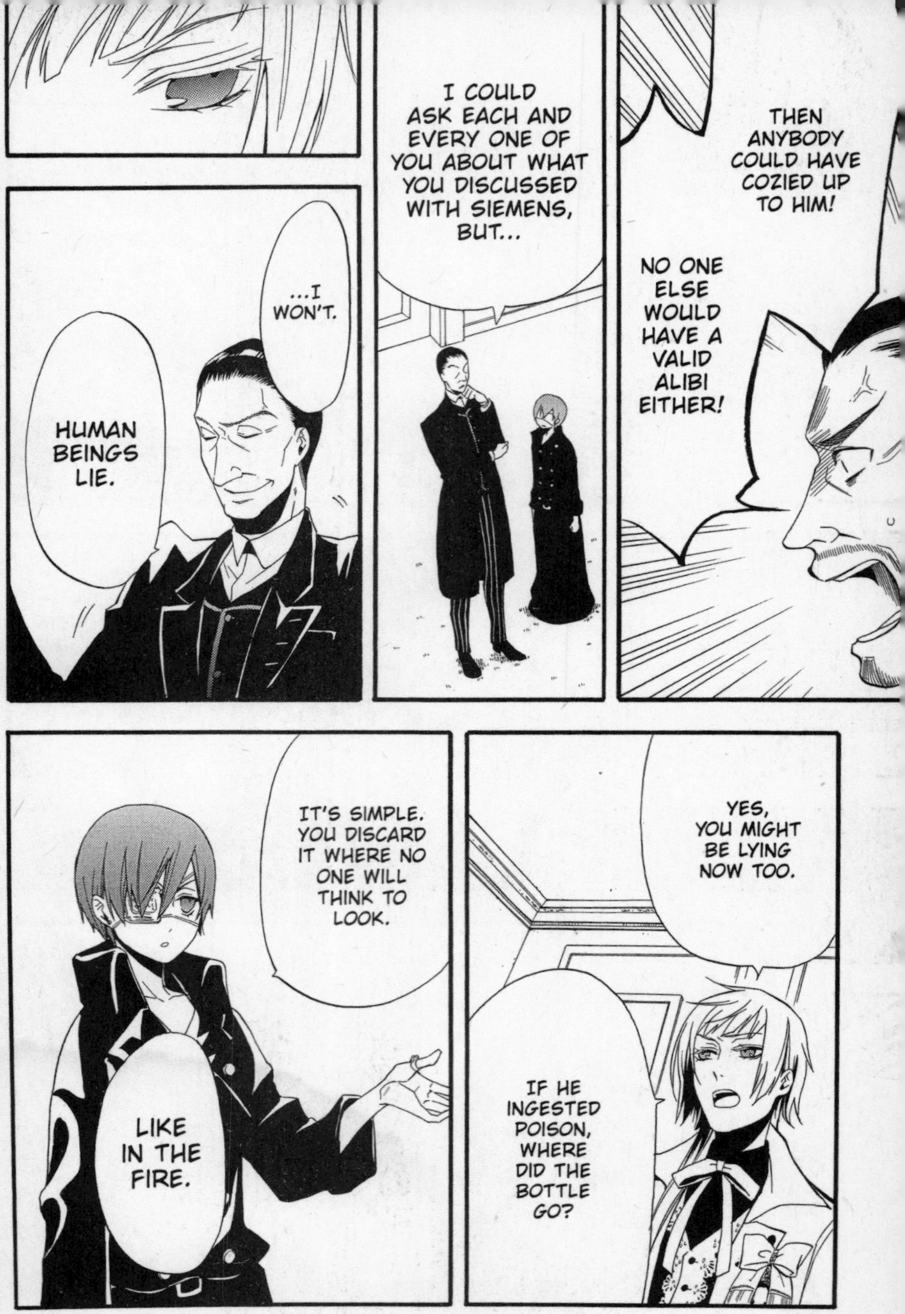
THEN ANYBODY COULD HAVE COZIED UP TO HIM!
NO ONE ELSE WOULD HAVE A VALID ALIBI EITHER!
I COULD ASK EACH AND EVERY ONE OF YOU ABOUT WHAT YOU DISCUSSED WITH SIEMENS, BUT...
...I WON'T.
HUMAN BEINGS LIE.
YES, YOU MIGHT BE LYING NOW TOO.
IF HE INGESTED POISON, WHERE DID THE BOTTLE GO?
IT'S SIMPLE. YOU DISCARD IT WHERE NO ONE WILL THINK TO LOOK.
LIKE IN THE FIRE.

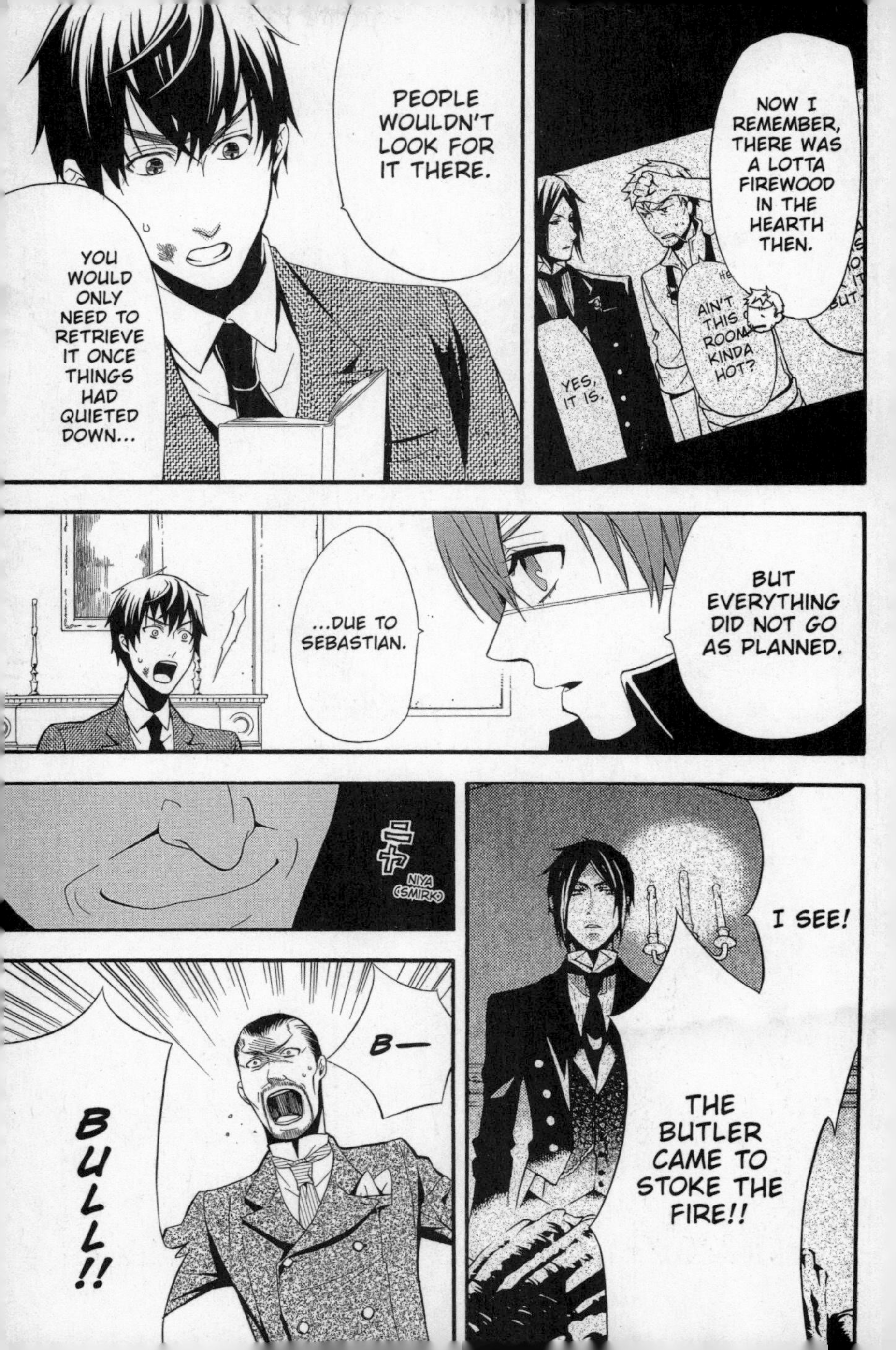
NOW I REMEMBER, THERE WAS A LOTTA FIREWOOD IN THE HEARTH THEN.
AIN'T THIS ROOM KINDA HOT?
YES, IT IS.
PEOPLE WOULDN'T LOOK FOR IT THERE.
YOU WOULD ONLY NEED TO RETRIEVE IT ONCE THINGS HAD QUIETED DOWN...
BUT EVERYTHING DID NOT GO AS PLANNED.
...DUE TO SEBASTIAN.
I SEE!
THE BUTLER CAME TO STOKE THE FIRE!!
ニヤ
NIYA (SMIRK)
B—
BULL!!

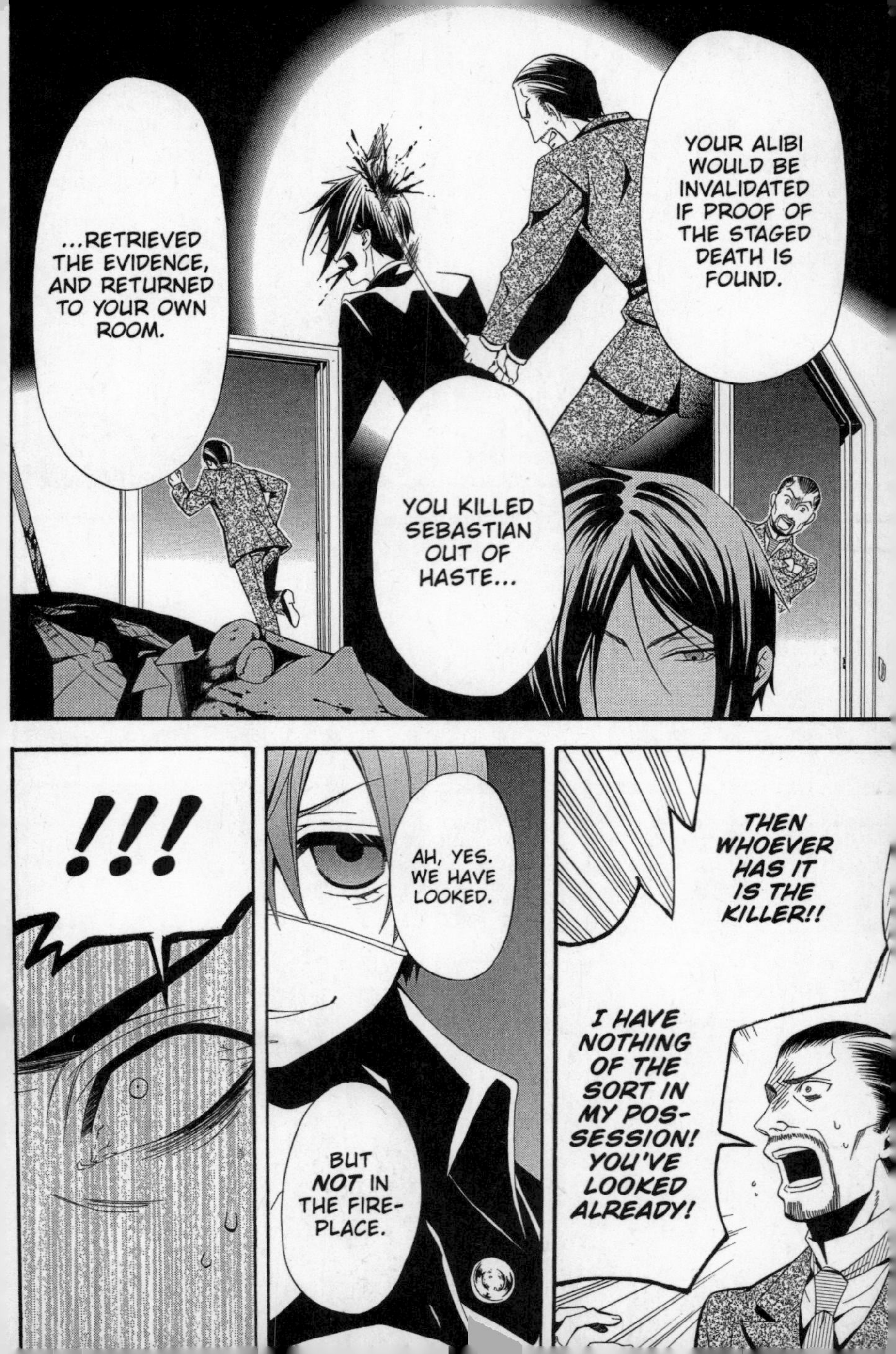
YOUR ALIBI WOULD BE INVALIDATED IF PROOF OF THE STAGED DEATH IS FOUND.
YOU KILLED SEBASTIAN OUT OF HASTE...
...RETRIEVED THE EVIDENCE, AND RETURNED TO YOUR OWN ROOM.
THEN WHOEVER HAS IT IS THE KILLER!!
I HAVE NOTHING OF THE SORT IN MY POS-SESSION! YOU'VE LOOKED ALREADY!
AH, YES. WE HAVE LOOKED.
BUT *NOT* IN THE FIRE-PLACE.
!!!

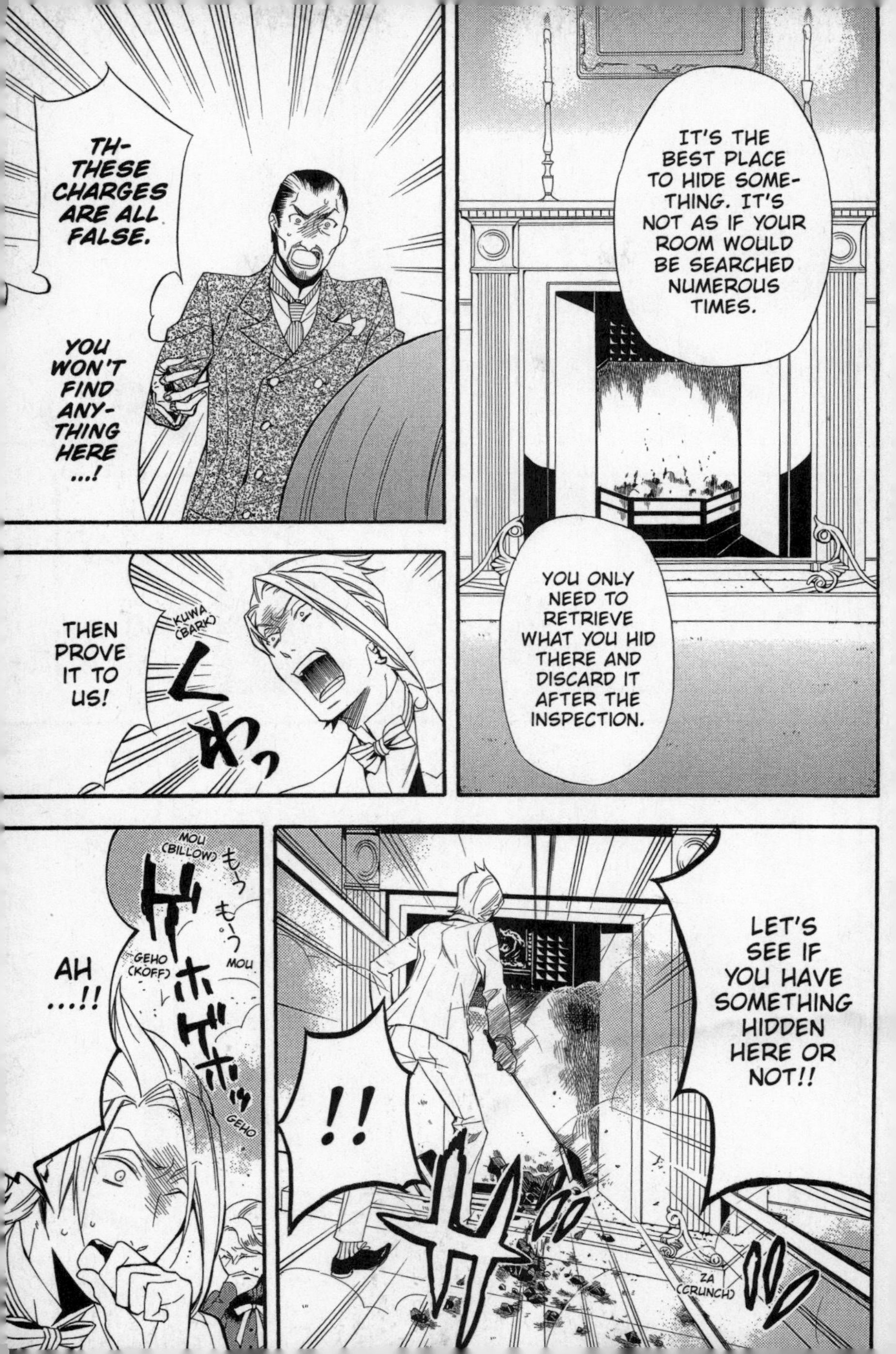
IT'S THE BEST PLACE TO HIDE SOME-THING. IT'S NOT AS IF YOUR ROOM WOULD BE SEARCHED NUMEROUS TIMES.
YOU ONLY NEED TO RETRIEVE WHAT YOU HID THERE AND DISCARD IT AFTER THE INSPECTION.
TH- THESE CHARGES ARE ALL FALSE.
YOU WON'T FIND ANYTHING HERE ...!
KUWA (BARK)
THEN PROVE IT TO US!
LET'S SEE IF YOU HAVE SOMETHING HIDDEN HERE OR NOT!!
!!
ZA (CRUNCH)
MOU (BILLOW)
MOU
GEHO (KOFF)
GEHO
AH ...!!

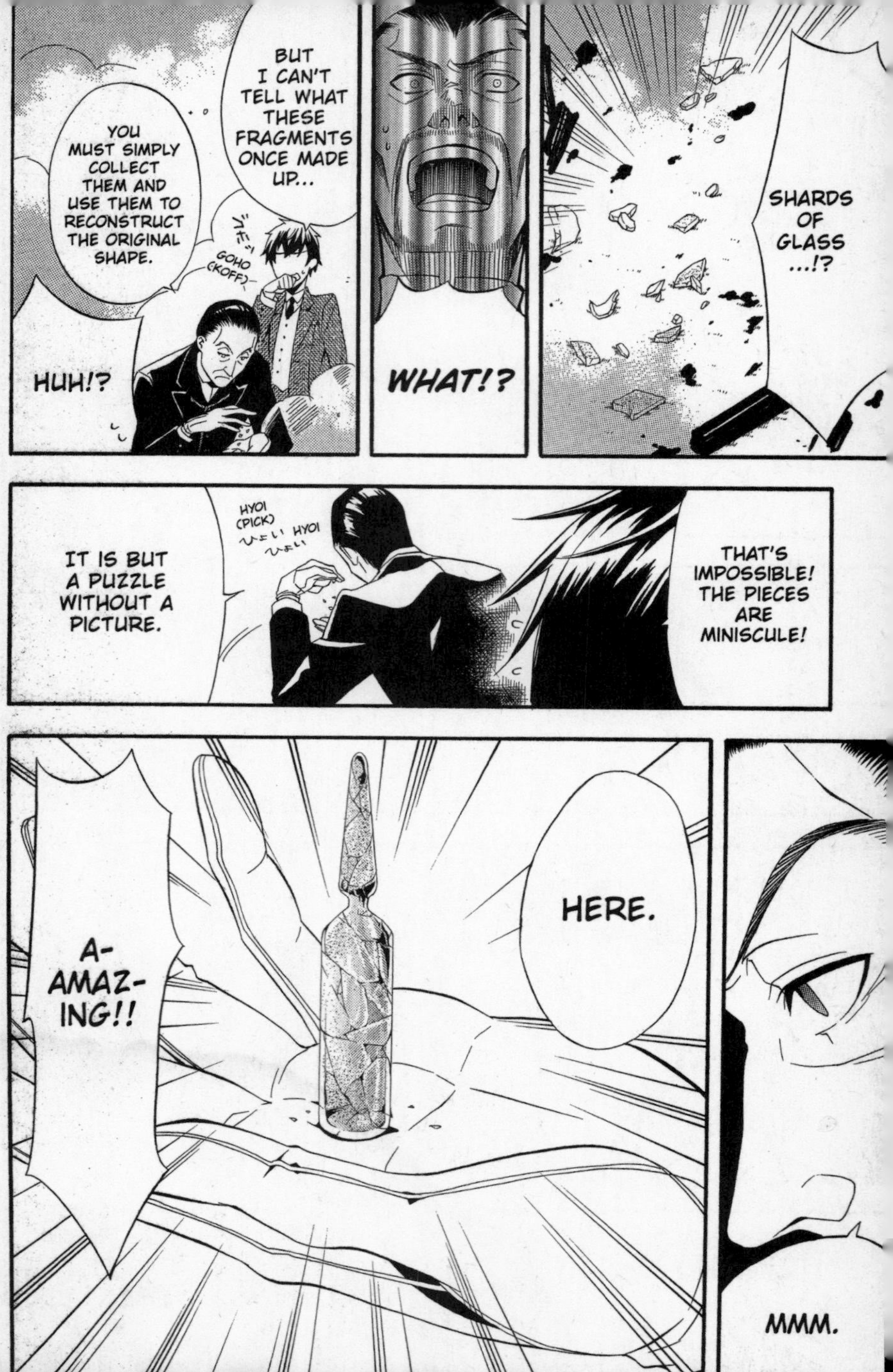
SHARDS OF GLASS ...!?
WHAT!?
BUT I CAN'T TELL WHAT THESE FRAGMENTS ONCE MADE UP...
YOU MUST SIMPLY COLLECT THEM AND USE THEM TO RECONSTRUCT THE ORIGINAL SHAPE.
GOHO (KOFF)
HUH!?
THAT'S IMPOSSIBLE! THE PIECES ARE MINISCULE!
HYOI (PICK) HYOI
IT IS BUT A PUZZLE WITHOUT A PICTURE.
MMM.
HERE.
A-AMAZ-ING!!

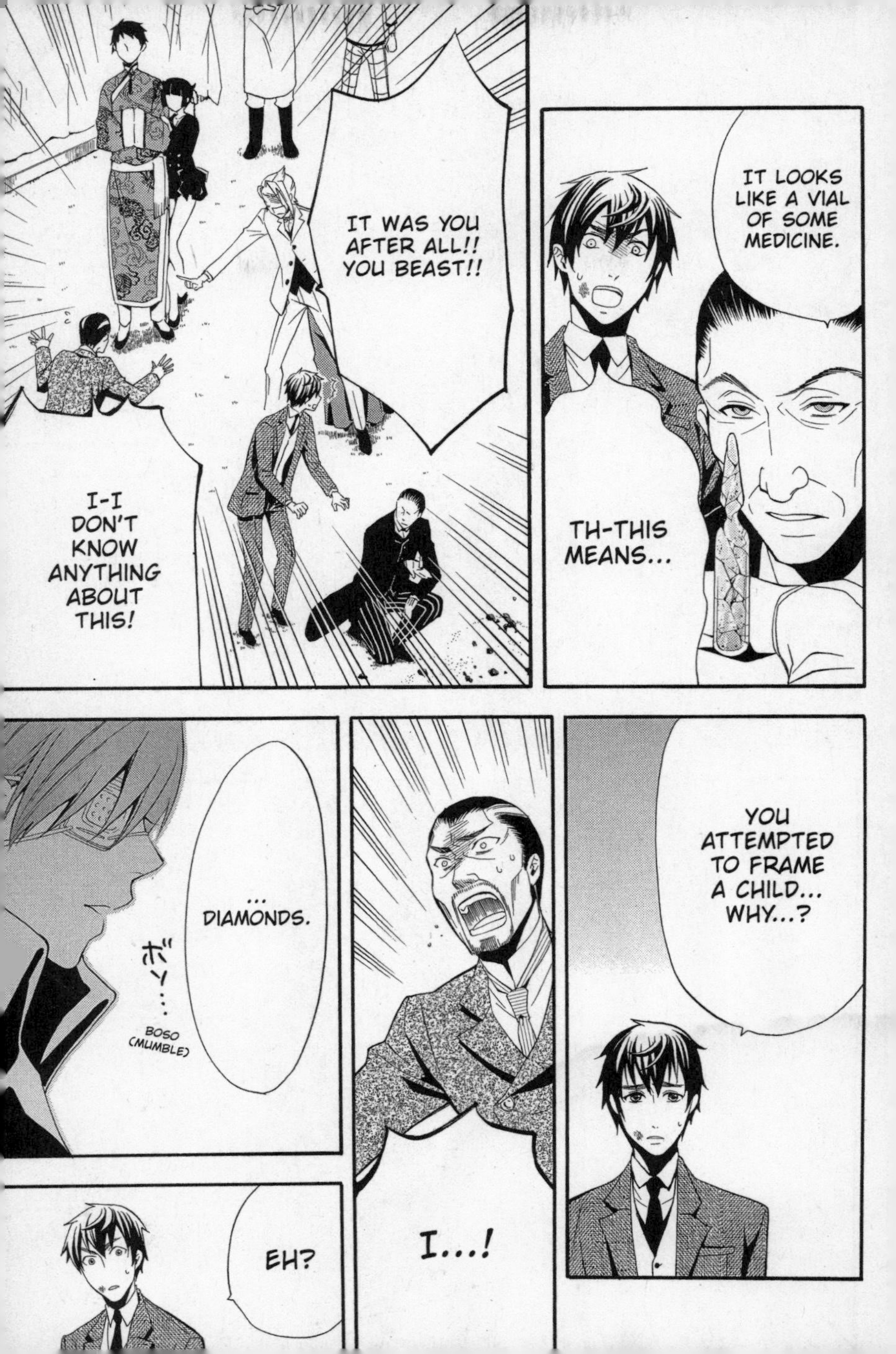
IT LOOKS LIKE A VIAL OF SOME MEDICINE.
TH-THIS MEANS...
IT WAS YOU AFTER ALL!! YOU BEAST!!
I-I DON'T KNOW ANYTHING ABOUT THIS!
YOU ATTEMPTED TO FRAME A CHILD... WHY...?
I...!
...DIAMONDS.
ボソ…
BOSO (MUMBLE)
EH?

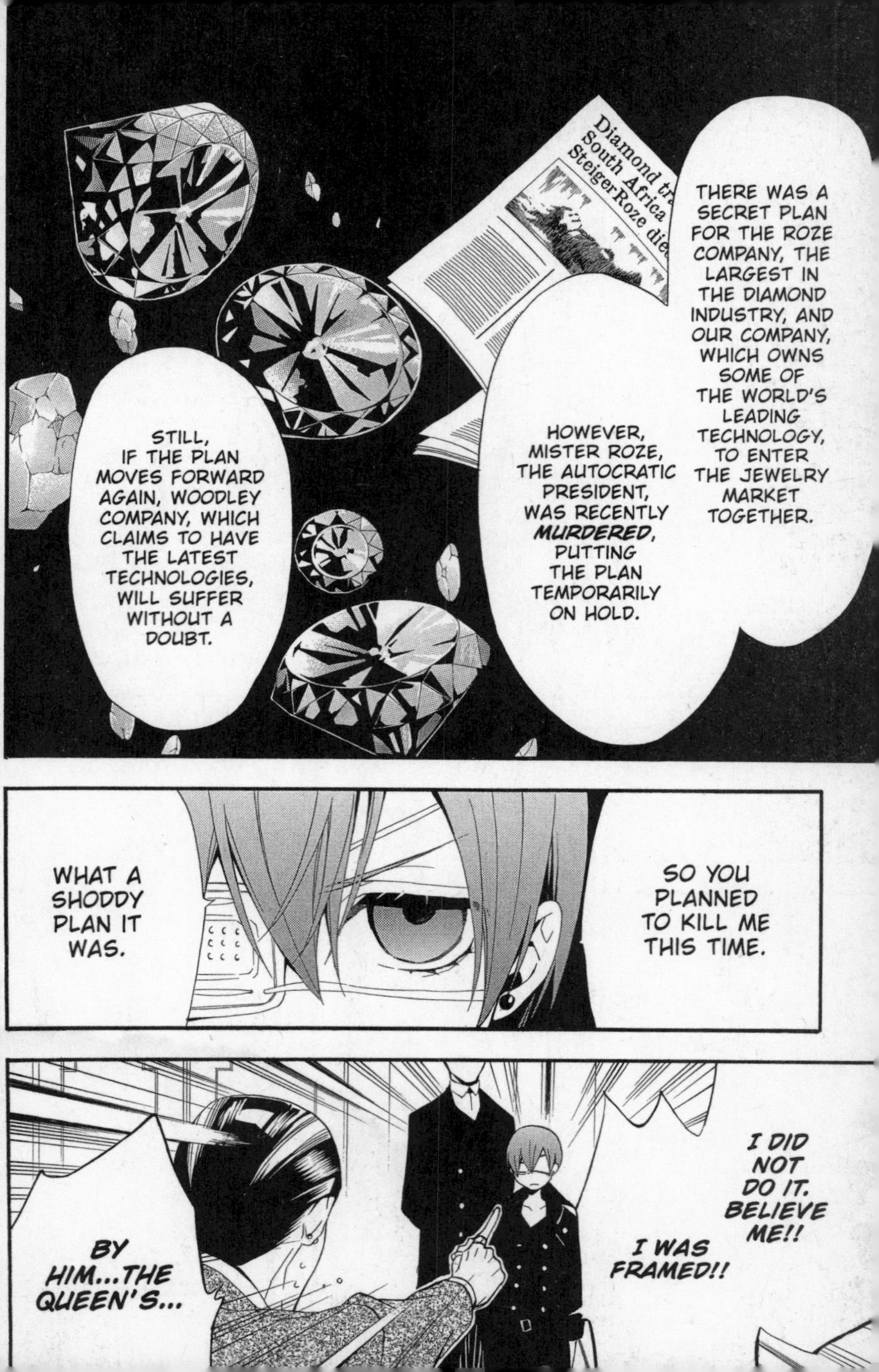
THERE WAS A SECRET PLAN FOR THE ROZE COMPANY, THE LARGEST IN THE DIAMOND INDUSTRY, AND OUR COMPANY, WHICH OWNS SOME OF THE WORLD'S LEADING TECHNOLOGY, TO ENTER THE JEWELRY MARKET TOGETHER.
HOWEVER, MISTER ROZE, THE AUTOCRATIC PRESIDENT, WAS RECENTLY *MURDERED*, PUTTING THE PLAN TEMPORARILY ON HOLD.
STILL, IF THE PLAN MOVES FORWARD AGAIN, WOODLEY COMPANY, WHICH CLAIMS TO HAVE THE LATEST TECHNOLOGIES, WILL SUFFER WITHOUT A DOUBT.
SO YOU PLANNED TO KILL ME THIS TIME.
WHAT A SHODDY PLAN IT WAS.
I DID NOT DO IT. BELIEVE ME!!
I WAS FRAMED!!
BY HIM...THE QUEEN'S...

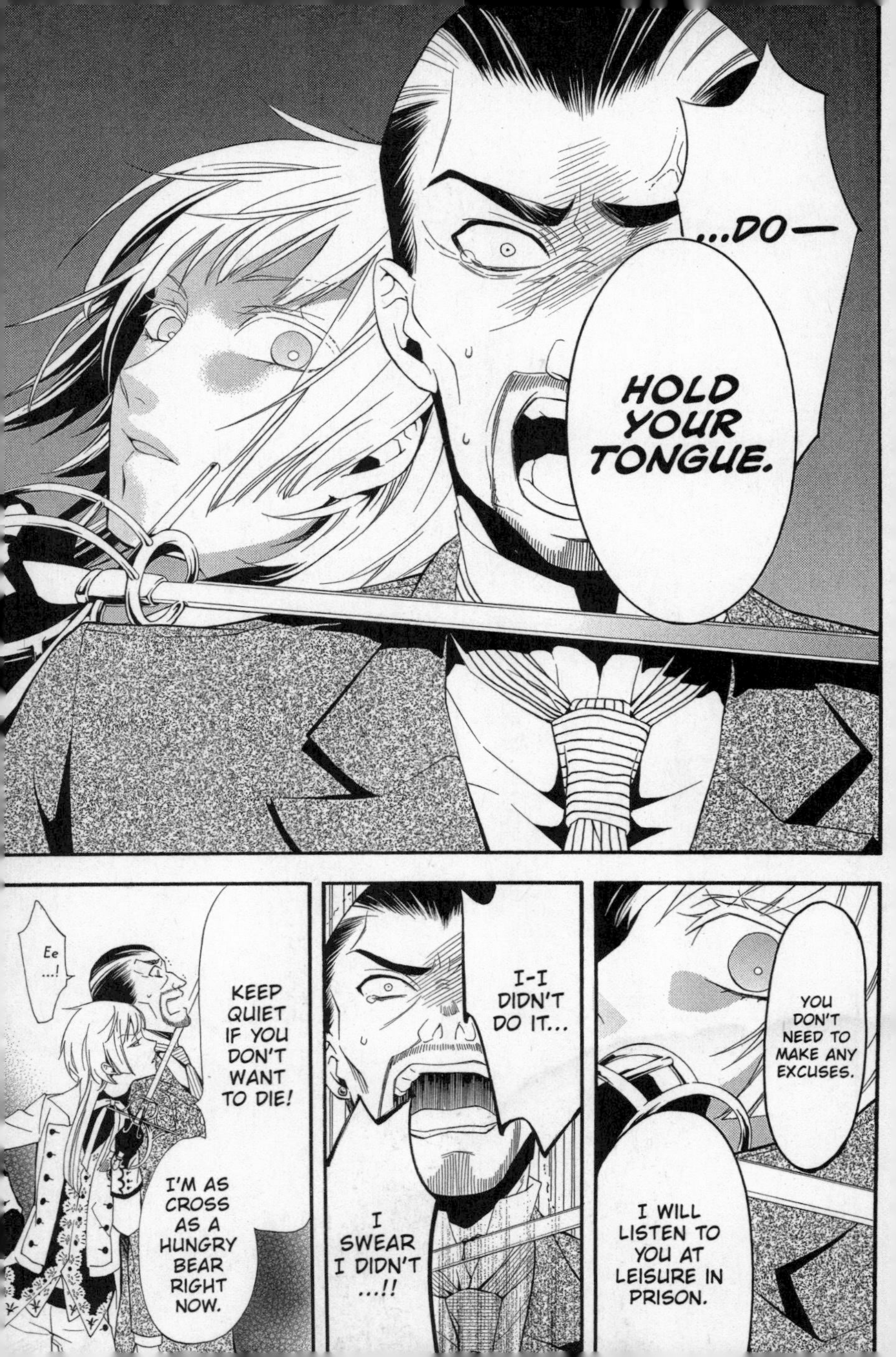

...DO—
HOLD YOUR TONGUE.
YOU DON'T NEED TO MAKE ANY EXCUSES.
I WILL LISTEN TO YOU AT LEISURE IN PRISON.
I-I DIDN'T DO IT...
I SWEAR I DIDN'T ...!!
KEEP QUIET IF YOU DON'T WANT TO DIE!
Ee ...!
I'M AS CROSS AS A HUNGRY BEAR RIGHT NOW.

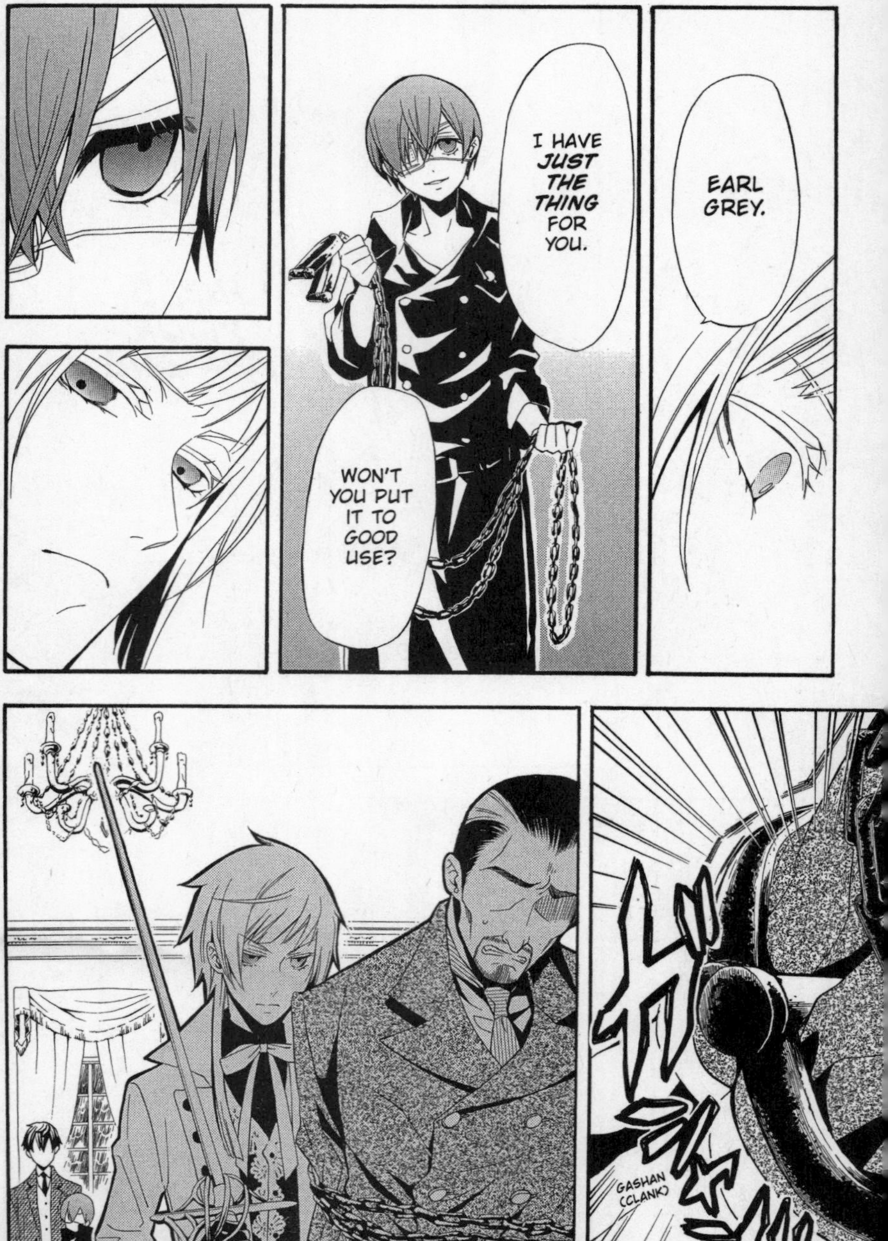
EARL GREY.
I HAVE *JUST THE THING* FOR YOU.
WON'T YOU PUT IT TO GOOD USE?
GASHAN (CLANK)

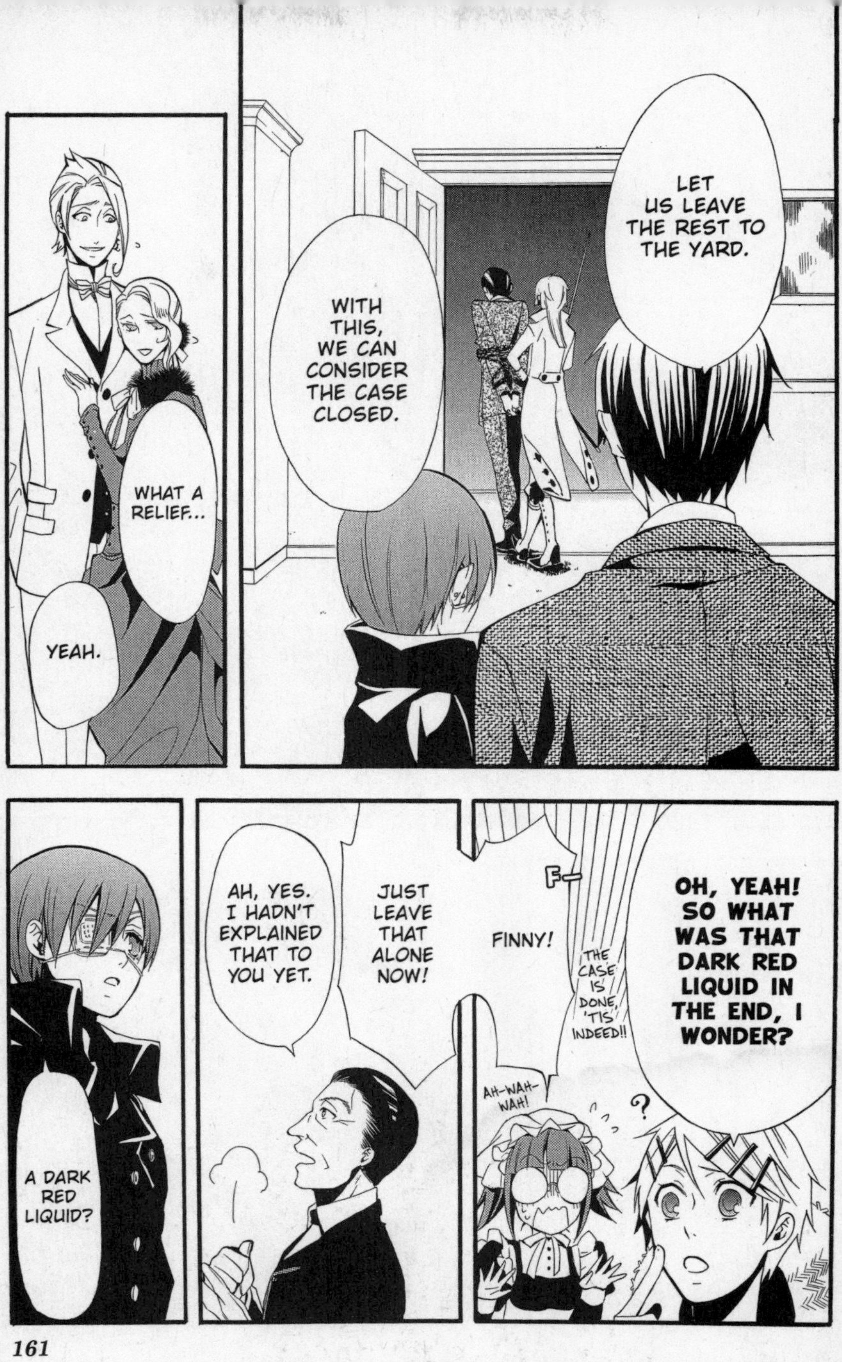

LET US LEAVE THE REST TO THE YARD.
WITH THIS, WE CAN CONSIDER THE CASE CLOSED.
WHAT A RELIEF...
YEAH.
OH, YEAH! SO WHAT WAS THAT DARK RED LIQUID IN THE END, I WONDER?
F—
THE CASE IS DONE, 'TIS INDEED!!
FINNY!
AH-WAH-WAH!
JUST LEAVE THAT ALONE NOW!
AH, YES. I HADN'T EXPLAINED THAT TO YOU YET.
A DARK RED LIQUID?

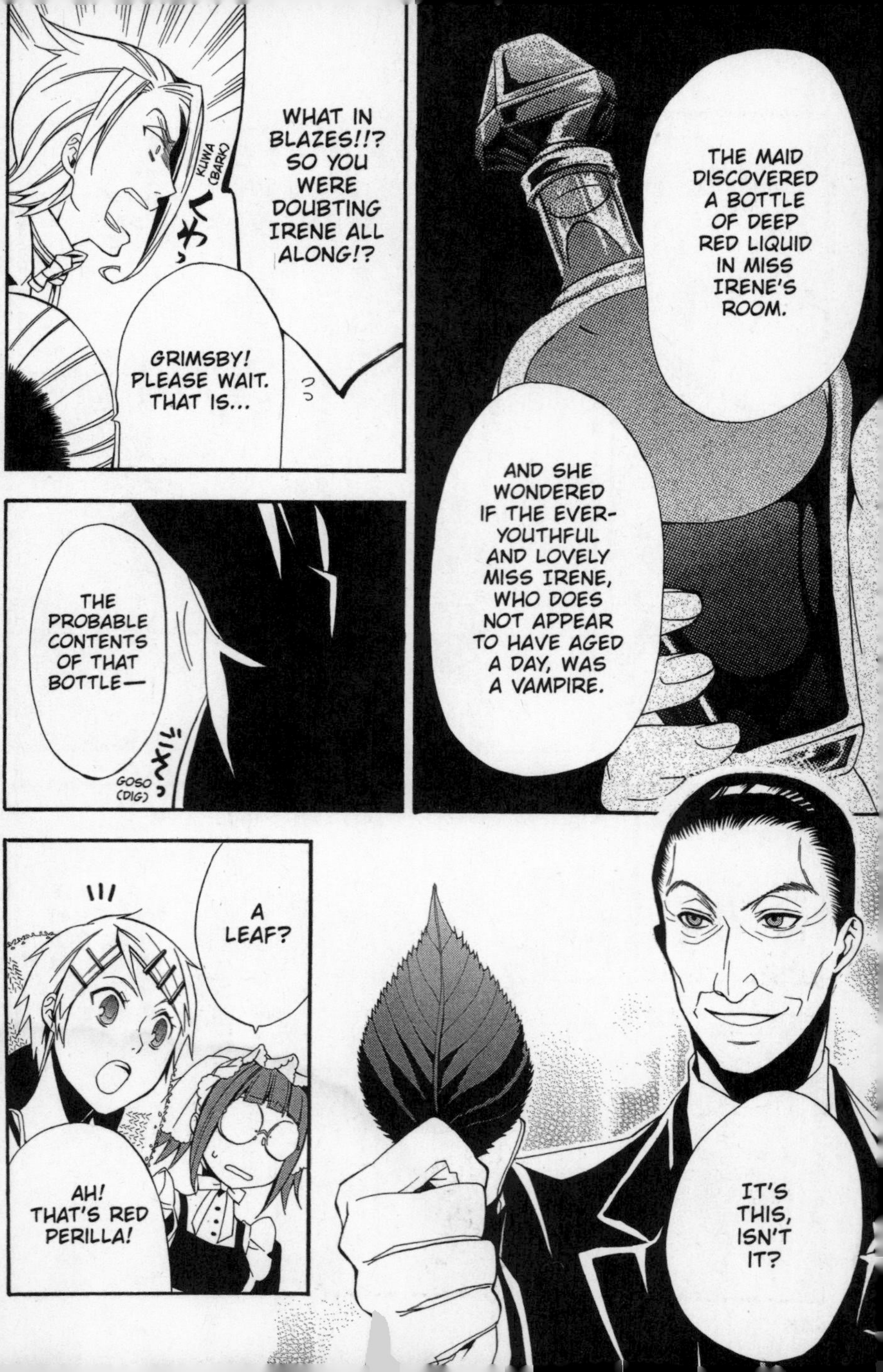

THE MAID DISCOVERED A BOTTLE OF DEEP RED LIQUID IN MISS IRENE'S ROOM.
AND SHE WONDERED IF THE EVER-YOUTHFUL AND LOVELY MISS IRENE, WHO DOES NOT APPEAR TO HAVE AGED A DAY, WAS A VAMPIRE.
WHAT IN BLAZES!!? SO YOU WERE DOUBTING IRENE ALL ALONG!?
KUWA (BARK)
GRIMSBY! PLEASE WAIT. THAT IS...
THE PROBABLE CONTENTS OF THAT BOTTLE—
GOSO (DIG)
IT'S THIS, ISN'T IT?
A LEAF?
AH! THAT'S RED PERILLA!

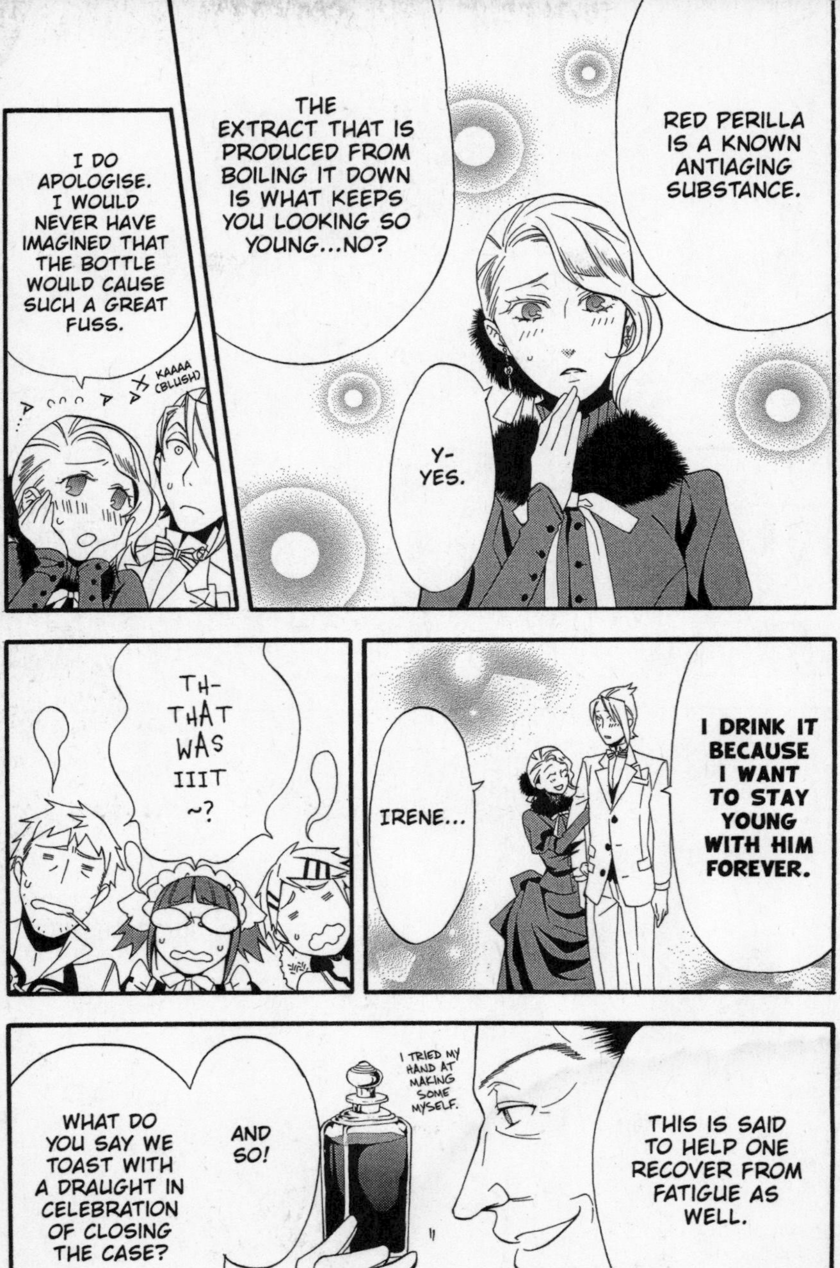
RED PERILLA IS A KNOWN ANTIAGING SUBSTANCE.
THE EXTRACT THAT IS PRODUCED FROM BOILING IT DOWN IS WHAT KEEPS YOU LOOKING SO YOUNG...NO?
Y-YES.
I DO APOLOGISE. I WOULD NEVER HAVE IMAGINED THAT THE BOTTLE WOULD CAUSE SUCH A GREAT FUSS.
KAAAA (BLUSH)
I DRINK IT BECAUSE I WANT TO STAY YOUNG WITH HIM FOREVER.
IRENE...
TH-THAT WAS IIIT ~?
THIS IS SAID TO HELP ONE RECOVER FROM FATIGUE AS WELL.
I TRIED MY HAND AT MAKING SOME MYSELF.
AND SO!
WHAT DO YOU SAY WE TOAST WITH A DRAUGHT IN CELEBRATION OF CLOSING THE CASE?

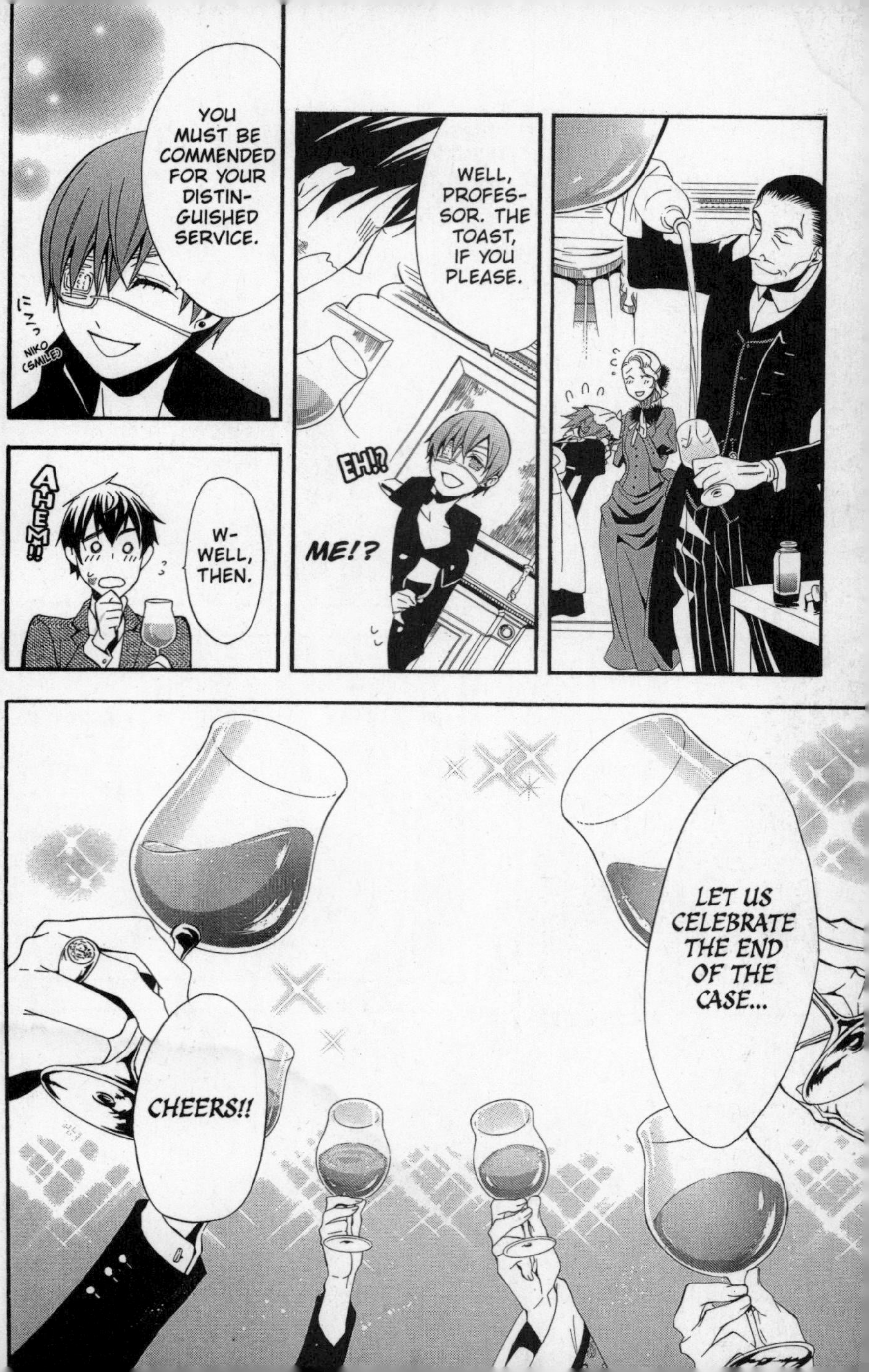
WELL, PROFESSOR. THE TOAST, IF YOU PLEASE.
EH!?
ME!?
YOU MUST BE COMMENDED FOR YOUR DISTINGUISHED SERVICE.
NIKO (SMILE)
AHEM!!
W-WELL, THEN.
LET US CELEBRATE THE END OF THE CASE...
CHEERS!!

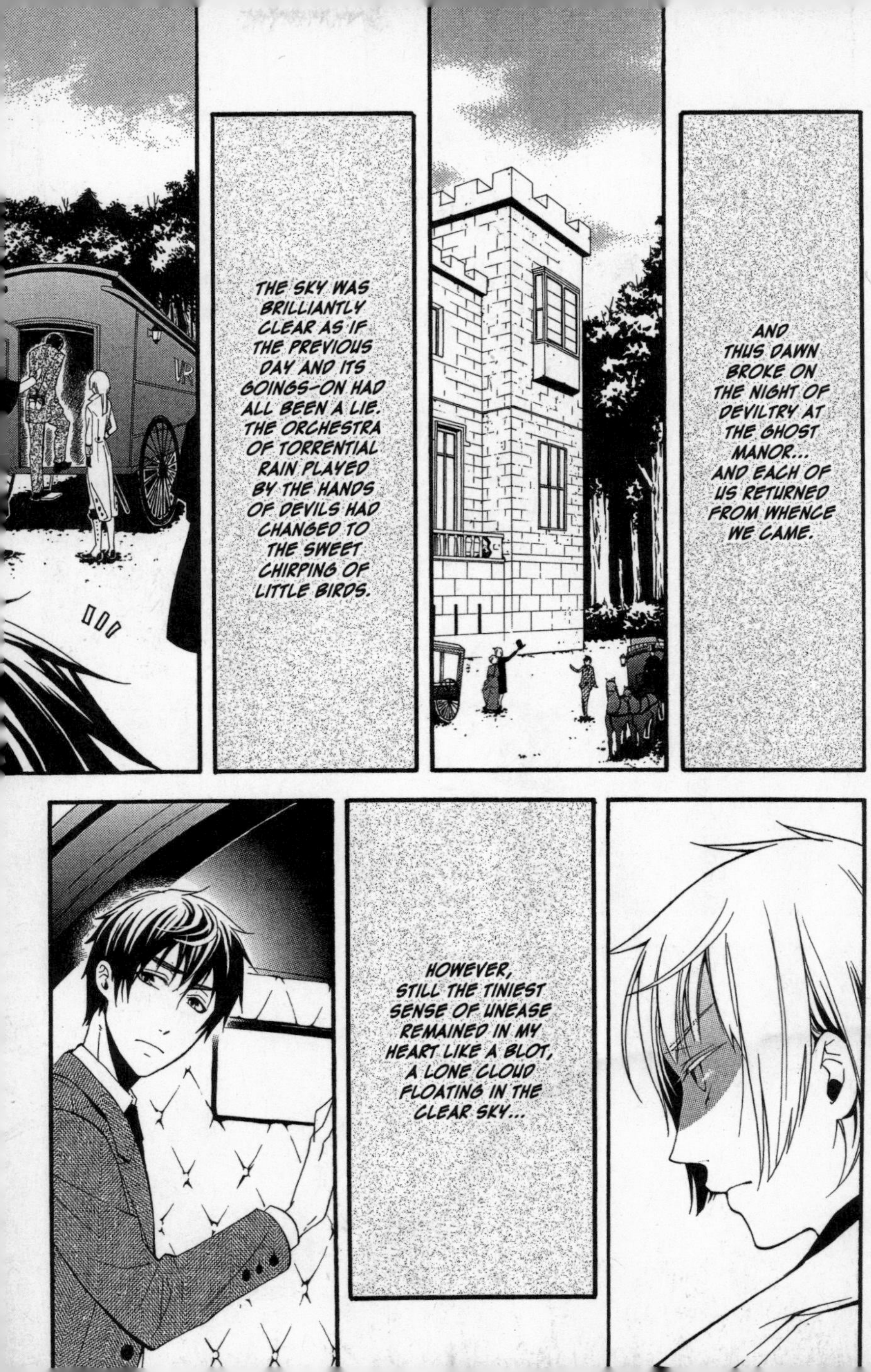
AND THUS DAWN BROKE ON THE NIGHT OF DEVILTRY AT THE GHOST MANOR... AND EACH OF US RETURNED FROM WHENCE WE CAME.
THE SKY WAS BRILLIANTLY CLEAR AS IF THE PREVIOUS DAY AND ITS GOINGS-ON HAD ALL BEEN A LIE. THE ORCHESTRA OF TORRENTIAL RAIN PLAYED BY THE HANDS OF DEVILS HAD CHANGED TO THE SWEET CHIRPING OF LITTLE BIRDS.
HOWEVER, STILL THE TINIEST SENSE OF UNEASE REMAINED IN MY HEART LIKE A BLOT, A LONE CLOUD FLOATING IN THE CLEAR SKY...

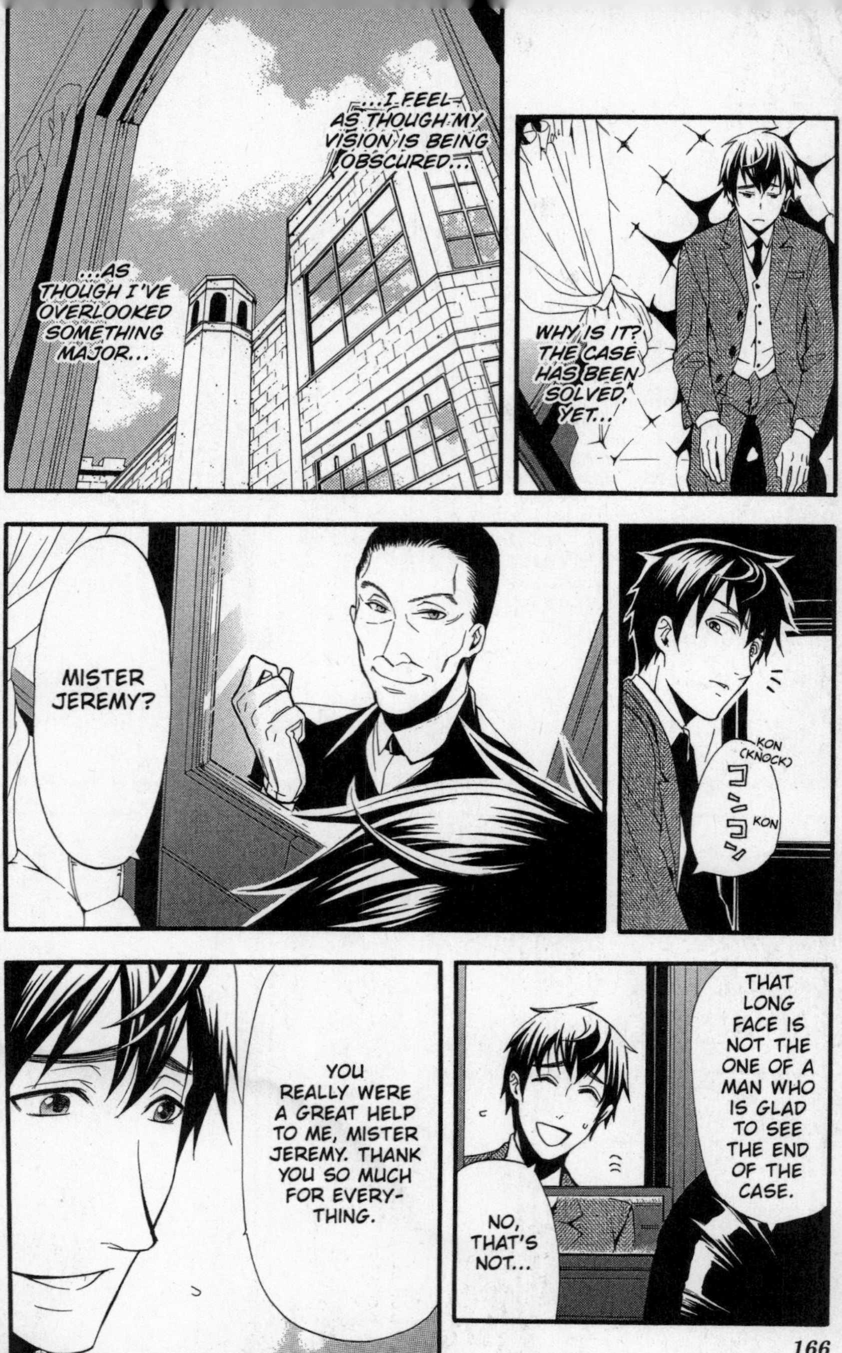
WHY IS IT? THE CASE HAS BEEN SOLVED, YET...
...I FEEL AS THOUGH MY VISION IS BEING OBSCURED...
...AS THOUGH I'VE OVERLOOKED SOMETHING MAJOR...
KON (KNOCK)
KON
MISTER JEREMY?
THAT LONG FACE IS NOT THE ONE OF A MAN WHO IS GLAD TO SEE THE END OF THE CASE.
NO, THAT'S NOT...
YOU REALLY WERE A GREAT HELP TO ME, MISTER JEREMY. THANK YOU SO MUCH FOR EVERY-THING.

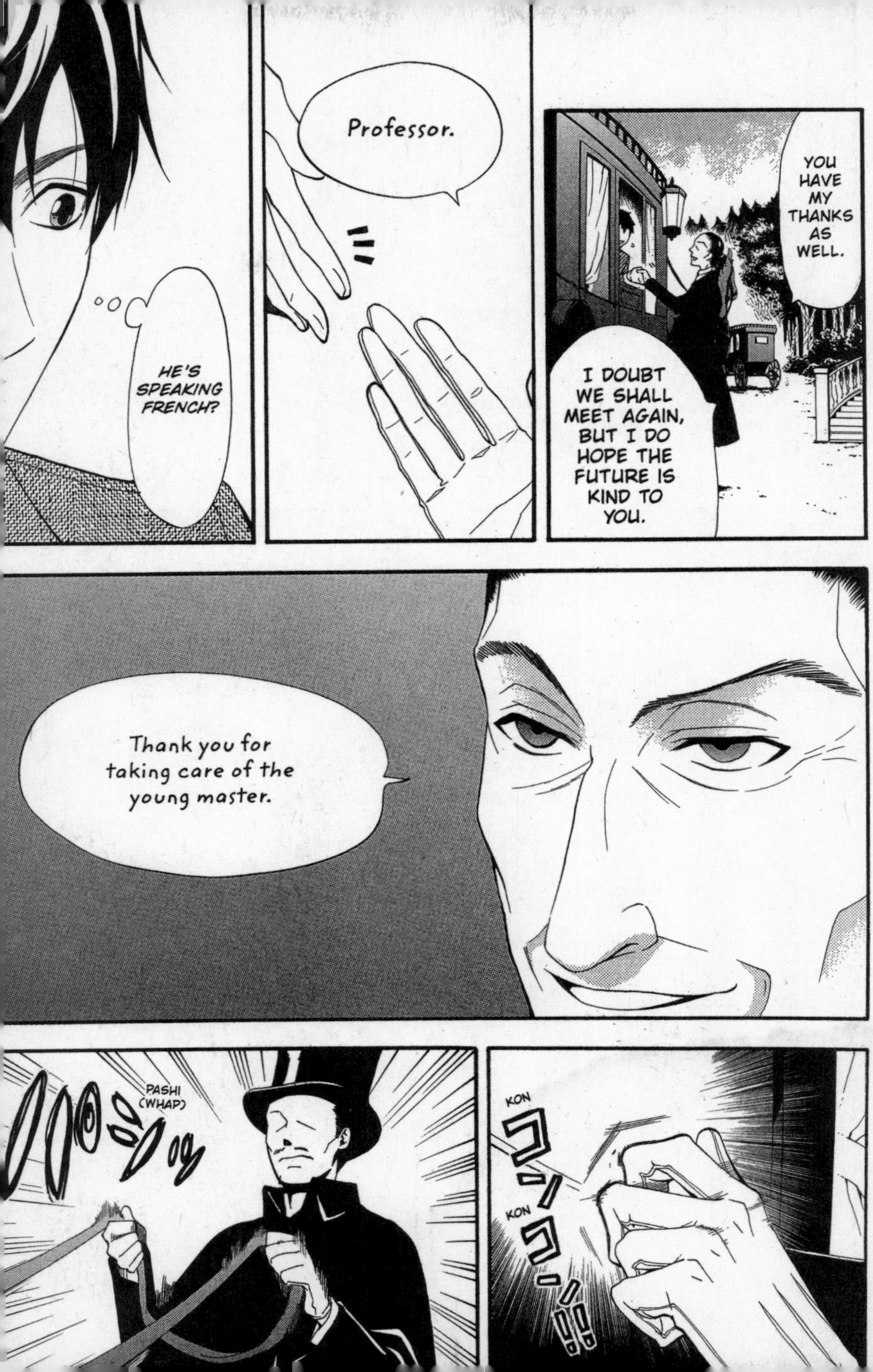
YOU HAVE MY THANKS AS WELL.
I DOUBT WE SHALL MEET AGAIN, BUT I DO HOPE THE FUTURE IS KIND TO YOU.
Professor.
HE'S SPEAKING FRENCH?
Thank you for taking care of the young master.
KON
KON
PASHI (WHAP)

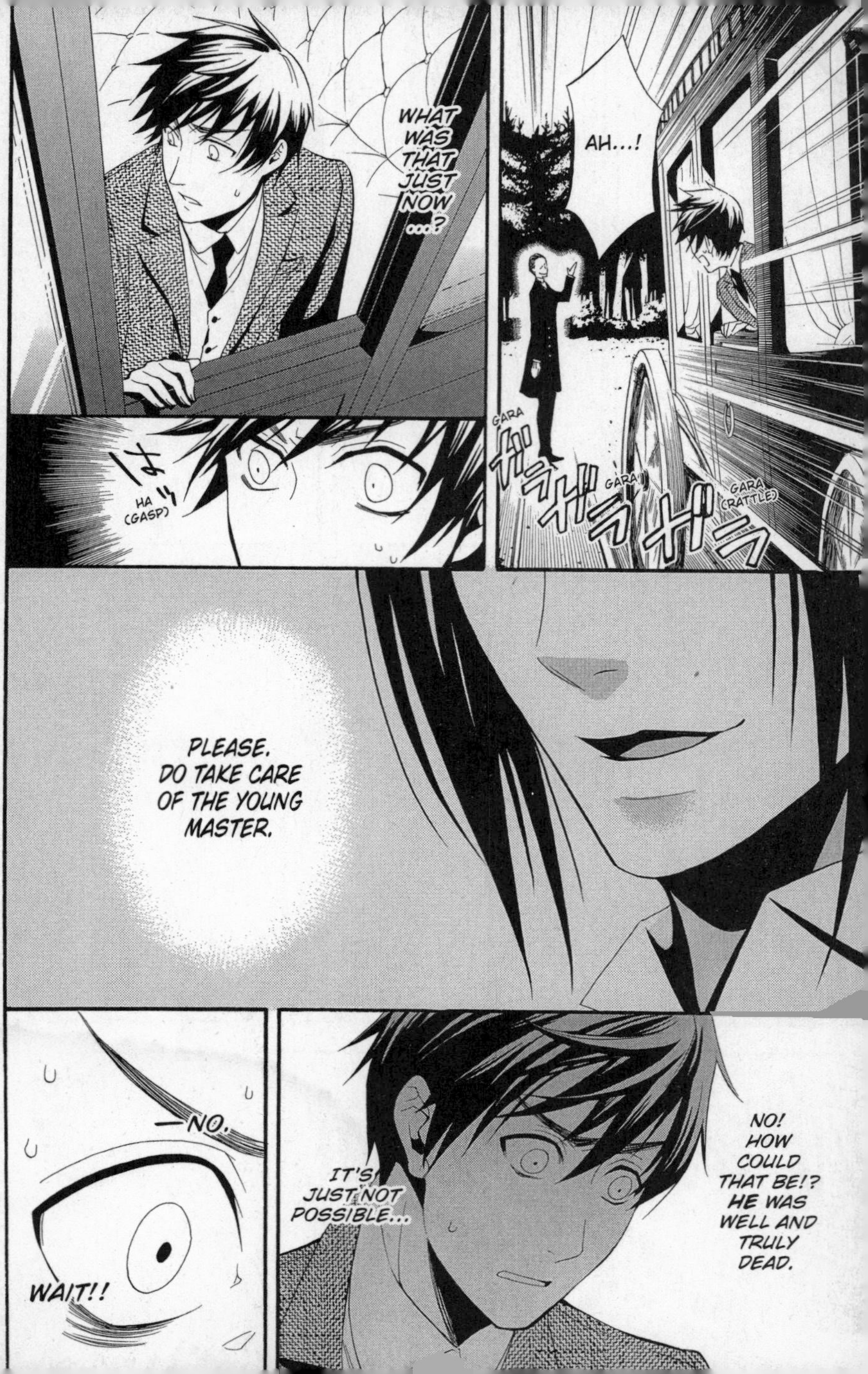
AH...!
ガラ GARA
ガラ GARA
ガラ GARA (RATTLE)
WHAT WAS THAT JUST NOW ...?
はッ HA (GASP)
PLEASE. DO TAKE CARE OF THE YOUNG MASTER.
NO! HOW COULD THAT BE!? HE WAS WELL AND TRULY DEAD.
IT'S JUST NOT POSSIBLE...
—NO.
WAIT!!

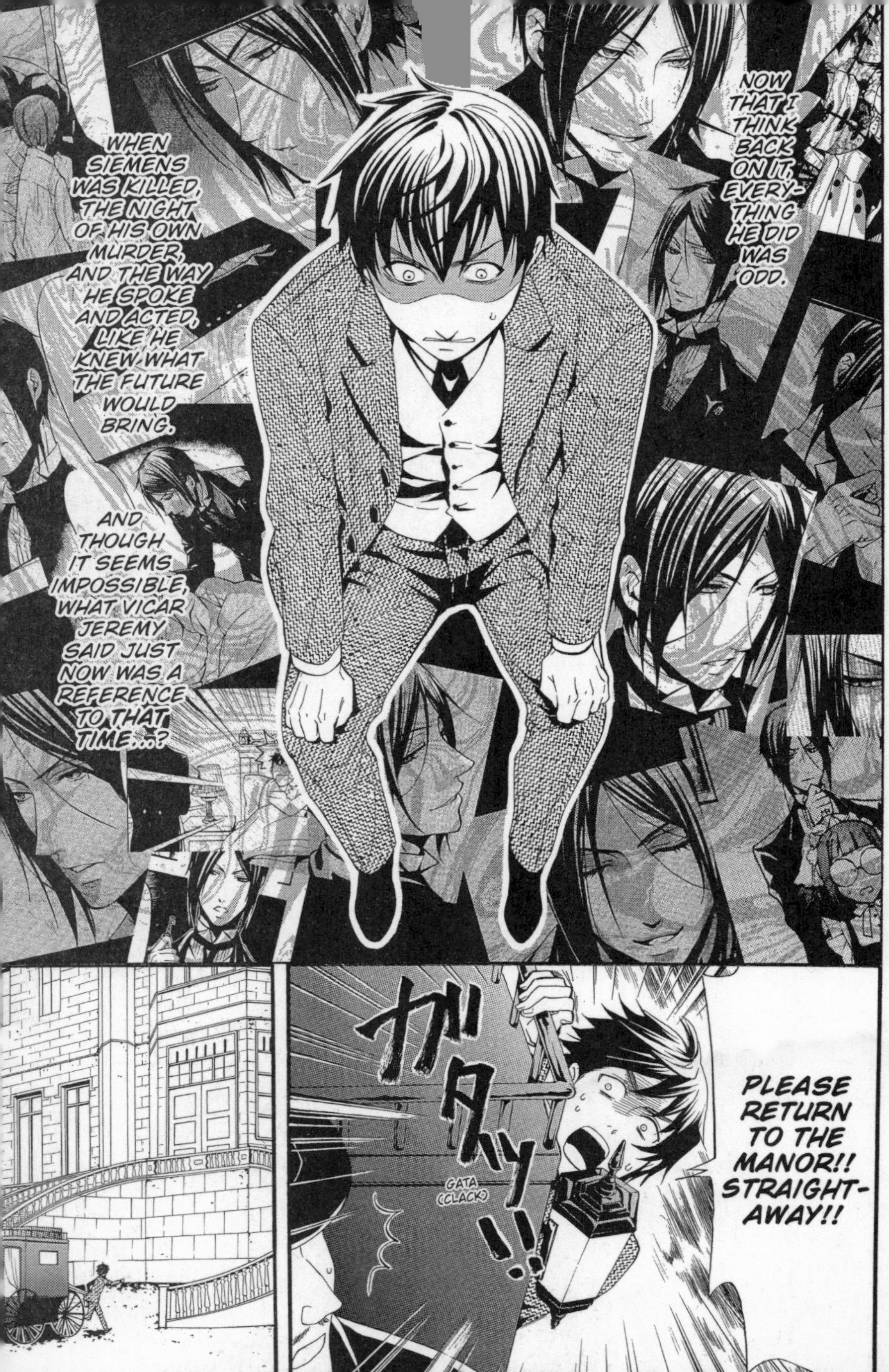
NOW THAT I THINK BACK ON IT, EVERY-THING HE DID WAS ODD.
WHEN SIEMENS WAS KILLED, THE NIGHT OF HIS OWN MURDER, AND THE WAY HE SPOKE AND ACTED, LIKE HE KNEW WHAT THE FUTURE WOULD BRING.
AND THOUGH IT SEEMS IMPOSSIBLE, WHAT VICAR JEREMY SAID JUST NOW WAS A REFERENCE TO THAT TIME...?
PLEASE RETURN TO THE MANOR!! STRAIGHT-AWAY!!
GATA (CLACK)

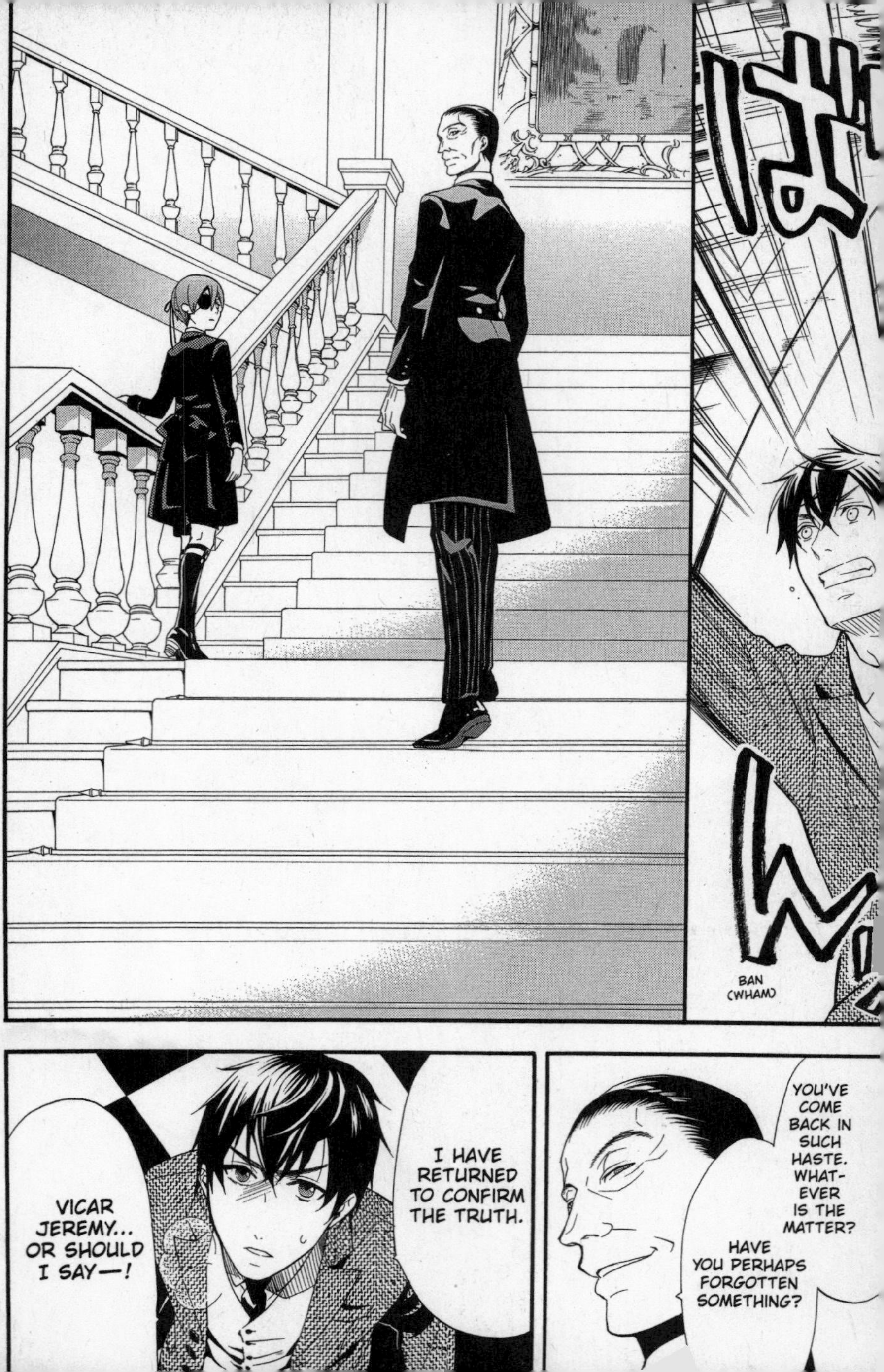
BAN (WHAM)
YOU'VE COME BACK IN SUCH HASTE. WHAT-EVER IS THE MATTER?
HAVE YOU PERHAPS FORGOTTEN SOMETHING?
I HAVE RETURNED TO CONFIRM THE TRUTH.
VICAR JEREMY... OR SHOULD I SAY—!

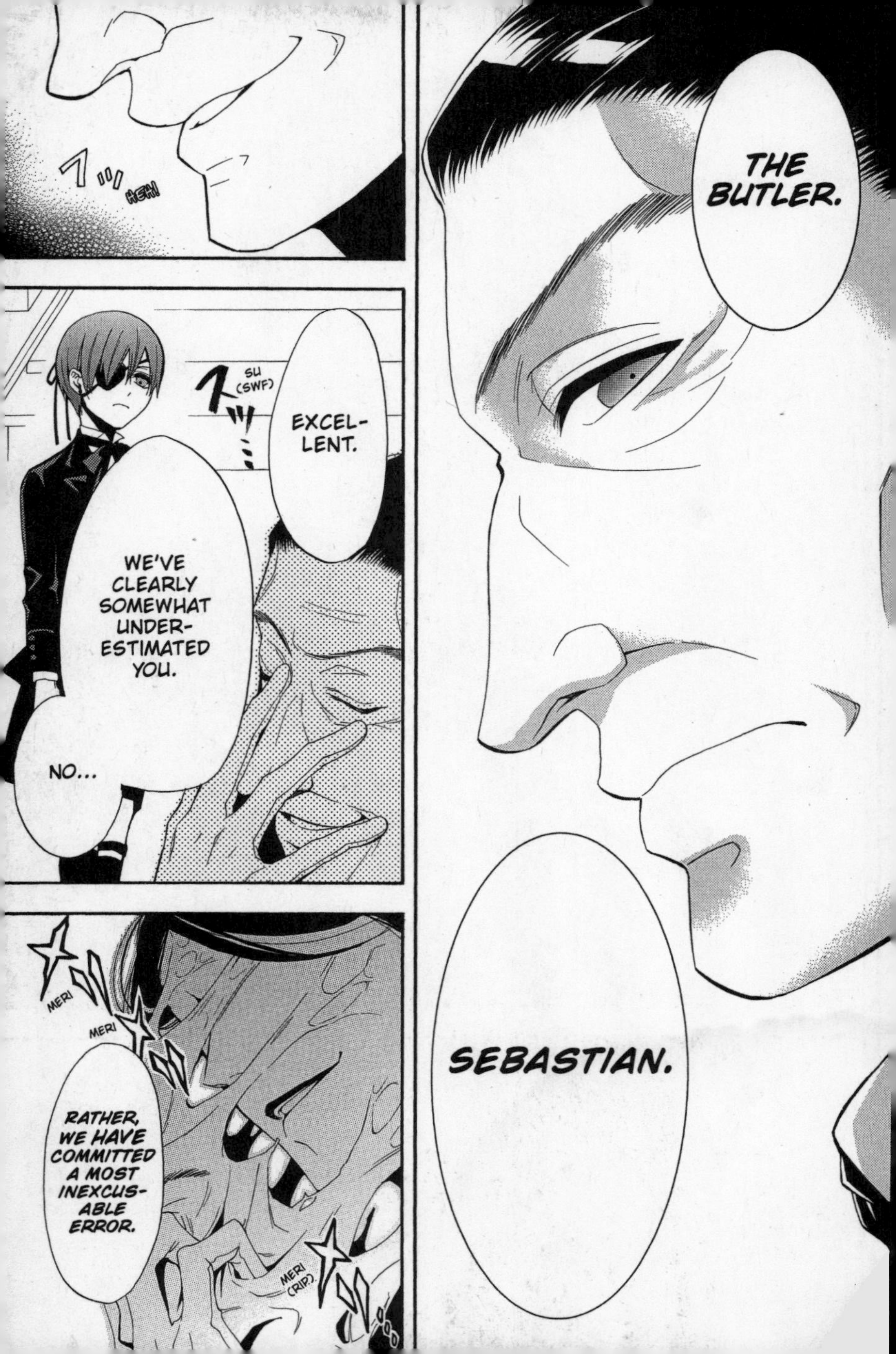
THE BUTLER.
SEBASTIAN.
HEH!
SU (SWF)
EXCEL-LENT.
WE'VE CLEARLY SOMEWHAT UNDER-ESTIMATED YOU.
NO...
MERI
MERI
RATHER, WE HAVE COMMITTED A MOST INEXCUS-ABLE ERROR.
MERI (RIP)

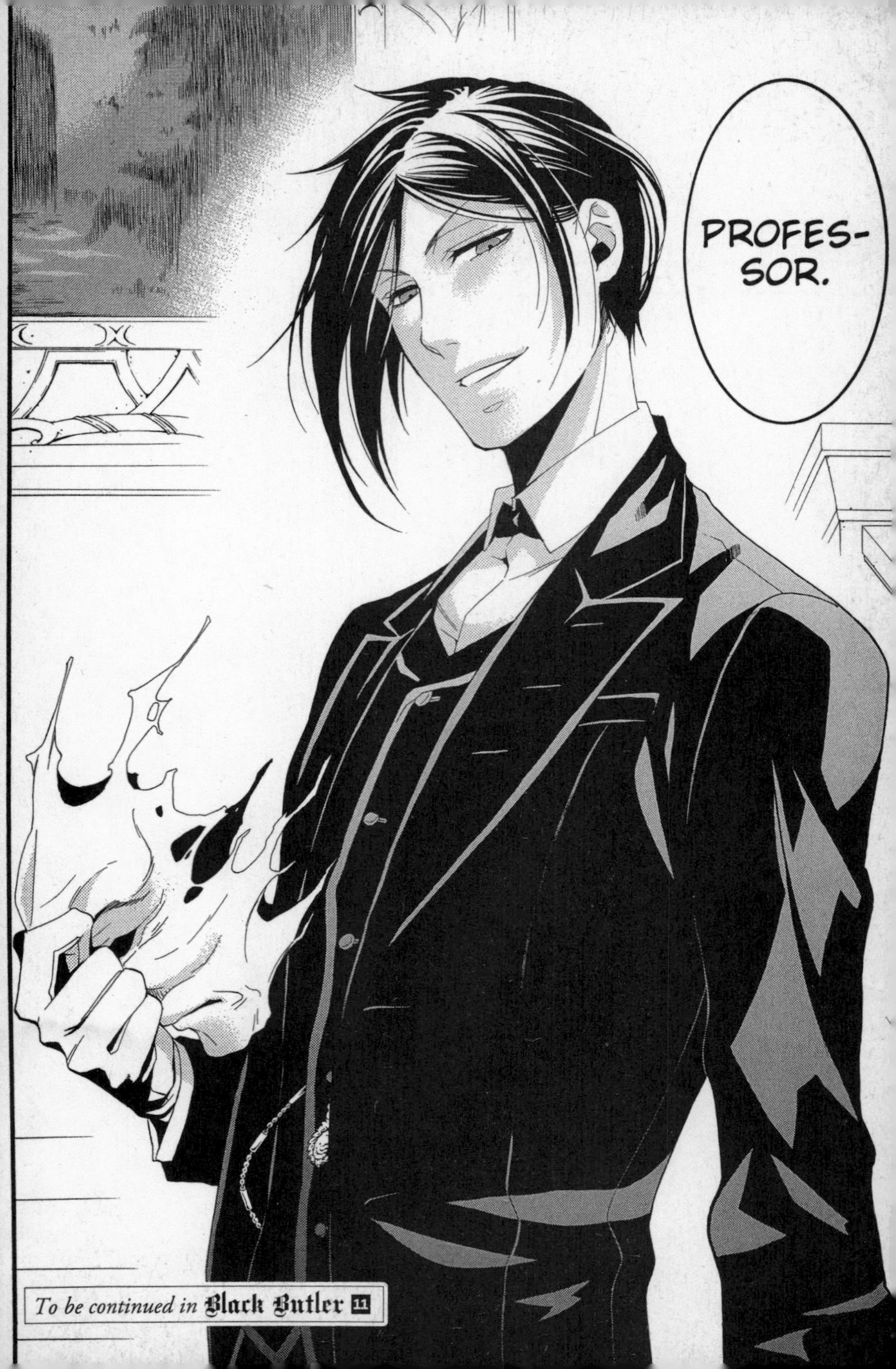
PROFES-
SOR.
To be continued in Black Butler 11

Black Butler

黒執事

Downstairs

Wakana Haduki

SuKe

7

Saito Torino

*

Takeshi Kuma

*

Yana Toboso

SpecialThanks

Yana's Mother

Sakuya

for You!

Translation Notes

INSIDE FRONT AND BACK COVERS
Mr. Sebas
In Japan, there is a magician named Mr. Maric, who calls himself a "super-magician." The name Maric is a combination of the words "magic" and "trick."

PAGE 7
Le Fanu's Carmilla
Joseph Sheridan Le Fanu's novella *Carmilla* is a classic of vampire fiction. Published in 1872, the novella about the vampiress Carmilla, who preys on a vulnerable young woman, was published prior to Bram Stoker's *Dracula*.

PAGE 28
Baritsu
Baritsu is a fictional martial art used by Sir Arthur Conan Doyle to explain how his great detective Sherlock Holmes survived his apparent death. It has been suggested that the term is a mishearing of "bartitsu," a mixed martial art which combined schools of jujitsu to create a gentlemanly art of self-defence for use in an urban setting, founded by Londoner Edward William Barton-Wright in 1899.

PAGE 43
Albert chain
A Victorian gentleman's watch chain popularised by Prince Albert, Queen Victoria's Royal Consort. It features a bar on one end which is slipped through the buttonhole of a man's vest, while the other end has a swivel hook for attaching a pocket watch, which is then kept in a pocket at the front of the vest, leaving the often elaborate chain and its decorative fob on display.

PAGE 83
Jeremy Rathbone
It is possible that the vicar's name and appearance are nods to two of the quintessential actors to play Conan Doyle's detective, Sherlock Holmes. Jeremy Brett was a British actor best remembered for his portrayal of Holmes in a British television series made between 1984 and 1994. Basil Rathbone was another British actor whose turns as Holmes in films between 1939 and 1946 are among the most memorable of his roles.

PAGE 84
Round brilliant-cut
The Belgian diamond cutter Marcel Tolkowsky is acknowledged as the father of what is known as the round brilliant-cut style of diamond today. The design was created in 1919.

PAGE 87
The Lady of the Lake
The Lady of the Lake is a tale of Arthurian legend, in which the eponymous lady is responsible for granting King Arthur the mythical sword Excalibur. Sir Walter Scott's 1810 poem on the subject provided material for a Gioachino Rossini opera, *La Donna del Lago*, which premiered in 1819 in Italy.

Page 87
Lyceum Theatre
A famous theatre in the West End of London, the present incarnation of the Lyceum was opened in 1834 as the Theatre Royal Lyceum and English Opera House.

Page 90
Doctor Bell
The Scotsman Doctor Joseph Bell was a private surgeon to Queen Victoria and a famed lecturer in medicine at the University of Edinburgh, where he and Sir Arthur Conan Doyle first met in 1877. Conan Doyle, who was a student at the University in medicine, served Bell as a clerk for a time, later stating that Sherlock Holmes was in part based on his teacher's observant ways. Bell also assisted Scotland Yard on cases, the most notorious of which is said to be the Jack the Ripper murders.

Page 120
Hamburg steak
Hamburg steak, which was then chopped, salt-cured, low-grade meat combined with breadcrumbs and onions and typically eaten by the lower classes, was brought into common parlance in the eighteenth century by sailors who called at the port of Hamburg, Germany, from where the dish derives its name, and places like New York, where the German immigrant population was considerable.

Page 140
Murder by snake
The method by which Mister Phelps is killed recalls the Sherlock Holmes story, "The Adventure of the Speckled Band," first published in 1892. The murder in the story is also a locked room mystery, the victim a young woman who is killed by a snake that climbs down the bell pull in her room.

Black Butler

Yana Toboso

AUTHOR'S NOTE

I've always loved experiments. Now that
I'm a *mangaka*, I have fun every day trying
out new techniques and tools. Every day I
experiment, thinking "Wouldn't I be able
to work more efficiently if I did this? Or
wouldn't my work improve?" I do realise
my work would get done faster if I worked
instead of wasting time experimenting.
Thanks to everyone, here is Volume 10!

BLACK BUTLER ⑩

Yana Toboso

Translation: Tomo Kimura • Lettering: Alexis Eckerman

Yen Press
1290 Avenue of the Americas
New York, NY 10104

Visit us!
† yenpress.com
† facebook.com/yenpress
† twitter.com/yenpress
† yenpress.tumblr.com
† instagram.com/yenpress

First Yen Press Edition: July 2012

Yen Press is an imprint of Yen Press, LLC.
The Yen Press name and logo are trademarks of Yen Press, LLC.

Library of Congress Control Number: 2010525567

ISBN: 978-0-316-18988-0

10

BVG

Printed in the United States of America